The Cooperstown Symposium on Baseball and American Culture 1999

The Cooperstown Symposium on Baseball and American Culture

1999

Edited with an Introduction by
Peter M. Rutkoff

Series Editor: Alvin L. Hall

McFarland & Company, Inc., Publishers
Jefferson, North Carolina, and London

Library of Congress cataloguing data are available

ISBN 0-7864-0832-4 (softcover : 50# alkaline paper)

British Library cataloguing data are available

Manufactured in the United States of America

*McFarland & Company, Inc., Publishers
  Box 611, Jefferson, North Carolina 28640
    www.mcfarlandpub.com*

To the memory of Robert Kronstadt and Abraham Marten
To Sylvia Kronstadt and Ann Marten

Table of Contents

Acknowledgments

To Jean Demaree, administrative assistant and fan of baseball, my thanks for your help and support. Special thanks to Sarah Demaree for preparing the index.

Preface

Alvin L. Hall

The First Cooperstown Symposium on Baseball and American Culture was held in June 1989, in conjunction with the fiftieth anniversary of the National Baseball Hall of Fame and Museum, Inc. Sponsored by the State University of New York College at Oneonta and co-sponsored by the Hall of Fame, the idea was to bring a few scholars of baseball together a couple of days before the anniversary celebration and talk about the impact of the national pastime on the nation's culture. Doing what academics do, we sent out a call for papers. None of the organizers expected a large response; maybe we would have enough papers proposed to have a credible one day meeting. We received 125 abstracts. Faced with a different kind of problem, we quickly assembled a jury and selected 18 papers to be presented over three days. The authors came from institutions like MIT, Southern Illinois University, Southern Methodist University, the University of Massachusetts, the University of Tennessee. The topics ranged from art history to women's studies, all related to the game.

We had intended to hold only one symposium. After all, there was only one fiftieth anniversary. But participants, nearly 100 altogether, thought the conference was good enough that it should be repeated at least one more time. The Second Cooperstown Symposium was held in June 1990, with only slightly diminished interest. We held the Third Symposium in 1991 and have held a symposium ever since, usually the second week in June. Since 1997, all sessions have been held in the Library of the Baseball Hall of Fame. The Twelfth Cooperstown Symposium is scheduled for June 7–9, 2000.

Over the years, the number of proposals received has remained relatively constant but we have increased the number of papers presented to
between 25 and 30. We have presented three original plays and one screen-
play and have spent several evenings listening to the poetry of the game.
Baseball impacts virtually every aspect of American culture while scholars in nearly all disciplines figure out a way to incorporate baseball in their
research.

As the organizer and coordinator of the Symposium, one who is not
a particularly avid baseball fan (until the Cincinnati Reds made their pennant run in 1999) nor a scholar of the game, my task has been to get it organized each year and let it run at its own speed. However, for several years,
I puzzled over the continuing attraction of the conference. About 75 percent of the participants each year have attended at least one other symposium. An equal percentage is college or university faculty members and
staff or graduate students. Twenty percent are women and about half of
the participants have played baseball seriously in the past up through the
minor leagues. Nearly all have managed to incorporate baseball into their
teaching. I think I have finally found an explanation for the continuing
interest.

In the 1940s, it took Harold Seymour two years to convince the history department at Cornell University to let him write a history of baseball as his dissertation. Baseball, in particular, and sport, in general, were
not considered serious enough topics for scholarly research. Seymour ultimately prevailed and his dissertation subsequently became the first scholarly account of baseball's history. Incidentally, Seymour served as the
keynote speaker at the Second Symposium, just months after he had completed *The People's Game*. When he died a couple of years later, we held a
ceremony in his honor as part of the Symposium, ultimately scattering his
ashes on first base at Doubleday Field. So now, dear reader, you know the
answer to that famous baseball question — "Who's on First?" At least in
Cooperstown, New York, at Doubleday Field, it's Harold Seymour, the
father of serious baseball scholarship. All who participate are indebted to
Dr. Seymour for paving the way.

This is my explanation of the continuing interest in the Symposium.
All of the participants, both those presenting papers and those simply
attending, are passionate baseball fans. They are also solid scholars in an
academic discipline. Baseball research provides the vehicle for them to combine their passions. Yet, although things on campuses are quite different
from the situation Seymour encountered in the 1940s, until quite recently,
baseball was still not considered a topic worthy of scholarship. Those who
practiced this heresy faced subtle and not so subtle discrimination. Research

on baseball was not viewed well during decisions for promotion and tenure. Researchers did not receive the same level of support to participate in scholarly meetings. Few graduate students settled on topics dealing with the game. They found themselves isolated on their home campuses. There is a subculture on American college and university campuses. But they persisted. Along came the Cooperstown Symposium, and they found respite from their isolation. Each June, about 80 gather in Cooperstown to talk about their love of baseball and its impact on their professional work. They are not alone but with several dozen kindred spirits. For one week each June, in Cooperstown, New York, at the National Baseball Hall of Fame, baseball as vocation and avocation are one.

Introduction

Peter Rutkoff

The game and the lake belong together. Because someone wanted to infuse baseball's origins with the pastoral setting of upstate New York, the two are now forever linked in image. The late afternoon sun of Lake Otsego does carry with it the charm of healing, of restoring what is missing in the present. And, in Cooperstown at least, so too does baseball. The national game, for both players and spectators, brings us back. Back to the shores of Otsego, its clear pale blue waters as cool as the night. Together, the game and the lake find common cause in their respite from the ordinary world.

To know Otsego's breeze on the back of your neck is to feel the ball's short-hop, to sense it, to apprehend it before it actually thumps home in your glove. And who does not recall their first baseball moment? It was as sensual as it was satisfying, as poetic as the white caps on the lake, lapping against the shore.

If you've ever been to Cooperstown you understand why they had to invent the invention of the game there. Abner Doubleday Field, the bronze statue at its entrance, the sweeping lawns that roll into Otsego, the lore of Cooper's imagination — these all work, they actually conspire to make us believe in them. Just as we believe in the spirit, in myth, in magic. Baseball in Cooperstown became all of these, and those whose words are included here participate in their reconstruction for a few days every June. There, when the air is blossom sweet we meet to talk about the game, its history, its meaning, its place in American culture.

For almost a century we have been asking the same question in one form or another. It is simple: "What is unique about American culture?"

Sometimes our intellect rouses itself and inquires, "What is American about our culture?" and some even ask, "What is different about our culture?" Somewhere, sometime, every answer to this core question about identity comes up against baseball. It really is our game.

It really is American. It has been a mirror, a silvery reflection, hard and clear of what makes our society both great and terrible. Baseball is male, white, full of greedy men pursuing dreams of aggrandizement. It is open and democratic, an emblem of the dream of equality. It is a game of social mobility and assimilation. Its history is riddled with racism.

Baseball is a window, it opens onto ourselves, tells us truths about who and what we are. It is distinct, of itself, timeless, and it is bound into the society which created it, nowhere separate, always connected. Baseball clarifies our very identity. And obscures it. Baseball teaches, teaches about spirituality, about myths and heroes, about work and ethics. But it also teaches ruthless competition, encourages violence, selfishness, and ignorance. Baseball is a city game played in a sylvan diamond; it is an immigrant game played like a modern form of bread and circus; it is a team game that upholds individual prowess; it is a game of heroes and goats, of statistics and panache, of boredom and glory.

But in Cooperstown, on the shores of Lake Otsego, it is also soft and quiet and dreamlike. It sits in our imaginations, stirring memory and remembrance, tugging quietly at our thoughts. When evening settles in this small corner of a world long past it is as if time has not transpired at all. The water greets the night air and coats that small world with a fine and silent mist.

Part 1

BASEBALL AND THE AMERICAN IMAGINATION

Solarball: Baseball, America, Time, and the Sun

George Grella

In the beginning was the ball, then later a stick and a ball: those two simple and universal objects lead to a multitude of human creations, including, if the pun may be forgiven, innumerable other big innings, and ultimately define almost all the games we play. The fundamental objects of stick and ball appear to lie behind a multitude of athletic endeavors, including of course our national pastime itself. Baseball began somewhere in the dark backward and abysm of time, probably in the form of some rudimentary play with a stick and a ball, in some sort of *Ur* game, perhaps deriving from some ordinary activity like the careless or random striking of a rock or even the head of an enemy with a club. When such an activity becomes regularized and ritualized, it changes from casual act to intentional conduct, from meaningless gesture to organized contest, from free play to a game, with connections to other sorts of ritual endeavors, particularly those involving various forms of religion, so that game and worship at times become synonymous.[1]

Even if no actual, single, original game exists, as Jungians and students of myth like myself would like to think, or more exactly, fantasize, certainly the proliferation of varieties suggests at least a universality of contests with stick and ball. In European civilization alone, stick and ball games include sports as varied as field hockey, ice hockey, hurling, tennis, cricket, golf, even pool and billiards. The possibilities in the two objects do not only exist in European societies, of course: the British discovered polo in India during their great imperial adventure, and adopted it for the amusement of the unspeakably rich; preppies in the United States engage in a modern version of the Native American game of lacrosse, and various indigenous groups and tribes all over the Western Hemisphere apparently played various, still not fully understood ball games. (One of the most important distinctions in the study of ball games probably involves the differences between the striking of a ball in the air, either thrown or batted toward the batter, and the striking of a stationary or moving ball on the ground; the distinction and what it means merit much further study, beyond the narrow limits of this paper.)

All those games, no matter how crude and simple in their origins and even practice, and though initially free and transitory, aspire to achieve the permanence of art, to become, in Yeats's phrase, monuments of unaging intellect, comminglings of truth and beauty with the timelessness of Keats's Grecian urn: all games create intricate strategies to defeat our common enemy, time, the subtle thief of youth. Within the confinements of their various lines, under the dominance of special rules peculiar to themselves, they formalize a space, the playing field, and submit to some defined time. Almost all the games that every modern culture plays conduct some immensely complicated transactions with the clock. Sports as different from one another as football, basketball, and hockey, for example, are played under the relentless pressure of minutes and seconds, their progress and outcome predetermined by the passage of time. Those contests do not end after a certain internal and organic structure is realized, but stop when time runs out. In their sad recognition of their mortality, those sports employ an arsenal of devices to extend their lives — timeouts, halftimes, stalls, delays, deliberate and sometimes desperate attempts to slow down the winged chariot hurrying near. When a contest ends in a draw, the extra period is called an overtime, as if it were somehow borrowed from a diminishing account, to be paid back with interest some dreary day. (Football calls its overtime "sudden death," which suggests precisely the negative aspects of a sometimes brutal game — after one's time is up, what else is there?) The great and glorious exception to the enslavement of time is America's national pastime, baseball, which is also America's own solar religion, perhaps a necessary invention in a country whose constitution expressly forbids the existence of an established church.

Baseball is the one major team sport played in America in which the participants conduct their activity completely outside the limits of time (note the adjectives, which disqualify, for purists, tennis or volleyball). It labors under no temporal limitation whatsoever, and its individual contests can take very little or a great deal of time for their completion. Baseball possesses an almost magical internal structure which exists apart from time — the unit of the inning, made up of three outs (the inning itself may be very short or long in duration), and the complete whole of nine innings, which constitutes a game. If a game is tied at the end of nine innings, of course, it must go on until one team triumphs; although such a thing is improbable, it is at least not inconceivable that a tied game could go on forever. As all fans know and many commentators tiresomly remind us, one of the most attractive qualities about the game is its commitment to life — it has extra innings rather than sudden death.

Yet, despite its freedom from the constraints of time, its independence of any regulations or minutes or seconds, its total rejection of the nonsense of two-minute warnings or 24-second buzzers, baseball may be, of all sports, the most closely attentive to the true essence of time. While ignoring temporality, the game, paradoxically, captures eternity. It is played out not so much against the clock, or even without a clock, as, in fact, upon a clock: it engages not ordinary time, but solar time. In its appearance and its reality, in its accidents and its essence, in its smallest and its greatest elements, the game appears to resolve itself into rituals, myths, and even worship of the sun, the master of all time.

The history of the sport reflects its development out of solar worship. Although archaeologists and anthropologists have discovered numerous traces of ancient ball games in many cultures, what may be called the pre-history of the game,[2] its actual recorded history begins, naturally, with the Egyptians. Like so much in Western culture, ball games originate in ancient Egyptian civilization, where ceremonial contests were held as a part of the annual fertility rites, connected of course with the veneration of the sun. The "games," which involved selected teams, probably of priests, consisted of moving a ball of some sort across a line, or through a temple door, or simply back and forth over a field, both represented and guaranteed the triumph of warm weather over cold, of life over death, of spring over winter, of good over evil, of the sun over the darkness of night.[3] In some interpretations of the rite, the ball is thought to be a vestige of the head cult, which revolved around the god's dismemberment. The head in question is usually believed to be that of Osiris, an important fertility figure. Apparently some versions of the ceremony used an actual head from some unfortunate sacrificial victim; rounding its features off smoothly turns it into a ball, a symbolic head, which may be the reason some batters speak of hitting one right on the nose. Most important, the ball, whatever else it may be, is also itself a useful and potent symbol of the sun, a small round object that could be kicked, rolled, thrown, or struck with a stick, a sphere that usefully served to represent the great ball that everyone could see burning in the heavens.

The very pattern of baseball's season shows its close connections with the solar rites of the past. It begins in April, with Opening Day, and ends in October, with the championship contests of the World Series. It flows thus from seedtime to harvest, encompassing our warmest, sunniest months, marking significant moments in the solar rhythm. Opening Day opens up more than a baseball season; it celebrates the renewal of the solar year, the beginning of spring, the rejuvenation of the human community. Reminding us of the manifold possibilities of life, growth, and joy, it also marks the vernal equinox, the dawning of the solar day of the season whose night will not fall again until autumn. Opening Day is the annual visible version of Thoreau's final sentence in *Walden*: "The sun is but a morning star."

Other events in the solar calendar occur in the movement of the baseball season from its happy dawn to its ambiguous twilight in the closing weeks to its sad evening in the gathering dusk of the autumnal equinox. In the middle of the season the National and American Leagues play their annual All-Star Game, an appropriate name to designate the brightest talents in the major leagues. By presenting a purely symbolic contest featuring lineups composed entirely of luminaries, the leagues celebrate Midsummer Eve, the summer solstice, again reminding us of the close relationship between the sport and its progenitor, between those stars and our great daystar.

Naturally enough for a sport so dependent upon the agricultural cycle, the season ends in the Fall. Baseball's World Series is its own version of the traditional harvest festival, as the accidental pun on Ceres, the goddess of the grain, so cleverly suggests. One reason for the sense of poignancy, the bittersweet quality, of the games of the Series is the knowledge in every fan's heart that these are not only the culmination of the long, happy season, but also the final contests before Winter once again descends on the land. Just as we know that Spring is here, no matter the weather, when Opening Day arrives, we also know that after the last game of the World Series Summer is over for another year. The whole season, contemplated in its entirety, constitutes a gallant solar pageant whose goal is the attempt to extend the calendar to its utter limits, to hold off Winter for as long as possible, to pretend somehow that the sun shines longer and brighter than it really does.

Understanding that attempt, one can easily understand (and thereby forgive) night baseball, which some critics contend has lowered the quality of play. A sun worshipper might initially contend that to play the game at night is to ignore its ancient heritage, perhaps even to commit an act of sacrilege. Night baseball, however, must be understood as yet another example of the attempt to lengthen the day by creating a midnight sun. For many years the Chicago Cubs enjoyed the distinction of being the only major league baseball team to refuse to perform at night, to do the deed of darkness; consequently, their supporters and numerous uninformed sportswriters lavished a great deal of sentimental blather on their decision to keep baseball pure and sunlit. In reality, of course, the team's owners had planned to light Wrigley Field before the demands of World War II obliged them to contribute the materials of the light towers to the war effort. The team may actually deserve to be regarded as timid savages afraid of the dark and unwilling to improve their condition. After finally installing lights to the accompaniment of even more blather some years ago, a gesture the club claimed would make them genuine contenders, they continued to fail in the same old ways, appropriately inhabiting a perpetual twilight of mediocrity. In a variant on Napoleon's comment that God is on the side with the most cannons, sun worship, of the natural or artificial sort, even for devout converts, apparently works best with a good team. No wonder with such confusion they haven't won a pennant in over fifty years.

(Though the recent practice of conducting some World Series games on decidedly frigid October evenings has drawn a great deal of negative comment, it too deserves at least a modicum of forgiveness. The commissioner of baseball, its high priest, usually appears at them in expensive summer suitings, rumored to conceal thermal underwear, trying in his own way to bless the proceedings; he pardonably attempts to prolong the season, preserving for a few short hours more the illusion of a sunny summer day.)

In addition to its seasonal involvement with the timeless solar rhythms, baseball's procedures and methods, its play and scoring, its shape and pattern, all demonstrate further, more complicated relationships with the sun. The first and most obvious of these is established by the simple geography of the ballpark. To make his difficult task a little more possible, the batter is situated so that he will not have to contend with the sun's bright beams shining in his eyes; the ballpark is constructed so that the sun sets behind home plate. The playing field itself, then, radiates out from the afternoon sun as it sinks behind home plate, becoming a sort of two-dimensional image of the sun's rays. The two foul lines, the only boundaries of the game, open up from that setting sun at a ninety degree angle to one another; those lines, on the left and right, symbolically represent the sun's rays, as they open up further and further in their progress away from home plate. The game, completely unlike any other, also opens rather than encloses space, radiating its arena across the continent. Since the structure of the game is based upon its nine innings rather than any limit of time, we see in baseball's space a symbol of its time: in its suggestion of infinity lies also the possibility of eternity.

Simultaneously with its presentation of an emblem of infinity, baseball also operates within a finite area that can indicate other aspects besides those of eternity. Although its structure may free it from the clock, the game depends in some remarkable ways upon the sun. This apparent paradox arises from changing one's perspective, viewing the game and its arena from some distance — say, several rows up from ground level, somewhere near the middle levels of the stadium; from up there the spectator can see that the so-called diamond can be circular as well as rectangular. The 360 feet around the basepaths from home plate and back again nicely coincide with the 360 degrees that make a circle. Baseball is the only game we play in this country where a man, not a ball, must accomplish the difficult task of scoring; the teams score their runs, therefore, through cyclical movement rather than penetration of territory. The batter, transformed by a successful swing into a runner, circles the bases, leaving and returning to home plate. That circular movement around a predetermined route repeats on a plane surface the sun's daily cycle as primitive men and women perceived it. Before he arrives at home plate the batter must emerge from a dark cave — the dugout — to which he returns after scoring (provided he does score); the movement out of darkness into light, the circular journey, and the return to darkness quite obviously parallels the solar cycle. No wonder that baseball players receive so much attention and adulation from the fans: each has the opportunity to become the incarnation of the solar hero, and many — the biggest stars, as they are rightly called — undergo that incarnation many times. (It may also be true that the alternations of being safe or out repeat the process of birth and death and rebirth of the solar hero demonstrated in the movement of day and night.)

If the spectator moves still higher up from the surface of the playing field — to the dizzying heights of the upper deck, for example, or the privileged vantage of the Goodyear blimp — he will find other significant truths in the shape of the field. The circular movement of the players around the bases plainly marks off a disk — along with the globe the most common sun symbol — displaying four particularly meaningful spots at home plate and first, second, and third bases, corresponding in fact to the common markings on a clock face at the numerals three, six, nine, and twelve. In the middle of this disk is a little circular hill, property of the pitcher, called his mound; on it, from above, the pitcher looks like a vertical shaft. The round infield with its four delineating marks and its central shaft, if we look again, appears, in fact, to be a large sundial with significant marks at predictable places and the pitcher serving as its gnomon, or style, whose shadow indicates the advancement of solar time. As the sun sinks lower behind home plate, of course, the pitcher's shadow lengthens across the playing field. The shape of the infield and that inexorably lengthening shadow imply that the game may not only be a struggle between two teams but between two teams that are also struggling against time, against the sun itself. (Rolfe Humphries, in "Polo Grounds," which may be the best of all baseball poems, captures the inexorable movement of another shadow as the marker of time:

> Time is of the essence. The shadow moves
> From the plate to the box, from the box to second base,
> From second to the outfield, to the bleachers.
> Time is of the essence. The crowd and the players
> Are the same age always, but the man in the crowd
> Is older every season. Come on, play ball!)

The team at bat tries to defeat not only the pitcher, but also his time; their journey around the basepaths is a movement against the sun — its direction is *counter clockwise*. Perhaps, then, each team attempts to impose its own time on that of its opponent: in the field each tries to prevent the counter clockwise solar journey and keep the pitcher's solar clock moving, while at bat each tries to send its members on that perilous circuit around the bases and back to home again.

The pitcher, of course, serves a number of other functions besides that of gnomon for the sundial of the field. Since pitching, as popular wisdom claims, constitutes 70 percent of the game, the pitcher is regarded as the most significant single personage on the playing field, its most heroic figure, the king of the little hill on which he stands. Standing on the mound, he holds in his hands not only what Roger Angell calls his little lump of physics, but also a great deal of the long history of the game; no wonder he alone is granted credit for a victory and, sadly, is burdened forever with the loss. When he pitches well and his team wins, his regal position is triumphantly intensified; he and his team and the community they represent bask in the glorious effulgence of victory. But if his role possesses the potential for great glory, it also includes the possibility of ignominious defeat. Like virtually every exalted ruler of every fertility cult, he is ultimately responsible for the happiness and prosperity of his community: when he rules well all men proclaim him king, but when he falters he must be replaced. Unlike the rituals of the past, this replacement is a bloodless and nonviolent procedure. No matter how much he might like to imitate the ancient Aztecs and stretch the poor man out beneath a burning sun and cut his heart out to propitiate the great god, the manager directs that a relief pitcher enter the game while the previous hurler must depart, hanging his head in sadness, defeat, and disgust, often the recipient of ambiguous utterances from the fans. The reliever stands on the mound, a new king, a surrogate ruler who tries to rescue the team from its apparent bad fortune or prevent a loss.

In one of the most interesting permutations of historic solar rituals in baseball, the surrogate fulfills other functions. Often, in games where his team needs a hit, a baserunner, some way of scoring, a pinch hitter impersonates the pitcher at the plate. He "bats for" the pitcher, as the familiar expression has it, specifically chosen as a temporary king, like the surrogates for innumerable kings in innumerable solar rites. Remarkably, this impostor may occasionally be called upon to carry out exactly the duties of the surrogates of ancient times and faiths — to act as the scapegoat for the king. The pinch hitter, in short, may be required to *sacrifice* himself for the good of his team. This bloodless sacrifice — usually a bunt toward either third or first base in order to move the baserunner up a notch on the sundial — remains one of the most convincing allusions to the methods of solar religion that baseball allows itself to make. Baseball is the only sport that practices a daily immolation, a concept that must be as old as the oldest myths of our race. (Note that the loathsome institution of the designated hitter in the American League significantly reduces the sacrificial gesture, a blatant act of solar sacrilege.)

In the relationship between the pitcher and the batter other indications of baseball's origins and meanings emerge. The contest between the two extends and intensifies the larger conflict of their respective teams. The pitcher grasps what we know to be a little sun, a symbolic sphere, which contains within itself both the history and potential of the game. His difficult task is to hurl that repository of the past, that little lump of physics, as hard or as deceptively as possible past the menacing club of the batter, who in turn desires to impart an entirely different and opposite trajectory to the speeding, spinning globe. Both play a sun game — an effective pitcher establishes the ball as his sun symbol, while a successful batter transforms the pitcher's symbol into his own by redirecting it away from its original destination.

When we remember once again the position of the playing field in relation to the sun, we understand still further functions of the pitcher. In throwing the ball toward home plate he is also, obviously, throwing it into the setting sun. In The Golden Bough[4] Sir James Frazer notes that the Ojibways of North America and the Sencis of eastern Peru would shoot flaming arrows toward the sun during an eclipse, in order to rekindle what they saw as a fire going out. It is not surprising, then, to realize that pitchers who throw with exceptional velocity are popularly termed "fireballers" or "flamethrowers": they throw small spheres of heats, gobs of flame, miniature suns, like the Indian archers, in order to keep the sun itself hot and bright and alive. Their actions, like all the actions of the game, are directed toward reversing the movement of the sun, keeping the summer afternoon endlessly bright and warm.

The batter who swings the lethal club initially seems less obviously significant in the solar ritual than the pitcher, upon whom so much depends and around whom the game literally revolves. He too serves important solar functions that must not be ignored. To begin with, the act of hitting is metamorphic: it can transform the batter into a baserunner, giving him the opportunity to move against solar time. In addition, he has a chance to duplicate something of the pitcher's task by providing a new direction for the ball, not rekindling the sun so much as reversing its path. All batters seek to achieve a safe hit, and all hits aspire to be home runs, not only because the home run is the quickest and most efficient way of scoring, but also because the home run's parabola imitates the journey of the sun across the sky. As the homer travels in one direction through space, its originator trots around the sundial of the field, providing two roughly simultaneous images of the solar journey, a complex geometrical, even topological figure that suggests that the game fully inhabits the Einsteinian four-dimensional space-time continuum. No wonder that so many sportswriters, with their pathetic fondness for elegant variation, often refer to home runs as "roundtrippers" and "circuit clouts"—the terms aptly describe that immediate accomplishment of a resounding backward tick on the solar clock.

The arc that a home run describes in the sky raises an important corollary point, that if the ideal hit is a home run, then the ideal home run is a perfect circle; all home runs may in fact be interrupted or disappointed revolutions. Perhaps the reason that fans express such awe over the distance that some batted balls traverse stems from their subconscious recognition that the greatest aspiration of the batter is to hit a ball hard enough to drive it into full orbit in perfect imitation of the solar cycle. (Baseball boasts many legends about some of its greatest hitters doing exactly that. In one version the great Josh Gibson of the Negro Leagues is alleged to have hit a ball out of sight in Pittsburgh; the next day, as he came to bat in Philadelphia, the story goes, a ball came out of the sky and was caught by the centerfielder. With absolute precision and a full understanding of the meaning of the whole experience, the umpire allegedly told Gibson, "You're out yesterday in Pittsburgh.") Back in 1977 the ceremonial first pitch in the traditional Opening Day ceremonies in Cincinnati involved a ball that had been carried in a space capsule by a team of American astronauts, circling the globe like the sun and amounting to something like the longest home run ever hit; it traveled more than four million miles, a roundtripper indeed.

In a sport so intricately connected with solar religion, it is not surprising to discover individual players who seem directly descended from the heroes of ancient myths. Not only does the game honor Ceres in its autumnal rites, but it also features in its rich and populous history two players named Demeter; like many others who resembled Phaethon more than Apollo, neither enjoyed an especially luminous career. In other incidental connections, it also boasts a number of appropriate names, no less than six players named May, two named Maye, one Mayberry, and a particularly outstanding performer, Willie Mays; although there are no Maggios, there are the three DiMaggio brothers, including of course the incomparable Joseph. (If George Steinbrenner, Zeus of the Yankees, in the tradition of his role rightly crowned Reggie Jackson as "Mr. October," he also derisively referred to Dave Winfield's postseason failures in calling him "Mr. May," appropriate sobriquets for solar sport.)

Other performers appear to fall into three major categories, each governed by an appropriate solar deity: the most memorable players seem to be avatars of Apollo, Dionysus, or Adonis. The Apollonian athlete is best exemplified by the austere, aloof Joe DiMaggio, who played with an effortless and understated grace, all classic precision and noble silence. The Dionysian, usually more interesting than his Apollonian counterpart, plays (and sometimes lives) with joyous abandon and overwhelming exuberance — a Babe Ruth or a Willie Mays or even a Pete Rose. In the full Bacchic frenzy he is represented by the fearsomely aggressive Ty Cobb or the troubled Jimmy Piersall. Most memorable perhaps is the Adonaic hero, the handsome, beloved, superbly gifted young man whose brilliant career ends before its time, shortened before its full and glorious cycle by some crippling wound — Pete Rieser, Sandy Koufax, and Herb Score rank among the most famous and touching Adonises, sun gods all. These are the most poignant of all heroes because in the premature ends of their careers are born all our dreams of what might have been.

The popularity of baseball in particular parts of the globe has often proved difficult to understand and explain. The sport is clearly, indelibly, natively American in its fullest and richest development, for numerous and various reasons; a great many histories, commentaries, and learned analyses have established the Americanness of the game in its present form. But the sport has traveled to other countries beyond the United States, some of them apparently rather unlikely places for baseball to flourish; its presence there underlines both the solar significance of the game and its potential for universality, looking forward to a time when it may become a truly global sport. In Japan, the land of sumo wrestling, samurai swordsmanship, and Zen archery, *besoboru*, as we all know, is the single most popular sport.[5] In Central and South America,[6] as the success of Latinos in the major leagues shows us, they play *el beisbol*; Romanians have a peculiar stick-and-ball game called *öjna*, and more important, the Finns, believe it or not, play a variety called *pesäpallo*, which results from a combination of a native game with the familiar American import. Such amalgamations of indigenous sports with those of other, often dominant nations occur throughout the world, suggesting yet another result of the various armed conflicts and imperial ambitions that have shaped our century.[7] The regions often appear to share very little in the way of common history, geography, or culture, which makes the popularity of the game even more inexplicable.

If we remember that the Aztec, Mayan, and Incan cultures preceded the Spanish conquest and that all three practiced rigid and extreme versions of sun worship, we then immediately comprehend that their heritage quite naturally provides the basis for the South American love and talent for the play of the game. The much maligned concept of the universal unconscious may indeed account for the context out of which the modern sport succeeded in Latin America. In fact, the pre–Columbian cultures played an unusual ball game whose structure remains a puzzle to archaeologists and historians. It may also be interesting to note that among the Mexican ballplayers, one of the most successful, the pitcher Fernando Valenzuela is a Toltec, descended from the rich and dazzling traditions of the Mayan civilization.

Finland, of course, is situated close to the Arctic Circle, and is one of those lands of the midnight sun, which means it is therefore a propitious place for the marriage of their native stick-and-ball game with the American version; the real wonder is that more northern countries don't play it, though with the end of the Cold War and the collapse of Communism, the Russians, who once claimed to have invented the game (and probably, in fairness, were referring to some rudimentary native sport), are also beginning to take it up. More obviously and probably more important, Japan has always been the land of the rising sun, dominated by sun images and a long history of sun worship. Though baseball was first imported early in the century, it increased in popularity after World War II, encouraged by the presence of the American occupation forces. After his nation's defeat, we must remember, Emperor Hirohito was not only forced to abdicate his position as ruler, but also to announce to his countrymen, most of whom had never seen him or even heard his voice, that he was no longer a god — a sun god, of course — but only a man like the rest of us, after all. Baseball logically, naturally, inevitably exploded in Japan, providing an entirely adequate version of sun worship for a nation deprived of its solar deity.

Although most Americans would resist the idea that our own history has any connection with sun worship — except perhaps among the indigenous inhabitants — the myth of the game's origin was probably accepted as truth (and in fact some still believe it, despite overwhelming evidence to the contrary) because its legendary inventor bore a perfectly American version of a perfectly appropriate name for a solar hero. Neither the wildest dreamer, the most inspired high priest, nor the most devoted worshiper could have come up with the name Abner Doubleday, clearly an American sun god, the Civil War veteran who helped to preserve the Union and therefore provide a peaceful context for the sport, the hero of a myth, the creator of a sport devoted to the sun, whose name prefigures the double-header and promises to extend the shining hours of the great globe toward which his game is directed. As Ernie Banks said one balmy afternoon in Chicago, "Let's play two." Further, of course, if it were not for the existence of that great hero-god, visitors, fans, students of baseball would not journey to Cooperstown, this lovely spot, this shrine to Doubleday, baseball, and America.

Even beyond the central image of the sun, baseball clearly depends upon the rhythms of the growing season, reflecting in its progress the passage of the months from seedtime to harvest, from its chilly early rainouts to Keats's season of mists and mellow fruitfulness. In addition, contrary to the realities of history, geography, industrial progress, or urban sprawl, Americans still sentimentally tend to regard themselves as inhabitants of an agrarian culture. Many of our most memorable images of the game, therefore, grow out of its profound relationship to the timeless agricultural cycle. The scene of immigrants playing their impromptu game in a vast field of wheat in movie *Days of Heaven* (1978) captures some sense of that relationship. More emphatically and complexly, a number of sequences in *Field of Dreams* (1989), indeed perhaps the whole movie, depend upon the connections between the two great sacred spaces — the spectral ballplayers frequently fade gracefully from ballfield to cornfield, often obliterating entirely the vague boundary between play and agriculture. The ghosts of dead athletes not only undergo the rebirth of baseball but also behave remarkably like some version of traditional corn gods. Perhaps even more beautifully, Roy Hobbs's final, triumphant home run in *The Natural* (1984) demonstrates the miraculous possibility in baseball. His colossal hit launches the ball into the night, then itself creates a Niagara of brilliance, in Shelley's phrase, "light dissolved in star showers thrown." The ball then continues its flight, finally metamorphosing into another ball in the middle of another field, this time bathed in sunlight, celebrating once again the solar ritual origins of the game and perhaps even hinting at that revolution around the earth that all hits aspire grandly to imitate.

All players, spectators, chroniclers, and students of the game of baseball, then, participate in a solar activity, working out in life and sport a variety of relationships with the sun. In its primitive and recent history, in its many echoes and replications of rituals, legends, myths, and cultural practices, baseball may be the oldest and purest of all our sports; it certainly is the one that most completely and coherently manifests the manifold possibilities in the fact of the sun. Its appeal unites players and fans in common worship, exerting a power unmatched by any other sport in America. No wonder those who love it love it so— playing it and watching it, we all become, for a fleeting moment, devoted and reverential children of the sun.

Notes

1. I discuss the connection between baseball and religion, particularly in terms of modern faith and sport, in a paper entitled "The Church of Baseball, Baseball and the Church," delivered at the Cooperstown Symposium on Baseball and American Culture in June, 1996.

2. For one of many examinations of prehistoric stick and ball games, see for example Erwin Mehl, "Baseball in the Stone Age," *Western Folklore* VII, 2 (April 1948), 145–161.

3. Some important discussion of the Egyptian games, with useful illustrations, appear in Robert Henderson, *Ball, Bat and Bishop: The Origin of Ball Games* (New York: Rockport Press, 1947) and in Wolfgang Decker, *Sports and Games of Ancient Egypt* (New Haven: Yale University Press, 1992).

4. Abridged edition (New York: New American Library, 1964), pp. 81 ff.

5. The most accessible and entertaining books about Japanese baseball are Robert Whiting's *The Chrysanthemum and the Bat* (New York: Macmillan, 1984) and *You Gotta Have Wa* (New York: Macmillan, 1989).

6. Among the many books on baseball in Central America are John Krich, *El Béisbol: Travels Through the Pan-American Pastime* (New York: Prentice Hall, 1989) and Alan M. Klein, *Sugarball: The American Game, the Dominican Dream* (New Haven: Yale University Press, 1991).

7. A major study of the merging of baseball with other, similar games in other cultures needs to be conducted; the narrow limits of this paper only allow some hints and suggestions.

Spirituality and Baseball

Richard Robison, Jr.

Baseball is much more than sport, or so we are led to believe by the host of books written about deeper aspects of the game. Thomas Boswell's *How Life Imitates the World Series,* Donald Hall's *Fathers Playing Catch with Sons,* and George F. Will's *Men at Work* ask us to see the game as symbolic play upon a field of meaning. And films about baseball carry us beyond mere reverence to mysticism.

In an opening voice over in the film *Bull Durham,* the character played by Susan Sarandon says, "I believe in the church of baseball. I've tried all the major religions, and most of the minor ones ... The only church that truly feeds the soul day in and day out is baseball."

And then later, Kevin Costner, as Crash Davis, declares his beliefs in this (edited) litany:

> I believe in the soul,
> the small of a woman's back,
> the hanging curveball,
> high fiber,
> good scotch.
> I believe the novels of Susan Sontag are self-indulgent,
> over-rated crap.
> I believe Lee Harvey Oswald acted alone.
> I believe there ought to be a constitutional amendment out-
> lawing astro-turf and the designated hitter.

The Costner character in *Field of Dreams* risks his family's farm, their well being, and his sense of respect within his community all for the chance to provide a venue for his father's reincarnation and a subsequent father/son connection through baseball. The theme of baseball as uniting force provides the tension and redemption in the story. Baseball becomes the medium for cosmic intervention where repair of the soul is needed.

In the September 1998 *Gentlemen's Quarterly*, writer Peter Richmond depicts Yankees owner George Steinbrenner as baseball's anti–Christ as much for his ignorance and buffoonery (are we really expected to believe the Yankees need a new stadium — in Manhattan — in order to compete?) as for his lack of reverence for the House that Ruth Built — the most fabled and recognizable baseball venue in the world (Fenway and Wrigley not withstanding). Even Yankee haters (and Steinbrenner has fueled the legions) feel a sense of awe strolling through Monument Park beyond the center field fence where the likes of Gehrig and Ruth and DiMaggio and Mantle are immortalized. I've heard children whisper in the presence of the monuments, in full belief that those players are actually buried there. Steinbrenner is perceived as evil because he has so little respect for the heritage of a team he merely owns.

But if Steinbrenner is the anti–Christ, then are we to believe there is a second coming of Jesus? Well, okay, maybe it's a stretch, and maybe we literary types get a little too hung up on metaphor, but how else to explain the dignity of Bernie Williams, the center fielder who quietly led the American League in hitting this year, or Joe Torre, the manager whose contemplative guidance evokes a unified spirit among players from all corners of the world, or mostly shortstop Derek Jeter, [Steinbrenner's] graceful antidote? Says Richmond, "I knew why he'd been summoned by the baseball gods: to carry the torch, to help save the team and the stadium, and maybe even the game of baseball itself" (359).

But let's not forget, baseball was a game before it was a profession, and will remain a game even if the Steinbrenners manage to destroy the profession. For it is in the game itself, not professional play, where meaning lies.

Without much effort one could articulate the game as the visible expression of a belief structure that we intuit with each play. We see a pilgrimage when the batter steps up to the plate and the momentary safety of home, and ventures forth. His path is determined and there are islands of safety, but in following the path he runs the risk of being picked off, forced out, doubled up, or stranded. But by good fortune (the baseball gods) or guile (with cunning he can steal), it is possible to return home triumphant.

Perhaps less apparent is home plate itself, a unique pentagram which may simply embody the evolution of the geometry of the game, but in

Western European tradition pentagrams are recommended for keeping evil forces at bay, five points representing the wounds of Christ on the cross. Is it purely coincidental that frequently we see players perform the sign of the cross before stepping up to bat?

Often we treat a ballpark as a cathedral, redolent with the incense of popcorn and cigars. Is it a stretch to perceive the watering of the infield before a game as a gesture of purification, the sins of yesterday wiped clean?

We observe rituals by individual players that bespeak of ceremony: the tapping of spikes and home plate, adjusting batting gloves, stepping over foul line, etc. And the fans participate too, like a choir singing the national anthem, or "Take Me Out to the Ball Game" during the seventh inning stretch, not to mention the maligned wave, a transplant from football that nonetheless verily screams, "Hallelujah." Is it any wonder then that we perceive the game in religious terms?

But somehow it does not seem enough, or it seems ingenuous, to sanctify a game simply by mining it from metaphor. The desire to see the sport as a repository of deeper meaning, a metaphor, is itself a part of the message — it tells us there is meaning for us there. But it is up to each of us to determine what that meaning is.

One thing baseball teaches us is the connection of generation to generation. Or perhaps more accurately, it connects generation to generation. As Donald Hall points out in his book, *Fathers Playing Catch with Sons:*

> Baseball is fathers and sons. Football is brothers beating each other up in the backyard, violent and superficial. Baseball is the generations, looping backward forever with a million apparitions of sticks and balls, cricket and rounders, and the games the Iroquois played in Connecticut before the English came. Baseball is fathers and sons playing catch, lazy and murderous, wild and controlled, the profound archaic song of birth, growth, age, and death. The diamond encloses what we are [30].

In 1929, in a small coal town in Pennsylvania, there was a man who played baseball with grace, power, and heart. The game was his life, or rather his escape from a life that promised little more than poverty and desperation. And yet, inexplicably, when the Cardinals offered my grandfather a tryout, he declined — not for love or family, and certainly not for money. His decision has spurred three generations of family debate: was he afraid, or did he simply fail to seize the moment?

My grandfather sits alone in a nursing home, sometimes strapped to a chair or bed. At 87 he weighs less than 100 pounds. When, as a child, I visited his hometown, the locals — his contemporaries, diminished to near extinction today — would regale me with tales of his baseball prowess. With each story, some mythic in proportion, I think of what he passed on to me — a love for the game, the athletic ability to enjoy it, the intellect to appreciate it. Baseball, with all of its attendant meaning is a gift he gave me — and it is a salvation for him today. Now he believes it is 1938. He thinks he has been playing ball every day. What more proof do I need of the spirituality of baseball than to find comfort in knowing it can deliver him from a world in which his body no longer fits, in which power is gone, and grace and heart have changed?

I have been doubly blessed in this life. I grew up having not only two grandfathers, but two grandfathers who loved baseball. My other grandfather, a man whose parenting skills were poor at best, seemed somehow willing to connect with me. Perhaps he acknowledged, consciously or not, what he had lost with his own son and saw in me a chance for parental redemption. Whatever the case, he nurtured me in the only way he could.

As a child I visited him (and my grandmother, of course, a small town justice of the peace who may have found solace in her husband's kind treatment of my sister and me) for two weeks, sometimes three in the heart of the summer. Every evening, after a hard day of being a kid, I sat with him on the porch swing. Together we listened to Pirate games fade in and out on his portable radio. For crucial moments in the game he would pull the Olds out of the garage and tune in, sitting with the door partly opened, one foot in the foot well, the other planted on the driveway gravel. I would work my way off the porch and into the passenger's side, a blanket for warmth, the radio light glowing more dimly than the ember of his cigarette. We rarely spoke those evenings, but I felt safe and warm and loved, the din of the Forbes Field crowd as comforting as dinner talk at home.

No wonder that today I prefer games on radio— there's time to savor the moment, to let the game ease its way into the soul, for the announcer to paint the moment with words, not instant replays. I smile when (Yankee announcer) John Sterling remarks that a young pitcher appears florid and enervated. Sometimes a word is worth a thousand pictures.

I sold my Lionel electric train (with smoking locomotive) when I was nine so that I could buy a transistor radio to listen to Yankee games in bed at night. Today my antique collecting friends ridicule me for the trade. But Maris hit 61 homeruns that summer, and New York demolished Cincinnati in five games to win the World Series.

And through baseball, the generations continue to connect.

> Baseball connects American males with each other, not only through
> bleacher friendships and neighbor loyalties, not only through barroom
> fights, but most importantly, through generations. When you are

> small, you may not discuss politics or union dues or profit margins
> with your father's cigar smoking friends..., but you may discuss base-
> ball [Hall 30].

During times when my father and I didn't communicate much (or
often), we'd play catch in the yard after dinner. Or he would take me to
the park and hit fly balls to me, fly balls I chased down with a joy I suspect he never knew I felt. But he would stay out there hitting ball after ball
when in my heart I knew he never particularly enjoyed baseball. And one
evening, after a session that lasted until twilight, when we returned to the
car for a drink from the thermos we always carried, he handed me the keys
and let me drive laps around the field. I was 14. We spoke no more than
my grandfather and I had years earlier, but for the moment we found a
common ground, a chance to catch our breath and steel ourselves for the
turmoil of times yet to come.

But as much as baseball connects us, mostly it teaches us. It teaches
us about heartache. Any Cubs or Red Sox fan can attest to that. For me,
the first heartbreak was in 1960. That was the first summer I was a true
Yankees fan. Each morning I rifled through the Rochester *Democrat and
Chronicle* for the sports section and the write-up and box score of the
previous evening's game. I memorized starting lineups, kept track of
favorite players (Did Mantle get any hits, any homeruns? How about
Yogi?), perused league standings with the solemnity of a doctor examining patient charts. To an eight year old this was true intimacy. But as
a child I did not realize that giving in to intimacy opened the door for
heartbreak. That October, on a glorious afternoon, I left school with
New York leading the Pirates 7–4 late in game seven. By the time I
arrived home, the game was tied in the ninth inning, and before I had
time to settle in and even so much as remove my jacket, Bill Mazeroski
ended the game and the series with a homerun. I read in the next day's
paper that the Yankee's locker room was morgue silent, that Mantle
cried in front of his cubicle. I was doubly devastated. Not only had my
heroes let me down, but they did so without dignity, or so I thought at
age eight.

It was not until just a few years ago, in an interview with Gil
McDougald at his home at the Jersey shore, that I was able to place the 1960
Series in perspective. He was on the field at the time of the Mazeroski
homerun, and though disappointed to have lost the Series, he was also
relieved. The long season was over and he was looking forward to spending time with his family again. The professional game robs players of the
chance not only to watch their children grow up, but to offer daily guidance, and to be a father. So the next year when he was unprotected in the

expansion draft, he opted to retire (at age 32) rather than move to California to play for the Angels.

Such perspective may not come easy to those enthralled with the game. When Don Zimmer was asked (during his tenure as manager of the Chicago Cubs) if the team's poor play during a pennant run worried him, he responded by saying (in reference to an injury suffered during his playing days) that lying in a hospital with a metal plate in your head, not knowing what's going to come of you, or how you'll support your wife and child, that's worry. This is only baseball.

Baseball teaches us about hope and possibility. Each spring is a new beginning. As fans, we speculate on our team's chances. If the pitching holds together, if the veterans play consistently and a rookie develops, well, come October we just might be there. We can hope, because in baseball there isn't much that isn't possible. There's much that is improbable, but springtime brings with it re-birth and belief. In April we might even believe in Roy Hobbs. It isn't until the harsh reality of autumn that the devil collects his debts.

I'm ten years old, playing in my first Little League game of the season. The field smells of cut grass, the foul lines white as confectioner's sugar. My uniform is cotton flannel with the sponsor's name embroidered across the chest. It is so large the lettering is obscured, tucked halfway into my pants cinched with a webbed belt that wraps around me nearly twice. I'm told I'll lead off and search for the lightest bat, then watch the pitcher take his warm-ups. In a prescient moment I picture myself hitting the ball over the center fielder's head. On the second pitch I do just that. Running is effortless, my shirt fills like a spinnaker; miraculously my helmet stays on. I reach third base standing. The next batter grounds a single through the left side and I jubilantly trot home with the season's first run, knowing the world is ripe with possibilities just waiting to be plucked.

Baseball also teaches us about diminished possibility. We must all eventually come to recognize when life's possibilities are narrowed. An English professor of mine once confided that if he were not granted tenure the only option he saw as viable was to play left field for the Boston Red Sox, forgetting (or failing to accept) that he was already older than Ted Williams at retirement. In baseball, the foul lines stretch toward infinity from the 90 degree angle of home plate. The playing field encompasses one fourth of the cosmos. As long as you are a part of the game, that perspective remains constant. It isn't until you leave the game that the field of vision is diminished. No wonder we cling to our heroes' careers, urge them silently to play just another year, scan spring rosters for players born before we were. For when they are all gone from the game, the rules change. The foul lines creep closer together. Our view of life and what we can be, though perhaps better focused, is more limited.

Baseball teaches us about family. We cannot shift loyalties from the team we've always rooted for anymore than we can change the family we are born to. As much as a team owner, or a specific player, group of players, or for that matter generation of players may anger or embarrass us, there is no escape. The heart cannot will itself. Like having a sleazy uncle, no amount of personal detachment can separate us from the gene pool.

Baseball is ultimately about redemption. It is not just Mark McGwire and Sammy Sosa demonstrating character and integrity during their mutual assault of the Maris record. (Though what more graceful balance to Piazza's rejection of 88 million dollars from the Dodgers, or the wholesale dismantling of the Florida Marlins?) Baseball certainly provides opportunities to redeem. We remember Aaron and Mays and Ruth, not so much for the times they struck out, but for the times they did not. An infielder may boot a ground ball one inning, but single in his next at bat, then score what is ultimately the winning run.

Baseball is not a symbolic puzzle, waiting to be solved once and for all, any more than it is about collecting memorabilia. Popular culture has it right: baseball is much more than sport. We can begin to see how much more if we allow ourselves to learn from it, accept the ways in which it connects us, and in so doing let the spirit in the game recapture our souls. In this way, baseball *becomes* meaning.

References

Bull Durham. Ron Shelton. Perf. Kevin Costner, Tim Robbins, Susan Sarandon. Orion, 1988.

Hall, Donald. *Fathers Playing Catch with Sons.* San Francisco: North Point Press, 1985.

Richmond, Peter. "Pride of the Yankees." *Gentlemen's Quarterly.* September (1988): 357–361.

The Baseball Diamond as American Landscape

Stanton W. Green and Gary M. Green

The landscape is loud with dialogues, with story lines that connect a place with its inhabitants — Anne Whiston Spirn, *The Language of Landscape*

Introduction

This paper examines several relationships between baseball as a carrier of American culture and the places and landscapes in which it is played. We bring two different but complementary perspectives to these issues. One is that of Stanton, an anthropologist with a background in landscape history and archaeology. The other is that of Gary, a photographer, whose work most often deals with issues and images of landscape. We both bring a lifetime of baseball interest and personal study shared as brothers brought up in and around New York City. We will explore how and why people tie such strong feelings to the places where baseball is played — places that range from city streets to rural lots, from Little League fields to multimillion-dollar stadiums. We will discuss the cultural significance and emotional resonance of the baseball field — in whatever ultimate shape it takes — as place and as landscape.

Landscapes evoke feelings. These feelings are tied to personal history, aesthetics and knowledge of place. This kind of tie between people and place would seem to be especially strong in baseball. Miranda's survey of Cooperstown Symposium participants over the past ten years shows that indeed one third of the participants tie their interest and loyalty to baseball to a first experience at a major league ballpark. Many baseball stories relate events to place, reflecting the emotional resonance of certain ballparks and playing fields. People both inside and outside baseball regularly describe personal stories and feelings tied to the baseball field. We can quote two examples from Gmelch and Weiner's study of people working in baseball entitled *In the Ballpark* (1998).

> There are certain ballparks that guys really like to play in — usually it's places where they have been successful or else they like the fans, the style ... The thrill of seeing those ballparks from the inside for the very first time was something. It gave me goose bumps. My first time to the Astrodome, I thought I must have died and gone to baseball heaven [p. 49].

— *Q.V. Lowe, Manager, Jamestown Expos.*

> How I got to be a groundskeeper goes back to when I was ten years old and growing up in Madison, Wisconsin.... I fell in love with the Wrigley Field and the Cubs at the same time. Eventually my dad took me down to Wrigley Field. It was that visit, and later trips as well, that made me think about becoming a major league groundskeeper. It was a magical feeling just walking into Wrigley. If you've ever been there, you know what I am talking about. You walk up the ramp into the seating bowl on a beautiful, sunny afternoon, with the breeze blowing and the ivy waving. And out there across a big expanse is that nice green grass. What a sight. I thought, boy, I'd love to take care of this [p. 93].

— *Paul Zwaska, Head Groundskeeper, Baltimore Orioles.*

People tie their desire and energy to work the long hours and the long season of baseball to the feeling they get when they see the ballfield. Many relate the surge of emotion they feel as they emerge from the bowels of the stadium to their first sight of the baseball diamond.

Let us get personal for a moment. When we think of our personal feelings about baseball, a picture emerges of our father and his friends playing stickball in the streets of New York. In fact, this snapshot is the inspiration for this paper. The players in this picture (our father is the catcher) were all first-generation Americans being raised in the tenements of the Lower East Side. They were being brought up in families who were probably living more like Eastern Europeans than New Yorkers. But the children were playing baseball. Their assimilation into their new place and the dominant culture was in large part reflected and shaped by baseball. The cultural changes that were occurring between immigrant parents and first-generation children were broad and deep. And this was carried on to the next generation of children such as our sister and us.

Roger Kahn's memoir, *Memories of Summer,* describes walks with his father through the Brooklyn Botanical Gardens, not knowing if the journey would end at Ebbets Field. His is a memory rich with references to place. Doris Kearns Goodwin's *Wait 'Til Next Year* likewise ties childhood to Brooklyn and to baseball. The first game Stanton remembers seeing was in the 1950s with our uncle, also at Ebbets Field. He still sees, in his mind's eye, the baseball diamond filled with the larger-than-life figures of Snider, Furillo, and Campanella. In fact, he feels Ebbets Field every time he enters a major league ballpark. And it is the mind's eye that is so interesting to us.

At the group level, culture becomes an intervening factor between people and place. Culture is shared, it is variable and it is always changing. It also takes from and gives meaning to its setting, and it is this meaning that brings us to the issue of landscape.

Landscape Theory

We can look to sensational landscapes to see the drama played out between culture and landscape. In his book *Imagining Niagara,* Patrick McGreevy (1994) shows how Niagara Falls, one of the natural wonders of the earth's landscape, both shapes the way people imagine it and is shaped by people's imagination. People imagine the Falls as both a place of beauty and a place of danger. And they behave in ways that reflect their imagination. Some people get married at the falls (beauty) and some cross the Falls on tightropes (danger). At the same time, people modify the Falls landscape by building gardens (beauty) while others build wax museums and spook houses (danger). McGreevy's uses of the verb "imagine" in both the active and passive sense expresses this mutuality of landscape and culture.

The Irish writer Seamus Heaney offers a penetrating description of this tie between people and landscape in his discussion of sensing place. He speaks of the literacy and historicism of landscape and notes two ways people sense place — the illiterate/unconscious and the literate/conscious. Speaking of a trip along the west Ireland coast, he writes:

> Irrespective of our creed or politics, irrespective of what culture or subculture may have coloured our individual sensibilities, our imaginations assent to the stimulus of names, our sense of place is enhanced, our sense of ourselves as inhabitants not just of geographical country but of country of the mind are cemented. It is this feeling, assenting, equable marriage between the geographic country and the country of mind, whether that country of mind takes its tone unconsciously from a shared oral inherited culture, or from a

consciously savoured literary culture, or from both, it is this marriage
that constitutes the sense of place in its richest possible manifestation.

For the purposes of this paper, we might think of the country of mind as
the ballfield of mind — or the "field of dreams." It arrives from experiences, readings, stories, and conversations over generations.

If we deconstruct some of these metaphorical notions of space and
landscape, we can move to a more social scientific perspective of landscape as having three main aspects: a) The integration of nature and culture, b) The perception and use of space by people and communities, c)
The affect of view.

The conceptual power of landscape results from its incorporation of
these three elements. First, it takes into account the integration of natural
and cultural factors. The place of a ballfield within its natural and cultural
landscape is a good example of this. Second, it takes into account the con-
tinuity of how people use space. We can look here to the way ballfields are
connected to their surrounding landscapes. The third aspect, the affect of
view, is to our mind most provocative.

The Landscape as a View of the Land

A view of the land can come from without or within. The geographer
Tuan (1974) characterizes these as vertical and horizontal views. The vertical view is that of the observer or analyst. The analyst interprets from a
particular perspective. The ballpark can be observed architecturally, or as
a place within a city or perhaps from the perspective of its unique characteristics and how it affects the game itself (for example, Fenway Park's left
field, known as the "Green Monster").

The insider (horizontal) view is the perspective of the people inhabiting the landscape. It is the view of ballplayers, the manager, and all of the
participants who choose to work at ballparks: beer vendors, mascots, ushers, groundskeepers, umpires, and broadcasters among them. It is the view
of the fan as participant. It was Stanton's view as he entered Ebbets Field
and it was our father's view as he played stickball on the streets of New York.

The affect of the insider view begins to tie people to place. This com-
bines with the aesthetic and historic (sometimes in a personal sense)
aspects of a place to bring out the emotions one feels as he or she thinks
about past experiences at ballgames or as he or she emerges into the landscape of the baseball diamond. Thinking of the baseball diamond and its
enveloping ballpark as landscape allows us to start understanding its affect.

What We See in the Landscape; What We Feel About What We See

We often look at landscape with a sense of yearning. This feeling may simply be a desire to take in what is around us, to understand where we are and, finally, who we are. Landscape provides the physical phenomena essential to describing the place in which we live. For instance, the ground covering (has it snowed? are leaves on the ground? is the grass green?) and the color and weight of the sky provide a backdrop for the time we spend outside, in our cars, or looking out of windows. That basic information colors our moods, evokes memories from our histories, and gives us specific clues to the time of day and the time of year — universal measurements that give our life order.

Perhaps looking at the landscape around us is simply a way of locating ourselves in the world and finding order where often none is apparent. When we break down the landscape to its essential elements of land, horizon, and sky, we are simply attempting to organize a much more complex set of facts that might otherwise be difficult to comprehend. Photographer Robert Adams (1981), who has often photographed the prairies and surrounding landscapes of his native Colorado, champions the necessity and practical nature of searching for order and the beauty it embodies.

> If the proper goal of art is, as I now believe, Beauty, the Beauty that concerns me is that of Form. Beauty is, in my view, a synonym for the coherence and structure underlying life.
>
> Why is Form beautiful? Because, I think, it helps us meet our worst fear, the suspicion that life may be chaos and that therefore our suffering is without meaning....

Baseball certainly provides that kind of meaning for many. Its structure has been used by writers, poets, philosophers, and anthropologists as the literal and metaphorical core of many explorations in art, science, and thinking. For our purposes here, it provides a structure and a language with which we can begin to appreciate and begin to describe how our landscape — social and physical — has colored our histories and emotions.

The diamond, itself a geometrical way of organizing a piece of land, utilizes lines, bases, and specific properties (dirt and grass) to further define the landscape and thus, the playing field. Form does indeed follow function here and the result is that the baseball field and stadium, created primarily to facilitate the game, present a paradigm of the kind of beauty — coherence and structure — described by Adams.

Another photographer, Terry Evans (1986), known for her extensive work involving the prairies of Kansas and the Great Plains, discusses the transformative nature of finding order in landscape by likening it to the history of America's Great Plains.

> As I looked at the forbs and grasses, continually searching for information about pattern and form, I believe that I had accidentally entered into a relationship with the prairie, considerably less developed than but similar to the relationship expressed by the plains Indians long before me in their daily life and in their rock art. In paying careful attention to the plants around them, they were living daily in two orders of reality — one of appearances and one beyond appearances. Barney Mitchell, Navaho, says, "The greatest sacred thing is knowing the order and structure of things."

When we make photographs, we are framing segments of the world in order to give it some kind of order, an underlying structure that has meaning. Even the small static snapshots of our families can hold clues to bigger truths and real emotions. Ordering those snapshots in an album, chronologically, for instance, allows a further understanding of the places and times that define our personal histories. If we see beauty in that kind of order, it's quite simple to understand the sheer pleasure involved in witnessing the baseball diamond with its geometrical precision, brilliant colors, and ultimate sense of order.

If our experience with the landscape of baseball is rooted in order, and thus — at least by modernist theories — beauty, it's a clear shot to understanding the emotional aspects of what we experience when we watch or play the game. Agnes Martin, a painter whose abstract grid paintings are often translated as landscapes, makes the short leap between beauty and emotion.

> When I think of art I think of beauty. Beauty is the mystery of life. We respond to beauty with emotion.... All artwork is about beauty; all positive work represents it and celebrates it. All negative art protests the lack of beauty in our lives.
> Beauty illustrates happiness; the wind in the grass, the glistening waves following each other, the flight of birds, all speak of happiness. The clear blue sky illustrates a different kind of happiness and the soft dark night a different kind. There are an infinite number of different kinds of happiness.... Happiness is being on the beam with life — to feel the pull of life.

When we first walk through the tunnel at Yankee Stadium to see the crowd and the great green pasture of the playing field, we most certainly feel the "pull of life," as Martin has described it. And we feel a pull as well, perhaps more quietly, when we drive by a Little League field that is decked out in the colors of merchant-sponsored teams and small crowds in summer clothes. And we most likely feel an emotional pull of another kind when we drive by an empty ballfield in the winter, with only the memory of the previous summer's events or perhaps the long-ago seasons of our youth.

The State of the Park: What Goes Up Must Come Down

If we look at the development of ballfields and the baseball diamond over the past century and a half, we begin to see a changing aesthetic and landscape (Lowry 1986, Ritter 1992, Kammer 1982, White 1996). The changing baseball landscape is in part reflected in the rotating list of names used to describe the place it is played: ballfield, ballyard, Elysian Fields, grounds, ballpark, stadium, etc.

Baseball began as townball. This was played within a square field marked by a set of stakes that marked a square in a common or pastureland. This square was surrounded by an unbounded field. This setup mirrored the agrarian pattern of land use of the times. The area within the stakes was the infield, while the outer reaches formed the outfield. A townball field may have looked something like a typically lush, green Nebraska field. The game involved a pitcher and batter and a number and scattered set of fielders. No gloves were worn to catch the somewhat softer townball, which, once struck in any direction or for any distance, had to be run out. Scores were tallied by touching the four stakes sequentially. Outs were recorded in two manners. One way was to catch the ball on the fly with both feet on the ground. The second was to hit a runner with the ball (called burning or soaking the runner) while he was away from a stake (base). Runners could avoid being burned by running anywhere in the field (and even loitering far enough away to be ignored by the fielders) or going to any stake in whatever order. Each side is allowed one out per inning. This less structured version of baseball reflects the more open, less structured playing field.

One of the earliest places the baseball diamond seems to have been inaugurated was in Hoboken, New Jersey, at Elysian Fields. Here the infield and outfield are laid out in the manner familiar to us with the diamond and arched outfield. Union Grounds in Brooklyn was the first enclosed field. This was followed by the building of a series of wooden ballparks including the original Polo Grounds in New York (1890) and Shibe Park in Philadelphia (1909).

The 1920s brought us the concrete and steel city parks that we now consider with some nostalgia: Wrigley Field, Fenway Park, Detroit Stadium and Yankee Stadium are among the ones still standing (although Detroit stadium has seen its last season and Fenway is soon to be re-created in an adjacent lot). These parks are notable for two reasons: They are located near public transportation (train stations, bus stops) for access from within the city, and they configure to their local terrain and cityscape. This latter attribute is what determines some of the unique characteristics of these fields.

The mid-twentieth century brought us the multipurpose stadium. Named Shea, Three Rivers, Veterans and Memorial stadiums, these ballfields were set out from the inner city and surrounded by parking lots accessible to the suburban commuter. They also melded the needs of football to those of baseball in their architecture. Hence, they are often cited as reflecting the homogenization of middle-class culture and are especially disliked by baseball fans because of their generic, cookie-cutter design.

The 1990s bring us back full circle to the traditional ballpark. Baltimore, Cleveland, Arlington, and Pittsburgh, Philadelphia and New York have built or will soon be building retro-parks. Camden Yards, Jacobs Field, and The Ballpark at Arlington will soon be joined by PNC Park and an Ebbets Field look-alike in Queens. Indeed this move back to traditional ballparks in itself expresses the strength of historic place in baseball.

The controversy over demolishing Fenway Park and replacing it with a look-alike field with upgraded clubhouses, indoor batting cages and, of course, skyboxes is a good illustration of the power of the past — Heaney's historicism of landscape — as it plays out in baseball. Not only is the new left field to be a replicated Green Monster, but the original left field wall will be saved and incorporated into a city park adjacent to the new Fenway Park. Replication in itself is not sufficient to maintain the tradition and the sense of place of baseball in Boston. The emotional attachment to Fenway Park's defining characteristic — the left-field wall where Yastrzemski held so many base runners to 400 foot singles — is so strong as to call for its preservation as part of Boston's landscape. Interestingly, the destruction of Memorial Stadium in Baltimore did not seem to call for the same action. As a multipurpose stadium from the 1960s, this home of the Orioles seems not as securely connected to the tradition and history of baseball to call for its remembrance and preservation in the same manner as Fenway Park. The sense of place, in Heaney's terms, which so strongly ties Fenway Park to the Boston landscape, does not appear to resonate in Baltimore as that city regards its own demolished park.

Conclusion

We would like to close by juxtaposing some baseball landscapes and traditional landscapes to express our thesis of emotional resonance. Ground, Horizon, and Sky in both the traditional and baseball form of landscape express a coherence, a history, and an aesthetic that evokes feelings of place and, in so doing, emotions that tie us to landscape and landscape to us. The Forbes Field horizon melds into the Pittsburgh sky with its outfield lights foreshadowing some city towers. The place, Forbes Field, evokes visions of Bill Mazeroski and Roberto Clemente while at the same time tying these to the Pittsburgh of the 1960s and 1970s. A vertical connection between horizon and sky similarly integrates the Columbia County landscape. Here a telephone pole coheres cultural and natural landscapes. In both cases, meaning is given and emotion derived through the history and view of the photographer and observer.

When shared by communities, the emotional resonance of baseball landscapes such as the classic view of the Yankee Stadium façade forms a part of the fabric of the culture that makes us feel comfortable as individuals within our complex and ever-changing world. The beauty of baseball is rooted in American history and place, a point essentially described by one of America's finest poets, Donald Hall.

> Baseball is fathers and sons.... Baseball is the generations, looping backward forever with a million apparitions of sticks and balls, cricket and rounders, and the games the Iroquois play in Connecticut before the English came. Baseball is fathers and sons playing catch, lazy and murderous, wild and controlled, the profound archaic song of birth, growth, ages and death. This diamond encloses us.

References

Adams, Robert. *Beauty in Photography: Essays in Defense of Traditional Values.* New York: Aperture, 1981.

Evans, Terry. *Prairie: Images of Ground and Sky.* Lawrence: University Press of Kansas, 1986.

Gmelch, George, and J. J. Weiner. *In the Ballpark: The Working Lives of Baseball People.* Washington, D.C.: Smithsonian Press, 1998.

Goodwin, Doris Kearns. *Wait 'Til Next Year: A Memoir.* New York: Simon & Schuster, 1997.

Hall, Donald. *Fathers Playing Catch with Sons: Essays on Sport (Mostly Baseball).* San Francisco: North Point Press, 1985.

Heaney, Seamus. "The Sense of Place." In *Preoccupations: Selected Prose 1968–1978.* New York: Farrar, Straus and Giroux, 1980.

Kahn, Roger. *Memories of Summer: When Baseball Was an Art and Writing About It a Game.* New York: Hyperion, 1997.

Kammer, David John, "Take Me Out to the Ballgame: American Cultural Values in the Architectural Evolution and Criticism of the Modern Baseball Stadium." Ph.D. Dissertation, University of New Mexico, 1982.

Lowry, Philip. *Green Cathedrals Cooperstown*. New York: SABR, 1986.

Martin, Agnes, "Beauty is the Mystery of Life." *El Palacio* 95 (Fall-Winter 1989).

McGreevy, Patrick. *Imagining Niagara: The Meaning and Making of Niagara Falls*. Amherst: University of Massachusetts Press, 1994.

Miranda, Michael, "Who Are We and Why Are We Here? A Survey of Participants of the Cooperstown Symposium." Presented at the 11th annual Cooperstown Symposium. National Baseball Hall of Fame, Cooperstown, NY, 1999.

Ritter, Lawrence. *Lost Ballparks: A Celebration of Baseball Legendary Fields*. New York: Penguin Studio Books, 1992.

Spirn, Anne Whiston. *The Language of Landscape*. New Haven: Yale University Press, 1998.

Tuan, Yi Fu. *Topophilia: A Study of Environmental Perception, Attitudes and Values*. Englewood Cliffs, New Jersey: Prentice Hall, 1974.

White, G. Edward. *Creating the National Pastime*. Princeton, New Jersey: Princeton University Press, 1996.

The 1913 World Series and the Epic Imagination

G. Ralph Strohl, III

Introduction

In the Sunday, October 5, 1913, edition of the *New York Times*, a fascinating topical cartoon appeared with the title, "The Annual Traffic Holdup."[1] A policeman, labeled "World's Series," stands in the middle of a busy street, a whistle in his mouth and his hand raised, palm out, stopping traffic. Come to a sudden halt are a variety of vehicles, labeled, respectively, "Affairs of the Nation," "Politics," "The Drama," and "Commerce." The policeman is allowing two boys, dressed in Little Lord Fauntleroy suits, to cross the street. These boys are labeled "Connie Mack" and "Johnny Mac," and they are carrying dolls labeled "Athletics" and "Giants," respectively.

The meaning is clear. All the usual activities of the nation come to a temporary halt to focus on these two boys and their dolls. They control the street for now. Lest anyone misunderstand, however, the *Times* hammers the point home in an editorial two days later, the Opening Day of the series, concluding

> For the remainder of this week, and perhaps longer, the world's series will absorb most of the interest of the American people. After the victory has been won there will be a chance for the consideration of other things, including business, the working of the new tariff, and here in New York, a somewhat important municipal campaign.[2]

For the *New York Times* and the *Philadelphia Inquirer*, newspapers representing the cities involved in the 1913 World Series, the series was far

41

more than a championship sporting event. As I will demonstrate, the World Series, by 1913, was seen as an annual national civic ritual, and this ritual bespoke

- The basic unity of the nation, bringing all economic classes, ethnic groups and dwellers of every region of the nation together in a celebratory event; and
- The quintessential American virtues which define the nation in contradistinction to the rest of the world, particularly Europe;
- Who properly had a share in this ritual, what their portion was, and, in the case of the African American, provided a chilling indication of just how much of an outsider he was perceived to be.

Good rituals, of course, are undergirded by crackling good stories, stories of epic dimensions. The journalistic task in October 1913, was, therefore, to provide a narrative worthy of the ritual and celebratory enterprise to be undertaken, on alternate days, at the Polo Grounds in upper Manhattan and Shibe Park in Philadelphia. This the *New York Times*, and, in a less deliberately calculated fashion, the *Philadelphia Inquirer* accomplished.

Why did these papers choose to unfold this World Series to its readers through the narrative style of the heroic epic? There were, after all, other narrative styles available to their editors. The year before, for example, the *New York Times* had told the tale of the series through the voices of Giants' players, the articles, of course, ghostwritten by professional newspapermen. In Chicago, in the pages of the *Tribune*, a young Ring Lardner was already honing the folksy, sardonic style which became his trademark. Then, there was the more neutral, more strictly reportorial style of writing, exemplified this year by Cy Sanborn, who covered the 1913 World Series for the *Chicago Tribune*.

By inference from the themes intoned in the pages of the *New York Times* and *Philadelphia Inquirer*, it may be surmised that the use of the epic style allowed these papers, first of all, to express the self-confidence and feelings of moral and social superiority of a nation "on the make." Only recently come into empire on the international scene as a result of victory in the Spanish-American War, politically stable and growing quickly, both economically and in population, the United States certainly was such a nation, and was acutely aware of its growing status.

At the same time, there was a certain malaise that arose from the nation's rapid diversification of population through the immigration of numerous ethnic groups, sharp economic stratification of society consequent upon rapid industrialization, and regionalism attendant upon settlement and consolidation of vast tracts of land in the west of the nation. Consequently, the basis on which national unity might rest was a reasonable question to posit.

Therefore, the papers seem to be addressing concerns arising from social and demographic forces that threaten the nation's sense of unity and purpose precisely at a time when it is generally felt there is reason for great national pride and optimism. They endeavor to do this by representing the World Series as a ritual of national unity and self-representation, in which all citizens of the nation have a stake.

To demonstrate how the papers set about its epic and ritual task, I shall first discuss the narrative accounts of the games, particularly as they occur in the *New York Times*, to demonstrate the epic character with which the sports writers clothed the contest. I shall then look at specific elements of these narratives, as well as the editorial and op-ed commentary made about the series, and small "filler" articles that deal with the disruption of American life due to the games, to demonstrate the civic ritual importance the papers attached to the World Series. I shall conclude with some observations about how baseball and the World Series served to differentiate the nation from the rest of the world, particularly Europe.[3]

The World's Series in 1913

This series engendered great anticipation among the respective teams' enthusiasts, and among baseball fans, generally. The Philadelphia Athletics and the New York Giants had met twice before in the series. The first time, in 1905, a young Christy Mathewson had turned in what remains the greatest individual pitching performance in World Series history, throwing three complete game shutouts in a five game series. All five games were shutouts, and, since the Giants lost the second game on unearned runs, the Giants' team Earned Run Average for the series was 0.00, still the finest team pitching performance in World Series play.

The teams met again in 1911, in a series won by the Athletics in six games. In this series the A's third baseman, John Franklin Baker, earned the moniker "Home Run" Baker by means of two dramatic blasts, against Rube Marquard and Christy Mathewson, respectively. These home runs were instrumental in Philadelphia victories in the second and third games of that series.

The teams were only a little changed from 1911, and, while few of the figures from the 1905 series remained on the teams in 1913, those who did were legendary:

- The managers, Connie Mack and John J. McGraw;
- Christy Mathewson, already winner of 331 games going into the 1913 series, and an idol throughout America; and
- The Athletics two most important pitchers, Charles Albert "Chief" Bender, and Eddie Plank, winner, at this point, of 269 career games, and a peculiar character known to talk to the baseball before pitching it.

Thus, there was a history here, providing an intense dramatic context. The Giants and the Athletics were about to meet for the third time in ten World Series, with managers and players who were already the stuff of legend on the American sporting scene.

A superficial glance suggests that the 1913 series did not live up to its billing. The Athletics won it in five games. The home team won only one of the five games — the A's in Game Four — and then barely hung on to win by a run after opening up a 6–0 lead. The Giants were bedeviled by injuries, losing their catcher, John "Chief" Meyers, to a freak injury just prior to Game Two, and with their starting first baseman, Fred Merkle, and center fielder, Fred Snodgrass, hobbled with ankle injuries. In addition, heavy wet weather bedeviled the series, with rain occurring most evenings all along the eastern seaboard, leaving the playing fields damp and slow in the ensuing afternoons.

For all that, however, there was quite a bit of drama in this series, with all the games save one, the third, being taut and closely played. The two newspapers, particularly the *Times*, did not fail to pick up on this drama in their writing.

The Epic Imagination at Work —
The New York Times *Accounts*

THE OPENING CADENCE

The *New York Times* accounts of the five games have a common structure. They open with a strident heroic cadence that announces the primary hero of the game, indicating what dramatic act cast him into that role. This is followed immediately by the introduction of the secondary hero(es) and the acts that place him in that position. Thus, the account of game two opens with the result of two old nemeses squaring off against one another:

> Christopher Mathewson, stout of heart and supple of arm, surmounted the obstacles of a crippled team and a deadly batting foe at Shibe Park to-day and pitched the Giants to a ten-inning shut-out victory over the slugging Athletics. He proved the master of Eddie

Plank in a gripping duel of curves, and when the teams seemed dead-locked he belted forth a stinging hit which broke the tie and blazed a tally of victory on the barren scoreboard. The Giants then fell upon the tottering Plank, drove in two more runs, and won the second struggle of the world's series by a 3 to 0 score.

Twenty thousand fans looked on, stunned and silent. No glad outcry of praise greeted the wonderful performance of "Big Six" and the fighting Giants. When "Home Run" Baker was retired for the last out in the tenth inning by the make-shift first baseman, "Hooks" Wiltse, Philadelphia's confidence in its batting heroes was shattered. Peerless Matty tramped to the clubhouse alone. On his broad shoulders he had carried the responsibility of the victorious strife, which redeemed the prestige of the New York Club. Matty is still the old master among the pitchers, and after thirteen years of yeoman service on the mound stands out as one of the most remarkable athletes the national game has ever known.

And two paragraphs further on:

The name of Wiltse will always be associated with Matty's in this victory. He fielded the territory around his station like Hal Chase at his best. And he wore a fingered glove, refusing to use a first sacker's mitt. Twice in the ninth inning, after two hits off Matty and Doyle's error had put Athletic runners on third and second with no one out, it was the cool, accurate fielding of Wiltse which shut off two runs at the plate. He played the position with grace and ease, and was Matty's greatest aid when the going was rough.[4]

COMIC RELIEF

After the opening cadence, the focus shifts to the hours before the game, when the crowd gathers. In the game one account, the focus was on who was in attendance, and has the flavor of a gossip column. The game two account focuses on the injuries to Giant players and an assessment of the Giants chances with the loss of their catcher, the "Chief" Meyers. But this portion of the account allowed for humor, as well, as exhibited by this tale of possible ticket-scalping prior to game four:

There was a good deal of commotion on Lehigh Avenue about 1:30 o'clock when "Germany" Schaefer of the Washington Club had two tickets, and was looking for somebody to sell them to at the regular price, $2. He did not see any familiar faces so he offered them to a deserving looking citizen. A policeman saw him in the act of turning over the tickets, and arrested him. The patrol wagon came and as the ball player started for the station house, the crowd guyed him unmercifully.

"Say, Germany, they can't arrest you for that," some one shouted.

"I told them that but they wouldn't believe me," answered Schaefer.

At the police station Schaefer explained the situation and was released. The officer on the desk first listened to his tale of woe and then said: "How do we know you're 'Germany' Schaefer?"

"Listen," said the comedian, "and I'll tell you a funny story. I'll make you laugh and then you'll know."

Schaefer told an old story, but it was new in Philly, and they let him go out to the game.[5]

After this *entr'acte*, the article gets down to inning-by-inning business, dwelling at length on the spots it deems crucial in deciding the game. In this section, the prose can range from dry to absolutely purple, and one sees a great deal of the melodramatic here, as in this description of a key double play in game one. The Giants have men on first and third with one out, down only a run, and their shortstop, Art Fletcher, at the bat:

From the gloomy recesses of the grandstands thundered the roar of thousands of fans, imploring, entreating, begging Fletcher to smash out the hit which would tie the score. Men set their teeth hard and clenched their fists. All eyes were glued on the stolid, unemotional Indian. Oh, if he would only crack or show some sign that the intensity of the situation was wearing on him. A howling multitude demanded his downfall, shrieked for his collapse. He cast a sneering, squinting glance over the mob. Again he looked back and saw that great $100,000 infield set and waiting. The personification of confidence the Chippewa was, and as cool as an arctic Winter.

Fletcher hit the ball with terrific impact and it bounded over the grass at Barry. Shafer raced down the third base path and the crowd jumped to its feet in one glad outcry, for they supposed that Shafer was carrying home the tieing run.

But wait. Barry jumped into the bounding ball. He fought it as it tried to slip from his hands. He clutched it tight, shot the ball to the waiting Collins, and Doyle was forced at second. Fletcher was tearing toward first, calling on every bit of speed at his command. Collins pivoted on one foot, swung easily and gracefully about until he faced first, and relayed the ball to McInnes. McInnes saw instantly that the throw was wide. With one toe on the cushion he spread himself out as far as his arms would reach. The white sphere came from Collins's hand like a rifle ball and sunk into the outstretched mitt of McInnes with a dull thud. The double play was completed, Shafer's run did not count, and the $100,000 infield saved the day and Bender's reputation.[6]

MORTALITY

The *Times* doesn't simply focus on the drama of the action in these inning-by-inning accounts. This is not just ball-playing; rather, it is where the young earn their stripes, the old see the handwriting on the wall, and every player comes face-to-face with either glory or ignominy. The *Times* intones the characteristically epic-heroic theme of mortality through its focus on youth and age, both plentifully present in this series. For example, the Athletics are dependent in game three on a rookie battery of pitcher "Bullet" Joe Bush and catcher Wally Schang, both of whom figure prominently in an 8–2 victory:

> As the game went along the value of Bush's pitching increased. Catching him was Wallie Schang, himself only 23 years old and new in world series games. This infant battery worked wonders. The enthusiasm of youth was in their work. After a time they forgot the rabid gathering which surrounded them, forgot that they were playing a game that meant gold and glory. They just settled down to natural, normal ball playing, and it was too much for the Giants.[7]

In contrast is this description of the two old masters of the mound, Mathewson and Plank, facing each other in Game Two. The game has entered the tenth inning scoreless, and we are set up to witness Achilles, in the person of Mathewson, slay Hector, played by Plank, in front of his own. The sequence begins with this sentence:

> Larry McLean, tall and clumsy, sounded Plank's death knell when he stepped to plate in the tenth.[8]

It transpires that Mathewson himself drives home the initial run with a single off his rival. Under the subtitle "Matty Crushes his Rival," we now read:

> Like a morning glory in the bright sun, Plank was fading. The deceptive hop on his curve ball and the tantalizing tangent of his famous cross-fire were missing. He had lost his cunning. The next ball he pitched hit Larry Doyle in the ribs and the bases were crowded.

Plank gives up another hit, leading to two more runs, and finally struggles out of the tenth:

> Dejected, tired, and bitterly disappointed, Plank walked slowly to the bench. They patted him on the back and tried to cheer him up. It was no use. He looked at Connie Mack and Connie looked at him. There was no word of reproach, no reference to the great southpaw's collapse. Plank was sorry he lost the game, but Mack was sorry for Plank.
>
> It's a tough thing to see Old Father Time stalk into the national pastime, touch a great performer like Plank on the shoulder, and tell him that his best pitching days are over. But they all get it sooner or later, in all walks of life, so cheer up, Eddie Plank, you were great in your day.

The Managers, The Teams, The Cities

An interesting motif in the *Times'* accounts is a set of paralleling contrasts drawn between the two managers, their respective teams, and their respective cities. In brief, it goes like this: McGraw's belligerence, pugnacious behavior and cantankerousness contrasts with Mack's reserved taciturnity, precisely the way the Giants' fiery, often brilliant but sometimes erratic play contrasts with the Athletics' systematic, thoughtful, "well-oiled" machine-like play. Extending the comparison, New York, brassy, always on the make, rough-and-tumble and scheming, contrasts, in similar fashion, with Philadelphia, a prim, proper, well-behaved, quiet and peaceable place.

Connie Mack's image as a stern, paternal sort with a firm grip on affairs is ubiquitous in these pages, as in this description from Game Three, when he counsels the young Joe Bush, who has just escaped an early-inning jam:

> After that trying moment, Bush sat next to Connie Mack on the Athletics' bench. Words of fatherly advice were given to the nervous boy. Bush listened and profited. The kind talk of the taciturn Mack did him a world of good. He went back into the fray with renewed confidence and an iron nerve, for he knew that he had a team behind him that would play their hearts out to return him a victor.[9]

McGraw, by contrast, is much more "one of the boys," in the coach's box urging his players on, and emotionally involved in the game. Missing from all depictions of McGraw, however, is the raw, hard, combative edge which personified him to the nation. His persona is "sanitized" in these pages; the contrast is between the hierarchical relationship that exists between Mack and the Athletics, and the *primus inter pares* relationship between McGraw and his Giants.

The Athletics' disciplined, "machine-like," and very effective play is symbolized by the "$100,000 infield" of Stuffy McInnis (1B), Eddie Collins (2B), Frank Baker (3B) and Jack Barry (SS). We have seen an example of what they could do already. By contrast, the Giants are capable of brilliant play, as exemplified by a spectacular leaping grab of a high line drive by the Giants' captain, "Laughing" Larry Doyle, and by Wiltse's heroics in game two, but are also capable of serious lapses, as indicated in this extraordinary passage from the fifth and final game:

> A lurid wild throw by Burns in the first inning paved the way for the first run. A foolish foozle by Larry Doyle, the Giant captain, and a monstrous misplay by the ill-fated Fred Merkle in the third inning, made possible the Athletics other runs and triumph.[10]

Finally, we can descry the difference between Philadelphia and New York with ease. Here is an image of Philadelphia:

> One of the best jobs in Philadelphia during a world's series is that of a policeman. The entire force sit about the outfield on soap boxes, just

inside the fence, and all they have to do is watch the game. Pretty soft. They don't even have to go into the crowd to recover the balls which are knocked foul, as they do in New York. Here the people are so honest that every ball is thrown back.[11]

Here is an image of New York:

The speculators grew rich on the baseball hungry crowd ... One man paid $20 for a $1 bleacher seat a half hour before the game. "I came 2,000 miles to see a world's series game," he said, "and I'm going to see it, no matter what it costs. Out West, where I came from, they used to hold up folks at the point of a pistol and take their money, but that system was very primitive compared to the way they get the money in New York."[12]

The Ritual Imagination

THE AMERICAN IDEAL

On October ninth, an op-ed piece appeared in the *New York Times*, which read, in part:

Serious-minded folk are inclined more than to doubt whether baseball played by hired professionals for money is a thing that really deserves the amount of interest it is just now receiving. Unquestionably, however, the interest is sincere and keen, and before condemning it as a manifestation of the public's frivolity it would be well to remember that when a large fraction of 90,000,000 people unites in getting excited over something there is likely to be a good deal of justification for its emotion.

That is particularly probable when the fraction includes people in every walk of life, and is by no means confined to the dull or vicious. Indeed, the appeal of baseball seems to be strongest to the active in mind and body — to those of broad sympathies and prompt reactions — while the disposition to question the validity of its claim to attention is found chiefly among those who are not very much interested in anything or who have no interest for more than a single object.

The charm of the game presumably lies in its close adaptation to the American temperament. It develops and illustrates many of the qualities we admire most, and when played, as now, by its recognized masters, the gratification it affords has a distinct aesthetic element.[13]

Here, then, is the meaning of the World Series, according to the *New York Times*. The game reveals the best qualities of the American temperament, and draws into its arena people who are "active in mind and body," and who have "broad sympathies and prompt reactions." Furthermore, this temperament is not possessed by an elite only — it permeates the republic and its entire citizenry.

This theme is hammered home repeatedly in the pages of the *Times*, beginning the Sunday prior to the series opener. An article, entitled "Famous Baseball Fans Who Haunt the Polo Grounds," commences, "Baseball's reputation as a thoroughly democratic sport and as a leveler of persons is well deserved ... Baseball enthusiasm thrills humanity in all walks of life, from the staid professional to the street gamin...."[14] It goes on to list the politicians, lawyers, businessmen, people of the theater, high society and Wall Street who frequent the games, "rubbing shoulders" with the common man. Several of the people named in this article reappear in the crowd in the account of the opening game.

We have seen how the ballplayers live or fail to live up to the glory that is offered them in the games. Their role in this national ritual is clear. They are, as it were, the high priests of the annual demonstration of the American character and temperament. What is the role of the rest of us in this agonistic ritual? What is our share? How is it brought about?

PARTICIPANTS IN THE RITUAL

Certainly the fans in attendance, whether within the ritual enclosure of the park, or witnessing from nearby rooftops or hilltops, are important ritual participants. They provide the emotional drive for each game; their day's satisfaction or dissatisfaction hangs on the outcome. Mention has already been made of the *Times'* assessment of the crowd and its makeup, but one more feature should be noticed:

> Nor is the baseball frenzy confined to the men. Women fans crowd the grounds, the average woman fan being far more demonstrative than the average man. Somewhat surprising is the amount of technical knowledge shown by women fans. They are excellent judges of hits and errors, and follow each play with close attention.[15]

The newspapers seek to extend the range of the crowd to the readership not in attendance. The *Times* accomplishes this by switching into the present tense at important moments of the game. In this manner, the game is re-created in the present, giving the reader the sense of being witness to events as they actually occur. Thus, we read in the Game One account:

> Now that this picture-taking appetite has been satisfied, let's have a little baseball ... Eddie Murphy is the first citizen up, making his debut as a world's series performer.[16]

Then, there is this moment at the end of Game Four:

> And now, Red Murray, if there ever was a time when you should deliver
> a hit, this is it. Slug it, chop it, murder it, but for goodness sake, whale
> it somewhere out of reach of those crouching, Mackian infielders.[17]

Both papers extend the participants in this ritual to the entire nation, and through that widespread participation, the nation, for all its differentiations of geography, ethnicity and economic status — not to mention the intense individualistic ethos that is identified with it —finds a common identity, a kind of unity. The *New York Times* accomplishes this in little ways, primarily by overtly linking a ballplayer with his hometown. Thus, we hear of "Gettysburg" Eddie Plank, "Georgie Burns of Utica, New York," "Tillie Shafer of Los Angeles," and Jeff Tesreau, "the Ozark Ajax, massive and powerful." These heroic figures are our neighbors, they live among us, and only highlight positive qualities we are all deemed to share.

The *Philadelphia Inquirer* establishes the national character of this eastern seaboard contest in an editorial after the fourth game entitled "Brainerd is on the map." Brainerd, Minnesota, was the birthplace of Bender and Joe Bush who, between them, won three series games for the Athletics in 1913. The editorial establishes a common bond between the metropolis and the little northern Minnesota town, which "only in recent years has arisen to the dignity of ten thousand population," due to the stimulus of the Northern Pacific Railroad. The editorial concludes:

> This is a nation of opportunity. Four years ago Bush was pitching on
> a high school team. Now none are so great as to refuse him reverence.
> Not long ago Bender was struggling with the English language. Now
> King Philip, Logan Powhattan, Osceola, Sitting Bull and Geronimo
> pale into insignificance.
>   We are opposed to the proposition to make Brainerd the capital of
> the United States, but we join most heartily in her present joy, seeing
> that so much of it is our own.[18]

Two more notes regarding the ballplayers themselves. First, the role of Native Americans is interesting. Clearly, the media perceive a role for them in this celebration of American life and society. Charles Bender, a Chippewa, is very highly regarded for his ability. Equally, the injury to John Meyers, a Cahuilla from California (whom the *Times* takes pains to note is "not a reservation Indian"[19]), early in the series is perceived to damage seriously the Giants' hopes by depriving them of a savvy, accomplished veteran hitter and handler of pitchers.[20]

The prejudicial character of the whites' interactions with the Native Americans is present in these accounts, and in commentary articles. "Chief" Bender has "the Indian memory," according to Hugh Fullerton, that allows him to remember the pitching sequence to a specific hitter years later. "Mack's Chippewa Scalps Giants in Fourth Game," proclaims the *Inquirer*.[21] Even so, the regard for these players as players is high, and some alteration in attitude appears to have occurred since the 1905 series, when the *Times* referred to Bender as "the tall, gaunt, swarthy, aboriginal speed incubator."[22]

Denied a share in the ritual is the African American. This is, of course, not news, but, especially in the *Times*, it is striking how outside the "American Dream" the African American is perceived to be. In the week of the series, two stories appeared in which African Americans figured prominently. One, entitled "Negro Killed in Race Riot," appeared on page one in the column adjoining the account of the opening game of the series. It involved the shooting death of a black man in Joliet as he led a group in storming the jail where a young black woman had been held for drunkenness. The other, entitled "Walter Johnson Loses," had the subheading "Senators' Pitcher Drops Game to Colored Team After Near Riot" and appeared in the sports pages the day before the series opened. It tells of an exhibition game almost canceled because of a protest by black players who had not been paid for at least six weeks. The *Times* states that the situation nearly developed into a "full-fledged riot," and that "it was with difficulty that the squad of police prevented disorder."[23]

In other words, in these *New York Times* articles, the African American is portrayed as the antithesis of the ideal represented on the baseball field. The African American is associated with disorder, rioting, and violence, and is kept at bay by the authorities only with difficulty.

RITUAL TIME

Recall the cartoon of the policeman holding up the nation's traffic for the World Series, and its stress on the suspension of ordinary time on behalf of the World Series. The intention here is clearly to supplant the daily routine with a ritual one, and the ordinary consideration of time with ritual time. Both papers planted numerous small news items around the baseball game accounts to make clear to the reader that this cartoon was not entirely in jest.

- Both papers comment on the Senate minority leader's disruption of majority attempts to gain a quorum by interrupting with updates of the opening game, provided him by a page.[24]
- The *Inquirer* informs us that "Baseball and woman suffrage divided the attention of the Committee on Elementary Schools of the Board of Education," necessitating adjournment and reconvening to attend to business.[25]

• The *Times* talks of Wall Street's closing due to the lack of floor traders,[26] the inattentiveness of a Columbia University class on the lecture to hand, due to the students daydreaming about the ongoing fourth game of the series,[27] and how President Wilson tired of bulletins updating him on the progress of the game and left to play golf. President Wilson's secretary, Mr. Tumulty, left the White House, "to mingle with the crowd in front of the newspaper bulletin board, finding the White House bulletin service less interesting."[28]

The papers agree. The national attention is well focused on a single object. At the same time, that object is the national ritual that celebrates our broad-mindedness, our creativity, our vitality and our diversity. We undertake that celebration in common, shoulder-to-shoulder with whoever is next to us, regardless of rank, privilege, geographic or ethnic background, whether at the park, or in front of an electronic scoreboard in Times Square or in the window of the local newspaper office. In this ritual we find the common bonds that constitute our national unity.

Conclusion: U.S. and the World

The 1913 World Series occurred during the highly publicized visit to North America of England's Lord Northcliffe.[29] Lord Northcliffe, it appears, had much to say about American life and customs, not excluding baseball and the World Series. He attended the first game of the series on October seventh, held at the Polo Grounds, and, while admitting he enjoyed himself ("He had a jolly good time,"[30] reports the *Times*), was surprised at the small attendance and felt the game was too technical and intricate to supplant soccer in popularity anywhere else, particularly in England.

The *Times* took these observations somewhat personally, and responded with an editorial suggesting that baseball's inability to be popular elsewhere had more to do with the lack of mental acuity on the part of the common man of more benighted nations such as existed in Europe, than with the game itself.[31] Thus, it was with evident glee that the *Times* published a news item on October eighth, entitled "Baseball in Finland: National Game 'One of Chief Elements of Physical Education,'" in which it quoted Helsingfors University Professor Lauri Pikhola as saying, in a letter addressed to an official of the Amateur Athletic Union, "It is the opinion of those interested in baseball in Finland ... that the game will gain a stronger foothold in two years than the game of soccer has gained in seven years."[32]

The underlying, and often overt, theme in the discussion of the United States *vis-à-vis* the rest of the world, but especially Europe, is the vitality of the former versus the jadedness and torpor of the latter. America is a comer, Europe is coming a cropper. This democratic nation, symbolized by that most democratic of sports, ennobles every one of its citizens, in contrast to the monarchies of Europe, the elitist nature of which ennobles only a few and can oppress many.

The importance of distinguishing the nation from the rest of the world has a far deeper and more sober importance than is seen in the bandying of words with Lord Northcliffe. To understand this, one needs to look at another cartoon, one or another version of which appeared in a number of papers a year later at the time of the 1914 World Series. Here we see a baseball stadium, the field of play bathed in sunlight. In the stands sits a solitary fan, gazing intently on the field of play, his coat pulled tightly around his shoulders and his arms clasped tightly around him. Outside the stadium, all is black. The field of light is labeled "U.S. and World Series." The black that threatens to engulf it is labeled "Europe and World War."[33]

Notes

1. This cartoon appeared at the top of page 1 of the "Sports."

2. *New York Times*, October 7, 1913, column 3. Hereafter, all *Times* citations will be as follows: NYT, month/day/13, page number, column number. Citations from the *Philadelphia Inquirer* will follow the same format, prefaced with PI.

3. It is interesting to speculate to what degree the writers for these papers were aware of the excitement being generated in academia at this time by the "Myth and Ritual" school of archaeological, anthropological and mythology scholarship, and may have applied the insights of that scholarship in their interpretations of the World Series. Jane Ellen Harrison, perhaps that school's most well-known exponent, was at the height of her career in 1913. She had written the *Prolegomena to the Study of Greek Religion* a decade earlier, and published *Ancient Art and Ritual* through H. Holt & Company, New York City, in 1913. It seems to me very likely that Hugh Fullerton, a graduate of The Ohio State University who had majored in English and Classics, and who was covering the series for the *Times* in 1913, was well aware of this scholarly movement. Nevertheless, this is mere speculation and beyond the bounds of this paper.

4. NYT, 10/9/13, p. 1, col. 1.

5. NYT, 10/11/13, p. 3, col. 1.

6. NYT, 10/8/13, p. 4, col. 1.

7. NYT, 10/10/13, p. 3, col. 1.

8. This, and the ensuing two quotes, are found at NYT, 10/9/13, p. 2, col. 1.

9. NYT, 10/10/13, p. 1, col. 1.

10. NYT, 10/12/13, p. 1, col. 1.

11. NYT, 10/11/13, p. 3, col. 1.

12. NYT, 10/10/13, p. 3, col. 1.

13. NYT, 10/9/13, p. 12, col. 5.

14. NYT, 10/5/13, p. 3, col. 1.

15. *Ibid.*

16. NYT, 10/8/13, p. 4, col. 2.

17. NYT, 10/11/13, p. 3, col. 1.

18. PI, 10/11/13, p. 8, cols. 1–2.

19. This comment appears in a biographical blurb beneath a picture of Meyers in a special photographic section on the World Series in the Sunday, October 12, 1913, *New York Times.* The caption to the page is "Record Hitters of the Giants." The pages of this "Baseball Section" are unnumbered.

20. On the Giants' squad for this series, although not playing and mentioned only in passing by the *Times,* was perhaps the most famous Native American athlete of all — Jim Thorpe.

21. NYT, 10/5/13, Section 5, p. 2, col. 3; PI, 10/11/13, p. 1, col. 7.

22. NYT, 10/5/13, p. 1, col. 1.

23. NYT, 10/6/13, p. 8, col. 4. The article entitled "Negro Killed in Race Riot" appears at NYT, 10/8/13, p. 1, col. 1. It is not being claimed here that the *New York Times,* as a paper, had a particular social or editorial perspective on the African American, negative or otherwise, in 1913, although it may well have had. Rather, it is being asserted that the paucity of articles concerning the African American, and the placing of such articles as these within proximity of either the World Series accounts or other baseball articles, makes it easy for the casual reader to contrast the African American's situation with respect to this national ritual with the position of everyone else — whites of either gender, American Indians, even foreigners as an appreciative external audience. By extension, it would be easy to understand the African American as an outsider to the entire social and political enterprise.

24. See especially NYT, 10/8/13, p. 5, col. 3, entitled "Baseball in the House: Mann Read the Bulletins, Though out of Order."

25. PI, 10/9/13. I regret that I failed to jot down the page number before returning the microfilm of this paper, which I had obtained on interlibrary loan. The article appears on an interior page, in columns 6–7, however.

26. NYT, 10/8/13, p. 14, col. 3, "Topics in Wall Street: Floor Traders and Baseball."

27. NYT, 10/11/13, p. 4, col. 6, "He Meant Something Else: Columbia Lecturer Was Not Referring to World's Series." This is quite an amusing little article. The professor is lecturing on the legacy of energy and creativity bequeathed the West by the early Anglo-Saxon peoples, and indicates that an excellent example of that legacy is to be made evident that very afternoon. The class, according to the article, imagines the athletic feats of the two baseball teams, until the lecturer states that President Wilson has just pushed the button destroying the Gamboa dike, the last barricade between the Atlantic and Pacific Oceans, thus officially opening the Panama Canal. The article ends, "And in the lecture room there was the audible rustle of readjustment."

28. NYT, 10/8/13, p. 5, col. 5, entitled, "Golf Lures Wilson Away."

29. Alfred Charles William Harmsworth, Baron (in 1913; later Viscount) Northcliffe (1865–1922), was a renowned newspaper proprietor in England. He and his brother acquired the *Evening News* in 1894, and Lord Northcliffe started the *Daily Mail* in 1896. In 1903 he started the illustrated *Daily Mirror,* and he acquired control of *The Times* of London in 1908. Thus, we have here the *New York Times* covering the North American tour of the owner of *The Times* of London and bantering with him through its pages for the enjoyment of the New York reader.

30. NYT, 10/8/13, p. 4, col. 2.

31. See NYT, 10/11/13, editorial page. The specific editorial is entitled, "Topics of the Times: He Thinks We Don't Care for Baseball."

32. NYT, 10/8/13, p. 12, col. 4.

33. Alas, although I have seen this cartoon in the *New York Times* many years ago, I have been unable to relocate it to provide a proper citation here. A variation on this cartoon, however, can be found in the *Chicago Tribune* of October 10, 1914, at the top of page 14. In this variant, the single-seated fan is Uncle Sam, and the caption for the cartoon is "The Sunny Side of the Fence."

Part 2

Baseball and American Culture

Baseball Short Stories: From Lardner to Asinof to Kinsella

Paul D. Staudohar

Baseball short stories were first published in pulp magazines about a century ago. They became part of the lore of the national pastime, and both reflected and influenced its historical development. Ring Lardner, more than anyone, popularized the genre. His baseball fiction appeared in slick journals like the *Saturday Evening Post* around the time of World War I. Since then, numerous prominent authors have penned baseball stories, either about the game itself or as a backdrop for other aspects of life. More stories have been written about baseball than any other sport.

Americans have an enduring fondness for short fiction and revere our great literary sources like *Post, Collier's, Harper's, New Yorker, Atlantic Monthly*, and *Esquire*. Stories have the advantage of allowing completion by the reader in brief episodes of leisure. We may lose interest in lengthy, encompassing books, or forget what we have read as we pick one up a few days later. While no one would contend that short stories are a literary rival to the great novels, they do provide a succinct package of visual goodness that has particular appeal in our helter-skelter world.

The subject of this paper is the ten baseball short stories that the author considers to be the best ever written. This is a subjective undertaking. But the choices are consistent with an examination by the author of baseball and sports anthologies. In each of the ten choices the story has been recognized as a classic of the genre by numerous reprintings over the years. The reader familiar with this literature may instinctively join me in his or her own critique. (Why was this story included? Why not that one?)

Readers who are less informed about the stories may wish to read them, which promises a literary treat. All these stories, plus dozens more of high quality, may be found in the anthologies listed at the end of the paper.

"Alibi Ike," by Ring Lardner (1915)

The stories are presented chronologically, and the first is Ring Lardner's well known "Alibi Ike." This is about a delightfully goofy ballplayer who has an excuse for everything, even what he does very well. Here is an example:

> "What do you think of Alibi Ike?" ast Carey.
> "Who's that?" I says.
> "This here Farrell in the outfield," says Carey.
> "He looks like he could hit," I says.
> Then Carey went on to tell me what Ike had been pullin' out there. He'd dropped the first fly ball that was hit to him and told Carey his glove wasn't broke in good yet, and Carey says the glove could easy of been Kid Gleason's gran'father. He made a whale of a catch out o' the next one and Carey says "Nice work!" or somethin' like that, but Ike says he could of caught the ball with his back turned only he slipped when he started after it and, besides that, the air currents fooled him.
> "I thought you done well to get to the ball," says Carey.
> "I ought to been settin' under it," says Ike.
> "What did you hit last year?" Carey ast him.
> "I had malaria most o' the season," says Ike. "I wound up with .356."
> "Where would I have to go to get malaria?" says Carey, but Ike didn't wise up.
> I and Carey and him set at the same table together for supper. It took him half an hour longer 'n us to eat because he had to excuse himself every time he lifted his fork.
> "Doctor told me I needed starch," he'd say, and then toss a shovelful o' potatoes into him. Or, "They ain't much meat on one o' these chops," he'd tell us, and grab another one. Or he'd say: "Nothin' like onions for a cold," and then he'd dip into the perfumery.
> "Better try that apple sauce," says Carey. "It'll help your malaria."
> "Whose malaria?" says Ike. He'd forgot already why he didn't only hit .356 last year.

Lardner (1885–1933) was a master of satire and humor. He wrote in the slang commonly used by real players in his day, providing a quaint realism to his prose. In "Alibi Ike" Lardner lampoons the apologists, complainers, and prevaricators among us. Ike is one of the great characters in baseball literature. He's actually a very good ballplayer, shoots a terrific game of billiards, plays poker like Nevada Slim, and gets the girl in the end.

But he's also a double-talking wag who never takes himself or anything else seriously.

Many modern sportswriters, like the late Jim Murray of the *Los Angeles Times*, Rick Reilly of *Sports Illustrated*, and Scott Ostler of the *San Francisco Chronicle*, lace their columns with clever witticisms in the Lardner mode. Lardner himself made his early mark as a sportswriter for the *Chicago Tribune*. One of his most important assignments was the World Series of 1919 and the subsequent Black Sox scandal. While at the *Tribune*, Lardner wrote his first "You Know Me, Al" stories, which caused a national sensation when published in the *Saturday Evening Post*. Four wonderfully funny and well written baseball stories by Lardner are "My Roomy," "Harmony," and "Hurry Kane."

In his later stories Lardner branched out into other sports. His boxing story "Champion" was made into a movie starring Kirk Douglas, and his golf story "Mr. Frisbie" is an amusing tale of a rich duffer and his resourceful caddie. Lardner's books include *The Big Town* (1925), *Round Up* (1929), and the *Collected Stories of Ring Lardner* (1941). Altogether, Lardner is considered one of the great American writers, especially of short stories, and "Alibi Ike" is his best known story.

"Baseball Hattie," by Damon Runyon (1931)

Judging from the number of times that it has been anthologized, "Baseball Hattie" is as popular as any baseball story. And though it was written long ago during the Great Depression, it has aged well, like a fine wine. Hattie is a dyed-in-the-wool New York Giants fan who, to the consternation of umpires, sees all of the games in the Polo Grounds and a good many on the road. She loves the team so much that she marries one of its pitchers; a big, tall, lefthanded phenom named Haystack Duggeler. Haystack is so good he pitches a no-hitter and wins fourteen straight games. He is, alas, also what Runyon waggishly refers to as a "hundred-percent heel." Poor Hattie tries to reform Haystack's drinking, gambling, and carousing. But it's hard to change a reprobate. Haystack cooks up the idea of a fix with a gambler to intentionally lose a game he is pitching, giving added meaning to the phrase "throwing a game."

When Hattie gets wind of this scheme she shoots Haystack in his pitching arm, ending his career. Despite this unfortunate circumstance, the story has a happy ending, as, some years later, Hattie and Haystack's offspring becomes the latest lefthanded pitching marvel. Naturally he plays for the Giants, and of course Hattie is there to see her son shut out Brooklyn on three hits.

Damon Runyon (1880–1946) was a contemporary of Ring Lardner's. He may have gotten the idea of the gambler putting in the fix in "Baseball Hattie" from the 1919 Black Sox, the Chicago White Sox players who intentionally threw World Series games with the Cincinnati Reds.

Runyon's formal education extended only through the sixth grade, yet he became one of the greatest newspaper people, and achieved initial fame as a columnist for the old *New York American* and as a nationally syndicated writer for the Hearst newspaper chain. Runyon loved baseball and was a close pal of Giants' manager John McGraw. He became one of the best short story writers ever, with numerous contributions on sports. Both as a humorist and a dramatic writer, many of Runyon's characters are shady New York tough guys with a flair for gambling, nightlife, and pretty ladies. Among his best known works are the trilogy of collected stories: *Guys and Dolls* (1929), *Money from Home* (1931), and *Blue Plate Special* (1931). Broadway play and film buffs will remember *Guys and Dolls*, with Marlon Brando, Jean Simmons, and Frank Sinatra in the movie version.

"You Could Look It Up," *by James G. Thurber (1941)*

The year is 1941 and a story is written about a midget named Pearl du Monville, who goes to bat in the major leagues. The team is slumping and looking for something to pick them up. Enter Pearl. Here's how author James Thurber describes the little fellow:

> Now, most people name of Pearl is girls, but this Pearl du Monville was a man, if you could call a fella a man who was only thirty-four, thirty-five inches high. Pearl du Monville was a midget. He was part French and part Hungarian, and maybe even part Bulgarian or somethin'. I can see him now, a sneer on his little pushed-in pan, swingin' a bamboo cane and smokin' a big cigar. He had a gray felt hat with one of them rainbow-colored hatbands onto it, like the young fellas wore in them days. He talked like he was talkin' into a tin can, but he didn't have no foreign accent. He might 'a' been fifteen or he might 'a' been a hundred, you couldn't tell. Pearl du Monville.

It takes some legal finagling with the baseball powers to get Pearl eligible to play. This done, the midget is outfitted in a miniature uniform and sent up to pinch-hit by Manager Squawks Magrew in a tight game.

> Magrew pushed the midget toward the plate and he says to him, he says, "Just stand up there and hold that bat on your shoulder. They ain't

a man in the world can throw three strikes in there 'fore he throws four balls!" He says.

"I get it, Junior!" says the midget. "He'll walk me and force in the tyin' run!" And he starts on up to the plate as cocky as if he was Willie Keeler.

Instead of walking, however, Pearl puts the ball in play, a little dribbler down third. He is thrown out at first, and that's when the fun starts, as the players on the opposing team commence to play "catch" with the midget and fans swarm onto the field to join the festivities.

> I seen Pearl du Monville strugglin' in the arms of a lady fan with a ample bosom, who was laughin' and cryin' at the same time, and him beatin' at her with his little fists and bawlin' and yellin'. He clawed his way loose finely and disappeared in the forest of legs which made that ball field look like it was Coney Island on a hot summer's day.

The story has a happy outcome. The team ends its losing streak and wins the pennant. But Pearl du Monville is never seen or heard from again.

It was August 19, 1951, ten years after Thurber's story, when Bill Veeck, showman owner of the St. Louis Browns, sent Eddie Gaedel, 43 inches tall and weighing 65 pounds, to bat in a game against the Detroit Tigers. In a batboy's uniform (currently on display at the Hall of Fame), Gaedel strode to the plate wearing ⅛. He walked on four straight pitches and was taken out for a pinch-runner. A protest was lodged and it was ruled no further such chicanery would be allowed.

So life delightfully imitated art, making Thurber's story even more memorable and creating one of the great legacies of the game. What is more, in the 1960s Casey Stengel, manager of the New York Yankees and Mets, was fond of saying in interviews, after making reference to the past, "You could look it up."

Author James Thurber (1894–1961) is famous for his stories about people and dogs. A master of satirical humor and fantasy, he was exceptionally versatile as a writer, even penning prized cartoons. His stories frequently appeared in the *New Yorker*. Thurber's major literary works include *My Life and Hard Times* (1933), *Middle-Aged Man on the Flying Trapeze* (1935), and *My World and Welcome to It* (1942).

"Goodwood Comes Back," by Robert Penn Warren (1948)

This is a story seen and told by a fellow who, as an undersized and bookish kid, was the friend of Luke Goodwood, a precocious athlete but indifferent student who makes it to the big leagues and even pitches in the World Series. Goodwood falls into drinking, however, and begins a downward spiral that winds up in premature death. It's a story less about baseball than friendship and twists of fate and, looking back, a different era in America. In the half century since the story was written so much has changed.

The characters in the story come from small towns, essentially country boys who spend their leisure time hunting, fishing and playing ball. For a youngster of such modest means and simple tastes to be thrust into the bright lights of the big-league cities was quite a shock. Both pleasurable and unsettling. Some could handle it. Luke Goodwood couldn't. The author embellishes the stereotype of the nonconformist pitcher who, as Goodwood says in the story, "are crazy as hell one way or another."

> He told me about some other pitchers too. There was one who used to room with him when the club went on the road. Every time they got to a new city, that pitcher made the rounds of all the stores, then the boxes would begin coming to the hotel room, full of electric trains and mechanical automobiles and boats, and that grown man would sit down and play with them and after the game would hurry back so he could play some more. Luke said his friend liked trains pretty well, but boats best, and used to keep him awake half the night splashing in the bathtub. There was another pitcher up in Indiana who went to a roadhouse with Luke, where they got drunk. They got thrown out of the place because that other pitcher, who was a Polak, kept trying to dance with other people's women. The Polak landed on a rock pile and put his hand down and found all the rocks were just the size of baseballs, and him a pitcher. He started breaking windows, and stood everybody off till the cops came.

Author Robert Penn Warren (1905–1989) is one of the nation's most distinguished literary figures, with an unparalleled reputation as a novelist and poet. He was cofounder of the *Southern Review*, a prominent literary quarterly. Among Warren's best known novels are *Night Rider* (1939), *All the King's Men* (1946), which won the Pulitzer Prize, and *Band of Angels* (1955). He also authored several books of poems, two of which won Pulitzers. In 1986 Warren was named the first poet laureate of the United States.

"One Throw," by
W.C. Heinz (1950)

This is another story that has been frequently anthologized. It's a wonderful morality play on the diamond, about a talented young shortstop in the Yankee organization who is stuck in the low minors playing for an unfeeling manager. The ethical dilemma posed by the author is whether the shortstop should intentionally make a bad throw, in order to goad the manager into shoving him up to a higher league.

In contemporary baseball, a gifted young player would not want to make anything but good plays to get moved up the ladder. But in 1950 the Yankees were the dominant team in baseball, which a farm system loaded with budding stars. So the kid is approached at his hotel by a hardware salesman and they talk a little baseball. The salesman suggests making the bad throw. (At various intervals in the story the name of a great Yankee scout, Eddie Brown, is mentioned. Brown has the kind of eye for talent that could get the kid moved up the ladder, but unfortunately he wouldn't come around a hick town like the one the kid is playing in.) It turns out that when the occasion arises, despite the power of suggestion, the shortstop makes a good throw instead of a bad one.

The story seems predictable in a sense, but it comes with a surprise ending. Not only does the kid take the moral high road with his one throw, but his reward is that the "hardware salesman" is really the famous scout, Eddie Brown. As Mel Allen used to say: "How about that?" This is an exceptionally fine character-building story for youngsters to read. The shortstop whose "virtue is its own reward" gets an added bonus for his honest effort.

Author W.C. Heinz was one of the top sportswriters of his day, perhaps best known for his book with Green Bay Packers coach Vince Lombardi called *Run to Daylight* (1963). He also wrote *The Professional* (1958), one of the greatest boxing novels, and coauthored a book that led to the popular movie and television series *M*A*S*H*.

"The Rookie," by Eliot Asinof (1953)

This story captures the stark realism and sacrifice that many players face in struggling to make the major leagues. It's about fate and fading youth, guts and dreams, as a thirty-five-year-old rookie finally gets his big chance for glory after sixteen frustrating years in the minors.

Each year we typically hear about a longtime minor leaguer who gets his shot with the big club. Often these players have had brief "cups of coffee" in the majors before, only to be sent back down. Fans instinctively warm to the grizzled veteran who tries to snatch glory from the jaws of mediocrity, because it is a common human experience to fail to rise to the top. "The Rookie" uses baseball as a metaphor for experiences that are beyond the sport itself. It captures the intensity of desire for success and the agony of failing to achieve it.

Author Eliot Asinof was the keynote speaker at the Cooperstown Symposium on Baseball and American Culture in 1999. He is a celebrated figure to baseball aficionados for his book *Eight Men Out: The Black Sox and the 1919 World Series* (1963), which is as good a book on the sport as one can find. A successful movie was made out of the book. Asinof is also well known for his screen and television writing. Among his many fiction and nonfiction books are *Man on Spikes* (1955), *The Name of the Game Is Murder* (1968), and a book about the Wilson administration and the post–World War I era called *1919: America's Loss of Innocence* (1990).

"Brooklyns Lose," by William Heuman (1954)

There are certain things which make this story attractive. One is that it has the distinction of having appeared in *Sports Illustrated* in the first year of that magazine's existence. Second, it concerns Brooklyn, and there are few longtime baseball fans who do not have a soft spot in their heart for "Dem Bums." These are the *Boys of Summer* that Roger Kahn wrote his illustrious book about. Another thing is that the story includes a lot of "Brooklynese," a distinctive American dialect that manages to be both offensive and endearing at the same time.

But most of all, "Brooklyns Lose" is a great story, about a father and son going to see the Dodgers play a day game at Ebbets Field. The sting of a loss to the Reds is revealed in the heart of a diehard Bums fan as he plods home after a long day at the ballpark. And who should be at the house to greet the man and his son but Uncle Nathan, a gloating Giants fan. None of this seems fair, but tomorrow is another day. Unfortunately, the "Wait Till Next Year" rallying cry of the Brooklyn fans was not heard much longer after this story was written, as only a few years later the team headed west to Los Angeles.

Author William Heuman is quite a humorist. This passage conveys some gems:

> Madge says when we come into the house at about six-thirty:
> "What were you doing-standing outside the field asking for their autographs?"
> She has that look on her face. The pots are still on the stove, all covered up, and they've been there for some time, I can see.

"It was a long game," I tell her.

"It's always a long game down there," she says, and the way she says "there" you'd think she was talking of some gin mill somewhere.

She should be married to a heavy drinker or a guy who plays the horses like some of them in the shop. I don't have any bad habits; I have a glass of beer now and then; I go to Ebbets Field. That's wrong?

"Sit down and eat your supper," Madge says.

"Pop wouldn't buy me a hot dog," the kid tells her.

"I'm not surprised," Madge says. "He probably didn't even know you were with him,"

"I bought him two in the park," I snap. "He wants another one on the way home. What am I — Rockefeller?"

"He'd have had a better time at Brighton Beach," Madge says as she's banging pots around on the stove.

"My vacation," I tell her. "Monday we go to the beach. Wednesday we go to the beach. What am I — a seal?"

"The Thrill of the Grass," by W. P. Kinsella (1984)

This story is familiar to many baseball fans. It was inspired by the 1981 baseball strike. That was the first of the big work stoppages in professional team sports. It lasted for fifty days and caused the cancellation of 713 games. In the story, a stellar fan takes particular umbrage at the denial of his summer pastime. What also rankles him is the artificial turf that covers the field at the local ballpark. He decides to take out his frustrations by hatching a plot to replace the synthetic grass with the real stuff.

As word of the idea spread, hundreds of fans join in surreptitiously ripping out the plastic and planting sod. By moonlight they come with their rakes, hoes, and bags of soil: "Row by row, night by night, we lay the little squares of sod, moist as chocolate cake with green icing." When their clandestine work is finished, the protagonist of the story says:

> Alone in the stadium in the last chill darkness before dawn, I drop to my hands and knees in the center of the outfield. My palms are sodden. Water touches the skin between my spread fingers. I lower my face to the silvered grass, which, wonder of wonders, already has the ephemeral odors of baseball about it.

No one writes with more lyricism about baseball than W. P. Kinsella. He was the keynote speaker at the Cooperstown Symposium in 1996, delivering a memorable talk that was ample sprinkled with delectable readings from his work. Kinsella's most famous baseball novel is his first, *Shoeless Joe* (1982). This is the book that spawned the popular movie *Field of Dreams*. *Shoeless Joe* also inspired the title for this story, when Joe

Jackson says, "I'd wake up in the night with the smell of the ballpark in my nose and the cool of the grass on my feet. The thrill of the grass."

Kinsella's other books on baseball are a collection of stories called *The Thrill of the Grass* (1984), a novel called *The Iowa Baseball Confederacy* (1986), and an edited collection of quotes by baseball personalities called *Diamonds Forever: Reflections from the Field, the Dugout and the Bleachers* (1997).

"The Hector Quesadilla Story," by T. Coraghessan Boyle (1986)

Los Angeles Dodger fans will remember an outfielder euphoniously known as Manny Mota, a Latin player who went on to become a coach. Mota was called a "pinch-hitter deluxe" by Dodger broadcaster Vin Scully, and it was said that he could get out of bed at midnight on Christmas Eve and stroke a base hit. Mota played old, he was unostentatious, and he was good at his job. He is the kind of player that inspired the fictional Hector Quesadilla.

One of the memorable characters in baseball literature, Quesadilla is described as follows:

> HE WAS NO JOLTIN' JOE, no Sultan of Swat, no Iron Man. For one thing, his feet hurt. And God knows no legendary immortal ever suffered so prosaic a complaint. He had shinsplints too, and corns and ingrown toenails and hemorrhoids. Demons drove burning spikes into his tailbone each time he bent to loosen his shoelaces, his limbs were skewed so awkwardly his elbows and knees might have been transposed, and the once-proud knot of his frijole-fed belly had fallen like an avalanche. Worse: he was old. Old, old, old, the graybeard hobbling down the rough-hewn steps of the Senate building, the ancient Mariner chewing on his whiskers and stumbling in his socks.

A quesadilla is a wheat tortilla that is filled with a savory mixture, folded, fried in deep fat, and topped with cheese. Hence Hector's nickname is "Little Cheese," and the cry in Dodger stadium when he comes up to pinch-hit is "Cheese, Cheese, Cheesus." He is so old and infirm that his wife begs him to quit.

> But he doesn't. He can't. He won't. He's no grandpa with hair the color of cigarette stains and a blanket over his knees, he's no toothless old gasser sunning himself in the park — he's a big leaguer, proud wearer of the Dodger blue, wielder of stick and glove. How can he get old? The grass is always green, the lights always shining, no clocks or periods or halves or quarters, no punch-in and punch-out. This is the game that never ends.

In a big game, he is finally called on to pinch-hit in the bottom of the thirty-first inning and delivers what appears to be the game-winning blow. Amazingly, however, the opposition comes back to tie the score. But there are no remaining pitchers on the Dodgers to go out for the thirty-second inning. Hector, who pitched in his earlier baseball life, gets the call, and the story goes on. Author Boyle provides a mise-en-scène, character sketches, and big-game description that are as good as one finds in baseball short fiction. Plus, his sense of humor is unrivaled.

T. Coraghessan Boyle is the founder and director of the creative writing program in the English Department at the University of Southern California. His short stories appear regularly in magazines such as the *New Yorker*, *Harper's*, *Atlantic Monthly*, and *Playboy*. He has written several novels and collections of short stories. Two recent books are *The Road to Wellville* (1993), which was made into a movie, and *The Tortilla Curtain* (1995).

"Casey at the Bat," by Frank Deford (1988)

Nearly everyone is familiar with the great American poem, "Casey at the Bat." ("The outlook wasn't brilliant for the Mudville nine that day.") It was written in 1888 by Ernest L. Thayer, a young newspaper writer for the *San Francisco Examiner*. "Casey" has given rise to endless commentary and imitation — in poems, stories, and art. A hundred years after the publication of Thayer's poem, Frank Deford did an "update" in the form of a short story. Deford's "Casey at the Bat" has become something of a classic in its own right. It is the most recently published of the top ten stories, yet it covers a period that predates the other stories.

Sports Illustrated published the story, which was preceded by a reprint of Thayer's poem. In particular, the famous last stanza sets up the story:

> Oh, somewhere in this favored land the sun is shining bright;
> The band is playing somewhere, and somewhere hearts are light,
> And somewhere men are laughing, and somewhere children shout;
> But there is no joy in Mudville — mighty Casey has struck out.

Is there a reader in this favored land who has not pined over Casey's fate, wishing it could have been otherwise? Part of the attraction of Deford's piece is that the pitch that Casey struck out on darted down and under the catcher's glove, rolling to the backstop. Casey is safe at first, and when he eventually scores there *is* joy in Mudville.

Writing about the mighty swinger's life before and after that fateful day in Mudville, Deford creates a bawdy hero worthy of the "Casey" myth. His story links Casey with real-life characters like heavyweight champ John L. Sullivan, and James Naismith of peach basket fame, providing fascinating glimpses of turn-of-the-century America.

Deford, the nation's premier sportswriter during his many years with *Sports Illustrated*, also founded the critically acclaimed but ill-fated daily sports newspaper, the *National*. He has written popular books with tennis personalities Arthur Ashe, Billy Jean King, Jack Kramer, and Pam Shriver, and published *The World's Tallest Midget: The Best of Frank Deford* (1978). A recent book is *Love and Infamy* (1993). In 1998 Deford returned to *Sports Illustrated* as a correspondent, writing a much-praised piece on basketball's Michael Jordan.

Anthologies of Baseball Fiction

Listed below is a collection of baseball anthologies that include short stories. In some cases, such as Charles Einstein's *Fireside* books, nonfiction material is included as well. It should also be noted that there are sports anthologies that include baseball fiction. For instance, *The Norton Book of Sports* (New York: W. W. Norton, 1992), edited by George Plimpton, is a collection of fiction and nonfiction material from all major (and some minor) sports. Included in Plimpton's book are the stories by Lardner, Thurber, Kinsella, and Boyle.

References

Bjarkman, Peter C., ed. *Baseball and the Game of Life* (Otisville, NY: Birch Book Press, 1990).

Bowering, George, ed. *Taking the Field: The Best of Baseball Fiction* (Red Deer, Alberta: Red Deer College Press, 1990).

Einstein, Charles, ed. *The Baseball Reader — Favorites from the Fireside Books of Baseball* (New York: McGraw-Hill, 1980).

Einstein, Charles, ed. *The Fireside Book of Baseball*, fourth edition (New York: Simon & Schuster, 1987).

Graber, Ralph S., ed. *The Baseball Reader* (New York: A. S. Barnes, 1951).

Greenberg, Martin H., ed. *On the Diamond: A Treasury of Baseball Stories* (New York: Bonanza Books, 1987).

Grossinger, Richard, ed. *The Temple of Baseball* (Berkeley, CA: North Atlantic Books, 1985).

Holtzman, Jerome, ed. *Fielder's Choice: An Anthology of Baseball Fiction* (New York: Harcourt Brace Jovanovich, 1979).

Hyman, Laurence J., and Laura Thorpe, eds. *Tales of Diamond: Selected Gems of Baseball Fiction* (San Francisco: Woodford Press, 1991).

Kerrane, Kevin, and Richard Grossinger, eds. *Baseball Diamonds — Tales, Traces, Visions and Voodoo from a Native American Rite* (New York: Anchor Books, 1980).

Shannon, Mike, ed. *The Best of* Spitball, *the Literary Magazine of Baseball* (New York: Pocket Books, Simon and Schuster, 1988).

Staudohar, Paul D., ed. *Baseball's Best Short Stories* (Chicago: Chicago Review Press, 1995).

Thorn, John, ed. *Armchair Book of Baseball* (New York: Charles Scribner's Sons, 1985).

Thorn, John, ed. *Armchair Book of Baseball*, Vol. 2 (New York: Charles Scribner's Sons, 1987).

Reflections on Baseball and Poetry

Ed Ward

I am going to begin my talk today about baseball and poetry by describing where my personal "journeys" have taken me since approximately April 1979, when I was teaching Spanish, French, and Physical Education at a high school in Niagara Falls, Ontario. I think you will see clearly how what started as a "geographical thing" has become a "poetic thing."

In April 1979 I happened to notice a lengthy article in a Sunday edition of the *Buffalo News*. The article was written by Joel Garreau, who was displaying some of his thoughts on American cultural geography. He was writing that there are not fifty states in the United States, but nine regions. His book, *The Nine Nations of North America*, came out in 1981.[1]

I read Garreau and *Nations* day and night, and I was slowly falling in love with the various nations in America and the American "scene" in general: downtowns, highways, people of all colors, movie palaces, railroad depots, art deco buildings, etc. Although baseball receives little mention in *Nations*, my appetite was nevertheless whetted to find out more about the American people and more about how sports played a role in their lives.

Not so parenthetically, I started to see patterns, and the lack of them, in things and people around me. I grew to understand how and why Chicago people and Peoria people have differing values and attitudes. I noticed a big difference in lifestyles in Gary as opposed to Indianapolis. I saw similarities in the folks from both Cedar Rapids and Des Moines. I wondered about how those from Salt Lake City get along with those from Las Vegas. (They don't get along famously. One is quiet, the other loud!)

73

I became hooked on regionalism, and I started to see that life is in the first instance regional: economically, politically, religiously, in jobs, in a love for sports, etc. The regional nature of weather appealed to me, too. How it all fits together, or does not fit, began to fascinate me, even consume me.

I also found a few adversaries who became upset with me when I asked them their definition of the "Midwest." They included Chicago. I asked how Chicago and Kansas City are both called "Midwest," given that the two places appear and "behave" differently. Chicago people do not know a lot about soy products; Kansas Citians have difficulty discussing "ethnic churches." Chicago, it seems to me, "looks east." The Yankees and the Mets are despised. Money to re-create Chicago after the fire in 1871 came from the east. So did the railroads. Kansas City does not "look" to the east like Chicago. How could Chicago even pretend that it cares about Des Moines and Omaha to its west?

I went to places like Evansville, Madison, Chattanooga, Omaha, Pittsburgh, and dozens of other cities in order to study both the American experience and an important item that goes with it ... baseball.

In St. Louis, a "baseball first" city, I encountered a lot of great history: KMOX radio, the Fox Theater, Kiel Auditorium, etc. I came away thinking that St. Louis "looks south" in many ways. I also began to see the terrific hold the Cardinals have on the city and the region.

In Milwaukee, where I had graduated from Marquette University in 1969, I noticed two things, among others: 1) a distaste for Chicago and 2) an opposite agenda from Madison (to the west of Milwaukee). It also occurred to me that someone could write an article talking about beer and baseball in Milwaukee as well as in St. Louis. Did not the two cities share Bob Uecker, too?

I must admit, too, that basketball in the "old days" held sway with me. I grew up in Joliet, Illinois, and as a young person remembered when central Illinois (south of Joliet, of course) came to a standstill when the University of Cincinnati and Bradley University in Peoria played basketball against one another. Cincinnati had Oscar Robertson, but Bradley had Chet Walker. It was large city versus small, big school against small, and the Breadbasket versus the Foundry, to use Joel Garreau's terms. The excitement of the games was tremendous. UC won NCAA titles in 1961 and 1962 without Oscar Robertson, believe it or not. Bradley won the NIT in 1960, then again in 1964, without Chet Walker the second time. To add to the euphoria, Bradley played some very exciting games against the St. Louis University Billikens, too, in the old Missouri Valley Conference. (Some of you probably will be thinking that at 6'4" I must have had a strong devotion to basketball. That is true. However, like some people, I now have "crossed over" to see that baseball provides more "theater" than any other sport, it seems to me.)

People, not just buildings and events, began to be important, too. Remember Frank Hague, the mayor of Jersey City? Baseball's Addie Joss? Erastus Corning II, the mayor for many years in Albany? Jack Brickhouse, the announcer for the Cubs and the Sox? Roy Sievers of the old St. Louis Browns?

Soundscapes as well as landscapes mattered to me. Remember WOWO radio in Fort Wayne? KOA in Denver? Can't you get the "flavor" of Reading, Pennsylvania, a little bit by listening to the noise of the city while standing in the old cemetery a little south of the Phillies ballpark?

From all of this I came out with "memory" in all of its meanings: the games, the scores, the radio stations, names of the players, and even the smells of the parks and other venues. I still like to think that I remember the smells of the old Bush Stadium in Indianapolis and, for those who love indoor venues, the Memorial Auditorium in Buffalo. (The ballpark in Reading today has a certain scent to it. Notice that as you buy a program just inside the main door.)

I began, then, to read of the history and lore of baseball, and I started to compose a few things on paper poetically about baseball "in place." I think the first thing I wrote may have been about the game in Fort Wayne.

Try this yourself some day: go to a game and sit with a note pad and a cold soda and see what happens ... The game lends itself to poetry easily. I think you will see some of your life played out on a baseball diamond, and you can do some writing about that.

Here are a few selections from my book, *Where Memory Gathers: Baseball and Poetry.*[2]

We will start with "Nowhere but Peoria."

> Central to it all is Peoria — Heartland, Midwest, Breadbasket,
>   Midlands, (tallgrass) Prairie, Farmbelt ... where values are tested.
>
> Good or evil? Black and/or white?
> Rich v. poor? Mainstream or *for a day*?
>
> Presidential streets stand out.
> Bradley University outstanding.
>
> Chicago? Too far, and busy.
> St. Louis? Far, too, but calm.
> Indianapolis? Distant, but a cultural cousin.
> Roads to the Mississippi show little, except quiet.

Peorians enjoy life on the Illinois River.
(Rails, be gone!)

The game has been good ... study old Woodruff.
... is good ... see (newer) Meinen.
... will be good ... on warm alluvial soil.
Skies contain (minor) stars with (major) dreams.
Winds from the west blow warm. Pop-ups climb against
  some cotton. Softer still is a bunt along third.

Batter up!

It is important for me to say that I have attended more than a few
minor league games. I think I have been to all of the parks of the Midwest
League (1991 edition, that is).
Here is my "Minor Baseball."

The dollar differs. A revocable license easy.

Get programs.
Pencils, too.

Look for "a sphere formed by yarn" (Rule 1.09).

Names? Unknown.
Places? Durham, Davenport, Duluth, and Danville.
Times? Always.

Players play a game of probable.
Probably not to make it; yes to second, no to bigs.

The chance thrills.
The crowd fills.

To rally once more in Trenton, Tulsa, and Toledo ...

Perchance to dream? Every day.

Night comes, too.

The road is long, "with many a winding turn."
Little Rock to Midland a long go.
Omaha to Buffalo, too.
Not to mention Tucson to Portland.

Stars have been shining:
harmon killebrew @ Chattanooga,
carl yastrzemski @ Minneapolis,
jim piersall @ Scranton,
len tucker @ Peoria.

Maybe tomorrow.

This third piece I have already read at the 1997 Conference entitled "Jackie Robinson: Race, Sports, and the American Dream" at LIU–Brooklyn, directed by Joe Dorinson.

This is called "A Fevered Time."

> Clouds of war obscure the game.
> Worshipping fans flood Ebbets.
> Enter Monte Irvin? No.
>
> Enter Jackie (Roosevelt) Robinson.
>
> Talent shines amid white fans.
> His position? Second base.
> His race, too ... but Jackie wins.
>
> Some bases have been stolen.
> But a respect has been earned.
> Some complain ... but Jackie wins.
>
> Black cats and taunts do their thing.
> Brooklyn victories add up.
> Insults come ... but Jackie wins.
>
> Fans see double (black and white).
> Jackie sees too much, of course.
> Mates look down ... but Jackie wins.
>
> Numbers bear out basic skills.
> Hits outweigh errors for sure.
> Some look askance ... but Jackie wins.
>
> Today Jackie is at rest.
> A peace and some grace prevail.
> Skills outran hues ... and Jackie won.
>
> A new day dawns for the game.
> Balls, bats and games await.
>
> Does some understanding come?

It has been pointed out to me that the word "shines" in line five above may not be the best word in the world to use. That is correct. If I could write the line again I might add "sparkles." "Shines," of course, is very derogatory to black people.

Needless to say, it has occurred to me that skin color is a *large* issue in our country. Those who have a scientific bent may wish to read Carl Sagan's book *Billions and Billions*, wherein he explains that black and white are really and truly similar in a scientific sense. That comment may sound odd to some, but I think it is true. For example, if Al Hall, our co-ordinator,

asks me to look through the windows of the Hall of Fame here in Cooperstown at 10 P.M. tonight and I see nothing but darkness, I will turn around
and report to Al that I see nothing. What I see is "blank." "Blank" comes
from the Latin "blancus," of course, which means white.[3] But I don't see
whiteness. In fact, I see the opposite, darkness or, if you will, blackness.
The two seem related in practical, daily experience somewhat, as well as
in the mind of science, but not socially.

Those with a poetic sense about them may want to consult their dictionaries for the definitions of black, white, and brown. One will find that
our definitions of color are socially constructed. Black is at times defined
as dirty, white as clean, etc. I found fascinating Michael Lind's article in
the *New York Times Magazine* last year. The article talks of people who are
beige, and Lind explains how beige may be a way out of our society's fix
on black and white.[4]

Another area that has become of interest to me is cemeteries, believe
it or not. Even the word is interesting. It means "sleeping place" to the
Greeks, and has another interesting "spin" to it that goes like this. Did you
know that for French-speaking people the word for Hall of Fame is "pantheon," while for Filipino people "panjon," the same word etymologi-
cally, means cemetery? That is right: one person's cemetery is another
person's Hall of Fame. That is a good thought to keep in mind as our
loved ones pass away. Secondly, our deceased loved ones go ahead of us;
we do not leave them behind. *Much* can be learned by walking in a cemetery.

Further, we should be aware that there is a psychogeography in various places and landscapes. Cemeteries are an easy example. We enter them
and we see history, biography, architecture, blacks and whites buried separately, and so forth. I have read somewhere that the first thing a community does is to designate space in which to bury the dead. Casinos are a
second example. When we walk into one we are transported into a world
very different from the one "out on the street." We have therein a "limi-
nal" experience; we cross a threshold (Latin: "limen") and enter into a
different world. Also, "home" is another example. I think there are about
twenty ways of looking at the meaning of "home."

Here is one that I have written, punning a bit on the phrase "artificial
grass." It is called "Artificial Class."

> green
> multi-purpose
> hotter,
> like the Astrodome stuff.

blotchy
patchy
slick,
like the Pittsburgh and St. Louis stuff.

inexpensive
tough
removable,
like the Cincinnati stuff.

true hops
straight lines
more hits,
like the Seattle stuff.

fewer errors
faster cleanup
better drainage,
like the Philadelphia and Montreal stuff.

"I, too, dislike it."

Here is "Religion and the Game." Those who study religions may see some references to various and sundry faiths:

All rise and sing.
Warm winds comfort.

Two teams of nine (not seven-sided) strive.

E-6? Lord, Have Mercy!

Sins/errors a basic style.

Questions arise:
Gospel? To follow other steps (like Ruth, Mays, Mantle).
Rally time? A resurrection: soon (and very soon).
Two-run homer? It would have been enough.
Pitching? An amazing grace.
Preaching? It wins the day.
Salvation? Essential, though "not of your own doing."
Grace? It is for giving.

Solution follows.

Hope, like hurling, anchors all.

Collect memories: Ruth, Aaron, Bonds. Marvelous fellows(hip).
: 1969 Chicago White Sox? Pardon their offense.
: "Ping" Bodie, catcher. May he rest ...

Collect coins, too.

(Another) batter up! Vespers soon.

It should be with luck!

No pepper. No hubris, either.

How many caught the reference above to "seven-sided"? I did not think too many. The reference is to the Baha'i faith. If you fly into Chicago (O'Hare) from the east you may see the Baha'i temple (or church?) from the left side of the plane. The building, I think, is seven-sided. That number is important to people of the Baha'i faith. (It may be possible to see Wrigley Field, too.)

Perhaps some of you are familiar with Jeff Campbell and His Hungry for Music productions in Washington, D.C. Notice how his music about baseball is so different from, say, the music given out recently on a CD at the NBA games at Continental Airlines Arena in the Meadowlands of New Jersey. Baseball music is light and can be hummed; basketball music seems percussive and throbbing. There seems to be a big difference. How would "football music" be characterized, I wonder? God only knows what "Jock Rock 2000" might sound like...

I also have one here entitled "Music and the Game." Some of you may be familiar with the name of Howard Reich, who writes brilliant reviews of music in the *Chicago Tribune*. I used to love reading his reviews when I was living in the Chicago area. This is "Music and the Game":

> Four flats and 3/4 time bring the anthem. Pride, too.
> No heed for past places "where the field was warm and green."
>
> Take good notes.
> Read between the lines.
>
> Rock the pitcher and his staff. Look for "bent pitches."
>
> No rests.
>
> Ragged play makes for rag(ged) time, "white music played black."
>
> The blues, "every happening an inconvenience," follow.
> Foes are "looking up at down."
>
> Swing. Bunt. Hit. Run. Score. Count.
> One-syllable fun there.
>
> Key of D in 3/4 time: "Take Me Out." Sing moderately.
> Use improvisation. Resist composition.
>
> Bottom of 9th? Sharp single up middle (mid-range?) wins it.
>
> Gospel for some; the game is the way, truth, and life.
>
> Critics agree. There is expressive purpose, purity of tone,
>   propulsive rhythm, sinuous lines.
>
> Let's play two.

It goes without saying that many of us are already aware that there are three things that are "ours" in the United States: jazz, the Constitution, and baseball, of course. We should be proud of those three things.

Here are two that do not appear in my book, *Where Memory Gathers*. I finished these only the other day. The first may be attractive to those who majored in physics or one of the sciences.

This is "Toward Night."

> The daylit game starts ... amid blue.
>
> A blue not near, but in the distance ... (like victory?).
> The sun does it! The light bounces its rays off the air (like
>
> baseballs off the bat!), causing blue and beauty.
> The wavelengths (à la home runs)
> are short (blue) and long (red). Read those lengths
>
> and create color. The blue (livid?) gives way
> to red (rubrics?). Then dusk comes. Rhymes with "tough."
> Tough to see the ball. "Star Dust" chants "purple dusk."
>
> GMHopkins paints "whitebeams" and Penny Harter
> "monoliths of hydrogen and dust."
>
> But the stars are not right. Things are dis-astrous.
> To wish upon the moon, or the evening star?
> We watch the stars "till they're gone."
>
> Some reverie awaits. (Is God out there? or here?) White
>   ("colorless, transparent") vanishes and black ("the absence of
>   color") arrives. They seem the same, but socially different.
>
> ... all this from CSagan's "pale blue dot."
>
> The game and the score may not be so important.
>
> [fade to black]

The last is "Darnyankees." I think more than a few of us can relate to the tone of this one.

> No breath is left in Chicago, Baltimore, Cleveland, Boston, or
>   Detroit.
>
> They did it again. Dammit!
> They beat us, "creamed" us.
>
> What to do?
>   What to think?
>   What/how to feel?
>   Where to turn?
>   (Whom to blame?)

(Berra ... Ford ... Mantle ... born*yankees*)

We hope they err;
we hope we pitch;
we hope they don't remember.

We've memorized the (sad) story.

Next season we'll do it; next game, first pitch
... rain or shine. Then hope will return.

Dar*n*yankees!

Can't they lose, Lord?
Soon! Please!

The time is getting away on me now, so I will stop. In the future I will be working on some of the symbols, rituals and myths of the game of baseball, the greatest game ever played.

Many thanks to everyone here today, including Al Hall, our co-ordinator.

Notes

1. Joel Garreau. *The Nine Nations of North America* (Boston: Houghton Mifflin, 1981).
2. Edward R. Ward. *Where Memory Gathers: Baseball and Poetry* (San Francisco: Rudi Publishing, 1998).
3. Carl Sagan. *Billions and Billions* (New York: Ballantine Books, 1997), 50–51.
4. Michael Lind. "The Beige and the Black." *New York Times Magazine*, sec. 6, August 16, 1998, 38–39.

Baseball and Vaudeville and the Development of Popular Culture in the United States, 1880–1930

Richard Pioreck

Popular culture like revolution is a middle-class phenomenon requiring leisure time and disposable income. Popular culture seems to be a series of idiosyncratic choices without apparent connection. With this in mind, it is interesting to examine how baseball and vaudeville helped define popular culture in the United States between 1880 and 1930 in similar ways. The roots of both pre-date the Civil War. The modern versions of both were born during the boom decade following the Civil War. Initially these leisure time entertainments competed for the time and money of men. Between 1880 and 1930 when vaudeville dominated live entertainment, motion pictures and radio, baseball o'erleaped boxing and horse racing to become the National Pastime. Today baseball and vaudeville's offspring, television, are so joined that they are dependent on each other.

Yet there is more to it than the coincidence of ballplayers crossing over to play the vaudeville circuit during the off-season or when their playing careers were over. What baseball and vaudeville have in common is that they established twentieth century popular culture among the melting pot of immigrants who were creating the urban America of the industrial age. Each benefited from the railroad in its early establishing of nationwide appeal. Baseball and vaudeville were both born professionally in the decade after the Civil War. The National League was founded in 1876. Wine rooms, the forerunners of vaudeville houses, existed in New York and Philadelphia by 1875.

Examining vaudeville and baseball, the similarities become evident. The pacing of both includes intense periods of exciting action between brief periods of inactivity. And between innings or the rotation of vaudeville acts, the crowd is free to eat and drink and talk among themselves. Heck, the crowd is free to eat and drink and yell at vaudeville and baseball players during their performances, and even throw things at them, anything from tomatoes to roses if so moved. Yet baseball and vaudeville do not appear to be variations on a theme. And I believe they are not variations on a theme but rather two different groups or industries using similar means to achieve their goals.

First, their origins are dissimilar. Discussing the origins of each is worth a separate paper, so I will try to summarize their similarities and stay with the salient points. Baseball, as you know, began as an athletic exercise for young gentlemen organized into gentlemen's clubs (hence, perhaps, the etymological reason that only professional baseball teams use the term club, while professional football, basketball and hockey teams more often use the business term organization). Vaudeville did not share this governing ideal of clean living and hearty exercise for gentlemen. Unlike the town ball games that were the antecedents of Alexander Cartwright's organized baseball, vaudeville sprang from a combination of alcohol and out-of-work actors.

This is the era that gives us the now quaint sign, "Please Don't Shoot the Piano Player. He's Playing the Best He Can." Saloons and the wine rooms usually employed piano players both to enliven the atmosphere of men drinking alone together and to provide music for the dance hall girls (like *Gunsmoke's* Miss Kitty) who danced vertically with the patrons in the saloon before dancing horizontally with them in the rooms above the saloon. Occasionally, a dance hall girl would triple-up and sing. Saloon-keepers soon discovered that contributing to the convivial atmosphere increased alcohol sales. Unemployed actors were happy to sing and dance for whatever money they could get while the dance hall girls could concentrate on their primary responsibilities.

Once baseball became a sport for professionals rather than a game for gentlemen, it became part of the entertainment industry. By the 1880s both vaudeville and baseball entrepreneurs were looking for ways to wring additional profit from their enterprises. Alcohol sales were the first and most obvious way of increasing profits. A patron would only buy one admission a day, but he could drink more than one beer on that day. Eventually vaudeville houses separated the sale of alcohol from the performances. Drinks were available in the lobby but not in the theater. Baseball on the other hand has forged a strong tie with breweries that remains so until today. In fact, during the 1880s the American Association halved admission prices to $.25 compared to the National League, but doubled the price of beer to $.10.

While this strategy worked in getting men to attend baseball games and the vaudeville houses, it still left a large segment of the population untapped. As leisure time rose and women were allowed greater opportunities for education, the entrepreneurs looked to them to help fill more seats. The interests of men had been served since the mid–1870s. The target audience for both industries was the white-collar, middle to upper-middle professional and managerial classes and the small businessman. These men would have both the disposable income and flexible schedule necessary to take an afternoon off to attend a baseball game, or to arrange an afternoon or evening at the wine room or saloon. While these men were the ideal target market for these two industries, their numbers were modest even in the largest cities like Philadelphia, Chicago, New York and Boston. But blue-collar workers, which largely meant immigrants, women and children, and African-Americans were discouraged from attending games by price, content, behavior and atmosphere, and racial segregation. The presence of prostitutes in the saloons and wine rooms and gamblers at the ballpark kept respectable women and children away. The $.50 price of admission kept blue-collar workers from frequently attending, and when they did attend, they were confined to the bleachers (often known as Burkesville or Germantown). African-Americans, when they were admitted, were restricted to specific sections of the theater or ballpark.

As Ann Douglas discusses in *The Feminization of American Culture,* the Victorian sensibilities began to dominate the understanding of what was considered acceptable social behavior and entertainment. While it would be another forty years before women could vote, they began to accumulate political power beginning in the 1880s.[1] This new collective, moral power of women helped galvanize the general attitude about baseball and vaudeville so that these industries from the sub-culture in America came to the mainstream of popular culture. Their newspapers and magazines could be on display in a respectable home, and mothers could encourage their sons to spend time with these two industries for their physical and cultural benefits.

In light of these changes in attitude, vaudeville and baseball entrepreneurs needed to make changes in how their industries were run in order to court these new demographics. Vaudeville managers and baseball owners cleared the prostitutes and gamblers from their premises to make them acceptable to women and children. In New York, Tony Pastor, often called the Father of Vaudeville, advertised the first continuous clean vaudeville show on October 24, 1881.[2] Now respectable women shopping the Ladies'

Mile could rest and enjoy themselves at Pastor's vaudeville house while their husbands were working or at the Polo Grounds. Ladies could also go to the Polo Grounds unescorted if they wanted.

As baseball and vaudeville began to take hold of the popular culture, they served as more than a source of entertainment. While ostensibly entertainment for the middle class, both industries provided an outlet for lower class Americans and immigrants to improve their socioeconomic status. While women had no direct place in baseball, in vaudeville they were able to rise to be headliners earning thousands of dollars a week. One of the most influential women in vaudeville never appeared on the stage or hired an act. Yet Mary Catherine Branley, a devout Roman Catholic from Providence, Rhode Island, who was Mrs. B. F. Keith, wielded incredible influence in the acts hired for the Keith-Albee circuit. By Mr. Keith's order and posted backstage in all 400 Keith-Albee theaters were the rules about decorum in performance. Performers could be discharged for using offensive words in their acts such as "slob," "son-of-a-gun" or "hully gee." To be fired in one theater meant a performer was banned from all Keith-Albee theaters.[3]

The rising influence of women during this early period of the feminization of the culture did crossover into baseball even though women did not have a presence in the industry. Rowdy behavior was curtailed by the hiring of additional ushers and putting them in flashy, sometimes military looking, uniforms.[4] Prostitutes and gamblers were no longer allowed to ply their trade on the premises. And social pressure was brought to bear upon the patrons so that decorum in public became the expected social behavior. Crowds in both industries still voiced their displeasure — booing and hissing were still acceptable — but less frequently did patrons throw things at the performers. Those who would not behave or looked as if they would not behave were seated separately from their betters in upper balconies and bleacher sections. Some of those relegated to less desirable seats often was done because of their appearance.[5] Remember, this was the era of phrenology and the belief that clothes made the man.

This was also one of the contributing causes to segregation of African-American spectators and performers. In the vaudeville houses, African-Americans often had to use a separate entrance to reach the second balcony. Those African-Americans who were professionals or small businessmen and wanted pay for the highest priced seats were denied the opportunity, and were forced to sit among the rowdies and prostitutes. Many chose to not to attend even though they were allowed. Instead, they patronized the African-American vaudeville houses, much the same way that later they choose the Negro League games to American and National League games were they were treated shabbily. Thus, as in baseball, a parallel circuit solely for African-Americans was established, separate, but equal in name only.

Vaudeville did not as effectively ban African-Americans as baseball did from the days of Moses Fleetwood Walker to Jackie Robinson. Yet all was not good for African-American performers. While some achieved fame and success in vaudeville, only a few of the very best acts got to play the big vaudeville houses because managers usually would not book more than one African-American act per bill so as to not offend the white performers. In hindsight we know of the great contributions African-Americans made to both industries because of the influence their level of performance had on white counterparts when they performed together.

Yet once all these social forces were in motion, the notion of how they helped the popular culture to evolve has a lot to do with the references to each other outside the two industries. Each was dependent on the spectator for his livelihood, and the seasonal nature of the work in both industries required the performers and ballplayers to take advantage of opportunities. Unlike today, ballplayers of this era had to work during the off-season. Many were farmers, laborers, or small business owners of saloons, taverns and pool halls in order to cash in on their popularity. Some spent their off-seasons in vaudeville. Besides managing the Giants for thirty-one years, John McGraw belonged to the actors' fraternity, the Lambs Club; such was the interaction between actors and ballplayers. This could also give us an indication of how actors and ballplayers viewed themselves. Before he became a baseball player in 1898, Harry Steinfeldt, who was *not* immortalized in Franklin P. Adams's poem "Baseball's Sad Lexicon" along with his infield mates Joe Tinker, Johnny Evers and Frank Chance, was an actor. Steinfeldt's acting troupe played exhibition games against local teams to attract audiences. Steinfeldt performed so well that he gave up acting to play professional baseball.[6] Adams later presided over the famed Algonquin Round Table during the 1920s, many of whose members were connected to show business. Among the Algonquin Round Table's sometimes members was Ring Lardner who provides a very strong link between baseball and vaudeville.

Chuck Connors, who played for the Boston Celtics as well as the Chicago Cubs and was better known as TV's *The Rifleman*, would, according to Ralph Kiner, "recite Casey at the Bat at the drop of a hat."[7] Denny McLain, who wore out his welcome in baseball, was an accomplished enough musician that he played the organ on *The Ed Sullivan Show* and in Las Vegas casino lounges. The "What a Game" TV advertising campaign featuring Aretha Franklin, LL Cool J, Mary-Chapin Carpenter and The Goo

Goo Dolls along with Ken Griffey, Jr., Barry Bonds, Rafael Palmiero, Cal Ripken and Mike Piazza, draws upon the baseball and vaudeville tradition of teaming popular entertainers with baseball players. The Nike "Chicks Dig the Long Ball" commercial with Greg Maddux, Tom Glavine, Ted Williams, Tony Gwynn and Heather Locklear (recently called by Murray Chass in the *New York Times* "the greatest commercial of all time"[8]) also draws on this tradition.

While the connection between baseball and vaudeville is forgotten with vaudeville's demise in the 1930s, in the fifty years between 1880 and 1930 both baseball and vaudeville had much more in common than they appear to have at first glance. Every time "Take Me Out to the Ball Game" is played at a ballpark, the connection between baseball and vaudeville is reiterated. "It's show biz. God, I love it!" George Steinbrenner declares in *The Scout.* He brings into focus what the owners and players have known for over a century, while the public for the most part has viewed the game as a romanticized, semi-religious ceremony where skill, honesty and fair play offer the opportunity for a player to be judged on the content of his character rather than on the glitziness of his exploits. And the idea of sports and entertainment is not new, Willie Mays wore his cap a size too small so it would fly off when he was making a running catch because Mays said he considered himself as much an entertainer as a ballplayer.[9] And Babe Ruth said baseball is a business and a player needs to get out of it all he can.[10] Pizzazz coupled with accomplishment makes players great.

From the beginning of both industries, players crossed over from the playing field to the vaudeville circuit trying to combine diamonds with limelight. Most of these players' names are unknown to today's fans although the players were popular in their day. Ballplayers such as Tony Mullane, Arlie Latham, Cap Anson, and Mike "King" Kelly, perhaps the first ballplayer to try to parlay his on-field popularity into a show business career (to get around the salary cap of his day, Kelly was paid $3,000 "for the use of his likeness" when he was traded back to Boston). Kelly was also among the first baseball players to have his exploits immortalized in song in the rousing "Slide, Kelly, Slide." Then there are Rube Marquard, who played vaudeville with his vaudevillian star wife Blossom Seeley, and "Turkey" Mike Donlin, who was married to vaudeville star Mabel Hite. Another is Marty McHale, who played vaudeville while he pitched for the Red Sox, founded the Red Sox Quartette, and later toured vaudeville with Mike Donlin. Waite Hoyt, the only twenty game winner on the 1927 Yankees (and whose father was a vaudevillian), also played vaudeville. And there is also McHale and Hoyt's teammate Babe Ruth.

By the beginning of the twentieth century vaudeville was "the unri-valed king of entertainment"[11] and baseball had become so popular that a second major league was born. Both industries attempted to court the family entertainment dollar by removing the rowdy element from their audiences and making it acceptable for women and children to attend their exhibitions. Chris Von der Ahe, the most dictatorial and baseball ignorant owner of his generation, came the closest to putting vaudeville on in the ballpark. Von der Ahe once offered the Buffalo Bill Wild West Show, includ-ing Sitting Bull and half price children's admission, along with a St. Louis Browns game. He also added among other things a merry-go-round, a race track and a wine room to the ballpark, billing it as "The Coney Island of the West."[12] According to historian David Nasaw, the demographics were essentially the same for the baseball crowd and the vaudeville audi-ence: white collar and middle class.[13]

While the audience for both industries was middle class, both drew the majority of their performers from the lower class. Both baseball and vaudeville allowed access to the American dream of success to people who had limited education, and who lacked the social and business connections to get anything more than the most menial jobs. What both fields offered their workers was an opportunity to achieve success through their talents and skills. The *Billboard* review of vaudeville acts at The Palace could aptly apply to baseball players: "here genius not birth your rank insures."[14]

Curiously bearing this out is the parallel between the lives of Babe Ruth and Eddie Cantor, two of the biggest stars of baseball and vaudeville. Cantor was orphaned at two and lived with his grandmother in a series of crowded tenement apartments on New York's Lower East Side; Ruth was placed in St. Mary's Industrial School for Boys when he was eight. As chil-dren both men ran the streets and were involved in petty thefts, although Ruth seems to have been the more harshly treated, being committed to the orphanage by his parents for being incorrigible.[15] In the end each achieved majesty in his field as the Sultan of Swat and the King of Vaudeville. A pho-tograph of a vaudeville marquee proclaiming "Babe Ruth Now Here" pro-vides a connection between the two most popular entertainments of the early industrial age.[16]

Yet there is more than the coincidence of ballplayers crossing over to play the vaudeville circuit during the off-season or when their playing careers were over. What baseball and vaudeville have in common is that they began helping to establish twentieth century popular culture in the last quarter of the nineteenth century.

Perhaps the earliest link between baseball and vaudeville is "Casey at the Bat," first performed by DeWolf Hopper on May 13, 1888, at Wallack's

Theatre on Broadway. Hopper would perform his dramatic recitation more than 10,000 times during his career. Albert Spalding states that crowds would demand Hopper perform "Casey at the Bat" whenever Hopper made a public appearance.[17] Hopper's recitation of "Casey at the Bat" proved to be so popular that Hopper performed it for the opening of Radio City on December 27, 1932. What contributed to the popularity of Ernest Thayer's poem, that had gone largely unnoticed when it was initially published, was the presence of Hopper's friends on the New York Giants who were in the theater that evening; some sources indicate the poem was added for their benefit.[18] The rest is history.

Arlie Latham, who skipped the White Sox world tour in 1888–89 to appear on stage, was known as "The Freshest Man on Earth" in part because of the specialty song written for him to sing.

> I'm a daisy on the diamond;
> I'm a dandy on the stage.
> I'd ornament a horsecart
> Or look pretty in a cage...
> I'm a Hustler from Hustletown,
> The Freshest Man on Earth.

Latham was the tiniest man in the major leagues.[19] He was not the least bit respectable by nineteenth century standards. He was a merciless heckler who was always involved in fights with opponents and teammates. Latham's first wife attempted suicide. His second sued for divorce for perversion, assault, and infidelity.[20] Yet he was a fan favorite because of his clowning on and off the field. As one story goes, as darkness threatened, Latham wanted the umpire to call the game and award his team the victory. When the umpire would not, Latham had the batboy line up twelve large candles before the dugout. Latham lit the candles and the crowd roared. The displeased umpire blew out the candles which Latham promptly re-lit. This farce was repeated for a few minutes until the umpire ordered the clowning to stop. With the home crowd in his pocket, Latham lit the candles once again. But this time instead of blowing out the candles, the umpire forfeited the game to the visiting team.[21]

Ruth was not unfamiliar with performing outside the ballpark. Marshall Hunt of *The New York Daily News* said he often performed with Ruth at charity shows in Palm Beach during spring training.[22] But why would Babe Ruth play vaudeville? Anyone could understand a ballplayer spending part of the winter in southern California making movies, but playing three-a-days, six days a week in a vaudeville theater in Minneapolis in the dead of winter — why?

For one thing, the money: "Babe Signs to Hit Home-Run Laughs on Vaudeville Diamond at $3,000 a Week" read the *Times* headline for the October 1921 article announcing Ruth's signing with the B. F. Keith circuit.[23] Most players did not make that much for an entire season. Granted, most ballplayers would not be paid to headline a vaudeville show because they couldn't, in the inimitable words of George Steinbrenner, "put fannies in the seats" the way Babe Ruth did for his entire adult life. As Waite Hoyt said, "He was the greatest crowd pleaser of them all."[24] Newspapers ran the syndicated column "What Babe Ruth Did Today" to satisfy the public's hunger for information about the most popular man of his day.[25] the *New York Daily News* covered Babe Ruth twelve months of the year with pictures and stories because he was such a good circulation builder.[26]

Ruth was perfect for vaudeville because people generally liked him no matter what he did. Fred Lieb reports that once Ruth was stopped for going the wrong way on a one-way street. A rather common occurrence as Ruth was a notoriously bad driver. Instead of rebuking or ticketing Ruth, the officer said, "Oh, it's you Mr. Babe," and with the lights on and the siren wailing, he led Ruth safely to an intersection.[27] Thus, B. F. Keith must have felt fairly certain of the return he would be getting on his investment.

Now Babe Ruth did not seek to play vaudeville in the off-season. He particularly wasn't much interested in show business even though he had spent most of August 1920 commuting to Haverstraw, New York, to make *The Babe Comes Home*.[28] As he did after most seasons, Ruth intended to barnstorm until the weather no longer permitted it. Players like Ruth could make $1,500 to $2,500 for each post-season barnstorming game.[29] Unfortunately for Ruth, the owners had a new rule against members of World Series teams barnstorming because they felt it would diminish the value of their premiere event.

The owners, who originally did not want a World Series, quickly established the rule to keep interest and income focused on the World Series.[30] Commissioner Landis vigorously enforced the barnstorming rule because he said a rule is a rule, but some thought Landis did so more on racial lines because he did not want a black team to beat major league players from the season's best teams.[31] Similarly, vaudeville was just as segregated. White performers tried to limit or keep black acts off the bills in order to avoid being overshadowed.[32]

Ruth disagreed with the rule and barnstormed anyway. Without going into detail about Ruth's first clash with the new commissioner, the confrontation over the barnstorming rule, about which Ruth said he had been poorly advised,[33] led to Ruth's first vaudeville tour. Ruth was happy for the opportunity to get out of the rest of the barnstorming tour and appear. He was attempting to make peace with Landis, for the 1921 barnstorming season was a bust for Ruth. Rain kept down both the crowds and revenue. Besides the financial loss, both the press and public opinion were against Ruth.[34] Faced with the loss of the barnstorming money, his 1921 World Series share and suspension for the 1922 season, Ruth signed with the B. F. Keith vaudeville circuit.

The Keith people were enthusiastic about Ruth's performing. Trying to decide on Ruth's billing and looking for the best way to publicize Ruth's appearance on the circuit, Tex Rickard, the G.M. of Madison Square Garden, cabled George Bernard Shaw, with the question, "Would it be quite proper to bill Babe Ruth as the superman of baseball?" Besides being a playwright and a critic, Shaw was regarded as a boxing expert, and thus knowledgeable about sports.[35] Shaw's immediate reply was, "Sorry never heard of her. Whose baby is Ruth?"[36] The front page story about Shaw's ignorance of Babe Ruth generated free front page publicity for Ruth's vaudeville debut.

That occurred at the Proctor Theatre in Mount Vernon, New York, on November 3, 1921, at what had been determined was going to be a sixteen week tour. Billed as "The King of Swat," Ruth was teamed with veteran vaudevillian Wellington Cross in a sketch entitled "That's Good: A Satirical Home Run." Armed with his easy way with the public and his "really fine baritone voice," Ruth sang a song written for the show: "Little by Little and Bit by Bit, I Am Making a Vaudeville Hit!"[37]

After Mount Vernon, Ruth and Cross played Boston on November 7.[38] Less than two weeks after playing Proctor's Theatre in Mount Vernon, Ruth made his New York debut at B. F. Keith's Palace Theatre — which might be record time for someone finally playing the Palace. Ruth "packed the Palace like he did the Polo Grounds during the baseball season.... His first appearance on the stage evoked applause that went on continuously for more than a minute while Ruth bowed back his thanks time and again."[39] While Ruth was by no means a polished performer, he was better by far than many baseball stars who had played vaudeville. According to the *Times* reviewer, "Ruth has good stage presence, a winning smile and he gets away with the singing part...."[40]

Ruth returned to barnstorming in the off-season until after the 1926 World Series. This time Ruth played the Pantages vaudeville circuit in Minnesota and California as a headliner. It would be conjecture that Ruth avoided playing the northeast because he had been branded the goat of the Series for having been thrown out attempting to steal second to end the seventh game of the 1926 World Series against the St. Louis Cardinals.[41]

The Pantages vaudeville tour was very successful in Minnesota. As always, everywhere Ruth played the crowds were large, loud and lionizing. On the California leg of the tour the crowds were just as adoring as those in Minnesota, but the public officials were another matter. Along with the patter and the songs in his vaudeville act, Ruth brought children from the audience onstage to josh with them, ask them questions and then give them baseballs. The California Deputy State Commissioner of Labor charged Babe Ruth with violating the child labor law concerning employing children in theaters because he did not have a permit for children to appear in his vaudeville act.[42] The case was settled as a misunderstanding because Ruth was unaware of the child labor law.

Yet while Ruth did not play vaudeville after the 1926-27 tour, he did make at least one vaudeville record with Lou Gehrig.[43] Many of these records were made by Warner Bros., who announced a policy on talking pictures in April 1925 to bring "the voices of the most popular stars of the operatic, vaudeville and theatrical fields" to the movie theater. Warner Bros. made these records to accompany filmed operatic, vaudeville and theatrical acts so these could be played in their theaters around the country. Warner Bros. briefly pursued this strategy because most of their theaters were too small to compete with the major studios' first run movie palaces that had movies on the bill along with vaudeville acts.[44] Whether the Ruth-Gehrig record was made to accompany a filmed act, or whether the Warner Bros. campaign inspired others to make talking records for their fans is unknown.

The record gives some insight into Ruth's capacity for vaudeville, Gehrig asks about Ruth's farm which leads to an Abbot and Costello–like discussion of celery and salary. Gehrig next asks about Ruth's driving and the lack of recent stories about Ruth's dubious expertise behind the wheel. Ruth responds, "There are too many motorists after the same jaywalker...." And to avoid driving troubles, "When a policeman stops me I autograph the car and give it to him as a souvenir."[45]

While Babe Ruth's connection to vaudeville might be the grandest, it is not the only connection. "Who's on First?" the routine that helps keep the names of Abbot and Costello alive, was a vaudeville perennial before they immortalized it in the movie *Naughty Nineties*.[46] Jack Norworth, vaudevillian and composer of "Shine On Harvest Moon" and the husband of the vaudeville star Nora Bayes, wrote Harry Carey's anthem "Take Me Out to the Ball Game" in 1908. When Norworth wrote "Take Me Out to the Ball Game," he had never seen a baseball game. Perhaps Norworth's ignorance of baseball goes toward explaining the line "Buy me some peanuts and Cracker Jack / I don't care if I never get back." While the song was initially not popular when Norworth played it (perhaps because the fans did care about getting back to family and home, or whatever else they were leaving for an afternoon at the ballpark), very shortly it was in demand all over the country, helped by sing-along slides in the nickelodeons.[47]

Nora Bayes provides another point where baseball and vaudeville intersect, although the Bayes connection is not to a player but to Ring Lardner, who first gained fame for his baseball writing in Chicago and Boston. Lardner's biggest musical success was the song "Prohibition Blues" written in 1919 for Nora Bayes for *Ladies First*, her farce about the feminist movement.[48] While Ring Lardner is forever remembered as the writer of humorous baseball stories, his heart belonged to show business. Lardner wanted to write songs for Flo Ziegfeld's Follies and the Shuberts' vaudeville shows more than he wanted to write about baseball.

Lardner's love of music and vaudeville inadvertently began him on his career as a sportswriter. Sent to Chicago in January 1902 to study mechanical engineering, Lardner's constant attendance at the vaudeville houses and musical halls of Chicago led to Lardner's invitation to discontinue his mechanical engineering studies.[49] Back home by the spring of 1903, Lardner did odd jobs until, following his brother Rex's footsteps, Lardner found work as a baseball writer in 1905. Steady work as a baseball writer did not deter Lardner from pursuing his first love. Lardner concentrated on plugging songs. While he was a beat writer for a number of Chicago papers covering either the Cubs or the White Sox, Lardner made the rounds of music publishers in New York to try to "fool any publisher with one ... for New York [is] the only place to try anything like that in."[50]

In 1908, Lardner found a kindred soul in White Sox pitcher Doc White, and together they collaborated, with White writing the music and Lardner the lyrics. The next year they published their first song, "Little Puff of Smoke, Good Night," best described as "a Southern 'croon' in the Bert Williams manner ... sentimental and imitative."[51] Next, Lardner and White tried to best "Take Me Out to the Ball Game" with their "Gee! It's a Wonderful Game." While Lardner and White's song was far more ingenious and baseball savvy than Norworth's "Take Me Out to the Ball Game," it was difficult to sing and did not sound good when played by a loud brass band.[52]

Here is the lyric for the first verse and chorus of "Gee! It's a Wonderful Game."

Who discover'd the land of the brave and the free?
I don't know, I don't know.
'Twas Christy Columbus is what they tell me;
May be so, I don't know.
There's only one Christy that I know at all,
One Christy that I ever saw,
He's the one who discovered the fade away ball,
And he pitches for Muggsy McGraw.

Baseball, baseball, ain't it a wonderful game?
Old Christy Colum' found this country by gum
But the extras don't carry his name.
If old man Columbus had sat in the stand,
Had seen Matty pitching that "fader" so grand,
He'd have said, "Boys I'm glad I discovered this land.
Gee! It's a wonderful game."

Lardner explores the wonders of the game in the comedy sketch "The Bull Pen," performed in the 1922 Ziegfeld Follies. This skit starred Will Rogers as a veteran Yankee pitcher in conversation with a busher during a game against the Indians at the Polo Grounds. The rookie pitcher is full of himself and ignorant of his baseball. He declares that the regular pitchers don't know how to pitch to Tris Speaker. Asked how he would pitch to Speaker, the busher replies, "First I'd give him my fast one —" To which the veteran says, "Hold on! Now you're pitching to the next batter. Speaker's on third."[53]

When Babe Ruth comes up, the busher says, "He wouldn't bust one if I was pitching!" Asked how he would pitch to Ruth, the busher declares, "High and on the outside." To which the veteran replies, "And that's just where it would go." Oblivious to the jibe, the busher states, "Just the same, I bet Ruth's glad I ain't with some other club." When told that the Babe doesn't know that the busher isn't with another club, the busher asserts that the Babe will not break the home run record this year because of all the time he missed. "I bet if I went barnstorming, Landis wouldn't of dast suspended *me* that long." The veteran assures the rookie he is right, Landis would not have suspended him, Landis "wouldn't of never heard of it."[54] While the rest of the skit is not as topical and plays off many of the veteran/busher themes found in Lardner's other baseball fiction, it does prove that baseball was so ingrained into American life that it was even part of the Zeigfeld Follies, the epitome of vaudeville class.

The connection between Lardner's baseball writing and vaudeville continues with "Harmony," his thinly disguised short story about The Red

Sox Quartette and Marty McHale, who Babe Ruth called "the best god-damn singer I ever heard."[55] McHale played in the majors from 1910 to 1916. In Lardner's story McHale becomes Mike McCann, the pitcher who sings in vaudeville during the off-season.[56] As the tenor, McCann is the center-piece of the quartette formed by the Boston star outfielder Art Graham, who is obsessed with singing. Once McCann hurts his arm and is released, Graham is inconsolable because no one on the team can sing well enough to be the fourth member.

Then Graham, on a trip to his uncle's farm on an off day in Detroit, meets his cousin's beau, Waldron, who sings beautifully. Graham, who is scouting a young outfielder for the team on the day trip to his uncle's, claims that Waldron is a better ballplayer than the one he was sent to scout. Waldron joins the Red Sox and Graham tries to give him a few pointers so he will look good enough to stick with the team. Then Waldron proceeds to play "better than any player since Cobb" and take Graham's centerfield job away. Everyone is then amazed by Graham's generosity for helping the young player who takes away his job, but as one character remarks, Graham is a friend to everyone who sings.[57]

Perhaps Lardner chose this ironic ending because nothing like that happened to Marty McHale. He left baseball to join the Army Air Corp in 1917. After the war McHale returned to vaudeville. During his time with the Red Sox and the Red Sox Quartette, he compiled a 0–2 record with an E.R.A. of over seven which indicates that McHale was better at hitting the high C than he was at hitting the corners. McHale's partners in the Red Sox Quartette were Buck O'Brien, Hughie Bradley and Larry Gardner, although Gardner gave up after a while and was replaced by Bill Lyons. McHale explains that Lyons was not much of a ballplayer. The only reason the Red Sox signed him was to keep the name of the act proper.[58]

Neither *The Baseball Encyclopedia* nor *Total Baseball* show a Bill Lyons playing for the Red Sox at this time. Either McHale's memory was faulty, or he was really "not much of a ballplayer" that Patsy Donovan never put him in a game. Perhaps Lardner was privy to this information and thought it highly amusing to turn Lyons into the player who was "better than any player since Cobb."

McHale relates how he spent five years touring with "Turkey" Mike Donlin, who got his nickname because whenever "he'd make a terrific catch or something he'd do a kind of turkey step and take his cap off and throw it up like a ham." According to McHale, he and Donlin, who McHale calls the Babe Ruth of his day, played the Keith circuit. He notes with pride that one year they were booked into the Palace twice. McHale recalls their act consisted of a lot of baseball and double entendres highlighted by the sentimental song, "When You Are Standing on Third, You're Still a Long Way from Home."[59]

As the husband of vaudeville star Mabel Hite, Donlin had considered a vaudeville career for a long time. In fact, Donlin held out for the 1907, 1909 and 1910 seasons and played vaudeville instead of taking pay cuts.[60] Donlin signed a contract on August 5, 1908, to play vaudeville with Mabel Hite beginning on October 26 in New York, Brooklyn, and perhaps as far west as Chicago.[61] The tour was successful enough that Donlin continued on in vaudeville and did not return to baseball until 1911. After Mabel Hite died of intestinal cancer in 1912, Donlin teamed with Marty McHale.[62] Donlin finally left vaudeville for Hollywood, where he appeared in a number of silent movies.[63] Donlin retired from the movies and never returned to either baseball or vaudeville.

Baseball and vaudeville have a long and entwined history. With television as the natural heir to vaudeville, the relationship continues. Seeing that baseball has always been a facet of show business is important to understanding the development of popular culture.

Notes

1. Douglas, *The Feminization of American Culture*, 34.
2. Gilbert, *American Vaudeville*, 113.
3. *Ibid.*, 202.
4. Nasaw, *Going Out*, 32.
5. *Ibid.*
6. Johnson and Ward, *Who's Who in Baseball History*, 413.
7. Kiner, WWOR–Mets telecast, June 2, 1996.
8. Chass, *New York Times*, sec. 2, 6, 6/6/99.
9. Healy, Fox-Yankees telecast, 5/16/99.
10. Creamer, *Babe*, 255.
11. Di Meglio, *Vaudeville U.S.A.*, 11.
12. Seymour, *Early Years*, 199–200; Voigt *American Baseball*, Vol. 1, 138–141.
13. Nasaw, *Going Out*, 99.
14. Snyder, *The Voice of the City*, 52.
15. *Ibid.*, 49–52; Creamer, *Babe*, 29–32.
16. Ritter and Rucker, *The Babe: A Life in Pictures*, 148.
17. Spalding, *America's National Game*, 449–450.
18. Seymour, *Early Years, Vol. I*, 356; Ward and Burns, *Baseball: An Illustrated History*, 38.
19. Smith, *Baseball in the Afternoon*, 86–87.
20. Voigt, *American Baseball*, Vol. 1, 140–141.
21. Davis, *Baseball's Unforgettable*, 106–108.
22. Holtzman, *No Cheering in the Press Box*, 18.
23. *New York Times*, 10/28/21, 20:3.
24. Nelson, *Baseball's Greatest Quotes*, 42.

25. Ward and Burns, *Baseball: An Illustrated History*, 164.
26. Holtzman, *No Cheering in the Press Box*, 17.
27. Lieb, *Baseball As I Have Known It*, 165–166.
28. Creamer, *Babe*, 232.
29. *Ibid.*, 236.
30. Seymour, *Golden Age*, Vol. II, 392.
31. Okrent and Wulf, *Baseball Anecdotes*, 91.
32. Nasaw, *Going Out*, 53–61.
33. *New York Times*, 10/22/21, 16:1.
34. *New York Times*, 10/24/21, 20:3.
35. Spitzer, *The Palace*, 108.
36. *New York Times*, 10/28/21, 1:7.
37. Smith, *Babe Ruth's America*, 117.
38. Creamer, *Babe*, 250.
39. *New York Times*, 11/15/21, 16:5.
40. *Ibid.*
41. Gallagher, *Day by Day in New York Yankees History*, 63.
42. *New York Times*, 1/26/27, 23:7.
43. Trimble recording given to author.
44. Schatz, *The Genius of the System*, 58–60.
45. Trimble recording.
46. "Who's," *Armchair*, Thorn 24.
47. Samuels, *Once Upon a Stage*, 82–85; Ward and Burns, *Baseball*, 96.
48. Lardner, Jr., *The Lardners*, 96–97.
49. Yardley, *Ring*, 60.
50. Lardner, Jr., *The Lardners*, 53.
51. Yardley, *Ring*, 101.
52. Elder, *Ring Lardner*, 248.
53. Lardner, "The Bull Pen," *The Portable Ring Lardner*, 722.
54. *Ibid.*, 722–723.
55. Ritter, *Armchair*, Thorn, 253.
56. Lardner, "Harmony," *Bases*, 318.
57. *Ibid.*, 313–330.
58. Ritter, *Armchair*, 253–254.
59. *Ibid.*, 254.
60. Seymour, *Early Years*, 107.
61. Fleming, *The Unforgettable Season*, 156.
62. *Ibid.*, 323.
63. Ritter, *Armchair*, 254.

Reading List and Works Cited

"Babe Ruth Warmly Greeted in Debut on New York Stage." *New York Times*, 15 Nov. 1921, 16:5.

Cooperstown. National Baseball Hall of Fame and Museum, Inc. Babe Ruth Clip File. (Articles dating from 1911 to 1958 concerning Babe Ruth's life and career. Many unattributed or indexed solely by publication date.)

Creamer, Robert W. *Babe: The Legend Comes to Life*. New York: Penguin Books, 1983.

Davis, Mac. *Baseball's Unforgettable*. Toronto, New York, London: Bantam Pathfinder Editions, 1965.

Di Meglio, John E. *Vaudeville U.S.A.* Bowling Green, Ohio: Bowling Green University Popular Press, 1973.

Douglas, Ann. *The Feminization of American Culture.* New York: Noon Day Press, 1977.

Elder, Donald. *Ring Lardner.* Garden City, NY: Doubleday & Company, Inc., 1956.

Fleming, G. H. *The Unforgettable Season.* New York: Holt, Rinehart and Winston, 1981.

Gallagher, Michael. *Day by Day in New York Yankees History.* New York: Leisure Press, 1983.

"George Bernard Shaw Wants to Know 'Whose Baby Is Ruth.'" *New York Times,* 29 Oct. 1921, 1:7.

Gilbert, Douglas. *American Vaudeville: Its Life and Times.* New York: Whittlesey House, 1940; reprinted Dover Publications, 1963.

Healy, Fran. Comments made during a Fox-NY Yankees telecast, May 16, 1999.

Holtzman, Jerome, ed. *No Cheering in the Press Box.* New York: Holt, Rinehart and Winston, 1973.

Honig, Donald. *Baseball America: The Heroes of the Game and the Times of Their Glory.* New York: Macmillan Publishing Co., 1985.

Johnson, Lloyd, and Brenda Ward. *Who's Who in Baseball History.* New York: Barnes & Noble Books, 1994.

Kiner, Ralph. Comments on Chuck Connors heard during Kiner's color commentary during the WWOR broadcast of the New York Mets game, June 2, 1996.

Lardner, Ring. *The Portable Ring Lardner.* Ed. with an introduction by Gilbert Seldes. New York: The Viking Press, 1946.

____, *Ring Around the Bases.* Ed. with an introduction by Matthew J. Bruccoli. New York: Charles Scribner's Sons, 1992.

Lardner, Ring W. Jr., *The Lardners: My Family Remembered.* New York: Harper & Row, 1976.

Lieb, Fred. *Baseball As I Have Known It.* New York: Grosset & Dunlop Inc., Publishers, 1977.

Nasaw, David. *Going Out: The Rise and Fall of Public Amusements.* New York: Basic Books, 1993.

Nelson, Kevin, ed. *Baseball's Greatest Quotes.* New York: Simon & Schuster, A Fireside Book, 1982.

Okrent, Daniel, and Steve Wulf. *Baseball Anecdotes.* New York: Harper & Row, 1989.

Ritter, Lawrence S. "Ladies and Gentlemen, Presenting Marty McHale" *The Armchair Book of Baseball.* Ed. by John Thorn. New York: Charles Scribner's Sons, 1985.

____, and Mark Rucker. *The Babe: A Life in Pictures.* New York: Ticknor & Fields, 1988.

"Ruth Makes Debut as Vaudeville Star." *New York Times,* 4 Nov. 1921, 20:6.

"Ruth Top-Liner on Keith Circuit." *New York Times,* 28 Oct. 1921, 20:3.

Samuels, Charles, and Louise Samuels. *Once Upon a Stage.* New York: Dodd, Mead & Company, 1974.

Schatz, Thomas. *The Genius of the System.* New York: Pantheon Books, 1988.

Seymour, Harold. *Baseball: The Early Years.* Vol. I. New York: Oxford University Press, 1960.

____. *Baseball: The Golden Age.* Vol. II. New York: Oxford University Press, 1971.

Smith, Robert. *Babe Ruth's America.* New York: Thomas Y. Crowell Company, 1974.

____. *Baseball in the Afternoon.* New York: Simon & Schuster, 1993.

Snyder, Robert W. *The Voice of the City: Vaudeville and Popular Culture in New York.* New York and Oxford: Oxford University Press, 1989.

Spalding, Albert. *America's National Game.* New York: American Sports Publishing Co., 1911; reprinted Lincoln and London: University of Nebraska Press, 1992.

Spitzer, Marian. *The Palace.* New York: Atheneum, 1969.

Trimble, Patrick. Audio tape of the Ruth-Gehrig record supplied to the author from Professor Trimble's collection. Date of the recording is unknown, but from the inferences in the Ruth-Gehrig patter, it appears to be after 1929 because of Ruth's comment on the uniforms now being numbered.

Voigt, David Quentin. *American Baseball*, Vol. I. University Park and London: The Pennsylvania State University Press, 1983.

Ward, Geoffrey C., and Ken Burns. *Baseball: An Illustrated History*. New York: Alfred A. Knopf, 1994.

"Who's on First?" *The Armchair Book of Baseball*. Ed. by John Thorn. New York: Charles Scribner's Sons, 1985

Yardley, Jonathan. *Ring*. New York: Random House, 1977.

Baseball and Country Music

Don Cusic

There is nothing more quintessentially American than baseball and country music. Each has its roots in England — the games of rounders and cricket for baseball and the British folk songs for country music — but each was developed in the United States during the nineteenth century.

During the twentieth century both baseball and country music expanded into truly national entertainment. Until 1953 there were 16 major league teams in 10 cities. None of these cities were further south than Washington and none further west than St. Louis. At the start of the 1999 season there were 30 major league teams in 24 cities, in every region of the country. Country music was a regional music before World War II, limited to the South, but since the War it has become a national music with country music radio stations all over the country. Country music artists tour throughout the country and it is possible to find albums by country music artists in every city in the United States; that was not possible during the first half of the twentieth century.

As baseball and country music developed into big business, three basic major revenue streams developed for each — and these sources of revenue are essentially the same for both country music and baseball. First is paid attendance at either ball games or concerts. Next is money from broadcasting — radio and TV income — and finally is the sale of "product" which, for country music, means compact discs and cassettes while for baseball this means the sale of merchandise with team logos.

In the preface to the book *Baseball: An Illustrated History*, Ken Burns and Lynn Novick write "The story of baseball is also the story of race in

America, of immigration and assimilation; of the struggle between labor and management, of popular culture and advertising, of myth and the nature of heroes, villains, and buffoons; of the role of women and class and wealth in our society."[1] The same could be said for country music.

In terms of "race," the story of baseball is part of the story of Civil Rights; first the segregation of baseball before 1947, the creation of the Negro leagues and black baseball stars, then the introduction of Jackie Robinson to the major leagues. For country music the story is not so clear; country music has never really been integrated to any great extent, but it doesn't bar African-Americans from its ranks either. During the 1960s, country music had its first black superstar, Charley Pride; however, unlike Jackie Robinson, a number of black country music superstars did not follow. It is easier to see Elvis Presley as the Jackie Robinson in popular music, because the music became "integrated" with the success of rock 'n' roll.

The story of immigration and assimilation in baseball comes from European immigrants — particularly those from Ireland and Germany — finding a place in baseball to fulfill the American dream. For country music the Irish brought fiddle tunes and other music that would be a foundation for commercial country music. The Germans would bring the beer hall and dances which would evolve in country music dance clubs, the two-step and line dancing.

The struggle between labor and management in baseball is the struggle of autocratic owners who kept baseball players in servitude through the "reserve" clause, which was interpreted by the owners to mean a lifetime bondage until player representative Marvin Miller came along and helped break that hold. For country music there hasn't been that kind of conflict, although record companies and artists are always locked in a struggle of entertainment versus business. The recording contract has its faults and drawbacks, but country artists have generally felt the benefits outweighed the disadvantages in these contracts, which usually favor the recording companies.

In terms of advertising we must look at the influence the media has had upon baseball and country music. Since each is a business venture as well as entertainment, both country music and baseball have enjoyed a unique position. Every recording and every baseball game is, essentially, an advertisement, but because they are also "entertainment," they are given "free" time in the media. The growth of radio and television has assured that each received national coverage as the twentieth century progressed.

In terms of the role of women, country music has done much better than baseball. Professional baseball only allowed women's leagues during World War II and immediately after, when it was feared that men's leagues would fold because of the wartime draft. But baseball, as a whole, has excluded women. Not so with country music. A number of women have become country music stars and, by the 1990s, around 65 percent of all country music recordings were purchased by women. Female country music stars, from Kitty Wells to Patsy Cline, Loretta Lynn, Tammy Wynette, Reba McEntire, and Shania Twain, have spoken to the public from the woman's point of view, and this has been key to their success. Even in the executive ranks there have been a number of successful women — something which cannot be said for baseball.

The story of "class" and "wealth" in American society is a touchy one because Americans, by and large, generally do not want to admit to a class society. But the simple fact remains that baseball and country music both have their roots in the white working class and were looked down upon by upper class Americans. Baseball and country music were both considered entertainment for roughs and rowdies, the great unwashed masses. And both have fought against this stereotype and become the sport and music of the middle class.

The executives in both country music and baseball often aspired to social success and acceptance and worked hard to obtain it. Their success in business made them legitimate in the eyes of more traditional businessmen, even when the traditional businessmen didn't quite understand the business of baseball or country music. But as baseball and country music proved themselves to be profitable businesses, social acceptance of executives in these fields followed. The same cannot be said for the players and performers, who often come from the working class and who often do not have social ambitions. Their lives revolve around their profession and, when they leave their profession, usually return to their working class roots. For those players and performers who do aspire to social acceptance it is a long, uphill struggle and, with few exceptions, they never quite fit in, even when they are at the same gatherings with the social elite.

Finally there is the myth of the hero. There is no doubt that many youngsters look up to baseball players and country music stars and want to emulate them. And it is no doubt that the accomplishments of baseball players and country music artists touch the lives of their followers, who invest much of their lives towards following the exploits of their heroes. Youngsters stand in awe of their heroes, who always appear larger than life. But adult fans, too, are touched by baseball players and country music artists because these players and performers articulate their own dreams and aspirations. Country artists often articulate the thoughts and feelings of their fans through lyrics in their songs while baseball players keep their fans in touch with the youngster deep inside each adult by providing heroic actions that adult fans, often living lives of quiet desperation, only dream about.

In April, 1861, when the first shots of the Civil War were fired at Fort Sumter, South Carolina, the seeds for baseball and country music had already been firmly planted. What evolved into commercial country music songs were, at that time, known as minstrel songs, set in shows done in blackface by itinerant entertainers, and British and European folk songs, which were sung particularly in the South and whose basic tunes and melodic structure were used for the minstrel songs.

The seeds of baseball evolved from the English games of cricket and rounders and the game had already developed into something uniquely American, first through base ball clubs in New York and then as an informal field sport in the rest of the country. At this point what linked the two—and would continue to link country music and baseball for the next century—was that they served as entertainment for white, working class Americans.

The "look" of baseball players and country performers was also established just after the Civil War. For baseball it was player-captain Harry Wright, who served as head of the Cincinnati Base Ball Club in 1868. Wright "permanently altered baseball attire when he had his men abandon the pantaloons players everywhere had worn up to then, in favor of flannel knickers and woolen stockings. Combined with jockey-style caps ... and half-sleeved flannel blouses with soft collars, the Cincinnati garb established the basic elements of the baseball uniform that would still be worn a century later."[2] For country performers the "look" was developed in vaudeville and consisted of bib overalls, often some teeth blacked out, and the hayseed image that would still appear on the TV program *Hee Haw* a century later. Vaudeville increasingly stereotyped "country" people as rubes and hayseeds and this image continued to be part of country music and was even used within country music. Performers in the early years affected the "mountaineer" image until the image of the cowboy began to take over during the 1930s after the popularity of singing cowboys in the movies.[3]

In terms of the *business* of baseball and country music, the first step for each was as live entertainment and entrepreneurs organized these sports and musical events for paying customers. Thus the financial base for both baseball and country music was developed in the nineteenth century from businessmen who organized an event—either a musical concert or baseball game—promoted it to the community, invested in performers and players, and then made a profit if enough paying customers came.

However, even though each endeavor—baseball games and musical concerts—was a business venture *within* the field, to the audience they were *entertainment* and the "performances" of baseball players and musical performers took on a meaning beyond mere commerce. According to Edward White, "baseball was thought of as a business, a form of entertainment for profit, but implicitly presented as a much more engaging spectacle than a circus or an opera or a play. It conjured up idyllic rural and pastoral associations, although staged in an urban setting."[4] Musical performances of early "country" music also transported the audiences to a past with idyllic connotations and fans attached themselves to these performers, who often served as idealized versions of those not on the stage.

Still, it was the *business* aspects of these endeavors that caused them to thrive. First, businessmen became involved and sought to market their "product." Second, it meant that players in each field would be paid and thus could become professionals with the implication that a professional ballplayer or a professional entertainer had achieved a level of ability beyond the ordinary.

The media that first linked the two ventures was print, particularly the newspaper. Since both sports and music fulfill two roles in the public — that of a business venture and popular entertainment — the businessmen involved in sports and entertainment took out advertisements to attract customers while the newspapers wrote stories about these events to satisfy the demand of readers. This coverage also attracted readers who would purchase newspapers in order to keep up with the games, concerts, players and performers in their area. From these business concerns as well as public demand developed the sports section and the entertainment section of the newspaper.

The key link between baseball and country music during the 1920s was radio. Baseball got there first. Shortly after the nation's first commercial station, KDKA in Pittsburgh, went on the air (November 2, 1920), they broadcast a baseball game. The date was August 5, 1921, and the place was Forbes Field, where the Pirates and Phillies played. Also in 1921 was the broadcast of the first World Series, although only the first game, announced by *New York Herald Tribune* reporter Grantland Rice, was broadcast. Ironically, Grantland Rice was born in Murfreesboro, Tennessee, about 40 miles from downtown Nashville, and went to college at Vanderbilt, then began his career as a sportswriter in Nashville where the baseball park was only a few blocks away from the National Life and Accident Insurance Company, which would begin radio station WSM and the Grand Ole Opry in the 1920s.

By 1922 WSB in Atlanta had "country" performers on the air; in January, 1923, a square dance began at WBAP in Fort Worth, Texas, and sometime around 1925 WBAP carried a regular Friday night "barn dance" which was the term generally used for early live country music programs. Meanwhile, in Chicago at WLS, a station owned by Sears, Roebuck and Company, a barn dance began on April 19, 1924. The "official" beginning of the "WSM Barn Dance" in Nashville was November 28, 1925, although it was not called the Grand Ole Opry until 1927.

Chicago was a center for radio broadcasts of both country music and baseball during the 1920s. In 1925 the White Sox and Cubs had all their home games broadcast over WMAQ, which was owned by the Chicago *Daily News*. That same year WGN began broadcasting games. Cubs owner William Wrigley loved radio broadcasts as a way to promote his chewing gum company as well as his Cubs team. In 1940 Wrigley would play a major role in broadcasting country music, sponsoring Gene Autry's *Melody Ranch* broadcasts over the CBS network.

Both baseball and country music benefited from national stars who emerged during the 1920s. For baseball it was Babe Ruth and his home runs; for country music it was Jimmie Rodgers and his blue yodels. Also, two key executives emerged from these two fields during this period; in baseball it was Commissioner Judge Kenesaw Mountain Landis and for country music it was recording producer and publisher Ralph Peer.

The dead ball era was over and the long ball era had begun but Babe Ruth was more than just a great hitter, he was one of those colorful, larger-than-life lovable characters who come along once in a lifetime. Fans not only loved his towering home runs, they loved his outgoing, exuberant, devil-may-care attitude. Kids made him their hero as he became a national figure both on and off the field.

Ruth's emergence as a baseball hero came at a critical time in the history of that sport. In 1919 the infamous Black Sox scandal occurred when a number of White Sox players made deals with gamblers to throw the World Series against the Cincinnati Reds. At this point, the baseball owners, realizing their sport as well as their livelihood was in danger, hired a commissioner to oversee the game. Because the owners were in such desperate straits, the man they chose, Judge Kenesaw Mountain Landis, a federal judge from Chicago, assumed a lot of power the owners would have normally been reluctant to give up. Landis was an autocratic ruler and many can fault his imperious manner; however, he did restore integrity to the game and ruled the sport with an iron fist until his death during World War II.

Country music received its first initial exposure on the national stage in June, 1923, when record executive Ralph Peer traveled to Atlanta, Georgia, to record Fiddlin' John Carson. The recording of Carson fiddling and singing was commercially successful, which led to other recording labels recording country music. In the summer of 1927 Ralph Peer traveled to Bristol, Tennessee, for recordings for the Victor Company; Peer had accepted a position with Victor for no salary if he could own the copyrights and publishing of the songs recorded. In Bristol he recorded Jimmie Rodgers, the first superstar in country music, and the Carter Family. Also, Ralph Peer established a royalty payment system for songwriters, and copyrighted a number of songs both old and new, which made the publishing of country songs lucrative for songwriters and publishers. Thus the financial structure for the business of country music was established with the sales of recordings and the copyrights of songs proving themselves good business ventures for New York executives.

In that same summer, 1927, the New York Yankees' famous Murderers' Row led their team to 110 wins (in a 154 game season) and a World Series victory over the Pirates. This was the season Babe Ruth hit 60 homes runs.

But the importance of the Yankee's season and the Bristol sessions extends beyond the commercial success that ensued for Victor Records because Jimmie Rodgers was to country music what Babe Ruth was to baseball. Like Ruth, who inspired countless young boys to pick up a bat and ball, Rodgers inspired countless rural boys to try singing for a living. The boys who looked at Babe Ruth as a hero swung for the fence; the boys who looked at Jimmie Rodgers as a hero sang blue yodels, a slipping into falsetto in key parts of the song. A generation of baseball players and country singers were influenced most by Babe Ruth and Jimmie Rodgers as these two men led their fields in the direction they would take in the coming decades.

Perhaps this is personified best in the story of a high school shortstop named Gene Autry who, around 1925, tried out for Tulsa, a farm club for the St. Louis Cardinals. He was offered a contract for $100 a month, but elected to work as a telegrapher for the railroad because they paid him $150 a month. Autry remembered that he never tried out for baseball again, "but that was a dream that didn't die easily. To play baseball, to reach the big leagues, that was the great national escape of my boyhood, especially for the poor ones looking for a way to get off the farm."[5] Later, he would become a singing star, modeling himself after Jimmie Rodgers at the start of his career.

The popularity of radio added another dimension to the business of both baseball and country music. First, it served as an advertising medium for the games and shows because those who heard a performance or game were more likely to want to see the event *live*. However, that is not how the businessmen of baseball or the recording industry saw radio at the time.

By the end of the 1920s neither country music nor baseball saw major revenue from radio. Both were essentially in the business of selling tickets to fans, who went to the ballpark or the show. The owners were interested in attracting a crowd and, although they saw radio as a means of advertising their wares, most power brokers in country music and baseball had an innate fear that radio would "steal" their audience.

The big money for baseball broadcasts did not arrive until 1934 when Commissioner Landis negotiated a four-year contract with the Ford Motor Company to sponsor the World Series for $400,000. Still, the owners generally did not see the benefits of broadcasting regular games.

The owners simply felt that if people could hear the games in their homes over the radio, they would not come to the ballpark. Sponsors who paid for the rights to broadcast games changed the owner's view because owners could see another source of revenue — indeed, a large source of revenue — by having their games broadcast. They were surprised to discover that not only the sponsors benefited by selling their product, the owners benefited because the games themselves were an advertisement that increased attendance.

The major recording industry companies also fought radio, essentially for the same reason baseball owners did. Network radio during the 1930s consisted of a number of live broadcasts of big bands who had sponsors. These bands and their leaders knew that radio appearances were lucrative because sponsors paid them and because these shows were good advertisements for live appearances. They wanted to assure sponsors the exclusive advertising rights — which sponsors demanded — so they saw recordings as an unwelcome intruder on radio. These acts did *not* want these recordings on the air because, the reasoning ran, why would the radio stations pay the act when they could get the recording for free? And why would fans attend a live concert as a paying customer when they could hear the recording on the radio for free?

In 1940 a very important thing happened that would affect country music on radio: the Supreme Court let stand a lower court ruling that when someone purchased a recording, all property rights belonged to the buyer. This made radio airplay for records legal and curbed the efforts of the record companies, who were fighting radio airplay and had hired a bevy of lawyers to enforce the ban on radio airplay.

In 1939 the Grand Ole Opry received its first national sponsor, Prince Albert Tobacco, and went on the NBC network. This would mark the beginning of Nashville and the Opry as major players in country music. Also in 1939 the Baseball Hall of Fame opened in Cooperstown, New York. What has this got to do with country music? Well, about 20 years later —

in late 1958 — the Country Music Association was formed in Nashville. One of their first ideas to promote country music and tourism was a Country Music Hall of Fame, which they based on the idea of the Baseball Hall of Fame.

The idea was rather obvious; the Baseball Hall of Fame was well known as both an institution and tourist attraction by 1958, so an "awareness" of Cooperstown was a given.

One of the important things that happened at the Grand Ole Opry because of the network connection was they began to move away from the original idea of the Opry show itself as the major attraction to a star system where an act would be promoted over the others. Prior to this time it was the *show* that was central and the artists were interchangeable; after this, the *star* would be the central figure. This idea of the power of an individual star would shift the balance of power at the Opry hierarchy as the Opry progressed through the 1940s.

The idea of a *star,* rather than just the team, attracting paying customers was also true in baseball. A lot of people came to see Babe Ruth, or Walter Johnson, or Ty Cobb and not just the team. But baseball would not have to face the drawing power of stars until the reserve clause in players contracts was struck down in the 1970s and made free agency possible.

By the end of 1939 Roy Acuff was the biggest star of the Grand Ole Opry and Acuff had a connection to baseball. Acuff played baseball until he was felled by a sunstroke in 1929; this resulted in him spending 1930 in bed, where he learned to play the fiddle his father owned. And this, in turn, led to his career in country music.

Another baseball fan, Bill Monroe, joined the Opry in October, 1939, with his group "The Bluegrass Boys." Monroe would go on to create "bluegrass" music, named after his group, and would form a baseball team with his traveling troupe that would play exhibition games before his concerts. Monroe pitched and played first base and his group played a number of minor league teams in the South. Because he was so infatuated with baseball, Monroe often made his decisions about hiring musicians for his band with additional consideration based on how well they played ball. Banjo player Stringbean was a good pitcher — which added to his value as a musician.

Monroe's group played six or seven nights a week and drove up to a hundred miles between shows. "The Bluegrass All Stars" got some good physical exercise and also used the game to help promote their shows, challenging local teams or anybody who could get up a team. In an advertisement in *Billboard* magazine in April 30, 1949, the ad copy states, "Bill Monroe will carry a baseball team with him again this summer in conjunction with his personal appearance tour. Monroe intends to line up 15 players, some of who will double in his show, to play all comers on afternoon dates, with his show set for the evening."[6]

In his 1950 songbook, *Bill Monroe's Blue Grass Country Songs*, the introduction states that in 1949 the baseball team had an 80-50 won-lost record and that two players "were spotted by big league scouts, signed, and placed with farm clubs."[7] Later, Monroe told author Jim Rooney, that if it wasn't for his weak eyesight, "I [would] have liked to be a baseball player. I could hit good and could've been a fair player."[8]

This idea of traveling entertainment is true of both baseball and country music, with the teams or musical performers going from town to town to put on a "show." Fans of both looked at the traveling show as "exotic," like the vaudeville and circus performers who also traveled from town to town. This idea of a gypsy-like life is part of the image of both baseball players and country music singers.

Another country music star in the 1930s who would play a major role in baseball was Gene Autry, who starred on Chicago's WLS Barn Dance before going to Hollywood in 1934 to become the leading singing cowboy star. Although Autry was a baseball fan, his direct connection to baseball would not come until December, 1960, when he became a baseball owner.

The St. Louis Cardinals were the favorite major league team of many Nashville residents, dating back to the Gas House Gang years in the 1930s because St. Louis was the most southern city in major league baseball and because Nashvillians could pick up the signal from the St. Louis radio station that broadcast Cardinals games on the radio. The Gas House Gang Cardinals also loved country music; a group of players led by Dizzy Dean called themselves "The Mudcats" and played and sang country songs like "Birmingham Jail" in the Cardinal clubhouse.

During the 1950-52 period baseball was finding its center in New York; the '51 playoff between the Giants and Dodgers was decided by Bobby Thompson's home run and the Giants faced the Yankees in the Series; in 1952 it was Brooklyn against the Yankees. If you were a baseball fan in New York it was heaven — either the Giants or Dodgers faced the Yankees in the World Series. But the rest of the country soon lost interest in rooting for teams that never made it to the Series and it was increasingly difficult for baseball fans outside New York to remain enthusiastic about their teams.

Meanwhile, down in Nashville 1950-52 the country music industry was steadily finding its center, led by the Grand Ole Opry and the songs from Acuff-Rose publishing. The biggest hit in 1951 was "Tennessee Waltz" by Patti Page, a song published by Acuff-Rose that, more than any other song up to this period, showed the pop music world that Nashville was a good source for songs and established it as "Music City U.S.A."

Although paid attendance at major and minor league baseball declined throughout the 1950s, at the same time baseball achieved a national audience. The culprit and the hero for baseball's problems during this period was television.

Baseball TV broadcasts followed the pattern of radio broadcasts; the commissioner negotiated network coverage of the World Series and All Star game, with all the clubs sharing in the revenue, while each individual club negotiated broadcast rights in their own market.

In 1955 the Columbia Broadcasting System (CBS) took over the *Game of the Week* on television and brought in Dizzy Dean to do the play-by-play for the Saturday (and sometimes Sunday) games. Dean, a Southerner, was known for his fractured English — and "Dean-isms" such as "slud into third" are still known — but he was also known for belting out Roy Acuff's hit "Wabash Cannonball" over the air. In fact, Dean cut a record of "Wabash Cannonball" and as many people probably heard Dean's version of the "Wabash Canoonball" as heard Acuff's country classic.

Like baseball, country music appeared on television through local shows in major cities with some occasional network exposure.

While television helped both baseball and country music by giving each a mass audience and bringing them into American living rooms, they also hurt baseball and country music by undermining their appeal for a live audience. For baseball this meant less fans paying to see games; for country music it meant saddling it with an image of yokels and rubes that the country music industry would work hard for years to overcome.

In terms of broadcasting, country music had an advantage over baseball because country music's major medium was radio; as the networks moved their emphasis to TV, radio was left to carve a separate niche. They did this by using recordings on the air and concentrating on a particular kind of music. Unlike baseball, country music was not seasonal — it could be broadcast year round — and country music could be broadcast 24-hours a day while baseball was limited to game times. Thus country music thrived on radio while that medium became less important for baseball.

Both country music and baseball ran into major roadblocks during the 1950s; for baseball it was television, for country music it was rock 'n' roll.

The emergence of rock 'n' roll and Elvis Presley in 1956 almost dealt a death blow to the country music industry. First, the young white audience — many of whom may have been attracted to country music — wanted to see rock 'n' roll performers who were young and attractive. That meant that the demand for live appearances for country music performers virtually dried up overnight.

Next, radio stations dropped country music and played rock 'n' roll instead. Television was the major catalyst in this trend as well. Prior to TV, radio was dominated by the networks, who programmed a number of live shows. However, as viewers shifted to television, the advertising dollars followed quickly and soon radio stations could not afford to hire live talent. So, increasingly, records were played instead of live acts booked.

In many ways, what Jackie Robinson was to baseball, Elvis Presley was to the music industry; both shook up the existing order in their respective fields. Jackie Robinson led the integration of baseball while Elvis, although he was white, led the integration of pop music. A number of talented black ball players and musical artists entered the mainstream because of this integration, but the mainstream wasn't comfortable with all the developments. The level of play was raised, but so was the level of unease.

By 1960, television was firmly established as an essential and central piece of furniture in American homes. It was the media with the greatest mass appeal and both baseball and country music faced a common problem: how to appeal to the television audience. Neither succeeded very well and the story of the struggle of both baseball and country music to reach a large, national audience is tied to their exposure on television. Country music had an advantage here; it would receive its major exposure on radio. Baseball also received exposure on radio but as more and more games were played at night in order to attract fans to the ballpark after work, the broadcasts suffered because they competed with television.

But the history of baseball and country music on TV was rewritten in the 1980s when ESPN, The Nashville Network (TNN) and Country Music Television (CMT) went on the air. This entry of baseball and country music on cable television coincided with the rise of cable television in the United States.

Cable television helped country music by bringing the artists directly into American homes, thus freeing country music from the national networks who presented country music sparingly or, when they did, altered it to fit stereotypes perpetuated by New York and Los Angeles TV executives.

Cable television helped baseball because it could give fans a steady diet of baseball, appealing to core fans without having to attract the big numbers from a diverse audience. The "superstations" in Chicago and Atlanta have made national teams of the Cubs and Braves while ESPN's core of sports fans are happy to watch a variety of teams throughout the season. Like country music, baseball is on television on its own terms, appealing to baseball or sports fans instead of trying to reach a broad, mass audience, and this has helped the game.

Also, the networks know that huge audiences are still there for country music and baseball each year with the Country Music Association Awards show and the World Series — both held in the fall. While baseball cannot pull big numbers throughout the summer for TV networks, it certainly attracts a huge audience for special events like the All Star Game, division playoffs and World Series. And while country music also does not draw big TV ratings week in and week out throughout the year, the big CMA Awards show is consistently one of the top rated shows on network TV each year.

Both country music and baseball have benefited from public financing through the years — a recognition from local governments of their importance. When the early stadiums were torn down, they were replaced with stadiums built through public financing. Of all the baseball parks built since the 1960s only one — Dodger Stadium in Los Angeles — was built with private funds. Country music has benefited from the concert arenas put up with public funds in large cities, allowing the music a major venue for fans to see the artists.

In terms of the future of baseball and country music, both enjoy a large fan base in the United States but see a large market with the Latino population. In the years since World War II there have been a number of Latin players who have starred in the major leagues; by the 1997 season about 30 percent of all major league players were Latinos. For country music, the large number of Latinos in Texas has produced a "Tejano" music that is appealing to country fans while commercial country music has always had an appeal to Hispanics in the Southwest.

The link between baseball and country music may seem tenuous at first glance but, upon closer examination, shows two forms of entertainment that have been linked throughout twentieth century America. Both started out as entertainment for working class Americans and evolved into an entertainment for the middle class. Both had to overcome a history of low social standing among upper class Americans to become accepted by all classes of Americans. And both have evolved from entertainment with a small, local appeal to become the national game and the national music.

Perhaps the most important contribution baseball and country music make to America is summed up by a quote from Sparky Anderson, former manager of the Cincinnati Reds and Detroit Tigers. He said, "This game has taken a lot of guys over the years, who would have had to work in factories and gas stations, and made them prominent people ... in this business you can walk into a room with millionaires, doctors, professional people and get more attention than they get."[9] The same can be said for those in country music. Both have taken people who were born with no social status, no money in the family or the right connections but with great talent and allowed them to rise to the top and become heroes. To come from a working class background and end up on top of the world, rubbing shoulders with the elite of the country is the American dream. Baseball and country music both deliver tickets to that dream and you can't get more American than that.

Notes

1. Ward, Geoffrey, and Ken Burns. *Baseball: An Illustrated History* (New York: Knopf, 1994). "Preface" by Ken Burns and Lynn Novick, p. xvii.

2. Alexander, Charles C. *Our Game: An American Baseball History* (New York: Henry Holt & Co. 1991), p. 18.

3. Malone, Bill C. *Singing Cowboys and Musical Mountaineers: Southern Culture and the Roots of Country Music* (Athens: The University of Georgia Press, 1993). This book discusses the issue at length.

4. White, Edward G. *Creating the National Pastime: Baseball Transforms Itself 1903–1953* (Princeton, NJ: Princeton University Press, 1996), p. 23.

5 Autry, Gene, with Mickey Herkowitz. *Back in the Saddle*. Garden City, NY: Doubleday & Company, Inc. 1978, p. 151.

6. Advertisement, *Billboard Magazine*, April 30, 1949, p. 36.

7. Monroe, Bill. *Bill Monroe's Blue Grass Country Songs* (Beverly Hills, CA: Bill Monroe Music, 1950), p. 1.

8. Rooney, James. *Bossmen: Bill Monroe and Muddy Waters* (New York: The Dial Press, 1971), p. 57.

9. Plaut, David, ed. *Speaking of Baseball* (Philadelphia: Running Press, 1993), p. 390.

As American as Cherry Pie:
Baseball and Reflections of
Violence in the 1960s and 1970s

Ron Briley

In an introduction to the paperback edition of *Rights in Conflict*, a report on the riots at the 1968 Chicago Democratic national convention, Max Frankel of the *New York Times* commented on the centrality of violence to American life, stating, "We are known for our violence, we Americans. The creative violence with which we haul down the good for what we fancy is better. The cruel violence with which we treated red men, and black. The intoxicating violence of our music and art. The absurd violence of our comics and cartoons. The organized violence of our athletic and corporate games."[1]

Frankel's commentary was the product of a time in American history when it appeared that the nation was on the verge of disintegrating into riot, rebellion, and revolution. Beginning with the murder of President John F. Kennedy in November, 1963, America was haunted by the specter of political assassination, with the shooting of such figures as Medgar Evers and Malcolm X, culminating in the 1968 assassinations of Martin Luther King, Jr., and Robert Kennedy. Evening news programs were dominated by images of violence in Vietnam, while the body bag count proliferated. The war in Vietnam, cultural changes, and a transition in university clientele led to violent confrontations between students and the educational establishment. Frustrations regarding the lack of economic progress made in fulfilling the promise of the civil rights movement helped ignite

America's cities; where high unemployment rates, the assassination of Martin Luther King, Jr., or an incident of police violence might produce the spark to set off an urban inferno.

Black activist Rap Brown shocked Americans, but perhaps accurately captured the mood of America in the late 1960s, by proclaiming, "Violence is necessary and it's as American as cherry pie."[2] Brown looked to the country's past for justification that violence was essential in the struggle for black liberation. While not prepared to join Brown in a call for revolution, many historians began to question the consensus historiography of the 1950s, documenting that violence has, indeed, played a significant role in American history. Richard Maxwell Brown maintains that militant individualism in American life is a reflection of the frontier tradition which eroded the English common law concept that a person has the duty to retreat from violence whenever possible. According to Brown, over time a legal revolution occurred in America allowing a threatened individual to "legally stand fast and, without retreat, kill in self-defense."[3] The historical studies and reports of the National Commission on the Causes and Prevention of Violence supported the conclusions reached by activists and scholars, while insisting, as the Kerner Commission report on racial unrest, that the key component to halting further violence in America's cities was the reconstruction of urban life.[4]

While many scholars looked to the American past in order to explain a propensity for violence, the American sporting tradition and institution of baseball, often described as the national pastime and identified with the American traditions of motherhood and pie, appeared to offer an example of assimilation where conflict could be peacefully resolved on the playing fields of the nation. However, during the 1960s and 1970s, many commentators were convinced that baseball was not immune to the violence sweeping the nation.

An examination of newspaper accounts and sports editorials during this era reflects concern that sport was not an island of tranquillity amid a sea of conflict washing over the nation. Sportswriters were worried that violence in the general society was spilling over into the playing fields of baseball, and the sport no longer reflected the values of a consensus society. Challenged by the growing popularity of the more violent sport of football, baseball writers and spokespersons were afraid that the self-proclaimed national pastime was both out of step with the culture of the 1960s and indicative of a growing tendency toward resolving differences through violence. Sportswriters expressed misgivings regarding confrontations among athletes off the field as well as between the foul lines. Any fight between black and white players was feared as possibly triggering racial unrest among spectators. And, indeed, there was considerable speculation that the ballpark was no longer a site where families could safely congregate. Baseball writers lamented that the sport's stadiums failed to provide an environment where a family could escape the social issues of violence, drug and alcohol abuse, and racial unrest. Commentators were apprehensive that the behavior of baseball players as well as spectators was mirroring a society in which violence was becoming the norm. Nonsense, replied such conservative columnists as New York's Dick Young, who proclaimed that, at least on the field, the sport had a rich tradition of beanball wars and physical confrontations. However, the amount of time and space devoted to the relationship between violence and baseball during the 1960s and 1970s certainly indicates that the sport was unable to escape the major social issues of the era, providing a microcosm through which to examine American society in a turbulent time.

As a recent article in *Baseball Digest* attests, violence on the baseball field usually evolves around the question of "beanballs," or pitchers throwing at batters. While some veteran players insist that pitching inside and knocking down batters was once an accepted part of the game, although now rejected by modern athletes, the history of baseball brawls does not necessarily support such an assumption. Thus, most of the confrontations between players during the tumultuous 1960s and 1970s fit well into the brushback tradition.[5]

Perhaps the most celebrated 1960s baseball altercation among players took place on August 22, 1965, during a heated pennant race between the Los Angeles Dodgers and San Francisco Giants. Giants pitcher Juan Marichal, whom the Dodgers accused of throwing at batters, took objection to the Dodger catcher John Roseboro zipping the ball near his ear on the return throw to the mound. An agitated Marichal proceeded to take his bat after Roseboro, opening a gash in the catcher's scalp, before both benches erupted. In an action which many criticized for its leniency, National League President Warren Giles suspended Marichal for eight games and fined the pitcher $1,750. Roseboro filed a civil suit, which was adjudicated in 1969.[6]

Deplored as one of the ugliest incidents in baseball history, the Marichal-Roseboro confrontation hardly reduced the sport's beanball wars. In 1967, the promising career of young Boston Red Sox slugger Tony Conigliaro was derailed by the fastball of Jack Hamilton. And the opening of the 1976 season was marred by a brawl when St. Louis Cardinals pitcher Lynn McGlothen hit Del Unser of the Philadelphia Phillies, who the night before had beaten the Cards with a homerun in the seventeenth inning. Columnist Dick Young protested when McGlothen was assessed a fine and suspension from the National League office. Stating that fighting was simply part of the competitive spirit, Young made adamant his contempt for liberals and the counterculture, insisting, "We are becoming a little too thin-skinned. Our athletes not only are wearing their hair like girls, they are screaming for cops like girls, as if they were being attacked. And the do-gooders, the bleeding hearts, who weep into their typewriter keyboards, are screaming right along with them." On the other hand, Melvin Durslag, writing in the *Sporting News*, maintained that those who, like Dick Young, perceived the beanball as part of baseball were simply ignorant. Durslag argued that baseball owners could put a stop to throwing at batters' heads by informing their managers that the practice would no longer be tolerated. However, the columnist surmised that the baseball establishment was reluctant to take strong action due to the perception that the fans were attracted to violent spectacles on the field. Thus, baseball management, like their counterparts in the National Hockey League, was placing profits above safety concerns.[7]

Durslag was certainly not the first individual to make the connection between an increasingly violent culture and baseball profits. The baseball establishment was apprehensive with declining attendance figures and the growing popularity of full contact sports such as football and hockey. Media analyst Marshall McLuhan insisted that baseball was out of step with American culture, observing, "When cultures change so do games. Baseball, that had become the elegant abstract image of an industrial society living by split second timing, has in the new TV decade lost its psychic and social relevance for our way of life.... Games are extensions of our immediate lives. And we are living in a violent age. Baseball has no violence." Management figures strongly dissented from the McLuhan prognosis. New York Yankees President Michael Burke, a former executive with the Columbia Broadcasting System, asserted, "Nowadays everyone is banging everyone else over the head. People will begin to gag on the violence in our lives, from the football field to the college campus. And the relative nonviolence of baseball will become attractive." Baseball Commissioner Bowie Kuhn proclaimed that neither baseball nor American society needed violence, pointing out, "You know, the Metropolitan Opera does not portray violence either. But it is a very dramatic performing art set on a very dramatic stage. So is baseball."[8]

In this quote Commissioner Kuhn displayed considerable ignorance regarding the violent themes in many German and Italian operas, while failing to recognize that the New York City's Met and America's baseball diamonds might not necessarily draw upon the same clientele. Both the Commissioner and media analyst overlooked the sport's tradition of brawling.

After all, as columnist and writer Don Atyea remarked, violence was an integral part of the sport which glorified the exploits of Ty Cobb. However, violence was not necessarily the panacea for sagging ticket sales. Hockey and basketball owners were concerned about the repercussions of mayhem on the ice and court. In 1975, the National Hockey League establishment was rocked by the civil case and criminal complaint lodged against Dave Forbes of the Boston Bruins, who attacked the Minnesota North Stars Henry Boucha during a game in Bloomington, Minnesota. As the two players were leaving the penalty box, Forbes knocked Boucha to the ice, while continuing to pummel the prone North Star, who was carried from the rink on a stretcher, suffering from cuts to his eye which required a twenty-five stitch surgery.[9]

While debates were rampant in the sporting community over whether confrontations between players were a reflection of a violent society or simply an extension of the competitive spirit, there was a consensus that a line was crossed during a 1977 spring training assault by the Texas Rangers Lenny Randle upon his manager Frank Lucchesi. Randle was angry that the Rangers second base position was apparently going to heralded rookie Bump Wills, the son of former Dodger star Maury Wills. Alleging that he was not given a fair chance at earning the position, although his 1976 batting averaged had dipped into the .220s, Randle threatened to leave the team, only to be talked out of it by teammates. When informed of Randle's discontent, manager Lucchesi quipped, "I'm sick and tired of punks making $80,000 a year moaning and groaning about their situation." According to Randle, a few days later and before an exhibition game in Orlando, he approached the manager, still dressed in street clothes, who was standing near the third base coaching box. When Lucchesi again called him a punk, Randle struck him, knocking the older man to the ground. Lucchesi, who denied repeating the offensive word punk, was hospitalized, having suffered a concussion and broken jaw. Randle was suspended and eventually dealt to the New York Mets, where he regained his batting eye.

Perhaps fearing for their own safety, baseball columnists were outraged that an athlete in his mid-twenties had assaulted a fifty-year-old man, although the racial implications (Randle was African-American and Lucchesi Italian-American) of the beating were downplayed. Melvin Durslag speculated whether any manager would now dare to discipline a player, while Bob Addie of the *Washington Post* maintained that the attack was a sign of the times. Addie wrote that the assault exemplified "the disrespect for authority that exists among modern athletes," predicting that even owners might become targets of physical aggression by players.[10] However, the Randle-Lucchesi incident did not establish a precedent for assault and battery against baseball management. The baseball establishment had much more to fear from Marvin Miller and the Major League Baseball Players Association's challenge to the reserve clause and other prerogatives enjoyed by ownership.

Nevertheless, serious issues of violence did plague the owners during the 1960s and 1970s. Rather than suffering from altercations between ball players on the playing field, management was confronted with incidents of violence in the stadium perpetuated by fans and often directed against the players. Ballpark violence was widespread, mirroring the violence of American society, shattering the notion of a sacred public place where the prerogatives of class and privilege could not be challenged, and cutting into the profits of ownership. Many fearful fans refused to venture out to night games in what they perceived as dangerous neighborhoods. Although not always articulated, these fears reflected America's racial divide during the 1960s and 1970s as the ballpark ceased to be a refuge for white privilege.

It would take considerable time and space to chronicle all accounts of violence in the major league stadiums during these troubled decades. However, a sampling of incidents spread over time and from differing locations offers evidence of the dangers confronting the baseball establishment. Of course, violence had entered the ballpark before the unrest of the sixties. For example, in 1929, a disputed call during a game in Cleveland between the Indians and Philadelphia Athletics resulted in a barrage of bottles being tossed on the field. Third base umpire Emmett Ormsby suffered a concussion, while one spectator from Akron later died from head injuries inflicted by a thrown bottle. The seventh game of the 1934 World Series was disrupted when Detroit fans unleashed a deluge of fruits and vegetables aimed at St. Louis Cardinals outfielder Joe Medwick. And on July 4, 1950, a spectator in the Polo Grounds was killed by a bullet supposedly fired from outside the ballpark.[11] Nevertheless, violence in the 1960s was different, demonstrating the generational, class, and racial divisions exposed by the civil rights movement and Vietnam War.

On April 24, 1964, the Pittsburgh Pirates advertised a special youth admission price of fifty cents. According to the *Sporting News*, over thirteen thousand teens made the ballgame miserable for the nearly eight thousand older fans paying full price. Ushers who had worked at Forbes Field for over thirty years reported that they had never witnessed such unruly behavior. The first aid room was full of youths being treated for sprained ankles and cuts, while other young people stole a huge mustard jar and sprayed the stands. On a more serious note, three other young men were arrested after they assaulted and robbed another youth in the bathroom. And, noted the *Sporting News*, such behavior occurred in a ballpark which did not even serve beer.

Similar manifestations of violence were reported at Milwaukee County Stadium in the spring of 1964, and a young college student attending a game at Busch Stadium in St. Louis was stabbed and killed outside of the stadium. The *Sporting News* editorialized upon the need for curbing youth violence, calling for the law and order policies which would later permeate the political platforms of presidential candidates George Wallace and Richard Nixon. Warning of "packs of juvenile hooligans and punks," the paper of the baseball establishment pleaded for beefed up security forces at the ballpark, insisting, "People will not risk a beating or worse to watch baseball or any other sport."[12]

Not that they needed any new excuses to lose, but similar concerns with youth violence led some in Boston to acknowledge that the city was better off with the Red Sox dropping the 1967 World Series. Deputy Superintendent Eddie Mannix of the Boston Police Department predicted that if the Red Sox had won the seventh and deciding game in Fenway, rioting would have stared with the five to eight thousand "vicious" kids hanging around the ballpark. Police on horseback had scuffled with the crowd during the game, and authorities were girded for a full scale confrontation. But as usual the Red Sox came through, and the Cardinals won the game 7–2. A relieved head usher Amby Anderson asserted, "If the Red Sox had won that seventh game, I'm positive 400 people would have either killed or injured. That's how bad the crowd was outside the park. As much as I wanted the Red Sox to win, I was almost hoping they wouldn't."[13]

During the 1968 season which culminated in a world championship for the Detroit Tigers, Joe Falls of the *Detroit Free Press* deplored what the reporter labeled as thuggery in the ballpark. Falls was incensed at Tiger fans, who threw five "cherry bombs" at Red Sox outfielder Ken Harrelson, almost costing Detroit a forfeit. Falls also had little use for what Yankee management labeled a poverty day promotion. Displaying his disgust for the cultural changes taking place in the country, the Detroit columnist concluded that the underprivileged kids in the left field bleachers at Yankee Stadium had tossed so much debris on that field that "the outfield looked like Central Park after a love-in." A *Sporting News* editorial voiced similar concerns about the conduct of bleacher bums in Chicago's Wrigley Field, who poured beer and threw tennis balls at Cardinal outfielders Roger Maris and Curt Flood. The self-proclaimed Bible of baseball concluded, "Unruly conduct should not be tolerated by club officials, because there always is the danger that passions on the field might lead to excesses in the stands. The hooligan who throws an ice cube one night might switch hands to a brick in another game."[14]

However, while the War on Poverty was being dismantled and the Vietnam War dragged on under a president who was elected in 1968 on a promise to end the conflict; the social, cultural, and generational clashes in America, and in ballparks mirroring the apparent deterioration of the country, only intensified. Following an April 12, 1970, doubleheader with the Indians, in which young fans swarmed on the field disrupting play, officials at Yankee Stadium were considering canceling future twin bills. Cleveland players complained of having full beer cans hurled at them, but the New York crowd played no favorites, making life miserable as well for the hometown Yankees. The Yankee mystique, which exemplified so well the affluent and conservative 1950s, offered little protection for New York relief pitcher Steve Hamilton who proclaimed, "I was hit by a sharp object, then I put my glove over my face. The situation in the bullpen is impossible. We get spit on, and billiard balls, nails, fruit, empty cans and just about everything is thrown at us." The chaos reduced Red Foley of the *New York Daily News* to a diatribe with implications beyond the "house that Ruth built." An agitated Foley wrote, "Instead of the plaques they dedicated to Joe DiMaggio and Mickey Mantle, the Yankees should have hung some of the kids on the center field wall at the Stadium yesterday. Considering the tumult that accompanied the split with the Indians, a show of muscle by the Establishment could be a deterrent against future outbreaks."[15]

But the political establishment simply never responded to sports rioting in such an authoritarian manner. Over-exuberant fans might still be placed within the context of bread and circuses, or as a safety valve through which the discontented and underprivileged might blow off some steam. Accordingly, in downtown Columbus, Ohio, the violent aftermath of an Ohio State victory over Michigan was tolerated, while the National Guard was needed in May 1970, at Kent State when protesters burned a political symbol such as the university's ROTC building. In a similar vein, the Associated Press's Pittsburgh bureau chief Pat Minarcin termed the actions of forty thousand revelers celebrating the Pirates 1971 World Series victory "a riot." According to Minarcin, "Police called the violence the worst in the city's history." But the National Guard was not dispatched as was the case in April, 1968, when the African-American community took to the streets in protest of Martin Luther King, Jr.'s, assassination. Instead, Pittsburgh Police Superintendent Robert E. Colville blasted what he termed the "gross distortion" of the media. Colville insisted that there was no riot, simply an over-exuberant celebration which got a little out of hand. According to Colville's account, there were no reported rapes and most arrests were for intoxication. While over a hundred injuries were reported, none were serious, and property damage and looting was minimal, with two cars overturned, damage to about twenty-five stores, and only two small fires.[16]

In 1973, the Mets' triumph over the Cincinnati Reds in a bitter National League Championship Series failed to produce rioting in the streets of New York, but the atmosphere at Shea Stadium was extremely tense. Tempers flared during the Mets 9–2 victory in Game Three, when Pete Rose barreled into Mets shortstop Bud Harrelson, setting off a bench-clearing fight. The crowd of nearly sixty-thousand reacted by booing and pelting Rose with bottles and debris when he returned to his left field position. After a threatened forfeit and a peacekeeping mission to the bleachers by the Mets' Yogi Berra, Tom Seaver, Cleon Jones, and Willie Mays, who had recently announced his decision to retire following the season, a semblance of order was restored. Following Pete Rose's game-winning ninth inning homerun in Game Four, which was punctuated by the controversial player's clinched fist raised in either triumph or defiance, the New York crowd was in a frenzy for the deciding Game Five of the series. As the Mets pulled away in the game and the crowd grew more unruly, Reds family members were taken out of the stands and escorted to safety. With the recording of the last out, New York fans surged on to the field and, in a scenario reminiscent of the 1969 Miracle Mets, inflicted severe damage to the playing surface. A disillusioned Tom Seaver lamented, "The sad part is that these fans would have done this to the field even if we had lost. I think a lot of them didn't care whether we won or not. They just wanted to rip up the field." An indignant *Sporting News* editorial asserted, "Shea Stadium patrons were terrorized and trampled by hordes of vandals who swarmed out of the stands and engulfed the field."[17]

However, self-righteous editorializing and calls for added security did little to quell ballpark violence, which appeared to reach a crescendo in 1974, as the nation reeled from the disillusionment of military defeat in Vietnam and political corruption at the highest levels with the Watergate scandal. Opening Day for the White Sox was marred by heavy drinking and fighting fans, as well as several streakers, both male and female, who pranced through the outfield grass clad only in baseball caps. The rowdy crowd caused White Sox pitcher Terry Forster to fear for his family's safety in the stands, while third baseman Ron Santo simply stated, "I never saw a crowd that bad. It took a lot of concentration away from us." White Sox management blamed the disturbance upon Opening Day hysteria and the thirty-seven degree temperature, although the cold day would appear to offer less than ideal weather conditions for streaking in the Windy City.[18]

Following the 1973 National League Championship Series with the Mets, Manager Sparky Anderson of the Reds had quipped that New York was not part of America. However, during the 1974 season Cincinnati proved to be little different from the Big Apple when it came to obnoxious fan behavior. On May 12, 1974, Houston Astros outfielder Bob Watson crashed into the left field wall at Cincinnati's Riverfront Stadium. With his sunglasses shattered and his face bloodied, Watson was afraid that any movement might endanger his eyesight. Meanwhile, some spectators in the bleachers began pouring beer over the prone and bleeding figure of Watson. Teammates such as centerfielder Cesar Cedeno engaged in a shouting match with unruly fans, while Watson was carried from the field. However, other Reds supporters helped identify the culprits, who, after being subdued by police, ended up in the same hospital emergency room as Watson.[19]

While deploring the behavior of those individuals who harassed the injured Watson, the ever-caustic Dick Young reminded his readers that the Astros' Cedeno might want to be careful about calling others hoodlums. In December, 1973, while playing winter ball in the Dominican Republic, Cedeno was involved in a hotel room shooting, which took the life of a young Dominican woman and mother. After initially fleeing the scene of the shooting, Cedeno turned himself into the authorities, explaining that his weapon had been accidentally discharged. With the intervention of Houston management, the charges against Cedeno were reduced to involuntary manslaughter, and the ball player was fined $100 for negligence in allowing the young woman to handle the weapon.[20] While barriers were being challenged in the United States, wealth and privilege certainly counted for something in the Dominican Republic.

The responsibility of fans, management, and players for baseball violence was evident in one of the sport's most infamous incidents; the June 4, 1974 forfeit of the Indians to the Texas Rangers on ten cent beer night in Cleveland. As the evening wore on, inebriated spectators began running on the field, and firecrackers were tossed in the direction of Manager Billy Martin and his Texas players. Despite interruptions, the game continued, with the Indians staging a two-out rally in the ninth which tied the score at 5–5. Cleveland had the potential winning run at third base when approximately a half-dozen drunken young men left the bleachers, surrounding Rangers outfielder Jeff Burroughs and tugging at his cap and glove. Led by Martin and armed with baseball bats, Texas players charged out of the dugout to protect Burroughs. Chaos ensued as the appearance of the angry Rangers team on the field induced many drunken spectators to throw debris at the visiting club or climb out of the bleachers to do battle. Now the Indians rushed onto the field in defense of the Rangers. In the resulting confusion and near riot conditions, Cleveland pitcher Tom Hilgendorf was injured when hit on the head with a steel chair, umpire Nester Chy-lak received a scalp wound, and the umpiring crew declared a forfeit, awarding a 9–0 victory to the Rangers. Burroughs maintained that he was afraid for his life, thanking the Cleveland players for coming to his rescue, "like John Wayne coming over the horizon." When the game was called, over five thousand people were on the field, and nine arrests were made for disorderly conduct.

In the game's aftermath, Cleveland management was censured for staging the beer promotion. The club's financial situation was precarious, and rumors were rampant that the troubled franchise would relocate. Popular promotions such as ten cent beer night were finally putting some people in the seats. However, critics suggested that management was placing profits above player and fan safety. The irrepressible Dick Young urged baseball owners to decide whether they were selling beer or baseball. Young maintained, "In this grab for the buck, they have shed all moral responsibility, then they have the gall to point a finger at the fans they encouraged to become stoned out of their minds." Echoing the sentiments of Young, James T. Carney, Safety Director for the City of Cleveland, stated, "Obviously these young guys went down there and for ten cents had a few beers, got stiff, became wild men and didn't know what they were doing. They just went berserk. It's just an act of God that nobody was killed. These kids get so wild and there were knives and everything else down there."

However, many Cleveland fans found the beer indictment a little too sweeping. After all, there were over twenty-five thousand fans in attendance, and the majority of spectators were not involved in the fisticuffs with the Rangers. Some Indian supporters blamed the media for focusing on a brawl between the Rangers and Indians a few weeks earlier in Arlington, urging fans to exact revenge on the Texas club. According to this line of thought, the Cleveland media played a major role in creating a climate of violence. Some in Cleveland, while condemning unruly individuals, found room to blame the combative Billy Martin. The Rangers were on the verge of losing the game when Martin led his team onto the field, agitating the belligerent fans and triggering the final outburst of violence.[21]

While the sport was engaging in considerable finger pointing after the Cleveland fiasco, players throughout the major leagues insisted that the climate at big league stadiums had changed. Sal Bando, third baseman for the Oakland Athletics, a quality team known for fighting in the clubhouse and whose mustaches and long hair appeared to exemplify the counterculture, maintained that violence in the ballpark was a manifestation of deteriorating values in the country. According to Bando, some fans lacked a proper family structure, "for no one with a decent background would abuse a player the way some have been treated this year." Apparently in agreement with Bando's analysis, Yankee management in 1976 moved to ensure that their spectators would have a more proper background, canceling a ten-year program in which Consolidated Edison distributed over one-million Yankee tickets to underprivileged youth. Yankee officials cited a lack of supervision and growing violence as motivating their termination of the popular program. The Yankees maintained a number of violent incidents had occurred in the Con Ed section, including the mugging of a fourteen-year old girl, a series of fires in the men's room, an assault upon a stadium security guard, and the intimidation of a seven-year-old boy whose head was held in a toilet until he surrendered his baseball glove.[22]

Nevertheless, excessive fan behavior continued to be a problem throughout the late 1970s as the nation attempted to cope with the legacy of Vietnam and Watergate, as well as an economic recession fueled by high energy prices. President Jimmy Carter referred to a cultural and political malaise in America, which was exemplified in baseball by sagging atten-dance figures, death threats against players, and the continuing rain of debris from the bleachers. Baseball executives, seeking to boost ticket sales, often exacerbated the situation. For example, on the evening of July 12, 1979, White Sox owner and promoter Bill Veeck was convinced by his son Mike to stage Anti-Disco Night. Sponsored by a Chicago radio station, the admission price for the doubleheader between the White Sox and Detroit Tigers was reduced to ninety-eight cents. Over fifty thousand fans filled Comiskey Park, while thousands of others milled around outside the sta-dium. Between games of the twin bill, things got out of hand when a disc jockey exploded thousands of disco records, setting off a frenzy in which many of the spectators, apparently high on marijuana, stormed onto the field, inflicting considerable damage and refusing to return to their seats. Veeck, afraid of violence and injuries, turned down the offer of the Chicago police to clear the field, accepting the umpires' decision to declare a for-feit in the second game of the scheduled doubleheader.[23]

Baseball journalists devoted considerable energy and ink to explor-ing the reasons for violent behavior in the nation's ballyards, offering var-ious solutions to stem what was perceived as an orgy of violence threatening the national pastime. Joe Falls of the *Detroit Free Press* and a columnist for the *Sporting News* was especially concerned with what he termed a lowering of standards in American society and culture. In a May 16, 1970 column entitled "Insults and Obscenities," Falls acknowledged that he was the voice of the Establishment, embarrassed by the language and obscene signs at the nation's ballparks. Falls chided college students and administrators for fostering a sense of permissiveness on university campuses. Falls complained, "I just can't get it through my head what kind of kicks the students get out of holding dirty signs. I guess it's a defiance of authority, or the right to say what you please. I just couldn't see myself feeling very proud of doing this."

Falls believed that violence among baseball spectators was a manifestation of a society in which many citizens, especially the youth of America, had lost sight of such basic values as civility and respect for property. While unable to reform the larger society, Falls called for law and order in the ballpark, applauding Detroit management for closing the bleachers when unruly fans tossed objects on the field. Like a candidate advocating beefed up police forces and more prisons as a cure for crime, the Detroit columnist campaigned for the baseball establishment to increase security forces at the stadium; the price of which could then be passed on to the fans, who in the final analysis would be paying to police themselves. An added bonus to this approach would be that ticket prices might become too steep for some undesirable elements.[24]

In a series of editorials and columns indicating alarm over the economic impact of violent fan behavior, the *Sporting News* expressed solidarity with the ideas espoused by Falls. However, the conservative slant of editorial policy suggested that problems within baseball would not be solved until the larger climate of violence and cultural change was subdued. Advocating a law and order approach, the *Sporting News* urged baseball management to get tough with unruly fans and expel them from the stadiums. Practical measures for curbing violence suggested by the editors included: limitations on alcohol sales, surveillance cameras, heavy wire fences to prevent the throwing of debris, and increased security. However, the baseball paper despaired of any significant improvements in the sport without a change in the larger moral and political climate. In concurrence with the opinion expressed by White Sox correspondent Edgar Munzel that a permissive society encouraged young people to get out of control and develop an "anti-law-and-order syndrome," the *Sporting News* concluded, "The sports world is confronted with its share of bad actors, but things could be worse. The trouble makers have yet to burn down a stadium. Maybe that's because they lack the advantage of a college education."

Larry Whiteside, the paper's Milwaukee correspondent, insisted that baseball parks would have to be taken back from the rowdy young fans causing mischief and terrorizing patrons. In order to restore baseball as a family entertainment, "every vestige of vulgarity, obscenity, and pugnacity must be stamped out in all parks." But why should such draconian measures be limited to the confines of baseball, editorialized the *Sporting*

News in the fall of 1976, observing, "Whatever the solution, sports events are vulnerable so long as the streets of America's cities remain unsafe."[25]

Other commentators, such as William Barry Furlong, writing in *TV Guide*, pointed out the role played by the media in creating an atmosphere for the glorification of violence. While deploring altercations on the field and stands, television executives, nevertheless, recognized that physical confrontations were popular with many viewers, and it was impossible to pretend that they did not exist. In addition to portraying fisticuffs, the new sports journalism of the late 1970s and post Watergate period emphasized the private life of athletes. This demystification of the athlete encouraged fans to become more familiar with players, and in some cases ball players, whose high salaries and lifestyle were common knowledge, were the targets of death threats and hate mail. The salary structure of baseball was especially frustrating to many fans as the American economy contracted during the late 1970s and early 1980s. Pirates outfielder Dave Parker noted that his "hate" mail and threatening telephone calls increased after he signed a 1979 contract extension calling for a salary of over one million dollars a season. Parker sadly related the message of a Chicago man who told the African-American player, "Regardless of all the money you make, you still ain't nuthin' but a stinkin' lousy nigger." To which Parker quipped, "You're right. But the money is good."[26]

The story of Dave Parker demonstrates how the *Sporting News* and columnists like Joe Falls often, in reality, ignored the larger culture about which they so profusely complained. They failed to consider the degree to which the Vietnam War and its atrocities, reported in detail every evening for the network news broadcasts, desensitized Americans to violence and perpetuated an outlook in which a high body count was evidence of victory and success. Also, the vulgarity and obscenity of racism, abandonment of the inner city, and high unemployment rates for minority youth were not the topics of journalistic diatribes. In fact, while issues of race were rarely mentioned in the sporting press, it by no means stretches credibility to read such terms as underprivileged youth and inner city kids, and sometimes stronger descriptions such as hooligan or thug, as euphemisms for young African-American or Latino males. According to the baseball establishment, these were the people who needed to be removed from the ballparks to make them once again safe for family values.

However, the broader historical and sociological implications of violence in American baseball and sport were evident to a growing number of scholars, whose opinions were rarely included in the pages of the *Sporting News*. University of Rochester psychologist Robert Nideffer, in an effort to explain the belligerent reaction of Mets fans to Pete Rose, observed that individuals use sporting events as outlets for frustration in their personal lives. For example, Nideffer asserted, "Someone who has had a hard day at the office or somewhere, who feels the country's falling apart, they can't take it out on the President, so they yell at an umpire or something else."[27]

Other scholars maintained that Nideffer's analysis was too narrow. In an op-ed piece for the *New York Times*, Ross T. Runfola, associate professor of social sciences at Mendaille College in Buffalo, argued that sport violence was a mirror of American culture and society. Concurring with the findings of the National Commission on the Causes and Prevention of Violence, Runfola described America as one of the most historically violent societies in the world. While the National Commission failed to incorporate the domain of sport in its study, the Buffalo professor found ample evidence to support his conclusion that the existing sporting structure in America fostered rather than alleviated violent behavior. Rather than advancing enhanced security and punitive measures, Runfola called for a deeper comprehension of the connections between sport and aggressive actions, writing, "Perhaps the first step in eradicating violence in sport is to work toward a full understanding of the roots of forms of violence in American society. It is, after all, the failure to balance basic goals with the humanistic process that lies at the base of many of the problems both of sport and of American society."

Building upon the arguments of Nideffer, Runfola, and the National Commission on Violence, Stanley Cheren, associate professor at the Boston University School of Medicine, testified before the House Judiciary Subcommittee on Crime, arguing for passage of a proposed sports violence bill. Cherin maintained that American sporting events contributed to a cycle of brutalization "wherein seeing violence reduces the impact of that level of violence, raises the general social atmosphere of violence and stimulates the need for more extreme violence." In his testimony, the professor was not calling for the eradication of sport, but rather suggesting that the Congress, media, player associations, and league management structures intervene and establish limits on how far increasing levels of violence will be allowed to go.[28]

While such ideas were an anathema for many in the sporting establishment, who feared federal interference and regulation of their businesses/games, the relationship between sport and American violence was increasingly evident to academics. In the fall of 1982, the University of Toronto sponsored a conference entitled, "War and Violence in North America." For a panel on sport and violence, Arnold Talentino, a professor at the State University of New York at Cortland, presented a paper equating the territorial acquisitions of manifest destiny with the values of competitive violence found in American sport.[29] However, while historians argued for the centrality of sport and violence to the American experience, violence at the ballpark began to subside in the 1980s and 1990s, with notable exceptions such as the riot following Detroit's victory in the 1984 World Series.

Various explanations may be offered for the decline of spectator violence in American baseball. Certainly, the 1980s, exemplified by the Reagan presidency, witnessed a conservative backlash to the excesses of the 1960s and 1970s. Others argue that crime rates were reduced by building more prisons and taking a tougher stance against criminals. On the other hand, declining rates of violence may simply be a reflection of an aging population lacking the energy for aggressive behavior. Despite lowered statistical evidence of violent crime, in the 1990s there remains considerable apprehension regarding mass slayings in the schools of America, culminating in the murder of thirteen students and a teacher at Columbine High School in Littleton, Colorado. Although in the Colorado shootings, athletes appeared to be the victims, there has been little analysis of how the "jock" culture of high school and American sport may have played a role in provoking the teenage killers into action. And there has not been enough consideration given to why these acts of mass violence are perpetuated by males rather than females. Does the violent world of male athletics play a role in this process?

But of one thing we may be assured. While the beanball wars continue to rage, the major league baseball park of the 1990s is far different from the monolithic stadiums of the 1960s and 1970s. Baseball's new parks, constructed upon the model of Baltimore's Camden Yards, offer luxury boxes for corporate America, economic revitalization of the urban center, plenty of shopping and food alternatives, along with expensive ticket prices. The "yuppification" of the American baseball environment has supposedly made it safe for families to return to the national pastime. Those minority elements in the inner city, which the National Commission on the Causes and Prevention of Violence credited with rebelling against the inequities of American life, have been removed from the sight of American baseball fans. Attendance of African-Americans at baseball games has declined steadily in recent years. Having weathered labor discontent and a canceled World Series, baseball is back due to the heroics of Sammy Sosa and Mark McGwire, along with upscale ballparks which have once again made the sport secure for women and children. But at what price?

Notes

1. A report submitted by Daniel Walker of the Chicago Study Team, to the National Commission on the Causes and Prevention of Violence, *Rights in Conflict: The Violent*

Confrontation of Demonstrators and Police in the Parks and Streets of Chicago During the Week of the Democratic National Convention (New York: Bantam Books, 1968), p. v.

2. Rap Brown quoted in Richard Hofstadter and Michael Wallace, eds., *American Violence: A Documentary History* (New York: Alfred A. Knopf, 1972), p. 39.

3. Richard Maxwell Brown, *No Duty to Retreat: Violence and Values in American History and Society* (New York: Oxford University Press, 1991), p. 1. For other studies on violence, see: Richard E. Rubenstein, *Rebels in Eden: Mass Political Violence in the United States* (Boston: Little, Brown and Company, 1970); and Richard Slotkin, *Regeneration Through Violence: The Mythology of the American Frontier, 1600–1860* (Middleton, CT: Wesleyan University Press, 1973).

4. Hugh Davis Graham and Ted Robert Gurr, eds., *Violence in America: Historical and Comparative Perspectives*, 2 vols. (Washington, D.C.: Government Printing Office, 1969); and National Commission on the Causes and Prevention of Violence, *To Establish Justice, To Insure Domestic Tranquility* (Washington, D.C.: Government Printing Office, 1969), p. xxii.

5. For the Marichal-Roseboro confrontation, see: *Sporting News*, September 4 and 11, 1965; and Dan Gutman, *Baseball Babylon: From the Black Sox to Pete Rose, the Real Stories Behind the Scandals That Rocked the Game* (New York: Penguin Books, 1992), p. 285–288.

6. Larry Stone, "Take Me Out to the Brawlgame: Fights on the Field," *Baseball Digest*, 58 (August 1999), p. 60–66. For a veteran pitcher who enjoyed throwing the brushback pitch, see Kirby Higbe with Martin Quigley, *The High Hard One* (Lincoln: University of Nebraska Press, 1998).

7. Dick Young, "Brawling a Part of Sport," *Sporting News*, April 25, 1976; and Melvin Durslag, "The Duster: A Sign of Ignorance," *Sporting News*, May 15, 1976, newspaper clippings, Violence File, National Baseball Hall of Fame and Museum, Cooperstown, New York.

8. Ira Berkow, "Does Baseball Need Violence?" *Utica Press*, April 4, 1969, newspaper clipping, Violence File, National Baseball Hall of Fame and Museum.

9. Don Atyea, "Blood Sports," *Tampa Tribune*, March 20, 1979, newspaper clipping, Violence File, National Baseball Hall of Fame and Museum. For the Forbes-Boucha controversy, see: Parton Keese, "Violence in Sports: What It Could Mean," *New York Times*, January 26, 1975; and Steve Cady, "Violence in Sports Is a Growing Concern," *New York Times*, September 25, 1975.

10. For Lenny Randle's assault upon Frank Lucchesi, see: *Sporting News*, April 16, 1977, and Melvin Durslag, "Next a Player Will Hit a Chaplain," *Sporting News*, April 27, 1977. Also, see Bob Addie, *Washington Post*, March 30, 1977, newspaper clipping, Violence File, National Baseball Hall of Fame and Museum; and Bruce Markusen, Senior Researcher, Baseball Hall of Fame, "Baseball's Precedent to Latrell Sprewell," unpublished paper, January 1998.

11. "Pop Bottle Victim Dies," May 15, 1929, newspaper clipping, Violence File, National Baseball Hall of Fame and Museum; and Gutman, *Baseball Babylon*, p. 316.

12. *Sporting News*, May 9, 1964.

13. Tom Horgan, "Some in Hub Happy Bosox Lost Finale," *Boston Herald*, November 4, 1967, newspaper clipping, Violence File, National Baseball Hall of Fame and Museum.

14. Joe Falls, "Thugs in the Ball Park," *Sporting News*, July 6, 1968; and "Get Rid of Bleacher Bums," *Sporting News*, August 31, 1968. For race relations in Detroit see Thomas J. Sugrue, *The Origins of the Urban Crisis: Race and Inequality in Postwar Detroit* (Princeton, NJ: Princeton University Press, 1996).

15. Jim Ogle, "Yanks Map Strategy to Deal with Mob Action," *Sporting News*, May 2, 1970.

16. "What Riot?" *Newsweek*, November 1, 1971, p. 82; and "Pittsburgh Deflates Riot Report," *New York Times*, October 19, 1971, newspaper clippings, Violence File, National Baseball Hall of Fame and Museum. For the 1968 violence in Pittsburgh, see: *Pittsburgh Courier*, April 13, 1968.

17. For the 1993 National League Championship Series between the Reds and Mets, see: *New York Times*, October 9, 1973; Bob Broeg, "Broeg on Baseball," *Sporting News*, October 27, 1973; Red Smith, "Feeney's Peace Brigade Calms Fans in Left Field," *New York Times*,

October 9, 1973; "Safety Valve or Time Bomb?" *Sporting News*, October 27, 1973; and Jack Lang, "Mets Clincher Marred by Maniac Mob," *Sporting News*, October 27, 1973, newspaper clippings, Violence File, National Baseball Hall of Fame and Museum.

18. *Sporting News*, April 27, 1974.

19. Joe Heiling, "Cincy Thugs Harass Astros' Injured Watson," *Sporting News*, June 1, 1974.

20. On Cesar Cedeno, see: Dick Young, "Rowdyism Erupts in Ballparks," *Sporting News*, June 1, 1974; and Joe Heiling, "Cedeno Tragedy Tosses a Cloud Over Astros," *Sporting News*, December 29, 1973.

21. For beer night in Cleveland, see: Russell Schneider, "Incident or Riot? That Depends on Who's Talking," *Sporting News*, June 22, 1974; and Dick Young, "Young Ideas," *Sporting News*, June 22, 1974.

22. "New Problem: Violence at Ball Parks," June 9, 1974; and "Yankees Halt Free Passes for Youth," June 22, 1976, newspaper clippings, Violence File, Baseball Hall of Fame and Museum.

23. For an amusing account of the White Sox's Anti-Disco Night, see John Helyar, *Lords of the Realm: The Real History of Baseball* (New York: Villard Books, 1974), p. 240–241.

24. Joe Falls, "Thugs in the Ball Park," *Sporting News*, July 6, 1968; "Insults and Obscenities," *Sporting News*, May 16, 1970; "Violence in the Ball Park," *Sporting News*, June 24, 1972; and "Rioting Crowd: It Can Happen in Any City," *Sporting News*, June 22, 1974, newspaper clippings, Violence File, National Baseball Hall of Fame and Museum.

25. "Trouble in the Grandstand," *Sporting News*, May 16, 1970; "Problems of Crowd Control," *Sporting News*, July 31, 1971; "Fears Stalks the Stadium," *Sporting News*, October 23, 1976; "Sports Violence ... A Disease?" *Sporting News*, December 18, 1976; and "Get Tough with Unruly Fans," *Sporting News*, May 30, 1981, newspaper clippings, Violence File, National Baseball Hall of Fame and Museum.

26. William Barry Furlong, "When a Fight Breaks Out..." *TV Guide*, December 10, 1977, p. 30–32; Melvin Durslag, "Temper! Temper! Why Today's Athletes Keep Losing Their Cool," *TV Guide*, November 10, 1979, p. 45–46; Terry Taylor, "Spectator Violence," *Utica Observer-Dispatch*, May 10, 1981; and "Death Threats Escalating," *New York Daily News*, October 18, 1981, newspaper clippings, Violence File, National Baseball Hall of Fame and Museum.

27. Steve Monroe, "Why Do Crowds Cause Trouble?" *Rochester Democrat*, December 2, 1973, newspaper clipping, Violence File, National Baseball Hall of Fame and Museum.

28. Ross T. Runfola, "Violence in Sports: Reflection of the Violence in American Society," *New York Times*, January 11, 1976; and Stanley Cheren, "Spectators and Violence: A Vicious Cycle Grows," *New York Times*, October 26, 1980.

29. Douglas Martin, "Sports Violence Seen as Ritual Amid the Chaos," *New York Times*, October 26, 1982.

"Three Strikes and You're Out": The Role of Sports Metaphors in Political Discourse

Dale A. Herbeck

Sports metaphors permeate political discourse in the United States. Politicians, we know, cannot resist appeals to sport. Consider some of the following chestnuts:

> He may well win the race that runs by himself.[1]

> In life as in a football game, the principle to follow is: hit the line hard.[2]

> My hat is in the ring. The fight is on, and I am stripped to the buff.[3]

> It's like a football game ... Mondale can't get the ball back with one big play. But the American people love a horse race. I would advise him to knock Reagan out.[4]

> Everything before has been a warm-up lap, a trial heat. But here in San Diego the real race begins. We're going for the gold.[5]

At the same time, those commenting on politics cannot help but to use the very sports metaphors they love to denounce. Knowing that these metaphors have meaning to their readers, journalists often acknowledge their own comic search to find appropriate sports language to character-ize political events:

> Superlatives, sports metaphors and every imaginable synonym for the word "surreal" jammed the airwaves yesterday as the television networks

jockeyed to do justice to a day described as a "political double-header" packed with events most historic, most incredible and, yes, most surreal. Would President Clinton "hit that home run" in his State of the Union Message, television hosts wanted to know. Would he "hit it out of the ball park?" Would his speech, combined with the opening of his impeachment trial defense, prove to be a case-clinching "one-two punch?"[6]

The coverage of Washington politics could be taken over by sportswriters and hardly anyone would know the difference. You hear so many sports metaphors here it's hard to know where metaphor stops and reality begins. Everyone's keeping score. This guy's winning, that guy's losing. Newt's on offense, Bubba's on defense.[7]

Coming into tonight's debate, fisherman George Bush needed to hook a whopper. Tennis player Bush was facing match point. Golfer Bush needed a hole in one. The former Yale baseball captain was looking to hit a grand slam. It was, for the man who installed a horseshoe pit at the White House, a time for ringers, not leaners. Bush heavy hitters weighed in. Samuel K. Skinner said it was "the bottom of the ninth." Jack Kemp called it "the fourth quarter." Lynn Martin, when the debate was over, said, "NBA games are won in the last five minutes. This campaign will be won in the last two weeks."[8]

Did Vice President Quayle score an ace when he declared that Bill Clinton "has trouble telling the truth," or did he step over the line and fault? Should Sen. Albert Gore Jr. have spent two minutes in the penalty box for high sticking with his sarcastic promise not to compare Quayle to Jack Kennedy? Did James B. Stockdale fumble the pigskin just as Ross Perot was mounting a serious fourth-quarter drive?[9]

Commenting on the pervasiveness of such metaphors in our daily lives, Hardaway claims that "the language of athletic competition has found its way as a metaphor into every phase of American life."[10]

Despite the prominence of these metaphors, Mio laments that "with a few notable exceptions, theorists in the area of political rhetoric have not devoted much more than passing mention to metaphor."[11] Even among those with a scholarly interest in metaphors, metaphors drawn from sports have received comparatively little attention. Recognizing this disparity, MacAloon has observed that "among no people known to us in history have sports models, discourse, and ways of thinking so thoroughly colonized politics, a fact often noticed but not yet investigated, much less understood."[12]

This essay, in a preliminary way, considers how sports metaphors are used in political argument. Although it would be possible to identify metaphors drawn from almost every sport with a substantial following, this essay focuses exclusively on one metaphor drawn from one baseball. While this choice may seem arbitrary, baseball is an especially appropriate sport to study as it is "especially emblematic of American society."[13] Stressing the unique cultural significance of baseball, Jacques Barzun has gone so far as to suggest that "whoever wants to know the heart and mind of America had better learn about baseball."[14] "Next to religion," President Herbert Hoover once claimed, "baseball has furnished a greater impact on American life than any other institution."[15]

In the pages that follow, this essay considers how the "three strikes and you're out" metaphor was strategically used by advocates during the mid 1990s to argue for tougher sentences for convicted felons. While the repeated use of this metaphor speaks to the lofty place of baseball in American culture, this essay develops the thesis that this particular baseball metaphor also constituted a powerful appeal for retribution. This conclusion is not meant to damn the sport, but rather to suggest that seemingly innocuous sports metaphors can, in fact, constitute complex forms of ideological argument. In this instance, the three strikes metaphor functioned to define argumentative ground, rationalize retribution, and constrain the discussion of potential policy alternatives.

Baseball and Crime

This case study has its origins in the late 1980s and early 1990s, an era when Americans grew increasingly anxious about crime. According to Wilson, crime "was not a major issue in the 1984 presidential election and had only begun to be one in the 1988 contest; by 1992, it was challenging the economy as a popular concern and today (referring to 1994) it dominates all other matters."[16] In a 1994 public opinion survey, Americans listed "crime and violence as the number-one problem facing the nation, far surpassing worries over the economy or health care."[17]

Given the public clamor, it is not surprising that politicians from "both parties, from cities and suburbs, and from all regions of the nation are scrambling to establish a tough position regarding crime."[18] While some advocated social programs stressing prevention or rehabilitation, retribution quickly came to dominate the political debate. National leaders argued, with considerable passion, that swift and certain punishment was more effective than social programs purporting to target the causes of crime. Even if such punishments did not deter would-be hooligans, convicted felons could not commit new crimes from inside prison.

In the race for political high ground, legislators from both parties sought visible ways to demonstrate their personal commitment to punishing criminals. In the debate that ensued, politicians quickly latched on to the image of the batter striking out and returning to the dugout. By comparing criminals to ball players, it was easy to argue for retributive sentences for repeat offenders. In a *New York Times* article that appeared in October 1993, Timothy Egan described Washington's Initiative 593, a measure called "Three Strikes and You're Out."[19] According to the article, this initiative "would mean that any person convicted of a third felony in a category labeled 'most serious' would go to jail for life without chance of parole."[20] Two months later, the *Times* reported on an effort to obtain signatures for a similar initiative in California.[21]

While there was limited discussion of three strikes in public argument about crime before 1993, three strikes quickly became the dominant metaphor in the crime debate. By January 1994, the *New York Times* was reporting that '3-Strike' Sentencing Is a Solid Hit This Season."[22] The same article reported that the idea had been enthusiastically endorsed by Governor Wilson in California, Governor Whitman in New Jersey, and Governor Cuomo in New York. In his 1994 State of the Union Address, President Clinton joined the chorus clamoring for such legislation:

> First, we must recognize that most violent crimes are committed by a small percentage of criminals, who too often break the laws even when they're on parole. Now those who commit crimes should be punished. And those who commit repeated violent crimes should be told when you commit a third violent crime you will be put away and put away for good. Three strikes, and you are out.[23]

By May of 1994, three strikes legislation was pending in 30 different states.[24] Meanwhile, the United States Congress, which had already enacted four major bills aimed at reducing the crime rate since 1984, hastily scheduled hearings on a new crime bill. While this measure included more money for police officers and prisons, it also contained the three strikes provision championed by the president.

Although the crime bill was the source of considerable partisan bickering, competing versions eventually passed both the House of Representatives and the Senate. After exhaustive discussion about the range of crimes covered by the three strikes clauses, legislators eventually reached agreement on compromise legislation that was adopted and signed into law by the president. In his 1995 State of the Union Address, President Clinton proudly announced new weapons in the war against crime: "But I remind you that last year we passed a very tough crime bill — longer sentences, three strikes and you're out, almost 60 new capital punishment offenses, more prisons, more prevention, 100,000 more police..."[25]

Baseball and American Culture

The preceding discussion illustrates the significance of the three strikes metaphor in the recent debate over crime. The metaphor was used by the President in his 1994 and 1995 State of the Union Addresses. Prominent politicians of both parties invoked the metaphor to demonstrate their resolve to combat crime. Even those who opposed harsher sentences relied on the language of baseball in their discourse. Indeed, the rhetorical appeal of three strikes was so strong that advocates to such legislation went to great extremes to invoke competing baseball imagery.

Some legislators felt that three strikes legislation lacked muscle. In Georgia, for instance, Governor Zell Miller claimed "three strikes" was too many for hardened criminals. As an alternative, he proposed a "two strikes and you're out" crime bill, and welfare reform based on "two strikes and you're off."[26] Making essentially the same point, Congressman Dornan complained that

> Another celebrated component of the crime bill is the "three strikes and you're out" provision. While this may sound tough, it is not. In fact, this sentencing provision will only apply to one percent of the crimes that occur throughout the country, since the third crime occurs on federal property for it to be eligible for this new punishment. If baseball adopted a similar rule, you would be out only if the third strike occurred in, say, Fenway Park.[27]

At the opposite end of the political spectrum, Reverend Jesse Jackson attempted to argue against three strikes by developing a competing baseball metaphor. "If the crime is vicious enough, and the person is sick enough, why not one strike?" Jackson sarcastically wondered.[28] Continuing with the baseball imagery, Jackson said he favored a "four-balls-and-you're-on" approach. According to Jackson, ball one would be adequate prenatal care and access to the Head Start program, ball two would be an affordable education, ball three would be job skills, and ball four would be a job. Instead of retribution, Jackson developed a metaphor based on a walk, a free pass to first base, to argue for more entitlements for disadvantaged groups.[29]

Taken together, the available evidence suggests that the three strikes metaphor dominated the public debate over penal reform. The three strikes metaphor was invoked in legislative debate, discussed at length by pundits and commentators, cited in thousands of newspaper and magazine articles, and became very much a part of daily conversation. At face value, the repeated use of this metaphor, generally without explanation or qualification, clearly proves that baseball jargon is an integral part of our language. As Kittell has observed, "Baseball has added significantly to the vocabulary of American English as well as adding colorful and descriptive terms to our language."[30]

The ability of advocates to invoke a baseball metaphor demonstrates that all Americans share a collective familiarity with the sport, and justifies the oft repeated claim that baseball truly is our national pasttime. Coffin argues that

> No other sport and few other occupations have introduced so many phrases, so many words, so many twists into our language as has baseball. The true test comes in the fact that old ladies who have never been to the ballpark, coquettes who don't know or care who's on first, men who think athletics begin and end with a pair of goalposts, still know and use a great deal of baseball-derived terminology.[31]

In this instance, the ability of political leaders to use baseball to explain a theory of punishment is a powerful testament to the lofty place of sport in our society.

Looking beyond the three strikes metaphor, the presence of sports metaphors in national politics reaffirms the place of sport in American culture. Smith grasps the obvious when he writes that "one measure of the stature of sports in the American scheme is the extent to which sporting terms are employed away from the playing fields."[32] "By keeping pace with the use of the sports metaphor in political discourse," Walk observes, "We may fully understand the collective meanings of sport in American society."[33] Likewise, by studying sport, Oriard suggests that scholars can discover "American ideas not just about sport and play themselves, but about all the things for which sport and play have become emblems — heroism, success, gender, race, class, the law, religion, salvation; the relations of Humankind, God, and Nature."[34]

Baseball and Argument

At first blush, the three strikes metaphor may seem an innocuous attempt to explain a penalty by representing a thing, sometimes called the tenor, in terms of another thing, often called the vehicle. In this instance, three strikes and you're out might be understood as another way of expressing the claim that three qualifying crimes means imprisonment for life. Approached from this perspective, language is seen as a neutral conduit used for conveying information. Thus, baseball metaphors are nothing more than a convenient set of linguistic devices for explaining a conflict.

Under closer scrutiny, however, it becomes apparent that this metaphor is much more than just a tired cliché. As Tannen has observed, "Words matter. When we think we are using language, language is using us."[35] The power of metaphors lies in their ability to frame a message. Among the first to recognize the power of such language, Edelman notes that

> Each metaphor intensifies selected perceptions and ignores others, thereby helping one to concentrate upon desired consequences of favored public policies and helping one to ignore their unwanted, unthinkable, or irrelevant premises and aftermaths. Each metaphor can be a subtle way of highlighting what one wants to believe and avoiding what one does not want to face.[36]

In this instance, the three strikes metaphor is more than an analogy for a particular sentence. Not only does it describe a proposed policy, it also argues for retribution.

It is not easy to discern the underlying ideological implications of such metaphors. "It is one thing to analyze societies that set up ministries of physical culture whose aims unblushingly reflect those of the ruling political party," Lipsky writes. "It is quite a different task to analyze sports in a society where the appearance of political or ideological purpose is minimized or carefully disguised."[37] This difficulty notwithstanding, a careful examination of the three strikes metaphor suggests that it draws its force from a powerful set of normative assumptions grounded in baseball. While the metaphor implies a fairly direct comparison between baseball and crime, it also contains a narrative story and offers a detailed prescription for action.

First, the three strikes metaphor suggests we live in an idealized world. In baseball, the batter stands in a fixed spot and uses a regulated bat to swing at an official ball thrown from a pitching mound of a prescribed height. While there are other players on the field, the batter alone faces the pitcher and the batter's success depends largely on the batter's own talent. If the ball is hit into play, the batter runs a clearly defined course around the bases with the goal of returning to the same spot from whence he started. "No game in the world," Gallico has written, "is as tidy and dramatically neat as baseball, with cause and effect, crime and punishment, motive and results so clearly defined."[38] In this sense, Messenger has observed that "baseball has a logic that appears almost Newtonian."[39]

There is, however, a great deal left unsaid in this simple description of America's pastime. The rules of baseball, for example, assume that all players share certain talents. While some might be more gifted than others, all players have an equal chance to hit the ball. No matter how inept, everyone in the lineup eventually gets their turn at the plate. Moreover, baseball is a team sport. While the batter alone faces the pitcher, all batters are part of a larger team that struggles together toward a common goal. In the interest of winning, individuals frequently sacrifice their place for the greater good. Since everyone benefits when the team wins, players do not seek individual glory at the expense of their teammates.

Second, the three strikes metaphor suggests a perfected system of justice based on the assent of the players. The official rules of baseball are codified in book form. Balls and strikes are clearly and reasonably defined by an objective set of criteria. In fact, arguing balls and strikes is against the rules and constitutes grounds for expulsion from the game. Deviations from rules necessitated by a particular ball park are communicated by the umpire as ground rules before the game. While the rules of the game must be applied by the umpire to specific situations, the rules themselves are not negotiated before the game, or even renegotiated during each game. The rules are sacred and timeless, explaining why statistical comparison from thousands of games compiled over decades are meaningful.

Not only are the rules of the game objectified, but the rules derive their power entirely from the consent of the participants. Players and managers occasionally protest calls made by the umpire, but even clearly erroneous calls cannot be reversed by an appeal to higher authority except under the most extraordinary of circumstances. The participants freely agree to abide by the rules and their acquiescence to the authority of the umpire is necessary to make the game possible. Observing this fact, Novak suggests "baseball is a Lockean game, a kind of contract theory in ritual form, a set of atomic individuals who assent to patterns of limited cooperation in their mutual interest."[40]

Finally, the three strikes metaphor suggests minimal, or even transitory, consequences for failure on the diamond. This is not to say that errors in baseball are soon forgotten. As Altherr has noted,

> Baseball lore abounds with inopportune bad hops, bad calls, pitchers throwing seventh games on too little rest, stumbles, falls, gopher balls, and second guesses. Several flubs are famous to many a fan: Merkle's Boner; Snodgrass's Muff; the 1919 Black Sox and "Say it ain't so, Joe"; three Dodgers on third; Hank Gowdy's mask; Lombardi's snooze; Mickey Owen's missed third strike; Kubek taking a bad hop in the throat; Bernie Carbo, Elrod Hendricks, and Ken Burkhart in the weirdest home plate ballet ever; and Bill Buckner as The Human Croquet Wicket.[41]

So too, failure as a batter is remembered. "Every play," Skolnik writes, "nearly every move is recorded, then registered, within a host of related categories deemed important for describing action and accounting for the out-come."[42] Since the average batting average in both the American and National League has been only slightly better than .250 in recent years, the typical bat-ter can expect not to get a hit three out of every four times at bat. While a routine ground ball might lack the highlight potential of a particularly inept fielding play, box scores methodically and brutally account for each at bat, while cumulative statistics reduce a career to a string of numbers.

But in baseball, errors in the field or poor hitting are neither unex-pected or fatal. Failure is inevitable; salvation is expected. Each time the ball is hit, a fielder has an opportunity to make a play. Poor hitters, like shortstop extraordinaire Mark Belanger, have been saved by particularly adept fielding. So too, the fallen hitter has another chance for glory the very next time he returns to the plate. As Ted Williams sagely observed, base-ball is the "only field of endeavor where a man can succeed three times out of ten and be considered a good performer."[43]

When one considers these assumptions, it becomes readily apparent that advocates who invoke the three strikes metaphor are doing more than simply describing the appropriate sentence for a crime. Upon reflection, it can be seen that the three strikes metaphor constitutes a powerful argu-ment for a particular view of our criminal justice system. By invoking the metaphor, advocates are able to argue that:

> Everyone in the line-up (all Americans) has a chance to bat (succeed in life).
>
> Every batter (all Americans) has an equal chance to make contact with the ball (succeeding in life) or to swing and miss earning a strike (committing a crime).
>
> All batters (all Americans) are strictly responsible for their own strikes (being convicted of a crime).
>
> Impartial umpires (judges) fairly call the game (conduct the trial).
>
> If a strike is called (conviction for a crime), the batter is not allowed to challenge the umpire's decision (appeal the con-viction).
>
> The appropriate penalty for striking out (committing three qualifying crimes) is returning to the dugout (life in prison).

When invoked in the crime debate, this line of metaphorical reason-ing legitimates a conservative judicial system. By citing the three strikes metaphor, advocates invoke imagery that justifies punishment. At the same time, advocates who use the metaphor are able to argue that individuals should be held responsible for their behavior, that the judicial system is fair and equitable, and that criminals deserve their punishment. When understood from this perspective, the three strikes metaphor constitutes a powerful ideological argument. The metaphor not only describes a sentence, it argues for a particular world view.

Sports Metaphors and Public Discourse

According to Diggs, "Baseball is American culture's most potent metaphor — so powerful an evocation of what Americans think of as best about America that its message is seemingly beyond criticism."[44] Given the enduring popularity of the game, it is not surprising that baseball metaphors are common figures of speech. Recognizing the importance of such usages, Lakoff and Turner have suggested that "to study metaphor is to be confronted with hidden aspects of one's own mind and one's own culture."[45]

Three strikes legislation draws heavily on the idealized world of sport. While this appeal to baseball explains a penalty, it also rationalizes retribution against criminals. This reasoning is potentially dangerous, as there are profound differences between sports like baseball and our criminal justice system. Unlike the batters envisioned by advocates of three strikes legislation, many criminals simply have no meaningful chance to hit the ball. A disproportionate amount of crime is committed by the uneducated, the disadvantaged, and the unemployed. While more might be said, it is readily apparent that many criminals are playing with numerous competitive disadvantages. In the game of life, players who have an education have a better chance of hitting a pitch than those without an education. Children raised in abusive situations, without appropriate parental roles, are far more likely to strike out. Given the disparity in opportunity and experience, analogies to the idealized confrontation between the batter and the pitcher on the baseball diamond become increasingly strained.

Further, our criminal justice system often bears little resemblance to the perfected rules governing civilized baseball games. Many crimes are never reported to the police. For the offenses reported, "clearance rates" — the rates at which the police identify and arrest suspects — have been dropping. Only a percentage of those arrested are actually convicted and only a fraction of those convicted of committing a felony are sentenced to prison terms. There are frequently wide disparities in sentences. All too often, justice is seemingly delayed by an endless series of appeals involving procedural technicalities. In the words of Diggs, "'Three strikes and you're out' plays ball on a field of dreams, but we live in an America that is undeniably real — a contemporary, largely urban scene of increasing unpleasantness, complexity, diversity, interdependency and, ultimately, of incomparable creativity and resourcefulness."[46]

Finally, and most significantly, a life sentence in a federal or state penitentiary is not akin to returning to the bench after striking out. While batters may be redeemed, a criminal convicted of a third qualifying felony will spend the remainder of life in prison. Baseball's history begins anew each time a game begins; each time a batter assumes a position in the batter's box. The game is ongoing, hence there is always a chance for salvation. Perhaps this explains why some of baseball's greatest hitters are fondly remembered as heroic figures, despite a penchant for striking out on a regular basis. In the epic poem "Casey at the Bat," the hometown hero strikes out to end the game. Reggie Jackson, Willie Stargell, Mickey Mantle, Harmon Killebrew, Lou Brock, Richie Allen, Frank Robinson, Willie Mays, and Bobby Bonds all struck out in excess of 1,500 times during their fabled careers. In contrast, under the mandates of three strikes legislation, a criminal convicted of three qualifying crimes is banished from the game and permanently imprisoned. If the life sentence is truly enforced, salvation is impossible as the player has been forever removed from society.

Because baseball is a sport, many believe it devoid of ideology. Such thinking is seductive, as it masks the powerful place that sports hold in our society. Invoking the three strikes metaphor does more than characterize a penalty; it argues for a particular view of justice. While this view may be reassuring to many Americans, it is potentially dangerous to informed discussion as the three strikes metaphor functions ideologically to reinforce our justice system, while simultaneously justifying harsh punishment for criminals. If we are to truly address the crime problem, we need to be fully cognizant of the ideological blinders imposed by the three strikes metaphor. In the words of Lipsky:

> The athleticization of politics is essentially a conservative device that prevents an adequate conceptualization of new policies and new directions. As our social and political worlds become more technically complex, it becomes increasingly difficult to imagine alternatives. The use of sports images to describe political action serves to camouflage this complexity and, hence, to perpetuate is reification.[47]

Recognizing the perverse consequences of sports metaphors in legal reasoning, some have suggested avoiding baseball metaphors altogether. Archer and Cohen, for example, claim that "frequent use of sports metaphors creates a linguistically unlevel playing field for those who are unfamiliar with sports or with sports metaphors' idiomatic meanings."[48]

Looking beyond the question of understanding, Oldfather cautions that since a baseball metaphor can function like an "invisible hand," we must "be wary of its use, and vigilant against its misuse."[49] Others have gone so far as to suggest that a conscious effort should be made to substitute non-adversarial metaphors into legal discourse. Thornburg, for instance, suggests a range of alternatives drawn from the arts, education, journey, food, and conversation.[50] A similar line of attack might be lodged against the general use of sports metaphors in politics.

Such criticism, however, is naive in that it underestimates the place of sports in our culture, while simultaneously overestimating the ability of academics to influence public argument. The three strikes metaphor was persuasive because baseball is a part of American culture. As such, appeals to the sport are an inherent part of our political communication. Rather than lamenting the prominence or the power of these metaphors, a more sophisticated response would be research that heightens our awareness of sports metaphors and dialogue that exposes the persuasive appeal of such potent linguistic frames.

Notes

The author is indebted to Edward M. Panetta for his substantial contribution to an earlier version of this essay.

1. Benjamin Franklin in Tim Constandine, "Starting from Scratch," *New York Times*, 27 July 1986, sec. 6, 6.

2. Theodore Roosevelt in Constandine, 6.

3. *Ibid.*

4. Lawton Chiles in Ellen Goodman, "Save Us from Sports Metaphors," *Boston Globe*, 14 August 1996, A23.

5. Bob Dole in Goodman, A23.

6. Janny Scott, "State of the Union: The Pundits — Media Notebook; Across Networks, Adjectives (Big Ones) Abound on a Day for the History Books," *New York Times*, 20 January 1999, A21.

7. Joel Achenback, "Sporting Metaphors Score Hits in Politics," *Arizona Republic*, 21 February 1995, B7.

8. David Von Drehle, "Win or Lose, Retire Poppy's Debate Tie; Sports Clichés Abound as President Bush Takes Final Step Toward Hall of Fame," *Washington Post*, 20 October 1992, A21.

9. David Mills, "Hardball Politics; Pundits at Bat with Sports Talk," *Washington Post*, 15 October 1992, C1.

10. Frances Hardaway, "Foul Play: Sports Metaphors as Public Doublespeak," in *Sport Inside Out: Readings in Literature and Philosophy*, eds. David L. Vanderwerken and Spencer K. Wertz (Fort Worth: Texas Christian University Press, 1985), 576.

11. Jeffrey Scott Mio, "Metaphors and Politics," *Metaphor and Symbol* 12 (1997): 114.

12. John J. MacAloon, "An Observer's View of Sport Sociology," *Sociology of Sport Journal* 4 (1987): 115.

13. Nick Trujillo and Leah R. Ekdom, "Sportswriting and American Cultural Values: The 1984 Chicago Cubs," *Critical Studies in Mass Communication* 2 (1985): 262.

14. Jacques Barzun in Michael Novak, *The Joy of Sports: End Zones, Bases, Baskets, Balls, and the Consecration of the American Spirit* (Lanham, MD: Madison, 1994), 63.

15. Herbert Hoover in Novak, 75.

16. James Q. Wilson, "What to Do About Crime," *Commentary*, September 1994, 26.

17. George Pettinico, "Crime and Punishment: America Changes Its Mind," The *Public Perspective*, September/October 1994, 29.

18. *Ibid.*, 32.

19. Timothy Egan, "Tax-Cut Backlash Swelling in California and Oregon," *New York Times*, 14 October 1993, 14.

20. *Ibid.*, 14.

21. Jane Gross, "Drive to Keep Repeat Felons in Prison Gains in California," *New York Times*, 26 December 1993, 1.

22. Ian Fisher, "Why '3-Strike' Sentencing Is a Solid Hit This Season," *New York Times*, 25 January 1994, B1.

23. William Jefferson Clinton, "State of the Union Address," *New York Times*, 26 January 1994, A16.

24. For more on the spread of three strikes legislation see Mario Cuomo, "'Three Strikes'— Two Views," *New York Times*, 29 January 1994, 19; and Steven Puro, "Three Strikes Is Out to Lunch," *St. Louis Post-Dispatch*, 6 May 1994, 7B.

25. William Jefferson Clinton, "State of the Union Address," *New York Times*, 25 January 1995, A17.

26. "Ever Tilting at Welfare Windmills," *Atlanta Journal-Constitution*, 5 April 1995, A12.

27. Robert K. Dornan, "The Crime Bill," *Congressional Record*, 11 August 1994, H7964.

28. Jesse Jackson in "Jackson Labels Crime Bill Criminal; Calls Portions Discriminatory," *Bergen Record*, 7 August 1994, A4.

29. Jackson's alternative is elaborated in Staci Turner, "Clinton Crime Plan 'Bumper-Sticker Gimmick,'" *Houston Chronicle*, 18 February 1994, A22; Michael Bunch, "Solve Crime Ahead of Time, Rev. Jackson to Say in S.D.," *San Diego Union-Tribune*, 3 March 1994, A1; and Hamil R. Harris, "Jackson Urges Spending on Prisoners, Not Prisons," *Washington Post*, 4 January 1995, D2.

30. Linda A. Kittell, "From Dreams to Diamonds to Dictionaries: Baseball as Acculturating Force," in *Cooperstown Symposium on Baseball and American Culture (1989)*, ed. Alvin L. Hall (Westport, CT: Meckler, 1991), 216.

31. Tristram Potter Coffin, *The Illustrated Book of Baseball Folklore* (New York: Seabury, 1975), 63.

32. Red Smith, "Spoken Like a True Son of Old Whittier," *New York Times*, 30 April 1973, 39.

33. Stephan R. Walk, "The Footrace Metaphor in American Presidential Rhetoric," *Sociology of Sport Journal* 12 (1995): 52.

34. Michael Oriard, *Sporting with the Gods: The Rhetoric of Play and Game in American Culture* (Cambridge: Cambridge University Press, 1991), ix.

35. Deborah Tannen, *The Argument Culture: Stopping America's War of Words* (New York: Ballantine, 1998), 14.

36. Murray Edelman, *Politics as Symbolic Action: Mass Arousal and Quiescence* (Chicago: Markham, 1971), 67.

37. Richard Lipsky, "Toward a Political Theory of American Sports Symbolism," *American Behavioral Scientist* 21 (January/February 1978): 346.

38. Paul Gallico in Richard Skolnik, *Baseball and the Pursuit of Innocence: A Fresh Look at an Old Game* (College Station, Texas A & M University Press, 1994), 192.

39. Christian M. Messenger, "Baseball and the Meaning of America," *Humanities*, July/August 1994, 13.

40. Novak, 59.

41. Thomas L. Altherr, "A Swing and a Myth: The Persistence of Baseball in the Amer-

ican Imagination," in *Cooperstown Symposium on Baseball and American Culture (1989)*, ed. Alvin L. Hall (Westport, CT: Meckler, 1991), 66.

42. Skolnik, 157.

43. Ted Williams, cited in Thomas Stinson, "100 Reasons Why We Love Baseball," *Atlanta Journal-Constitution*, 4 April 1993, B21.

44. Terry Diggs, "The Flaws of Baseball-Inspired Penology," *Legal Times*, 26 September 1994, 25.

45. George Lakoff and Mark Turner, *More Than Cool Reason* (Chicago: University of Chicago Press, 1989), 214.

46. Diggs, 25.

47. Richard Lipsky, "The Athleticization of Politics: The Political Implications of Sports Symbolism," *Journal of Sports and Social Issues* 3 (Fall/Winter 1979): 36.

48. Maureen Archer and Ronnie Cohen, "Sidelined on the (Judicial) Bench: Sports Metaphors in Judicial Opinions," *American Business Law Journal* 35 (1989): 226.

49. Chad Oldfather, "The Hidden Ball: A Substantive Critique of Baseball Metaphors in Judicial Opinions," *Connecticut Law Review* 27 (1994): 51.

50. Elizabeth G. Thornburg, "Metaphors Matter: How Images of Battle, Sports, and Sex Shape the Adversary System," *Wisconsin Women's Law Journal* 10 (1995): 225–281.

Baseball Meets the National Pastime: Baseball and Radio

Doug Battema

Despite what is often understood as a "natural" confluence of interests, the relationship between professional baseball and the U.S. broadcasting industry has not always been easy. While baseball might have
seemed an obvious source of programming for broadcasters seeking inexpensive yet popular programming that would reach a mass audience in the
1920s and 1930s, the question of how to proceed with baseball broadcasts
did not have a clear answer. Commercial broadcasters appreciated the
potential for baseball to reach a large audience, but did not fully embrace
the commercialization of the sport — especially for major events such as the
World Series. Moreover, concern about whether baseball broadcasts served
or exploited its audience sparked continued debate, while the potential
for baseball broadcasts to undercut the economic viability of both club
owners and radio networks provided a constant threat to industrial security and stability. Yet historical examinations of the relationship between
baseball and radio often simply romanticize the games or broadcasters
(e.g. Barber 1970, Smith 1987) or fail to explore their own assumptions.
While even minor details of television broadcasts of baseball have been
documented (e.g. Klatell and Marcus 1988; Rader 1988; Berkman 1988;
Gorman and Calhoun 1994), little has been written about the rationale
behind early baseball broadcasts on radio.

With respect to baseball, radio is typically considered important only
insofar as it helped to set the stage for television. Yet most authors taking
this approach also assert that telecasts followed the model established in

radio without explaining how or why that model was formulated. In 1953, for instance, Cozens and Stumpf asserted that "[t]here is every indication that televised sports will enjoy the same widespread popularity that radio sportscasting has enjoyed since the first event came over the air" (1953: 151), and their tone consistently suggests that television was ready to supplant, rather than supplement, radio. They also characterized the commercialization of baseball broadcasts as uncomplicated and straightforward: "The first World Series was broadcast in 1926[1] and today is considered the prize commercial program of the year. Behind this statement lies a story of baseball's stubborn resistance to radio" (1953: 145), though the only detail offered about this "stubborn resistance" is that it had been overcome by 1941, when radio contracts for *minor*-league baseball games totaled over $1 million.[2]

More recently, Klatell and Marcus dismissed radio's influence on sports broadcasting in two paragraphs, concluding that "[b]y the end of World War II, radio moved aside for television.... Radio became secondary to television for family entertainment, and local stations created new formats to replace lost network programming" (1988: 25–26). Similarly, Lever and Wheeler wrote that "[r]adio set many of the patterns for the television age,"[3] adding that "[t]he commercial possibilities of sports broadcasts were also recognized early" (1993: 129).[4] In neither case is there a sustained examination of precisely what patterns were established during radio's "golden age," nor any consideration of how the particular properties of radio or the particular political and economic pressures exerted upon the radio industry may have affected the style and/or content of baseball broadcasts. Instead, sports broadcasts seem unproblematic: "Major advertisers became aware of the benefits of connecting their products to big-time sports and to their large and growing audiences.... Club owners who literally gave away the rights to broadcast their games soon understood the commercial value of those rights. The long honeymoon had begun for the *ménage à trois* among owners, broadcasters, and advertisers" (1993: 130). Yet advertisers' interests and the audience for baseball broadcasts may not have coincided quite so smoothly, with the "long honeymoon" off to a rockier start than they believe.

Likewise, Gorman and Calhoun suggest that broadcasting is just a matter of "progression, and not so much the progression of technology but of cultural patterns" (1994: 88). They state,

> baseball broadcasts had no sponsors.... They began as a technological gimmick, then became a lever to draw people's attention into the game.... Sponsorship of games did not begin until the 1930s. In 1934, Mobil Oil began sponsoring the Detroit Tiger games; the average

annual amount of revenue from radio at that time was about $1,000
per team. It was also in 1934 that baseball commissioner Kennesaw
[sic] Mountain Landis signed a contract with the Ford Motor Company to broadcast the World Series for the next four years for
$400,000.... The games were major broadcasting events, to which the
entire nation listened [1994: 89].

This progress narrative, however, does not illustrate the problems faced
by broadcasters, particularly as stations increasingly affiliated with national
networks, creating conflicting obligations for the local stations that had to
be resolved; nor by sponsors, who at times remained unconvinced about
the efficacy of having their products linked with the national pastime.

Susan Smulyan claims that in the early days of radio, sports broadcasts "proved a natural for radio, which needed inexpensive programs to
fill empty hours," appealing primarily to "white middle-class males ...
whom radio broadcasters sought to attract" and who desired college sports,
as well as to "[w]orking-class fans" unable to afford tickets (1994: 27). And
the national pastime had an even broader audience: "the World Series was
an event with national appeal.... Baseball's appeal crossed racial, ethnic,
gender, and class lines, especially at World Series time, and fans whose
interest was stirred by a national contest joined those who had followed
hometown teams throughout the season" (1994: 29). Even Smulyan's examination of the commercialization of radio, however, does not explore the
controversies that affected the baseball-radio-sponsor relationship and the
controversies arising from baseball's "national appeal." Robert McChesney,
too, offers the uncomplicated assertions that "broadcasting continued the
nationalization of sports" and that "radio broadcasting had become dominated by two major networks," NBC and CBS, with advertising-supported
sports contributing to their national prominence (1989: 59). But affiliates
often upset the networks' schedule by broadcasting local baseball games,
threatening the relationship between the networks and their advertisers by
interfering with the networks' ability to ensure national audiences; and
internal NBC memos suggest that the networks preferred to keep many
major sporting events (such as the World Series) as sustaining features
rather than commercially-sponsored events.[5]

This paper, then, presents some preliminary observations about the
role of baseball during the formative years of radio broadcasting, focusing particularly on the 1930s. By noting the ongoing debate among network
executives about the value of baseball broadcasts; the tensions between
local affiliates and national networks over clearance for ballgames; and the
networks' reliance upon the World Series to establish their credibility with
a national audience and to keep in the government's good graces, we can

see not only how sports functioned as a cornerstone of network programming, but also (ironically) how fragile the commercial network system was as a result of relying on sports.

The NBC Ballgame: Network Needs vs. Affiliate Autonomy

The advent of NBC and CBS in the late 1920s created new opportunities for baseball to expand its appeal — and for radio stations and networks to carry potentially profitable programming. Network affiliates wanted the high-quality programming, national appeal and other benefits that a network could provide; however, they also wanted to retain a sense of local identity and appeal to a local audience, something that regular-season baseball broadcasts of local teams' games could accomplish. The networks needed these stations and the listeners they addressed if they were to establish themselves as stable business entities and attract advertising money, yet the networks were often reluctant to cede their affiliates time for local baseball games, since such broadcasts often conflicted with the networks' needs. Broadcasting baseball was one way in which affiliates and networks could demonstrate that they were not simply exploiting their commercial privileges, yet it was a strategy that occasionally backfired on the networks in particular. The tensions between national control versus local autonomy complicated the relationship between baseball, radio, and advertisers and became a lasting source of conflict throughout the decade.

One early example of the tensions baseball caused involved the Cleveland Indians and NBC. In 1930, NBC purchased rights to Indians regular-season broadcasts for its recently acquired O&O (owned and operated) station WTAM for $3,000. The Indians, however, prohibited Sunday broadcasts against WTAM's wishes; the station wanted to broadcast such games if the team was in the pennant race. Sunday ballgames drew the largest crowds of the week, and Indians general manager William Evans justified his stance by saying that "[i]f the fans got a taste of a Sunday broadcast at the more important games, it would make them feel that they should have the same right throughout the season" (NBC 1). Presumably, Sunday games were more lucrative for the team than weekday games, when most of baseball's core constituency was working, though Evans never publicly articulated why Saturday contests were not prohibited as well. Regardless, the club got its way, as WTAM broadcast all home games from Monday through Saturday only.

Prior to the next season, Cleveland's CBS affiliate WHF inquired about broadcast rights, giving the team additional leverage over both networks. Apparently the Indians did not tell NBC whether or not WTAM would be able to retain broadcast rights, prompting NBC's John F. Royal to explain to Evans that "[w]e cannot very well talk to sponsors unless we can get some idea of what our arrangements must be with you. We are very anxious to cooperate.... There is one thing that I do not want to do, and that is, to get into a bidding controversy with any other station" (NBC 2). The bitter rivalry between NBC and CBS, evident here, allowed Evans to use the threat of CBS's inquiry to extract $7,000 from NBC in exchange for his club's 1931 broadcast rights.

Despite the unique appeal of baseball, not everyone at NBC was enthused about paying for broadcast rights. The next year, a prescient L. Niles Trammell informed Royal that he could "see a very, very dangerous precedent established" (NBC 3) after another NBC executive, aware that the Cleveland owners had let other team owners know how much they received from NBC in 1930 and 1931, secured broadcast rights from one of the St. Louis ballclubs in order to keep it off St. Louis' CBS affiliate. Royal justified the previous decision to buy the Indians' broadcast rights by relying on two arguments: first, he had "to keep it from Columbua [sic], who was willing to pay, and at the same time to break down the resistance of some of the baseball managers who were opposed to broadcasting" (NBC 4); and second, he indicated that the network had been willing to more than double its payment because he and other executives believed they "might be criticised [sic] severely for losing the baseball the first year after NBC took it over" (NBC 4), suggesting the desire to service local interests. Royal added that WTAM surrendered its rights for 1932 only because the Indians' owners bought CBS affiliate WHK and would broadcast the games themselves.

This exchange did not clarify what Trammell's specific objections were, though it is possible to identify some of them in retrospect. First, Trammell may have objected to the potential preempting of network programming by local stations. This might have been a major problem if the daytime hours were purchased in large chunks by ad agencies, as was the case at least by the mid–1930s. If NBC could not even deliver audiences to sponsors on its own O&Os because they were broadcasting local baseball games rather than network programming, sponsors might lose faith in the network. Second, Trammell may have objected to paying for broadcasts, a rationale that would have been consistent with NBC's anxieties over government regulation — as legislation concerning government regulation of radio was still being debated, and any payment may have been considered inappropriate given the networks' attempts to depict baseball as public service broadcasting.

The first concern — the potential preempting of network commercials — may have been the most critical; it certainly describes the most sustained debate within the network and expressed the tension between national network imperatives and local station autonomy. In 1933, Trammell informed Roy C. Witmer, NBC's Director of Sales, that Chicago station WMAQ (another recently-acquired O&O) must be allowed to bump network programming in order to broadcast major-league baseball if the station was to retain its legitimacy with Chicago listeners:

> Chicago is a very definite and enthusiastic baseball town.... [The stations] have been broadcasting baseball for the last eight or ten years....
> To discontinue the broadcasting of baseball by WMAQ would mean that we are taking a definite step in obliterating what is left of this station's local identity, and association with local events in Chicago. We have always sold the baseball games on WMAQ, and as long as I have anything to do with it, we are going to continue to sell them. It means $30,000.00 to the Company for a broadcast we would be forced to do if we didn't have a sponsor [NBC 5].

Faced with the choice between broadcasting the games and losing revenue from sponsors, or not broadcasting the games but possibly losing the loyalty of Chicago listeners, NBC allowed its O&O to carry the ballgames. This policy may have allowed NBC to preempt claims that it was growing too large and losing touch with its audiences; Trammell's insistence on not "obliterating what is left of this station's local identity" suggests anxiety over NBC being seen as callous and uncaring about its audience's desires. Allowing the broadcasts to be sponsored seems not to have been a concern, suggesting that Trammell less worried about preempting other commercials than he was about potentially losing WMAQ's fan base.[6]

Chicago may have been an exceptional case, however, because of multiple station overlap. NBC affiliate KYW could ensure transmission of Red network programming while another outlet, WENR-WLS, could provide Blue broadcasts to the Windy City. Trammell's argument may also have been aided by the fact that WMAQ had been broadcasting Chicago baseball for eight to ten years, thus clearly identifying major-league baseball with the station in the public eye. Later in the 1930s, when the opportunity arose to regain major-league baseball broadcast rights in Cleveland, Witmer informed Royal that it was "too much of a hazard to attempt in conjunction with network broadcasting. The moment we sell a program of this kind [baseball] ... it means that network commercials must stand aside which is exactly the reverse of NBC policy" (NBC 8). By 1934, when

KYW was no longer available to ensure that Red broadcasts would be transmitted if WMAQ was tied up with a Cubs game, an NBC official stated that "if we arrange for a sponsorship of baseball on WMAQ ... the baseball broadcasts must be interrupted as, if and when necessary for network commercials" and that Sunday broadcasts must not be broadcast since "[o]n Sunday ... there are definitely a number of conflicts with network commercials" (NBC 9; see also NBC 10).

NBC, however, reserved the right throughout the 1930s to preempt entertainment programs for sports broadcasts defined as "in the public interest"—a policy which was evidently extended to affiliates and which ultimately caused headaches for the network. Against assertions that radio was "dominated" by national networks, NBC executive Frank E. Mason believed the network was highly vulnerable and dependent upon its affiliates: "If [affiliates] follow our World Series policy [allowing "public interest" sports to preempt entertainment programming], only the advertiser and the NBC suffer a loss, while the station selling the program substituted for our cancelled network commercial will gain approximately 3 times what they would get by taking the network broadcast" (NBC 35). The inability to prevent affiliates from refusing to clear time for network programs and instead broadcasting local sporting events that brought in greater local ad revenue threatened the network system; remaining consistent, claimed Mason, would ensure greater network stability.

In 1936, after some potential problems had been dodged with respect to baseball games in St. Louis (NBC 44) and despite Witmer's admonition to think of missing local baseball broadcasts not "in terms of approximately $35,000 net revenue loss, but rather in terms of what would inevitably be the infinitely greater loss to NBC were we to take it" (NBC 45), Detroit O&O WWJ decided to broadcast both the home and road games of the Detroit Tigers. NBC had approved WWJ's plan to carry home games on a sponsored basis; the road games, on the other hand, were to be sustaining broadcasts underwritten by the station, and WWJ petitioned NBC to allow the station to preempt for-profit network programming with the sustaining fare. WWJ's station manager argued that NBC's "clients would derive more benefit by releasing the time than they would be retaining their programs and bucking baseball on three other Detroit stations" (NBC 46); he also explained his position to the advertising agencies directly, successfully receiving the agencies' permission to exempt WWJ from the regular NBC schedule. Apparently, however, WWJ's station manager understated the amount of broadcast time that would be lost, and one sponsor (Quaker Oats) insisted "that the first time WWJ has to cancel they wish to drop the station for the entire season" (NBC 46). NBC ultimately lost money in the deal, and its failure to keep its own O&Os in line with network efforts suggests that NBC may not have been as stable as most accounts of the time purport.

Sponsors, according to a 1938 memo from Witmer, soon became "conscious of the fact that if they buy a late afternoon period, it will be interfered with by baseball" and claimed that "one of the most valuable and lucrative periods of the day is beginning to be frowned upon" (NBC 49). Witmer argued that NBC had to hew to a stronger line with its affiliates and insist that they broadcast network programming over local baseball, charging that NBC was "altogether too loose in the past in our concessions to stations in Network Time" (NBC 49). When William S. Hedges responded that baseball gave NBC affiliates a competitive edge over stations that did not carry the sport, stating that NBC should continue to "recognize local demands rather than insisting upon contractual arrangements" and that "baseball is really the only exception" to NBC's policy towards commercial programming (NBC 50), Witmer replied that local baseball and network broadcasts were simply incompatible. Baseball, he insisted, had to be handled "like any other local account — that is, on a removal basis" (NBC 51). As a live and externally-produced event, however, baseball was inflexible and therefore "much worse than the average local commercial which can be moved and still heard. You cannot move baseball. Either you have it or drop it entirely" (NBC 51).

NBC seemed willing to take the risk of preempting network broadcasts at times, however, particularly to boost ratings for affiliates of the Blue network. Blue, which carried less popular and more "public-service" programming than the Red network, benefitted from baseball in Pittsburgh (on KDKA) and San Francisco (on KGO), as the major-league Pirates and minor-league Seals respectively did "more to build up the afternoon audience of these two Blue stations and to change the listening habits of their communities towards them than anything the stations have done in the last few years of their operation" (NBC 53). Surveys showed that "[t]he effect of baseball on a station's popularity is not theory or guesswork"; baseball's popularity caused immense leaps in audience share, leading some NBC executives to argue that baseball was vital to Blue's survival (NBC 53). NBC Vice President Frank M. Russell stated that NBC would benefit "from the standpoint of income, but more particularly from the standpoint of program improvement," and that "if any network time is sold it would be a very simple matter to record the programs locally and schedule them at the close of the baseball broadcast" (NBC 54; see also NBC 55 and NBC 56).

Neither Crossley ratings nor a lack of interference with commercials, however, convinced Witmer of baseball's value to NBC. In 1939, Witmer cited a survey taken by WENR (Chicago) indicating that "at least 98% [of 2000 responses] asked for a continuance of the present programs" rather than having them replaced by baseball — an unexpected result in Chicago, which was "supposed to be such a red hot baseball city" (NBC 57). The issue seemed to come to a head in 1940, when NBC ran into scheduling difficulties across the country. In Pittsburgh, Providence, and other East Coast cities, NBC-Blue affiliates aired baseball games that conflicted with programming sponsored by Sterling Products; while NBC tried to "offer a record-rebroadcast, ... this 'meat-substitute' is not satisfactory" to the sponsor or its ad agency, Blackett-Sample-Hummert, since the time offered as compensation would give the agency "an audience which is not their audience, i.e. men or children" (NBC 63). Though this conflict was resolved by offering Sterling Products an earlier time slot on these stations (NBC 64), a similar and more serious situation developed on the West Coast, where night baseball caused "a total of 13 national Blue advertisers [to have to be] affected [moved] for a total of 15 periods of time" (NBC 65). More important to the network than the loss of revenue — approximately $4,400 (NBC 66) — was the damage to NBC-Blue's reputation:

> Here we are struggling to develop the Blue Network and about the time we seem to be making at least some little headway, we have to rush about suddenly to advertisers like Canada Dry, Westinghouse, General Foods, duPont, etc., and tell them that local baseball on the Pacific Coast Blue Network (of all things!) makes it necessary to change their schedules. This is a major disturbance.... It is very hard for the boys in Network Sales to understand why in some cases $29,000 or $30,000 worth of local baseball business seems to be worth more to [NBC] than several millions worth of network business [NBC 65].

These incidents caused NBC executives to rethink their policy and ensure that the "local baseball business on the [West] Coast Blue must be cut out next year" (NBC 67), affirming the primacy of the national network's advertisers and needs over the interests of local stations and their audiences.[7]

The debates over local baseball broadcasts thus suggest that NBC had put itself in a weak position vis-à-vis its affiliates, and in some cases O&Os even dictated policy to the network rather than the other way around. Advertisers also were of two minds about the unreliable, high-risk, seasonal local baseball product; those sponsoring the broadcasts enjoyed the relatively low cost and the relatively high Crossley ratings, but the potential for local stations to preempt network broadcasts caused advertisers to pressure the network to change its policy. The conflicting demands placed on NBC by these two entities, both necessary for its continued existence as a network, had yet to be worked through by the beginning of the 1940s, and suggests that NBC's ability to dictate terms to local programmers and ensure the stability of its synchronized national broadcasts was less coherent than it might seem. Given that local baseball broadcasts were so scattered, national network ties were often not mentioned in accounts of local sponsorship deals, and NBC's policy toward accommodating such deals was relatively flexible, the relative inattention afforded to these problems and the underlying tensions they suggest is understandable.

As important as local broadcasts seem to have been to the networks and their quest to provide public interest programming to their constituents, however, baseball's World Series was an even more vital component of network service. And unlike the local baseball issue, this event captured national headlines, thrusting radio's capacities — and its limitations — into the spotlight.

The World Series: A Public Service?

In 1929, NBC and CBS jointly broadcast their first World Series. According to *TSN*, the arrangements constituted "[t]he most extensive radio hookup ever carried out" to date; given the combined reach of the networks, "it was expected that the descriptive stories of the games would reach every section of the North American continent" ("Radio hikes..." 1929). At the time, there were no sponsors: the networks carried the World Series as sustaining programming, as part of their public service to all Americans. At this time, there was no recorded objection from sponsors having their programs moved to clear time for the World Series; no sponsors protested their inability to sponsor the series, and no executives at either network seem to have been bothered by the expense of providing this public service (possibly because carrying the games without sponsors facilitated their ability to assert that the broadcasts were a public service — and the fledgling networks garnered plenty of free publicity to boot). Both of America's commercial radio networks willingly carried the Series at their own expense during the early 1930s; both claimed that they acted solely in the public interest by presenting these broadcasts to the nation at no direct cost to anyone else.

This situation changed, however, in 1934. During the spring, ad agencies Lord and Thomas (representing Lucky Strike) and Ruthrauff and Ryan (representing B.F. Goodrich) asked if the World Series could be sponsored, and Commercial Program Director Bertha Brainard posed the question to other NBC executives, noting that "[o]f course it would have to be understood that it would be exclusive to NBC if we could sell it" (NBC 11). Benton & Bowles, representing an unnamed client, made a similar request at the same time (NBC 12). NBC's P.G. Parker responded that from his discussions with Baseball Commissioner Kenesaw Mountain Landis, it might be possible to have a sponsor if the sponsor bought the "complete Red and Blue and Supplementary networks" as well as independent stations, particularly since Landis reportedly had some "antipathy for the Columbia crowd" (NBC 13). A sticking point was "the advisability of this commercial sponsorship principally for the reason that if it were secured on an exclusive basis there might be a very bad reaction from the audience" by being limited to certain stations (NBC 13).

A subsequent meeting between Parker and Landis confirmed this latter concern: Landis was concerned about the potential public backlash against both the baseball establishment and the broadcast company carrying the Series, and "personally is opposed to a commercial sponsorship of [the World Series or the All-Star Game] and [Parker] told him we were in agreement with him that it would be better not to have a sponsor." Royal shared this concern, believing "that it would be detrimental to our interests to broadcast events such as this on a commercial basis" (NBC 14), and added as late as September 1, 1934, that NBC "will probably do the World Series sustaining. There was some talk about doing it commercially — that is something we should never do" (NBC 15).

The defensiveness about receiving money for the World Series or allowing a sponsor to underwrite the costs could have been linked to several overlapping concerns. First, NBC executives may have felt a true obligation to ensure the availability of baseball's greatest games without a commercial taint, particularly given that America was suffering through the Great Depression. Second, the radio industry was still on uncertain ground with respect to government regulation; the debates over the Communications Act of 1934 and its protections of commercial broadcasters were not yet resolved, and the broadcasting industry was concerned about possible antitrust charges (McChesney 1993). Carrying the World Series on a sustaining basis may have helped to deter the federal government from taking antitrust action against the networks and their affiliates.[8] Finally, defining the World Series as a public service ensured that sponsors whose programs were bumped couldn't complain that they were being preempted in favor of another sponsor — and for an event that may have attracted a larger audience to the time slot they had paid for. Regardless of motive, the networks had always *treated* the World Series as a public event on par with, say, national politics. In fact, in 1933 "both NBC and CBS permitted their facilities to be used during the recent speeches by President

Roosevelt and also during the world series [sic].... the addition of non-member stations for such events as the world series was a new departure for both networks" ("Nets let..." 1933), with the latter act of generosity perhaps linked to this concern for ensuring public service.

Landis' September 13, 1934, announcement that the Ford Motor Company would sponsor the World Series for four years by paying $100,000 annually for the rights came as a surprise even to the networks, which had to redefine their commitment to the Series quickly — no easy task. *Advertising Age*, noting the broadcast industry's tenuous position, asked, "How far can commercial sponsorship go without invading the special field which is held to be inviolate?" and suggested that the networks had to rethink "just how far they intend to go in letting down the bars to advertisers in connection with reports of big news and sports events" ("A problem..." 1934).

NBC, caught off-guard, responded publicly that Landis' announcement left the network with no choice but to change its policy. A memo to the Sales department provided instructions as to how to answer questions by reporters and by the public:

> [The deal between Ford, represented by N.W. Ayer, and Commissioner Landis] was such that they must broadcast the Series on at least one major network and if possible, two networks. [CBS] immediately accepted the Ford proposition.... [NBC] does not believe that this should be done, but we were placed in a peculiar spot whereby if we refused to take the Series commercially we could not have it on a sustaining basis.... while our principle of sustaining service was right, we could not afford to take a chance and refuse to take it commercially and thereby deprive our stations and listeners of this series.... we did not attempt to get the Series, commercially, but ... the Ford Motor Company and N.W. Ayer did it themselves and ... we were forced to accept the Series on a commercial basis... [NBC 16].

Privately, there was confusion and frustration over Landis' maneuver. Royal noted that "I cannot find any letter to me where the Judge [Landis] said to [NBC]—'We have finally decided to accept the best offer,'" and implied that Landis had neither involved the networks in his negotiations nor gotten the best deal from the most deserving sponsor (NBC 17). NBC scrambled to contact agencies and sponsors who had expressed interest in World Series rights, preferably "before they lose faith in any explanations we might give them" (NBC 19). Shuffling commercials, rescheduling programs, and pacifying advertisers on the Red network was difficult: "Our facilities contracts with these other advertisers provide that we may take their time 'for special events of importance,' but this is the first time that we have attempted such wholesale cancellation of commercials for other commercial programs" (NBC 21). As feared, both NBC and CBS encountered substantial resistance to clearing time for a sponsored Series; *Advertising Age* reported that "advertisers who hitherto have made way for the World Series as a sustaining event seem little disposed to bow themselves out in favor of Ford," forcing NBC and CBS to be "reticent as to the actual make-up of the networks to be used" ("World Series broadcast..." 1934), though NBC arranged to credit canceled commercials in a manner that seemed to satisfy sponsors (NBC 23).

In the short run, however, the deal turned out to be a boon for the networks. Though at least one NBC executive noted that "I still have considerable reservations as to our selling sporting events commercially" (NBC 18), the response offered by journalists and audiences was positive: "It was amusing to me to see that the newspapers carried the sponsoring by Ford on the front pages and sports pages without criticism ... instead of the newspapers resenting the sale of the broadcasting right [sic] to Ford, they handled it in quite a complimentary way throughout" (NBC 20), wrote NBC President Merlin Aylesworth. Moreover, he continued, baseball's own commercialism obviated the need for a public service explanation, since "after all our business is to obtain sponsors for our programs, except in education, religion and the President of the United States" (NBC 20). Regular advertisers might have grumbled about having to step aside for another commercial interest, but avoided significant public backlash for not funding the Series,[9] and NBC internal memos do not report any advertisers backing out on the network as a result. Strategically, Ford's decision to buy the rights for both networks, rather than simply one, had prevented CBS or NBC from having to compete with one another for the privilege and protecting — for the time being, at least — the rhetoric of public service articulated by both networks.

NBC especially had good fortunes with the broadcast. Ford had intended to have only CBS and NBC-Red carry the broadcasts, but NBC asserted that the weaker Blue network had to be included in order to ensure that all of America would be reached. P.G. Parker told N.W. Ayer and Ford representatives that NBC "had been placed in a very embarrassing position, on account of the fact that our Blue network had not been ordered," and that contrary to Ford's assumption, NBC "had always broadcast the World Series on our complete networks" (NBC 22). After reconsidering its stance (and more importantly after realizing that it may have been in violation of an NRA code), Ford not only agreed to utilize both of NBC's networks but also allowed independent stations to link up with the broadcast as had been done in the previous year ("Ford to link..." 1934), absolving NBC of the difficult decision as to which of its affiliates would not be able to carry the World Series.

Ford's purchase won it accolades within both the broadcasting and advertising industries. *Broadcasting* declared Henry Ford its biggest success story of the year, explaining that since Ford had begun using radio, "sales of his product more than double[d], and for the first time in three years oustripp[ed] all competitors — when before the radio campaign and with the same product, sales lagged behind competition" ("The biggest success..." 1934), citing the World Series as the capstone of his effort. *Advertising Age* admitted that "[n]o one seems to know just what it is costing Ford, but the prestige gained from being the first sponsor of a World Series broadcast is expected to be worth the price," which was estimated at about $350,000 all told ("Costs...." 1934). The broadcasts, however, were a disaster for Ford, which thought the expenses exorbitant protested to NBC about its announcers' fees and facilities charges (NBC 25, 26 and 27) even though Ford claimed it had "helped N.B.C. out of a very difficult position with its stations by purchasing the Blue network when there was no real advertising reason for the purchase of this network" (NBC 26).

After the 1934 Series, NBC executives considered the possibility of commercializing a national event previously defined as within the public interest. Especially since CBS had decided "to accept all sporting events on a commercial basis, NBC must necessarily acquire ... the major sporting events in order that we would be protected from the standpoint of our audience, associate stations and clients" even if it "substantially increase[d] the cost to NBC of the large sporting events in America" (NBC 24). Implementing this policy change, however, vexed the network; NBC's policy had been not to "buy sporting events for sustaining programs," and "neither CBS nor NBC will purchase a sporting event without a definite order for a client" (NBC 28), suggesting that while some executives wanted to take an aggressive posture with respect to their rival, they could not do so without considerable economic risk. Moreover, noted R.C. Patterson, Jr., such a policy might have put the network in the untenable position "of paying for every prominent sporting event in which the nation is interested." Aylesworth, in a handwritten response, responded that he agreed and did "not think we should go out and buy sporting events. But —?" (NBC 29), implying that NBC felt backed into a corner by CBS's quick acceptance of the Ford deal.

Another memo described the pitfalls of provoking a bidding war with CBS for sporting events that were deemed in the public interest, suggesting that no matter which way NBC turned, it might incur the government's wrath. David Rosenblum advocated an agreement stating that radio networks would "not compete with each other to buy the exclusive right to broadcast national sporting events either on a sustaining or commercial basis," a collusive policy that could have violated federal law. The primary problem with open competition, wrote Rosenblum, was that "any broadcasting company that tried to control the reporting of such [public service] events would probably in the end create resentment not only on the part of other networks and stations, and part of the public, but would probably incur criticism from the F.C.C." (NBC 30). Rosenblum suggested that it was not worth the risk to redefine public events such as the World Series or the Kentucky Derby; sports, he argued, should remain free from ownership by a specific entity. Aylesworth and Patterson, keeping Rosenblum's points in mind, worked out an agreement with CBS President William Paley that "we will not permit a sponsor to buy our facilities exclusively on either the Red or Blue Network for the World Series, nor will Columbia ... this is a national service which must be given over to the Red and Blue Networks of NBC as well as Columbia if the sponsor is to have the World Series. Otherwise, we will all do the World Series sustaining" (NBC 31).

Regardless of how major sports broadcasts were acquired, NBC expected to have them — and to have advertisers who understood the transcendent national importance of such broadcasts, whether sponsored or unsponsored. Royal, for instance, asserted that "[g]iving the poeple [sic] of America ... the World Series each year is more important in my opinion than any one client on our network ... and we should not accept Procter and Gamble or any other client who would not agree to step aside for the World Series" (NBC 32). The wisdom of alienating one of NBC's largest clients can be questioned, but the explicit willingness to do so in order to secure a broadcast such as the World Series is impressive. Royal, noting that "I doubt if [clients] would get any different decision on Columbia," even stated that it might be possible and prudent "to put such a clause in Proctor and Gamble's contract, or the contract of any other client" to ensure that NBC would "have the World Series, sustaining or commercial" (NBC 32).

The hard line Royal advocated with respect to sponsors also applied to relations with CBS, as he and other executives feared that NBC would be perceived as weak, ineffective, and second-rate rather than a leader within the radio industry if it lost broadcast rights for major events to CBS. Serving the public interest and serving NBC's interests were considered one and the same by network executives, and there was no harm in commercializing sports events if it meant that the public interest and the network's interests were widely acknowledged as synonymous. Edgar Kobak insisted that NBC could only expect to broadcast these events if the network purchased them as CBS had purchased the 1935 Kentucky Derby, even without a sponsor yet lined up, in order to avoid "the same trouble on the World Series. These things should be purchased by NBC and not by the advertiser or his [sic] agent.... NBC must maintain its leadership. If we lose anyone [sic] of these important events we will gradually lose our standing in importance with our stations, our listening audience and also our advertisers" (NBC 33). Royal expressed a similar opinion, not only criticizing the pact between the CBS and NBC presidents as not "worth the paper it's written on, if it was ever written,"[10] but also advocating that "we take the offensive and make them come to us with suggestions of agreements. I don't think we ever should be on the defensive. We are too big, or at least we ought to be" (NBC 34).

No policy changes were made in time to affect the 1935 World Series, which Ford again sponsored, this time with the Mutual network on board as well. Landis insisted on including Mutual, and Ford expected "expenditures of $500,000 or more for the network time and broadcasting right" in 1935, even though "[c]ommercial announcements [were] so short as to amount to little more than sponsor identification" and "[a]fter the first game probably will be made between all innings" ("World Series Again..." 1935). As internal memoranda suggest, NBC believed it reaped great benefits from the privilege of being allowed to broadcast the Series,[11] but it seems unlikely that Ford — laying out up to $500,000 for an occasional mention — viewed the benefits in quite the same way.

The automaker, too, was still upset at what it felt were exorbitant charges in 1934[12] and "refused to buy the Blue Network" in 1935, claiming that the networks "were forcing them to buy all three networks because of an agreement made by NBC and CBS and they felt that this was against the laws and constituted restraint of trade" (NBC 37). The N.W. Ayer agent representing Ford feared the loss of his biggest client and "asked [NBC] to broadcast the World Series on the Blue Network without charge to Ford, the broadcast on the Blue to be the same as on the RED [sic] and CBS," offering "to pay us our out-of-pocket costs to those stations on the Blue not owned or managed by NBC." A memo from Aylesworth stated that Ford and N.W. Ayer "bought a public service when they bought the Series," and in doing so "receive such great publicity they should take care of it by sending the Series over the three networks and not have some of the stations complaining that they are not getting it and blaming the Ford Motor Car Company or NBC" (NBC 36). But NBC, likely still attempting to have the broadcasts fulfill their public service obligations, carried the games on a sustaining basis on the Blue network in 1935, justifying the move in part by asserting that to do otherwise "would undoubtedly turn the Ford Motor Company against broadcasting, which would be bad for our business" (NBC 37).

Impending policy changes, however, might have opened the door for the competition that Rosenblum feared. Royal reported that in a meeting with CBS executive Lawrence Lowman after the Series, the agreements that had privately governed the networks' sports-purchasing capabilities had been dissolved. Royal asserted that NBC "must meet this competition" and "should give [CBS] a darned good licking. My suggestion is that we go out and buy all the important events now. Most of them we can sell. We might have to take a loss on one or two, but in the long run we will keep NBC out in front where it belongs" (NBC 38). Whether or not NBC attempted to obtain broadcast rights to the events it considered in the public interest and failed or simply did not pursue this new policy is unclear. With respect to the World Series, however, NBC remained temporarily tied to CBS, with both networks relying publicly on the same public service argument to reinforce their contention that neither one should be deprived of the ability to carry the Series.

In the meantime, the World Series broadcasts stumbled. All three networks again carried the Series in 1936, with the Blue network again carrying the games on a sustaining basis, but Ford was unhappy with the ratings and the high cost. Ford's disenchantment with the broadcasting expenses peaked in 1937, when the company ended its commitment to the Series by paying baseball $100,000 for the broadcast rights but refusing to sponsor the broadcast. According to Royal, "Ford's agents tried to find another sponsor to whom they might resell the radio rights, but could not do so" (NBC 48). *TSN* reported that Standard Oil and General Mills had been interested in sponsorship rights, but declined; the magazine emphasized that "no extra revenue [accrued] to players, clubs or leagues as a result" ("On the radio..." 1937). *Broadcasting* magazine noted that "[a] last-minute effort to secure sponsorship of the series was being made but the high cost of rights plus the expense of network facilities appeared to be standing in the way of prospective advertisers" ("No Series client" 1937). All three networks faithfully broadcast the Series, but the 1937 Series netted relatively dismal ratings: "An average of one out of every four radio homes listened each day to the World Series broadcasts," reported *Broadcasting*, reaching a "high figure of 27% for Wednesday and Saturday, with a drop to 20% on Friday"—significantly lower figures than the 1935 Series, in which "the average size of the audience for four week-days was about 32%" ("Series audience" 1937).

Ironically, NBC's commitment to a "public service" model and its unwillingness to carry the Series as a commercial event led to its losing broadcast rights to the Series. In August 1938, L. Niles Trammell responded to an inquiry by Commissioner Landis about the possibility of NBC carrying the World Series exclusively by stating that "the World Series in my opinion was the biggest feature available in America and it would be suicide to restrict its distribution to one third of the network stations" (NBC 52). Furthermore, Trammell told Landis,

> Baseball is such a part of American life it should be carried on a non-commercial basis and should be made available to all radio stations regardless of whether they were network stations or not. At this point he interrupted to inquire if he was to infer because he had such a tremendously popular feature he was to be deprived of the revenue derived from selling it.... I told him in my opinion [the Series] was too big to be commercialized [NBC 52].

Trammell returned to the issue of public service throughout the discussion, despite Landis' attempts to move the conversation back to the subject of an exclusive broadcast, which Landis pointed out would be cheaper and more attractive to a sponsor (and profitable for baseball, which received nothing if the broadcasts were unsponsored) than being forced to pay for CBS, NBC, and [Mutual] all carry the games.[13] Trammell seemed either unable to recognize baseball's economic interests, or so committed to the notion of the World Series as a public service, that when he suggested that "it might be smart for him [Landis] to get together with Columbia, Mutual and ourselves and come to a long term agreement on a sustaining basis at a very nominal fee," Landis replied that "of course he couldn't consider anything under $100,000" (NBC 52) and terminated the interview.

The 1938 World Series broadcast was routine. The absence of a sponsor for baseball's Fall Classic did not trouble the networks, who retained the prestige associated with the broadcasts and did not have to explain to advertisers that another sponsor would temporarily occupy their time slot. *Advertising Age* noted that the lack of a sponsor for the second straight year was understandable, given the difficulty of perfect "timing and ... phrasing of commercial announcements," "[t]he high cost of the world's series sponsorship, plus the usual expenses for time and wire service" and "more than the normal budget of policy and technical problems" ("No World's..." 1938). All three networks carried "play-by-play accounts of the World Series, the Yanks winning the thanks of every station and commercial manager along with the championship by defeating the Cubs in four straight games and making unnecessary the cancellation of any further commercial programs" ("Quick Series..." 1938), while ratings jumped from 25% in 1937 to 33% in 1938 ("One-third..." 1938).

But disaster struck for NBC and CBS on August 17, 1939. Not only had Landis lined up the Gillette Safety Razor Company to be the exclusive

World Series sponsor, but Mutual was named the exclusive network carrier, preventing NBC and CBS from carrying the World Series for the first time in a decade. Noted *Advertising Age*, "Mutual is planning to link 150 stations to carry the broadcast to the nation's fans in early October" and it was presumed that, "in view of advertisers' recent lack of interest in the classic, Gillette is supposed to have made a somewhat better bargain" than Ford ("Gillette signs..." 1939). The news only got worse for NBC and CBS: Gillette had "also signed an option with the baseball leagues and [Mutual] for exclusive broadcast rights of the 1940 World Series," ensuring at least a two-year hiatus for the older nets ("Gillette sponsors..." 1939).

NBC and CBS both protested the loss of their broadcast privileges to Landis, asserting that he was doing a disservice to the fans. CBS complained that "the broadcasting of World Series games exclusively over the Mutual Network would prevent many people from hearing them. That such a result would betray the public interest in a very serious way is ... self-evident. It is equally true that from the point of view of self-interest, as broadcasters ... we are most anxious that there be no public reaction against radio broadcasting" (NBC 59). CBS offered its network "on a non-commercial and non-exclusive basis," adding that "our offer would relieve baseball of a possible criticism of excessively commercializing the country's greatest and most closely followed sports event" (NBC 59). CBS also claimed that Mutual attempted to lure CBS affiliates to Mutual's broadcast and "disregard their commitments to a number of national advertisers in order to serve the interests of a single advertiser to whom they are under no commitment" (NBC 59). The familiar theme of national public service, considered imperiled by the relatively limited reach of Mutual's network, rather than commercialization, failed to convince Landis to change his mind or to accept CBS's offer.

NBC's Trammell sent Landis a similar and predictable letter, though his began by referring to the "licensing agreement between broadcasting stations and the government whereby stations are required to operate in the public interest" in an effort to highlight both the legal obligations of the jilted networks and the moral obligations of baseball and radio to serve the American public. After noting that only a multi-network broadcast would be able to reach the whole nation, Trammell referred to baseball's recent "Centennial Celebrations in Cooperstown," at which NBC and CBS "carried the lion's share of the broadcasts" publicizing the official opening of the Hall of Fame, and to the broadcasts of the Junior World Series. Trammell noted that he had offered to carry the Series on a sustaining basis, a possibility which piqued Gillette's interest but was rejected after checking with Mutual and Landis (NBC 60), and again warned against an angry outcry from a snubbed public.

Landis' rejection was based in the economic reality of the commercial system, a reality the networks attempted to deny when it did not suit their ends. The networks were the only entity to gain from the previously established Series broadcast system; they gained public confidence as well as listener loyalty to their station, which they could then use to build or keep an audience for their own profit. Series advertisers, as the Ford Motor Company had demonstrated, suffocated under the economic burden of the commercial/public-interest hybrid created from 1934 to 1936 by being forced to pay the line fees, announcers fees, and incidentals (even when NBC provided the Blue network on a sustaining basis as it did in 1935 and 1936). Baseball, finally, only realized a profit if there was an advertiser, which the networks' public desire for sustaining broadcasts and joint broadcasts discouraged. The haughty tones of CBS's and NBC's responses to the announcement that Mutual had obtained exclusive rights may only have fueled Landis' resolve;[14] baseball's inability to receive any compensation for the product it created for the networks made no sense in the context of an otherwise commercialized radio system. Landis reportedly "felt the Series to be of no greater [public] interest than the Kentucky Derby, Rose Bowl game, and numerous boxing events that have been carried exclusively on a single network" previously ("Staff for..." 1939). Without Landis' action, the networks could have continued the sustaining broadcasts indefinitely, depriving other industries — particularly baseball itself — from profiting from the Series broadcasts.

There was little, if any, complaint from the public or the government that the networks were not fulfilling their public service obligations by not carrying the Series, and concerns about Mutual's coverage were not loud enough to cause Landis to reexamine his choice of networks. *Broadcasting* documented Trammell's actions on behalf of the network ("Staff for..." 1939) and *TSN* described how spoiled the American public had become by free and easy access to the games, as demonstrated by "the bitter comment this year because the accepted sponsor did not blanket the country," while faulting "the officials of the game" for forgetting fans in the Southeast and Rocky Mountain areas, where Mutual did not reach ("Series a triumph..." 1939). Other than these latter concerns, however, the broadcast seems to have gone smoothly for Mutual in its first solo effort.

Compounding NBC's and CBS's error in judgment about the public service issue, the government responded to a Mutual complaint that the other networks refused "to permit certain of their stations to take the series"— a clear violation of network rights, since affiliates have the right to refuse to clear time for network programming if they so desire ("Refusal..." 1939). *Broadcasting* noted that there was "some controversy between the networks and their affiliates," citing a letter sent to the magazine by NBC's affiliate in Columbia, SC, stating that "'NBC is withholding permission for delayed broadcasts, but otherwise apparently appreciates our reasoning in accepting the Series'" ("129..." 1939). NBC apparently applied more pressure to other affiliates: William Hedges sent a telegram to several stations stating that NBC's "commercial programs will be broadcast at the same time as the [World Series] games and those commercial programs are of great importance to both you and us.... I am convinced we can assure our sponsors that all of our affiliated stations will live up to their commitments and abide by their contracts with us" rather than jumping to the Mutual World Series broadcast (NBC 58). Hedges also told Trammell that

> both Proctor & Gamble and General Mills by direct contact with stations are weakening in their support of our position in respect to the World Series.... Inasmuch as we have put pressure on our stations to adhere to their commitment to NBC and NBC's advertisers, I think it is equally important that we secure confirmation from General Mills and Proctor & Gamble that they will adhere to their commitment to us.... This is the only way we can exercise any degree of control of the situation [NBC 61].

Such correspondence prompted a letter from FCC Secretary T.J. Slowie to the head of NBC affiliate WMAL, asking about the 1939 Series broadcast controversy in light of General Order No. 37. Specifically, Slowie inquired as to whether or not "any attempt was made by any person or organization to influence or persuade you against broadcasting the programs" offered by Mutual (NBC 62). The responses collected from Slowie's letters — apparently sent to most, if not all, NBC affiliates — were apparently intended for use in connection with evidence given at hearings before the FCC from November 1938 to February 1939 as the basis for an FCC investigation into NBC's possible monopolistic operating practices. These developments suggest that, as noted above, the network was not in the dominant position it was assumed to be in vis-à-vis its advertisers and affiliates, and that the desire for additional control only complicated already-existing problems.

Conclusion

This cursory study of the early years of baseball's broadcast history suggests that the combination of baseball, commercial sponsorship, and broadcasting was neither predestined nor necessarily stable. Even when baseball team owners' technophobia diminished and radio broadcasts became increasingly common, tensions arose among actors within the broadcasting industry, between sponsors and broadcasters, between local and national interests and between the radio networks and major-league baseball. The battle for control and authority in the economic and socio-political spheres of radio's early days, often portrayed as stable, straight-forward, and predetermined, was in fact convoluted and much more fluid than most histories assert. Given these rocky origins, on which current tele-vision and radio relations are built, the subsequent growth and develop-ment of broadcast sports into the multibillion dollar industry of today seems far from inevitable.

This examination of how baseball broadcasts became commercial-ized also points to tensions within the radio industry, as well as within the network-affiliate relationship, that cannot be understood without acknowl-edging the central role that sports played in the radio industry during its early years. Adopting a perspective that centralizes and explores the roles that sports programming played, rather than one that marginalizes sports broadcasts or makes snap judgments about their importance, might lead to a revitalized understanding of broadcasting history.

Notes

1. This is, by the way, inaccurate. Archer (1938: 279) mentions WJZ's broadcast of the 1922 World Series, as well as the broadcast of the 1923 Series by WEAF and WGY (1938: 321–322). Douglas (1987: 117–118) describes play-by-play radio broadcasts of baseball in 1921 and 1922, as do Gorman and Calhoun (1994: 89). *Broadcasting*, in 1939, claimed that "[t]he first World Series broadcast was aired in 1926 by WJZ's nation-wide hookup" ("Gillette sponsors..." 1939), so perhaps the authors intended to specify the first nationwide broadcast of the Series.

2. An early draft of this paper traced the resistance to radio by baseball owners, using articles from *The Sporting News* to demonstrate that most major-league teams had effectively, if sometimes reluctantly, embraced radio by 1934 — but that minor-league teams were far more wary of the effect that radio broadcasts of major-league games might have on atten-dance. Minor-league owners, in fact, asked Commissioner Kenesaw Mountain Landis before and after the 1936 season to consider banning broadcasts ("Baseball magnates..." 1936), but their cries effectively went unheeded (c.f. "Minneapolis baseball" 1936; "Chicago base-ball..." 1936).

3. The authors erroneously state that "the threat [of television to attendance] was not perceived until long after the invention [of television]" (1993: 131). *The Sporting News* warned back in 1922 that attendance would be cut by something more insidious than radio: "When Ruth hits a homer or Sisler slides into the plate, a film will catch him in the act, wire-less will carry it a thousand miles broadcast and the family sitting in the darkened living room at home will see the scene reproduced instantaneously on the wall. No more impos-sible than what we now have seemed ten years ago" ("This our..." 1922). Such warnings occurred occasionally in the pages of *The Sporting News* throughout the 1920s and 30s (c.f. "Radio and..." 1939).

4. Lever and Wheeler (1993) also explore the gendered dimension of the audience, yet either contradict themselves in the process or fail to explore explicitly the process by which the female audience was addressed or not addressed. While asserting that "[t]he pattern of male dominance in the ratings was set early," as "63% of the male audience listened regularly to sporting events," this supposed dominance was undercut by other statements, such as the explanation that while "sports ranked lower for women, their potential appeal to women was already in evidence by the 30% of the female audience who reported listening to sports" (1993: 129) or the assertion that Cubs broadcasts "had so stimulated interest, especially among women, that, before another year had passed, they had established a 'Ladies' Day' at Wrigley Field" (1993: 129). This latter statement is also contradicted by evidence of "Ladies' Day" promotions which long predated broadcasting.

5. Smulyan, McChesney, and others also overlook a critical aspect of baseball broadcasting that challenges the historian's ability to presuppose a masculine audience: though sports was considered a male domain, baseball in the early 1930s was exclusively a daytime affair, and even early night games — introduced in the major leagues in 1935 — were fairly rare. Ballgames thus either supplanted or supplemented such "women's genres" as soap operas, and some evidence exists to suggest that women's interest in baseball increased as a result. Space limitations preclude a sustained examination of this issue in this paper, but audience research and editorial commentary in the 1930s (e.g. Kellogg and Walters 1932; Thomas 1936; "Chicago baseball..." 1936; and "Women and the game" 1938) clearly indicate a substantial audience for, and interest in, baseball for female listeners.

6. Another concern was the potential for games to run into extra innings and spill over into network commercials. According to a note by Witmer (NBC 6), this happened on at least one occasion in 1933, less than two months after Trammell's note to Witmer, when the Procter & Gamble–sponsored Cubs broadcast of a doubleheader was delayed by rain and wound up cutting off almost two hours' worth of programming by rival Chase & Sanborn. NBC began to pay particular attention to this possibility; on a note about the (unsponsored) broadcast of the first All-Star Game later that season, Royal scrawled, "If no confliction [sic] with Sales we should do it. Watch time. We cannot take chances of extra innings and run[ning] into commercials" (NBC 7).

7. Witmer's comments indicated his agreement "that baseball builds an audience but — it builds an audience *only* when baseball is being broadcast and not during the long lean weeks and months when there is no baseball" (NBC 67). The logistics of rescheduling required a near–Herculean task on the part of NBC's West Coast sales department (NBC 65, NBC 66) and memos suggest a loss of reputation among the involved sponsors.

8. Of course, the networks seem to have been in collusion throughout the 1930s with respect to sports broadcasts particularly; see NBC 17, NBC 19, NBC 34, NBC 35, NBC 41, NBC 42 and NBC 43 for allusions to private agreements with CBS that might have drawn attention from the federal government.

9. What public criticism there was seemed to be leveled at Ford and at Landis, rather than at broadcasters, for commercializing the Series. *Advertising Age* quoted newspaper publisher James Stahlman of the *Nashville Banner* as saying that "it is against the public interest '*for sports promoters* to sell exclusively to any commercial interest the news of a transcendentally important event such as the world series, whether that news be for publication or broadcasting'" ("Broadcast of World Series..." 1934).

10. Royal added that "I think it illegal and if either NBC or Columbia tried to enforce it, it would be very embarrassing" (NBC 34). See note 8 for other memos referring to possible collusion between the networks.

11. These were not always tangible benefits, though, as a pair of memos indicated that the Series broadcast was not good for all NBC stations. Surveys conducted during the Series indicated that "the Red is strong and that Columbia is right behind it, but it shows up some very weak spots on the Blue, particularly WJZ and WBZ" despite the sales department's claims that "[w]e are selling the Blue Network hard. It is a good network, but it is not good enough...." (NBC 40). The surveys, which NBC had intended to use as part of its sales

promotion package, were so embarrassing that they were deemed unworthy of publication or distribution outside the network (NBC 39).

12. According to Kobak's memo, several N.W. Ayer representatives explained that Ford "felt the price for rights, plus the time was excessive. They had several suggestions as to how this cost could be cut. None of these suggestions [not spelled out in the memo] were acceptable to us because they meant a cut in our basic rates.... Representatives from the agency on that day or the day before also called upon Mr. Klauber of CBS and presented the problem to him. Mr. Klauber's answer was the same as ours" (NBC 37). Whether or not the charges were "exorbitant" is not noted and precise figures as to how much Ford paid do not seem to exist; however, a letter from E.R. Hitz to a Young & Rubicam agent in 1937 suggests that the cost for NBC-Red alone would be approximately $181,600 before broadcasting rights fees, CBS — "as the agreement is that the Series be fed to both chains" — and NBC-Blue were added in, though Hitz indicated that "we would include the stations of the Blue Network without an increase of facilities cost," meaning that NBC-Blue would cost an extra $7500 (NBC 47).

13. Landis informed Trammell that "he had an obligation to the ball players ... and he could not afford to let the players down ... and here was the only chance the players had to capitalize on broadcasting and that he would not be able to explain to them his reasons for not selling it. He elaborated on this phase of his discussion a little bit, *but it is not important*" (NBC 52). Trammell's dismissal of Landis' concerns in adhering to the public service mandate, while likely not the sole cause of NBC's losing the Series in 1939, suggests the network's inability to recognize baseball's needs. Trammell also noted that Landis, a former judge, did not "mention collusion, monopoly or any violation of any law," suggesting either that Trammell had expected Landis to charge NBC with monopolistic practices and was relieved that Landis had not done so, or that Landis would have informed him if any of his statements had violated any of those laws. Given the subsequent removal of the Blue network from NBC by the government in 1943, it is possible that Trammell was aware that the federal government might look askance at NBC's practices and that Landis could use the threat of illegality as a lever to extract favors from the network.

14. A follow-up letter from Trammell to Landis in 1940 further demonstrated no awareness of the basis for Landis' choice of MBS for commercial broadcasting rather than NBC for sustaining purposes: "I now offer to you, as the head of organized baseball, the privilege of having these games broadcast over the Red network and the Blue network of the National Broadcasting Company on a sustaining basis.... A large percentage of the stations affiliated with [NBC] are owned by newspapers who have promoted baseball throughout the year and if they are to be deprived of carrying the World Series, it is my feeling that a grave injustice has been done them" (NBC 68).

References

BOOKS AND JOURNAL ARTICLES

Archer, G.L. (1938). *History of radio to 1926*. New York: Stratford Press, Inc.

Archer, G.L. (1939). *Big business and radio*. New York: Stratford Press, Inc.

Barber, R. (1970). *The broadcasters*. New York: The Dial Press.

Berkman, D. (1988). Long before Arledge ... sports & TV. *Journal of popular culture* 22 (2): 49–62.

Cozens, F.W., and Stumpf, F.S. (1953). *Sports in American life*. Chicago: University of Chicago Press.

Douglas, G.H. (1987). *The early days of radio broadcasting*. Jefferson, NC: MacFarland & Company, Inc.

Gorman, J., and Calhoun, K., with Rozin., S. (1994). *The name of the game: the business of sports.* New York: John Wiley & Sons, Inc.

Klatell, D.A., and Marcus, N. (1988). *Sports for sale: television, money, and the fans.* New York: Oxford University Press, Inc.

Lever, J., and Wheeler, S. (1993). Mass media and the experience of sport. *Communication research* 20 (1): 125–143.

McChesney, R.W. (1989). Media made sports. In *Media, sports, and society*, L. A. Wenner (Ed.). Newbury Park, CA: Sage Publications: 49–69.

McChesney, R.W. (1993). Conflict, not consensus. In *Ruthless criticism: new perspectives in U.S. communication history*, W.S. Solomon and R.W. McChesney (Eds.). Minneapolis: University of Minnesota Press: 223–258.

Rader, B.J. (1988). *In its own image: how television has transformed sports.* New York: The Free Press.

Smith, C. (1987). *Voices of the game: the first full-scale overview of baseball broadcasting, 1921 to the present.* South Bend, IN: Diamond Communications, Inc.

Smulyan, S. (1994). *Selling radio.* Washington: Smithsonian Institution Press.

Magazine Sources

"Baseball magnates seeking radio curb." *Broadcasting*, 1 May 1936, vol. 10 no. 9, p. 15.

"The biggest success story of 1934!" *Broadcasting*, 15 October 1934, vol. 7 no. 8, p. 11.

"Broadcast of World Series springs leak." *Advertising Age*, 6 October 1934, vol. 5 no. 40, p. 29.

"Chicago baseball teams to add talent charges for broadcasts in 1937." *Broadcasting*, 15 November 1936, vol. 11 no. 10, p. 36.

"Ford to link nets for World Series." *Broadcasting*, 1 October 1934, vol. 7 no. 7, p. 14.

"Gillette signs for sponsorship of World Series." *Advertising Age*, 21 August 1939, vol. 10 no. 34, p. 1.

"Gillette sponsors baseball on MBS." *Broadcasting*, 1 September 1939, vol. 17 no. 5, p. 14.

Kellogg, H.D., and Walters, A.G. (1932). "How to reach housewives most efficiently. *Broadcasting*, 15 April 1932, vol. 2 no. 8, pp. 7+.

"Minneapolis baseball." *Broadcasting*, 1 June 1936, vol. 10 no. 11, p. 18.

"Nets let independents pick up World Series." *Broadcasting*, 15 October 1933, vol. 5 no. 8, p. 20.

"No Series client." *Broadcasting*, 1 October 1937, vol. 13 no. 7, p. 73.

"No World's Series sponsor." *Advertising Age*, 10 October 1938, vol. 9 no. 41, p. 12.

"On the radio airlines." *The Sporting News*, 7 October 1937, vol. 104 no. 8, p. 5.

"One-third of nation's sets tuned in on Series." *Advertising Age*, 24 October 1938, vol. 9 no. 43, p. 10.

"129 are signed in World Series list, says MBS." *Broadcasting*, 15 September 1939, vol. 17 no. 6, p. 28.

"A problem for broadcasters." *Advertising Age*, 22 September 1934, vol. 5 no. 38, p. 10.

"Quick Series aids station business." *Broadcasting*, 15 October 1938, vol. 15 no. 8, p. 14.

"Radio hikes Series all over continent." *The Sporting News*, 10 October 1929, vol. 88 no. 1, p. 4.

"Refusal of World Series mentioned to FCC." *Broadcasting*, 1 October 1939, vol. 17 no. 7, p. 16.

"Series a triumph for pitchers." *The Sporting News*, 12 October 1939, vol. 106 no. 9, p. 4.

"Series audience." *Broadcasting*, 15 October 1937, vol. 13 no. 8, p. 81.

Thomas, E.S. (1936). "Capturing the beauty market by radio." *Broadcasting*, 1 August 1936, vol. 11 no. 3, p. 28.

"Women and the game." *The Sporting News*, 17 November 1938, vol. 106 no. 14, p. 4.

"World Series again will be sponsored on NBC, CBS and MBS by Ford Motor Co." *Broadcasting*, 1 October 1935, vol. 9 no. 7, p. 9.

"World Series broadcast is vexing chains." *Advertising Age*, 29 September 1934, vol. 5 no. 39, p. 4.

ARCHIVAL MATERIALS

Many of the sources used are materials in the NBC Archives (Central Files) collection at the State Historical Society of Wisconsin. Specific sources cited in this paper, all from the NBC Archives (Central Files) are as follows, arranged by date and numbered:

1. 18 April 1930. Memo from William Evans to John F. Royal. Box 2 Folder 49.
2. 4 March 1931. Memo from John F. Royal to William Evans. Box 2 Folder 49.
3. 5 March 1932. Memo from L. Niles Trammell to John F. Royal. Box 2 Folder 49.
4. 7 March 1932. Memo from John F. Royal to L. Niles Trammell. Box 2 Folder 49.
5. 24 March 1933. Memo from L. Niles Trammell to Roy C. Witmer. Box 16 Folder 6.
6. 3 May 1933. Memo from Roy C. Witmer to B.F. McClelland. Box 16 Folder 6.
7. 2 June 1933. Memo from A.W. Kaney to John F. Royal. Box 16 Folder 6.
8. 27 July 1933. Memo from Roy C. Witmer to John F. Royal. Box 16 Folder 6.
9. 17 January 1934. Memo from P.G. Parker to Bill Hay. Box 24 Folder 4.
10. 26 January 1934. Memo from Bill Hay to J.V. McConnell. Box 24 Folder 4.
11. 7 May 1934. Memo from Bertha Brainard to P.G. Parker. Box 24 Folder 5.
12. 10 May 1934. Memo from E.R. Hitz to Bertha Brainard. Box 24 Folder 5.
13. 10 May 1934. Memo from P.G. Parker to Bertha Brainard. Box 24 Folder 5.
14. 23 May 1934. Memo from P.G. Parker to Roy C. Witmer. Box 24 Folder 4.
15. 1 September 1934. Memo from John F. Royal to Edgar Kobak. Box 24 Folder 5.
16. 14 September 1934. Memo from Edgar Kobak to Roy C. Witmer. Box 24 Folder 5.
17. 14 September 1934. Memo from John F. Royal to Niles Trammell. Box 24 Folder 5.
18. 14 September 1934. Memo from Edgar Kobak to M.H. Aylesworth. Box 24 Folder 30.
19. 17 September 1934. Memo from John F. Royal to Edgar Kobak. Box 24 Folder 5.
20. 17 September 1934. Memo from M.H. Aylesworth to Edgar Kobak. Box 24 Folder 30.
21. 21 September 1934. Memo from A.L. Ashby to Edgar Kobak. Box 24 Folder 5.
22. 26 September 1934. Memo from P.G. Parker to Morton and Kobak. Box 24 Folder 5.
23. 27 September 1934. Memo from Edgar Kobak to D.S. Shaw. Box 24 Folder 5.

24. 15 October 1934. Memo from Mark Woods to Richard C. Patterson, Jr., Box 24 Folder 5.

25. 17 October 1934. Letter from E.R. Hitz to Francis C. Barton, Jr., Box 24 Folder 5.

26. 24 October 1934. Letter from Francis C. Barton, Jr., to Jack Overall. Box 24 Folder 5.

27. 21 November 1934. Letter from Jack Overall to Francis C. Barton, Jr., Box 24 Folder 5.

28. 19 November 1934. Memo from M.H. Aylesworth to R.C. Patterson, Jr., Box 24 Folder 30.

29. 22 November 1934. Memo from R.C. Patterson, Jr., to M.H. Aylesworth. Box 24 Folder 30.

30. 24 November 1934. Memo from David Rosenblum to R.C. Patterson, Jr., Box 24 Folder 30.

31. 28 November 1934. Memo from M.H. Aylesworth to R.C. Patterson, Jr., Box 24 Folder 5.

32. 25 March 1935. Memo from John F. Royal to R.C. Patterson, Jr., Box 34 Folder 29.

33. 26 March 1935. Memo from Edgar Kobak to R.C. Patterson, Jr., Box 34 Folder 29.

34. 15 April 1935. Memo from John F. Royal to R.C. Patterson, Jr., Box 34 Folder 30.

35. 8 May 1935. Memo from Frank E. Mason to Edgar Kobak. Box 34 Folder 30.

36. 17 September 1935. Memo from M.H. Aylesworth to R.C. Patterson, Jr., Box 34 Folder 29.

37. 23 September 1935. Memo from Edgar Kobak to R.C. Patterson, Jr., Box 34 Folder 29.

38. 1 October 1935. Memo from John F. Royal to R.C. Patterson, Jr., Box 34 Folder 30.

39. 18 October 1935. Memo from Roy C. Witmer to Edgar Kobak. Box 34 Folder 29.

40. 23 October 1935. Memo from Edgar Kobak to R.C. Patterson, Jr., Box 34 Folder 29.

41. 9 November 1935. Memo from John F. Royal to R.C. Patterson, Jr., Box 34 Folder 30.

42. 26 November 1935. Memo from Richard C. Patterson to John F. Royal. Box 34 Folder 29.

43. 29 November 1935. Memo from John F. Royal to Richard C. Patterson. Box 34 Folder 29.

44. 3 February 1936. Memo from Frank E. Mason to Lenox R. Lohr. Box 44 Folder 27.

45. 24 February 1936. Memo from Roy C. Witmer to Frank E. Mason. Box 44 Folder 27.

46. 14 April 1936. Memo from R.M. Brophy to R.C. Witmer. Box 44 Folder 27.

47. 27 August 1937. Letter from Edward R. Hitz to Carlos Franco. Box 58 Folder 80.

48. no date, 1937. AP wire and story from unnamed newspaper ("Ford Declined to Broadcast World Series After Paying $100,000 for Option Rights"). Box 52 Folder 4.

49. 7 July 1938. Memo from R.C. Witmer to W.S. Hedges. Box 58 Folder 78.

50. 8 July 1938. Memo from William S. Hedges to R.C. Witmer. Box 58 Folder 78.

51. 9 August 1938. Memo from R.C. Witmer to A.H. Morton. Box 58 Folder 78.

52. 29 August 1938. Memo from Niles Trammell to L.R. Lohr. Box 58 Folder 79.

53. 14 September 1938. Memo from Alfred H. Morton to Lenox R. Lohr. Box 58 Folder 78.

54. 17 September 1938. Memo from Frank M. Russell to Lenox R. Lohr. Box 58 Folder 78.

55. 10 April 1939. Telegram from S. Strotz to Niles Trammell. Box 66 Folder 35.

56. 11 April 1939. Telegram from Niles Trammell to Sidney Strotz. Box 66 Folder 35.

57. 18 April 1939. Memo from Roy C. Witmer to Lenox R. Lohr. Box 66 Folder 35.

58. 22 August 1939. Telegram from William Hedges to "All Stations." Box 66 Folder 35.

59. 25 August 1939. Letter from Columbia Broadcasting System to Commissioner Kenesaw Mountain Landis. Box 66 Folder 35.

60. 25 August 1939. Letter from Niles Trammell to Commissioner Kenesaw Mountain Landis. Box 66 Folder 35.

61. 7 September 1939. Memo from William S. Hedges to Niles Trammell. Box 66 Folder 35.

62. 2 November 1939. Letter from T.J. Slowie, FCC, to Dr. C.B. Jolliffe, NBC Station WMAL. Box 66 Folder 35.

63. 7 February 1940. Memo from F.M. Thrower Jr. to R.C. Witmer through I.E. Showerman. Box 74 Folder 60.

64. 20 February 1940. Memo from John H. Norton Jr. to William S. Hedges. Box 74 Folder 60.

65. 22 March 1940. Memo from R.C. Witmer to W.S. Hedges. Box 74 Folder 60.

66. 3 April 1940. Memo from F.M. Greene to R.C. Witmer. Box 74 Folder 60.

67. 29 April 1940. Memo from Roy C. Witmer to Niles Trammell. Box 74 Folder 60.

68. 25 July 1940. Letter from Niles Trammell to Commissioner Kenesaw Mountain Landis. Box 74 Folder 60.

Part 3

BASEBALL AND
AMERICAN SOCIETY

Slide, Kelly, Slide: The Irish in the Early History of Baseball

Richard Peterson

Baseball historians have long recognized the ascendancy of Irish players in the early history of baseball. By the end of the nineteenth century, Irish stars dominated baseball and its greatest teams. The legendary Baltimore Orioles, managed by Ned Hanlon, won consecutive National League pennants in 1894, 1895 and 1896 with Hall of Famers Big Dan Brouthers, Hugh Jennings, and John McGraw in the infield and Joe Kelley and Wee Willie Keeler in the outfield. A decade earlier so many New York Irish fans came out to see the stellar pitching of Tim Keefe and Smiling Mickey Welch, both winners of over 300 games in their professional careers, and the slugging of "The Mighty Clouter" Roger Connor, the Babe Ruth of his day, that the bleachers at the Polo Grounds were called "Burkeville." At other ballparks, the Irish sat in "Kerry Patches" to watch the colorful Mike "King" Kelly, generally regarded as the most popular baseball player of the nineteenth century. A. G. Spalding's sale of Kelly in 1887 from the Chicago National White Stockings to the Boston Beaneaters for the unheard of price of $10,000 was the biggest and most controversial deal of the era. Kelly's base running was so spectacular and his behavior on and off the field so flamboyant that he inspired the popular song "Slide, Kelly, Slide" and often performed on the vaudeville stage to packed houses during the off-season.

This predominance of Irish players in baseball's evolution into America's national pastime is most frequently interpreted within the traditional view of the game as both an opportunity for individual success and a melting pot for ethnic groups. Conventional historical wisdom has it that once organized baseball shook free of its amateur beginnings in the 1840s and the Knickerbocker hold on the game as a polite pastime for Protestant gentlemen, it opened its fields, especially after baseball became professional in 1869, to an increasing tide of immigrant players. The first immigrant wave of Germans and Irish supplanted the English and Scottish and transformed the game in the last few decades of the nineteenth century from a rural diversion and class signifier into an expression of America's democratic character and its competitive spirit. By the twentieth century, baseball had further evolved to the point where the ethnic origins of players had become an essential part of baseball's character and even a matter of pride. Of course, even as German and Irish players became assimilated into the national game and some of them emerged as ethnic heroes, other ethnic and racial groups, like the Italians, Jews and African Americans, would face the same prejudices and obstacles, but would have the same opportunity, when their time came, to prove themselves on the playing field. In a 1931 *Sporting News* editorial, baseball's bible declared, as if in anticipation of Joe DiMaggio, Hank Greenberg, and Jackie Robinson, that the "Sons of Erin" had "better beware.... They will be challenged to prove their racial superiority one of these days."

The problem with this theory of the melting pot and the ethnic hero, besides its paradoxical nature, is that it relies heavily upon a romantic vision of baseball as a moral and heroic proving ground, an immigrant field of dreams. This vision, while one of the formative principles for baseball histories, finds its perfect expression in Lucy Kennedy's *The Sunlit Field*, generally recognized as the first adult baseball novel written by a woman. Published in 1950, two years before the appearance of Bernard Malamud's *The Natural*, Kennedy's historical romance, set in 1857, follows its runaway sixteen-year-old Irish heroine Po (for Pocahontas) O'Reilly from Fall River, Massachusetts, where the capitalist Eaters and their thread mills threaten her spirit, to Brooklyn where she discovers that her dying father's dream of America as "a fabulous place — like a great open sunlit field" comes to life on a baseball field where "the men flashed about, stretching their bodies in long beautiful arcs, or leaped into the air to catch the ball with easeful sureness in bared cupped hands. Yes, these were the tall men!"

In *The Sunlit Field* baseball also becomes a battlefield for ethnic clashes and class rivalries when Kennedy turns one of the most celebrated events in early baseball history, the 1858 three-game Fashion Race Course Series, into a blood-letting, to-the-death contest between the hirelings of the Knickerbockers and Po Reilly's tall men. The real series, the nineteenth century precursor to the modern day World Series, was played over a span of three months and was remarkable not only for its fierce rivalry, but for the demand by its organizers for a fifty-cent admission fee and for the heavy amount of gambling on player performance and the outcome of the games. In her novel, Kennedy doesn't change the historical outcome of the series — New York won the deciding third game after the teams split the first two — but she does condense the series into a three-day event and transforms the games into a ruthless attempt by the upper-class Knickerbocker Club to buy baseball supremacy by hiring "shooting stars" or "revolvers" to beat the upstart, working-class Brooklyn nine by any means, including bribery, cheating, and dirty play.

In *The Sunlit Field* the dream of baseball as a field for individual opportunity and social assimilation survives Brooklyn's loss. By the end of the novel, the game of baseball as a professional sport emerges as the Irish immigrant's best hope for participating successfully in the democratic and competitive spirit of America. But Lucy Kennedy's closing vision of the Irish and baseball is the stuff of historical romance. Baseball historians, even as they celebrate the game as a national melting pot, have tended to view baseball's assimilation of ethnic and racial groups through the distorted lens of ethnic and racial stereotypes. Lawrence McCaffrey in *The New York Irish*, observes that "Irish players came to represent American adaptability and their skills in this arena gave them a more acceptable persona" but he also notes that their athleticism "reinforced nativist opinion that the Irish were strong of back and weak of mind."

One of the most blatant, if not outrageous examples of the historical stereotyping of Irish ballplayers occurs in one of baseball's most popular historical texts, *The Bill James Historical Baseball Abstract*. In writing about the Irish domination of baseball in the 1890s, James, at first, appears to reject nativism and stereotypes by declaring that "many people, in the same stupid way that people today believe that blacks are born athletes, thought that the Irish were born baseball players." But in the very next sentence, after observing that "of course people also associated the roughness and unruliness of the players with their ethnic background," he notes that "the Irish have, indeed, always been known for that." In other words, while it is stupid to think of the Irish as born baseball players, to think of them as born rowdies may be another matter.

Adding ethnic insult to injury, James, beginning with his section on baseball in the 1880s, a decade where the players were "mostly eastern, mostly Irish and a little rough," sets up a special category for baseball's Drinking Men. The category, with its listing of Charlie Sweeney, King Kelly, Curt Welch, and Duke Farrell among its eight most notorious drunks, is obviously tilted toward the Irish. In the next section on the 1890s, James, in writing about the decade most dominated by Irish players, continues his category for Drinking Men. By listing Tom McCarthy, Marty Bergen, and Willie McGill among his five baseball lushes of the 1890s, the category once again raises the glass to the Irish. When James gets to the 1900s, the decade when baseball "gradually began to shed its Irish flavor," his category for the game's Drinking Men disappears, apparently no longer required. And, notes James, with baseball becoming more temperate and respectable, baseball attendance dramatically improved: "whereas baseball in the nineteenth century was in danger of becoming a game of the Irish, by the Irish, for the Irish, it now began to appeal to a broader cross-section of the public."

The Bill James Historical Baseball Abstract obviously relies on stereotyping in its association of baseball's early rowdyism with the predominance of Irish players in the 1880s and 1890s, but in defense of James, there is ample historical evidence to support his attitude toward the Irish, an attitude shared by baseball historian Benjamin Rader, who in his own commentary on late nineteenth century ballplayers notes, "(at least for the Irish) drinking, brawling, and display were a conspicuous part of their male homosocial world." Curt Welch, listed among James's Drinking Men, once, purportedly, dedicated his season to beer. His heavy drinking forced him out of baseball at the age of 31, and he died three years later of alcoholism. Also on James's list, Charlie Sweeney, according to the biographical entry in SABR's *Nineteenth Century Stars*, "was vilified in the press for his public drunkenness and for assaulting another player." Several years after his career was over, Sweeney was convicted of manslaughter and sentenced to ten years in prison for killing a man in a barroom argument. But Sweeney's conduct and fate pale beside that of Marty Bergen, a brilliant but emotionally disturbed player, who, in the middle of an erratic career and nine days after the turn of the century, used an ax to kill his son and daughter, then cut his own throat with a razor.

Even baseball's earliest historians had no trouble finding and displaying examples of Irish misconduct on and off the playing field. In *America's National Game*, published in 1911 and generally regarded as the first official chronicle of baseball, A. G. Spalding uses, as one of the turning points in baseball's development into the national pastime, a meeting between William Hulbert, President of the National League, and Jim Devlin, one of four Louisville players banned from baseball for conspiring with gamblers to throw games. According to Spalding, Devlin, after being reduced to abject poverty by his expulsion, came to Hulbert's office and fell to his knees to plead for mercy on behalf of his starving family. Moved to tears, Hulbert put a fifty-dollar bill into Devlin's palm, but told him: "That's what I think of you, personally; but damn you, Devlin, you are dishonest; you have sold a game, and I don't trust you. Now go; and let me never see your face again; for your act will not be condoned as long as I live."

The banning of Devlin, despite the claims of Spalding, hardly kept baseball free of gambling and scandal, but, thanks to Spalding's chronicle, Devlin became baseball's most conspicuous example of the crooked ballplayer, at least until the fixing of the 1919 World Series. Devlin, a thirty-game winner for Louisville in 1876 and in 1877 and one of baseball's emerging stars at the time of his expulsion, was further proof that the Irish were prolific in the late nineteenth century, not only for their playing skills, competitive nature, and success on the ball field, but for their alcoholism, hoodlumism, and self-destructiveness. They have provided historians with the best examples of the "poor moral conduct and ... ill-mannered behavior both on and off the field" that Steven A. Riess in *City Games*, his study of sports in the Progressive Era, sees as the cause for ballplayers low prestige in the early history of professional baseball.

The epitome of the nineteenth-century Irish ballplayer for baseball historians is the colorful and controversial figure of Mike "King" Kelly. Listed by Bill James as the most handsome and dashing ballplayer of the 1880s, Kelly is described in SABR's *Baseball's First Stars* as "the brainiest, most creative, and most original player of his time." The most spectacular baserunner of his day, Kelly once stole the remarkable total of 84 bases in just 116 games. He was also an excellent hitter, leading the National League in batting twice and in runs scored three times. During his major league career, he led Cap Anson's Chicago club to three straight National League pennants from 1880 to 1882 and to two more in 1885 and 1886. He was elected to the Hall of Fame in 1945.

Yet when baseball historians portray Kelly, their accounts draw far more attention to his heavy drinking, his flaunting of baseball rules, and his troublesome and often unmanageable behavior than to his accomplishments. In *Baseball: An Illustrated History*, the book derived from Ken Burns's popular television documentary on the history of baseball, the narrative relates story after story of Kelly's drunkenness and trickery. Readers, after looking at a cartoon of Kelly in the clubhouse sleeping off a nightly bender, learned about the time Kelly, when asked if he drank while playing, replied, "It depends upon the length of the game," and the time he held up a game while Kelly and "several wealthy gentlemen in box seats toasted one another." The narrative also quotes the solemn words of Henry Chadwick, baseball's pioneer journalist and an early reformer of the game, condemning Kelly's outrageous conduct: "To suppose that a man can play properly who guzzles beer daily, or indulges in spirituous liquors, or who sets up nightly gambling or does worse by still enervating habits at brothels is nonsense."

The stories of Kelly when he was sober enough to play ball are usually about his trickery and cheating. On the base paths, he routinely skipped second base on his way to third if the umpire was watching the ball being retrieved in the outfield. When he was the catcher for his team, he would cover home plate with his mask to prevent the base runner from scoring. But the most apocryphal story of Kelly's on-the-field cunning has to do with his leaping, game-ending catch in the twilight gloom to save a Chicago victory. When he came off the field and was asked for the ball by his manager Cap Anson, Kelly supposedly replied, "The ball? ... It went a mile over me head." There is also the story of the time Kelly, sitting out the game because of a hangover, saw a foul pop fly heading toward the bench, cried out, "Kelly catching for Boston," and jumped up and caught the ball for an out.

Kelly, however, was a piker compared to the infamous Baltimore Orioles and their galaxy of Irish stars and miscreants. The Irish dominated Orioles were led on the field by the pugnacious John McGraw, who was called Muggsy by his enemies for his foul mouth and dirty play. In the Ken Burns history, McGraw is described in the words of the sportswriters of his day as "the toughest of the tough ... an abomination of the diamond." Bill James in his *Baseball Abstract* named McGraw the best third baseman of the 1890s, but also listed him as the decade's least admirable superstar. McGraw's own biographer, Charles Alexander, called him the worst umpire baiter in the history of baseball.

McGraw's Baltimore Orioles may have been one of the best teams in the early history of baseball, but they are also generally regarded as one of baseball's most infamous nines. While they were the era's most skilled team at playing inside or scientific baseball, they have been historicized for abusing umpires and intimidating, even maiming opposition players. In Harold Seymour's highly regarded history of baseball, he cites *The Sporting News* complaint that the Orioles were "playing the dirtiest ball ever seen in the country" and summarizes its description of such dirty tactics as tripping and spiking base runners, or grabbing their shirts as they went by. The Orioles would also bunt between the mound and first base to run into and spike opposing pitchers. They bowled over infielders as they rounded the bases, and crowded around and jostled any catcher waiting for a throw home. As for umpires, one of their favorite targets, John Heydler, who was an umpire during the 1890s and later became President of the National League, offers the following indictment of the Orioles, as quoted in Seymour's history:

We hear much of the glories and durabilities of the old Orioles, but the truth about this time seldom has been told. They were mean, vicious, ready at any time to maim a rival player or an umpire, if it helped their cause. The things they said to an umpire were unbelievably vile, and they broke the spirits of some fine men. I've seen umpires bathe their feet by the hour after McGraw and others spiked them through their shoes. The club never was a constructive force in the game. The worst of it was they got by with much of their brow beating and hooliganism. Other clubs patterned after them, and I feel the lot of the umpires never was worse than in the years when the Orioles were flying high.

The most obvious way to counter the historicizing of the Irish ballplayer in the nineteenth century as something of a cross between an irresponsible drunk and a vicious hooligan is to offer examples, and there are many, of Irish ballplayers who, in spite of the ethnic stereotype of the "Sons of Erin," were not alcoholics, rowdies, or blackguards. For every Irish ballplayer in SABR's two volume biography of nineteenth-century stars who fits the stereotype of the Irish born to drink, brawl, and break the law, there is a player like the idolized The Only Nolan, the respected Billy McLean, or the redoubtable Connie Mack, each greatly admired for either his skill, his integrity, or his career achievements. For every Irish ballplayer who qualifies for James's list of Drinking Men, there is an enshrined Hall of Famer like Orator Jim O'Rourke. A Yale Law School graduate, O'Rourke, when told that to sign a contract with Boston and its Protestant financial backers he would have to drop the "O" from his name, responded: "I would rather die than give up my father's name. A million dollars would not tempt me." For every Jim Devlin, banned from baseball for life for throwing games, there is a Kid Gleason, who retained his reputation for fairness and honesty as a manager even after eight of his Chicago White Sox players threw the 1919 World Series. Among the overflow crowd of 5,000 in attendance at Gleason's funeral were Baseball Commissioner Kenesaw Mountain Landis, who had banned Shoeless Joe Jackson and his fellow Black Sox from the game, as well as fellow managers and Irishmen John McGraw and Connie Mack.

Among the nineteenth-century greats listed position-by-position in Alfred H. Spink's *The National Game*, first published in 1911, are several Irish players praised for their "sterling character," "excellent disposition," and "splendid habits." James Deacon McGuire, who caught and managed for over thirty years and later coached at Albion College, was known to have "never been fined, never put out of a game by an umpire." Long John Reilly, one of the early power hitters in his years with Cincinnati, won public acclaim for his modest conduct and was widely regarded as a model for self-discipline and team play in an era characterized by its rowdiness. Tommy Burns, the third baseman for Cap Anson's pennant-winning Chicago teams of the 1880s, never drank or smoked and was respected for his fairness and his honesty as a player and a manager. Silent Mike Tiernan, who starred as a slugger and a base stealer with New York in the 1890s, earned his nickname for his dignity and his calm. In a 1902 article in *The Gael*, he was described "as honest as the sun, a sober gentlemanly professional player, ... a credit to his team, ... possessed [of] a record of never having been fined for disputing an umpire's decision."

Other Irish ballplayers in Spink's *The National Game* are singled out for their "braininess" and were instrumental in revolutionizing the professional game. Irish born Tommy Bond, who won forty or more games in three consecutive seasons from 1879 to 1881, was one of the first to "throw the ball rather than pitch it" and is credited with perfecting the curve ball after learning how to throw it from Hall of Famer Candy Cummings. Another Hall of Famer, Charles A. Comiskey, destined to become one of the most dominant and controversial baseball magnates in the twentieth century, revolutionized the position of first base in the late nineteenth century by playing far off the base when fielding his position. James Fogarty, a leftfielder described by Spink as one of the "greatest who ever lived" was one of the first outfielders to earn a reputation for his defensive play because of his great speed, powerful throwing arm, and his ability to make sensational catches. Tim Murnane, popular with his teammates because of his cheery disposition and credited with the first stolen base in National League history, eventually became, after a brief umpiring stint, one of the leading baseball writers of his day. He became renowned as a champion of the game's traditions and its old-time ballplayers and is credited with writing the first baseball column.

There were many stellar Irish ballplayers important to the early history of American baseball whose conduct did not conform to an ethnic stereotype, but the real historical issue of the Irish in baseball resides not in the character of the Irish but in the character of the professional game in the late nineteenth century. Steven Riess points out that "the professionalization of the sport did not begin in earnest until after the Civil War in response to the strong demand by upper-middle-class amateur clubs for winning teams." These ringers or revolvers were not only given money, they were often given jobs or placed on company payrolls. As baseball in the 1870s became a means to earn money, it attracted young men who were poor and uneducated and otherwise trapped economically and socially within their underprivileged class.

That baseball's origins were in the Northeast and that professional play was concentrated in seaboard cities, Philadelphia, New York, Brooklyn, Baltimore, and Boston, also had a major impact on the character of baseball in the nineteenth century. Riess notes that eighty-three percent of the players in baseball's first professional league came from cities and forty percent of those players from cities along the Eastern seaboard. With baseball's professional game emerging as one of the few ways of escaping urban slums, it is hardly surprising, considering the waves of Famine and Post-Famine Irish immigrants settling into shanty towns in America's cities, that the "Sons of Erin" seemed to have a natural affinity for baseball and its rowdy play.

As for the rowdyism in baseball, the obvious cause, rather than the ethnic character of the ballplayers, would seem to be the loosely organized, financially unstable, and fiercely competitive nature of the early professional game. With the biggest payouts and profits going to the most successful players and teams, with the most skilled players rotating to the highest bidder, and with less successful teams going bankrupt and failing to meet their payrolls, baseball quickly became a cut-throat business on and off the field. The Pittsburgh club earned its team name not because of its swashbuckling play but because it stole players under contract to another team.

When baseball formed the National League in 1876 and took its first major step toward becoming a business monopoly, the owners, who now saw themselves as magnates, instituted, within a few years, a reserve clause to gain absolute control over player movement and salaries. With players now in virtual bondage to the owners, the game became even more combative — Spalding applauded it as "War"— as victory or defeat determined a player's survival in the game and his livelihood. If extra money could be made by associating with gamblers, some players were willing to take the risk.

The early professional game may have been something like a war, but not because of the ethnic stereotype of the Irish as drunken brawlers. That the stereotype of the Irish seemed to fit the early character of baseball is undeniable, but it is also undeniable that the game's economics demanded a combativeness from its players and victories on its playing fields. Once baseball became a money-making opportunity, created ironically by the same class that had turned Irish immigrants into servants and day-laborers, the Irish were among the first and became the foremost in seizing upon the game as a means to rise out of urban slums. It is true that some Irish players in the first decades of professional baseball could not handle their new financial success and celebrity status and ended their careers and sometimes their lives in disgrace and tragedy. But it is also true that many performed so well and conducted themselves with such integrity that they became a major reason for the advancement of baseball into a major sport, a big business, and a national pastime worthy of the support and passion of the American public.

While baseball historians are fond of their stories of the wild Irish and the rowdy days of the early professional game, the Irish, in reality, played the game as they found it. Once they became a major part of early base-ball, however, the Irish played with such fierce determination and success that, though they were early targets for nativism, many of them also were eventually elected into Baseball's hallowed Hall of Fame. The Irish belong in Cooperstown, not for their notoriety, but for their achievements on the field and their contributions in the transformation of a leisurely pastime for gentlemen into America's national game.

"There Is Nothing Now Heard of, in Our Leisure Hours, but Ball, Ball, Ball": Baseball and Baseball-Type Games in the Colonial Era, Revolutionary War, and Early American Republic

Thomas L. Altherr

On April 11, 1824, Bowdoin College student and future poet Henry Wadsworth Longfellow wrote to his father, who was in Washington, about a surge in ball playing on the campus:

> This has been a very sickly term in college. However, within the last week, the government, seeing that something must be done to induce the students to exercise, recommended a game of ball every now and then; which communicated such an impulse to our limbs and joints, that there is nothing now heard of, in our leisure hours, but ball, ball, ball. I cannot prophesy with any degree of accuracy concerning the continuance of this rage for play, but the effect is good, since there has been a thorough-going reformation from inactivity and turpitude.[1]

Young Longfellow's analysis of the possible effects of baseball, or some variant of it, reflected the solid position the game had achieved in American

187

recreation fifty years into the young republic. Developing over the past centuries from a variety of folk games, baseball and its variants was well on its way to becoming the national pastime a couple of decades before the use of that term.

Although most current Americans probably still believe in the "immaculate conception" theory of baseball's origins, that one June day in 1839 in Elihu Phinney's farm field in Cooperstown, Abner Doubleday drew up the rules, laid out the diamond, and taught the villagers his new game, Americans had been playing baseball and its variants long before then.

In fact, bat and ball games, are actually quite ancient and in spite of Albert Spalding's fervid wishes, not even particularly American. In his 1947 book, *Ball, Bat, and Bishop*, Robert Henderson demolished the Cooperstown origins story by pointing to numerous examples of bat and ball-type games in medieval Europe and Great Britain before and during colonization of the Americas.[2] Soon Denver historian Phil Goodstein will place another nail in the coffin with more evidence about the unreliability of the Mills Commission's "star witness," Abner Graves, whose unsavory connections in the West were many.[3] Folklorist Erwin Mehl pushed the antiquity of baseball back even further than Henderson would. In a 1948 article "Baseball in the Stone Age," Mehl located evidence of ancient bat and ball games not only in western Europe, but also in North Africa, Asia Minor, India, Afghanistan, and northern Scandinavia. "The spectators at an American baseball game, cheering a Ty Cobb or a Babe Ruth, may have had counterparts in the Stone Age," he surmised.[4] The terminology for baseball may also be quite more ancient than expected. English vicar Robert Crowley, in his 1550s poem "The Scholar's Lesson," may have referred to baseball in his advice to pupils on the advantages of healthful recreation:

> To shote, to bowle, or caste the barre,
> To play tenise, or tosse the ball,
> Or to rene base, like men of war,
> Shal hurt thy study nought at al.[5]

English professor Robert Moynihan has suggested other examples of the antic linguistic derivations of baseball terms dating to ancient, medieval, and Shakespearean times.[6]

Along with other fragmentary evidence such as a hieroglyphic scene of a bat and ball game in ancient Egypt, a 1344 French illustration of nuns and monks lined up for a ball game, a 1400s Flemish painting showing women playing a bat and ball game, eighteenth-century English diary writers' references to the game, and mention of "baseball" in Jane Austen's novel, *Northanger Abbey*, Henderson and Mehl's writings make it clear that baseball existed long before and outside an American context.[7] So, then, why not the probability of the existence of the game and its variants within the American context?

Problems of definition arise. As O. Paul Mockton pointed out in *Pastimes in Time Past*, "The very fact that so many early pastimes were all played with balls, causes great confusion, in attempting to investigate the history of these old games. Old historians were very loose in their descriptions of the way the different games were played in mediæval times."[8] Some of the "ball games" may have been actually soccer or a combination of foot-and-hand ball sports, but in the absence of firm proof, it is just as reasonable to assume that "ball play" among Euroamericans involved a stick and a ball.

Indeed, in my research for an encyclopedia of pre–1820 North American primary source sports documents, I found that the sources made distinct references to football, cricket, bandy (a type of field hockey), and fives (a forerunner of modern handball) when they meant those sports. In a couple of instances they referred to "base," "baste ball," or "baseball," leaving the possibility that the term "ball" or "to play ball" referred fairly regularly to baseball-type games.[9]

Certainly Europeans, perhaps mostly the children, but probably even adult men and women, took a swing at a variety of pre-baseball folk games: stool ball, trap ball, catapult ball, which became one o'cat (and two o'cat, three o'cat, etc.), kit-cat, munchets, tip-cat, round ball, sting ball, soak ball, burn ball, barn ball, rounders, town ball, and base, or baste, ball, and possibly others called whirl and chermany.[10] Balls were easy to make out of rags and leather and wood and feathers, and bats were paddles or tree branches.[11] Farm fields or the cozier confines of streets and alleys sufficed for the playing field. Bases were trees, chairs (hence "stool ball"), stones, and stakes. Rules were immensely flexible. For example, sources described trap ball as a "simple batting game," in which a batter hit a ball resting on a stake, much like in modern T-ball, and fielders attempted to catch the ball in order to come to bat themselves, much as in the modern game of work-up.[12]

Yet other sources, namely children's books in the 1810s depicted trap ball as a much more elaborate game in which batters tried to outhit their opponents over a series of consecutive hits, guess the lengths of their opponents' hits, or hit or pitch the ball into a special trap.

The games then were mostly spontaneous. There were no long, grueling playing seasons nor extended tournaments. But the quality of spontaneity and irregularity did not signify whimsicality. The games held importance for the players and the community. These folk games fit into the interstices of work patterns, ceremonial days, and longer leisure stretches.[13]

The first recorded instance of a baseball-type game in Anglo-America took place in 1621, in of all places, Plymouth, Massachusetts, on, of all days, Christmas Day.

Plymouth may have a spurious claim to being the starting place of "American" history, but it may have a solid claim on the start of baseball in the English colonies. The Separatists, as with many other English Reformation dissenters, did not celebrate Christmas, but rather saw it as any other day. Thus the governor, William Bradford, took a work crew out that morning. The non–Separatist English in the group begged off and Bradford relented, only to find them hard at play, playing stool ball among other sports. Bradford scolded them and recalled the episode in his journal:

> One the day called Chrismasday, the Governor caled them out to worke, (as was used,) but the most of this new-company excused them selves and said it wente against their consciences to work on that day. So the Governor tould them that if they made it a mater of conscience, he would spare them till they were better informed. So he led-away the rest and left them; but when they came home at noone from their worke, he found them in the streete at play, openly; some pitching the barr, & some at stoole-ball, and shuch like sports. So he went to them, and took away their implements, and tould them that if they made the keeping a mater of devotion, let them kepe their houses, but ther should be no gameing or revelling in the streets. Since which time nothing has been atempted that way, at least openly.[14]

Bradford and his successors may have had some success in curtailing ball games, but probably never totally suppressed them. The Dutch also played, according to Esther Singleton, in her book, *Dutch New York*, "all varieties of ball games" in New Netherlands.[15] After the turn of the century, Boston magistrate Samuel Sewall reported games of "wicket" and made one tantalizing reference to trap ball in 1713: "The Rain-water grievously runs into my son Joseph's Chamber from the N. Window above. As went out to the Barber's I observ'd the water to run trickling down a great pace from the Coving. I went on the Roof, and found the Spout next Salter's stop'd, but could not free it with my Stick. Boston went up, and found his pole too big, which I warn'd him of before; came down a Spit, and clear'd the Leaden-throat, by thrusting out a Trap-Ball that stuck there."[16]

Caesar Rodeney, an East Dover, Delaware, resident, mentioned playing trap ball, indeed quite well, twice in his journal for August, 1728. On August 24th, he scribbled, "Hart and I & James Gordon went to a Trabbal [trap ball] Match In John Willsons old feild I out Plaid them all," and a week later, he noted, "To Tim Harons: Where James Gordon & I Plaid at Trabbal against John Horon and Th Horon for an anker of Syder We woun We drunk our Syder."[17]

Clearly the British were familiar with these games, as evidenced in Irish doctor John Brickell's comment about a bat and ball game that indigenous people in North Carolina were playing about 1737: "They [indigenous peoples] have another Game which is managed with a *Battoon*, and very much resembles our *Trap-Ball....*"[18] It is tempting to wonder if this was a pre-contact game or the tribal people adapted it from early European Carolinians.

About mid-century, however, the frequency of references to baseball and baseball-type games increased. Three groups in particular, children's book writers, soldiers, and students, seem to have made the most major contributions to spreading the game. In his study of sport in colonial and Revolutionary Era New England, Bruce Daniels contended that ball sports gained less acceptance than other sports such as horseracing, but that due to "soldiers in the militia, mischievous adolescents, and the students at Harvard and Yale," the games "were on the verge of legitimacy." Daniels did not refer specifically to baseball and its variants, but mentioned wicket, bowling, shinny, fives, and football.[19] Baseball-type games were definitely in the mix. Future Philadelphia physician Benjamin Rush played so much that it caused him to lament all the time spent: "I have been ashamed likewise, in recollecting how much time I wasted when a boy in playing cat and fives...."[20]

Indeed it was a children's book that gave Americans their first *American* visual expression of the games of stool ball, baseball, and trap ball. A 1767 revised edition of a 1744 book, *A Little Pretty Pocket-Book, Intended for the Amusement of Little Master Tommy and Pretty Miss Polly*, featured engravings of scenes of boys playing each of the three games and appended the following moral verses below them:

STOOL-BALL

THE *Ball* once struck with Art and Care,
And drove impetuous through the Air,

Swift round his Course the *Gamester* flies,
Or his Stool's taken by *Surprise.*

RULE *of* LIFE

Bestow your Alms whene'er you see
An Object in Necessity.

BASE-BALL

THE *Ball* once struck off,
Away flies the *Boy*
To the next destin'd Post,
And then Home with Joy.

MORAL

Thus *Britons* for Lucre
Fly over the Main;
But, with Pleasure transported,
Return back again.

TRAP-BALL

TOUCH lightly the *Trap*,
And strike low the *Ball*;
Let none catch you out,
And you'll beat them all.

MORAL

Learn hence, my dear Boy,
To avoid ev'ry Snare,
Contriv'd to involve you
In Sorrow and Care.[21]

It is impossible to gauge just what effect a children's book had on the growth of baseball-type games, but by 1771 the province of New Hampshire felt compelled to prohibit boys and adolescents playing ball in the streets on Christmas Day for fear of damage to windows. The law, as opposed to

William Bradford's 1621 remonstrances in Plymouth, did not outlaw the game, but rather asked the players to remove to a safer location. Ball playing had apparently become an accepted Christmastide recreation. The New Hampshire law read as follows:

> An Act to prevent and punish Disorders usually committed on the twenty-fifth Day of December, commonly called Christmas Day, the Evening preceding and following said Day, and to prevent other Irregularities committed at other Times.
> *WHEREAS as it often happens that many disorders are occasioned within the town of Portsmouth,...by boys and fellows playing with balls in the public streets:....*
> And any boys playing with balls in any streets, whereby there is danger of breaking the windows of any building, public or private, may be ordered to remove to any place where there shall be no such danger.[22]

Yet it would be inaccurate to assume that only children, lazy adults, and indigenous people played baseball-type games. Revolutionary war troops were apparently enthusiasts for ball, even walking for miles to find a place level enough to play.

In the spring of 1779, Henry Dearborn, a New Hampshire officer, was a member of the American expedition in northeastern Pennsylvania, heading northwards to attack the Iroquois tribal peoples. In his journal for April 3rd, Dearborn jotted down something quite different than the typical notations of military activities: "all the Officers of the Brigade turn'd out & Play'd a game at ball the first we have had this yeare.—" Two weeks later he entered something equally eye-catching. On April 17th, he wrote: "we are oblige'd to walk 4 miles to day to find a place leavel enough to play ball."[23] On the face of it, the two journal entries might not seem all that startling, but to baseball historians they should be sort of front-page news. For Henry Dearborn was one of several, if not more, soldiers who played baseball, or an early variant of it, during the Revolutionary War, a good sixty years before another military man, one Abner Doubleday allegedly invented the game in the sleepy east central New York village of Cooperstown. Dearborn's two notations, meager as they were, suggest that the game of ball they played was more than whimsical recreation.

Tom Heitz, the longtime historian and librarian at the National Baseball Library at the Hall of Fame, has speculated that baseball-type games at this stage were like pulling a hacky-sack out of a backpack and kicking it around or playing frisbee on the college quad.[24] But what if the game was more serious, more important than that? Indeed Dearborn's writings warrant a second look. First, the earlier one reveals that the men were familiar with the game, having played it before, at least during some previous year.

Moreover the remark hints that they were eager to play again, that the weather or other circumstances had delayed their "opening day," if you will. The second entry also reflects on the place of the game in their lives. Any historian of the Revolution knows that average soldiers, and even some of the officers, despite their well-known heroism, grumbled about carrying out daily duties.

In this case, however, the prospect of playing ball was so important that they hoofed it four miles, during a time when a good day's march might have been fifteen miles, to locate a spot flat enough to get in the game. Clearly this game meant something more to Henry Dearborn and his assemblage.

The Revolutionary War contained, as do most, long stretches of boredom and busywork, camp duty and drill for the troops. They sought out recreation to alleviate this tedium. As long as the game did not involve gambling, which George Washington prohibited and prosecuted, or trample on public safety, soldiers could resort to such exercises. Presumably, as their diaries and memoirs show, baseball was in that category. The level of formality to the games was probably low. Certainly there were no organized teams nor leagues, but the embryonic pattern for such may have lain behind what soldiers saw played and played themselves at Valley Forge, in the Wyoming valley of Pennsylvania, and elsewhere. The notations were often simple, as in the case of Sharon, Connecticut, soldier Simeon Lyman, who recorded his ball playing in New London on September 6, 1775, quite tersely: "Wednesday the 6. We played ball all day."[25] Even a quick entry, however, is revealing in its information that they played *all day*. Similarly, Joseph Joslin, Jr., a South Killingly, Connecticut, teamster, observed ball playing, on April 21, 1778, while carrying out his duties for the army: "I took care of my oxen & then I went to Capt grinnels after oats and for a load of goods and then S W Some cloudy and I See them play ball...."[26] In like manner, Samuel Shute, a New Jersey lieutenant, jotted down his reference to playing ball in central Pennsylvania sometime between July 9 and 22, 1779: "..., until the 22nd, the time was spent in playing Shinny and Ball."[27] Incidentally Shute distinguished among various sports, referring elsewhere in his journal to "Bandy Wicket." He did not confuse baseball with types of field hockey and cricket that the soldiers also played.

Other soldiers made several references to playing. For example, Lieutenant Ebenezer Elmer, a New Jersey officer, chronicled ball playing in New York state, in September, 1776, and in New Jersey, in May, 1777. On

September 18, 1776, he wrote: "...The Regiment exercised 'fore and after-noon, and in the afternoon the Colonel, Parsons, and a number of us played whirl...." Two days later the troops played again and Elmer suffered a jaw injury: "At 9 o'clock, A.M., the Regiment was paraded, and grounded their arms to clear the parade; after which we had a game or two more at whirl; at which Dr. Dunham gave me a severe blow on my mouth which cut my lip, and came near to dislocating my under jaw...." "In the after-noon again had exercise.... Played ball again." A week later Elmer returned to the theme in his September 28th entry: "We had after exercise a con-siderable ball play — Colonel, Parsons and all. Parade again at 2 o'clock, but soon dismissed." Two days later, the ball play resulted in a rhubarb: "The day was so bad and so much labor going on, that we had no exercise, but some ball play — at which some dispute arose among the officers, but was quelled without rising high." The next spring, Elmer was playing ball again. His diary citation for May 14, 1777 noted: "Played ball, &c., till some time in the afternoon, when I walked up to Mr. DeCamp's, where I tarried all night."[28]

Benjamin Gilbert played ball with about the same frequency. Gilbert, a Brookfield, Massachusetts, sergeant who ironically settled later near Cooperstown, recounted ball playing in the lower Hudson River valley in the Aprils of 1778 and 1779. On April 28, 1778, he entered in his journal: "In the fore noon the Serjt went Down the hill and plaid Ball." Two days later, duty hindered his desire to play: "In the Morning I went Down the Hill to play Ball and was Called up immediately to Gather watch coats."

The next April, however, found him hard at play. On April 5, 1779, he wrote: "Our Regt Mustered at 3 oClock after noon. After Muster went to the store and plaid Ball with serjt. Wheeler." And the next day: "In the after noon the serjt. of our Regt. Went to the Comsy. store to play Ball." A week later, on the 14th, Gilbert wrote about ball again: "Fair and Clear. In the afternoon we went to the Comissary Store and Plaid Ball." Three years later, on April 7, 1782, Gilbert noted once again: "plaid at Ball severely." Whatever "severely" meant is anyone's guess; it may have been a misspelling for "severally."[29]

Indeed baseball is associated with the heights of patriotism in the war. In 1778, at Valley Forge, after that terrible winter of deprivation, George Ewing, a New Jersey ensign, recorded that the troops played baseball. In what might have been the first written use of the term "base" in North America, Ewing wrote that April: "Attested to my Muster Rolls and deliv-ered them to the Muster Master excersisd in the afternoon in the inter-vals playd at base...."[30] Even the commander of the whole Continental

Army apparently had a penchant for throwing the old horsehide around. Commenting on George Washington's character while observing him at camp at Fishkill in September, 1779, the newly-arrived secretary to the French legation, François, Comte de Barbé-Marbois, wrote, "To-day he sometimes throws and catches a ball for whole hours with his aides-de-camp."[31]

The patriots, however, did not have a monopoly on baseball; even loyalists played. Enos Stevens, a Charlestown, New Hampshire loyalist lieutenant serving near New Utrecht on Long Island, mentioned baseball several times in his journal. On May 2, 1778 he penned: "at hom all day play ball sum" On May 31st: "Lords d^y. I omit puting down every dy when their is nothing meteriel happens good weather for ball Play" Apparently Stevens saw ball play, even when the Sabbath prevented it, as more important than "nothing meteriel." On June 2nd: "fine plesent weather play ball" On June 5th: "play ball" And on June 8th: "play ball in afternoon" The next May 3rd, he recorded "in the after noon [illegible words] play ball" And in 1781, he returned to the game. On March 22nd, the entry read: "in the after noon played Wickett" And a week later, Stevens wrote "playd ball."[32]

Some of the soldiers and officers observed ball playing while they were prisoners-of-war. Lieutenant Jabez Fitch, a Connecticut officer, witnessed ball playing during his imprisonment in the New York city area in March and April, 1777.

On March 14th, he wrote: "In the Morning Lt. Blackleach made us a short Visit; this forenoon I went with Capt. Bissell down to Capt. Wells's Quarters where I procured some paper &c; on our way we lit of a number of our Offrs. who were Zealously Engaged at playing Ball, with whom we staid some time; We came home to our Quarters at about one." The next day the scene was much the same: "This Forenoon Col. Hart & Maj. Wells came to our Quarters, & we went with them down Street as far as Johanes Lotts, where there was a large number of our Offrs. collected, & spent some Time at playing Ball." About a month later, on April 12th, Fitch again saw the officers at play: "Toward Night I took a walk with Lt. Brewster down as far as Capt. Johnsons Quarters, where there was a number of our Offrs. Assembled for playing Ball; I came home alittle after Sunset."[33]

Some Americans watched or played the game while imprisoned in England. Charles Herbert, a Newburyport, Massachusetts, sailor, thus referred to ball playing as a prisoner-of-war in Plymouth, England, on April 2, 1777: "Warm, and something pleasant, and the yard begins to be dry again, so that we can return to our former sports; these are ball and quoits, which exercise we make use of to circulate our blood and keep us from things that are worse."[34] Jonathan Haskins, a Connecticut surgeon who was also in an English prison, witnessed one of the odder occurrences of a baseball-type game. On May 23, 1778, a game of ball took an odd and potentially deadly twist. Haskins wrote in his journal for that day: "23rd. This forenoon as some of the prisoners was playing ball, it by chance happened to lodge in the eave spout. One climbed up to take the ball out, and a sentry without the wall seeing him, fired at him, but did no harm."[35] Note that it was the prisoners, that is, the Americans who were playing the ball game, not their colonial overlords.

Perhaps the most intriguing evidence about soldiers playing during the Revolution came from the memoirs of Samuel Dewees, a Pennsylvania captain, who in 1781 and 1782 was a teenager guarding the British prisoners-of-war at Lancaster, Pennsylvania. Dewees recalled that the Convention Army officers had a passion for ball playing:

> These officers were full of cash, and frolicked and gamed much. One amusement in which they indulged much, was playing at ball. A Ball-Alley was fitted up at the Court-House, where some of them were to be seen at almost all hours of the day. When I could beg or buy a couple of old stockings, or two or three old stocking-feet, I would set to work and make a ball. After winding the yarn into a ball, I went to a skin-dressers and got a piece of white leather, with which I covered it. When finished, I carried it to the British officers, who would '*jump at it*' at a quarter of a dollar. Whilst they remained at Lancaster, I made many balls in this way, and sold them to the British officers, and always received a quarter a-piece.

Dewees's passage is remarkable for a number of reasons. It suggested that ball playing was quite common and an activity that players could invest with a passionate intensity. Second, skill in making balls was also apparently commonplace, as a fifteen-year old boy easily knew how to fashion them. And it is astonishing to find out that players were playing with white leather balls as early as 1781 or 1782! Dewees also recorded a brouhaha among the officers during a ball game: "Whilst the game of ball was coming off one day at the Court House, an American officer and a British officer, who were among the spectators, became embroiled in a dispute."[36]

It is unclear whether or not the Revolutionary War accelerated the familiarity of baseball in North America, as the Civil War clearly did sixty some years later. It would be useful to ascertain if prisoners-of-war taught their captors how to play the games and learned from each other during those incarcerations. Similarly, did officers play the games more often than enlisted men, or vice versa? Were the officers' games more formalized than those of the troops? The sources indicate that both sets of soldiers played, but don't make any detailed distinctions. What is discernible is that during the war, baseball-type games provided needed recreation for troops within a matrix of other sports. As Montague, Massachusetts, farmer Joel Shepard recalled baseball at a bivouac near Albany, New York, late in the war, about 1782: "We passed muster and layed in Albany about six weeks and we fared tolerable well, and not much to doo, but each class had his amusement. The officers would bee a playing at Ball on the comon, their would be an other class piching quaits, an other set a wrestling,...."[37]

Like the soldiers, students, such as Henry Wadsworth Longfellow quoted above, at the academies and colleges took a shine to the ball games. Students probably played the games, taking advantages of study breaks and lapses in college discipline to pour out onto the common for a match or two. The practice apparently could get quite rowdy. Some colleges attempted to ban the ball games because of potential property damage to windows and buildings. As early as 1764, Yale College tried to restrict hand and foot ball games. The statute, in Latin at first, and in later laws in English, read: "9. If any Scholar shall play at Hand-Ball, or Foot-Ball, or Bowls in the College-Yard, or throw any Thing against [the] College by which the Glass may be endangerd,..., he shall be punished six Pence, and make good the Damages." Later renditions changed the monetary amount to eight cents and this restriction carried into the next century with little change.[38] Dartmouth College followed suit with its own ordinance in 1780: "If any student shall play at ball or use any other diversion the College or Hall windows within 6 rods of either he shall be fined two shilling for the first offence 4 for the 2d and so no [on] at the discretion of the President or Tutors —"[39] In 1784, the University of Pennsylvania acknowledged that the yard was "intended for the exercise and recreation of the youth," but forbid them to "play ball against any of the walls of the University, whilst the windows are open."[40] Williams College followed suit in 1805: "...the students in the College and scholars in the Grammar School, shall not be permitted to play at ball, or use any other sport or diversion, in or near the College Edifice, by which the same may be exposed to injury." Violations would result in fines and possibly dismissal.[41]

Students continued to play, however, as this excerpt from diarist John Rhea Smith at Princeton College in March, 1786 shows: "A fine day, play baste ball in the campus but am beaten for I miss both catching and striking the ball."[42] Daniel Webster referred to "playing at ball" during his Dartmouth College years at the turn of the century.[43] Williams Latham played at Brown in the mid–1820s. On March 22, 1827, he declared, "We had a great play at ball to day noon." But a couple of weeks later, on April 9th, he was comlaining about the quality of the play and pitching: "We this morning ... have been playing ball, But I never have received so much pleasure from it as I have in Bridgewater They do not have more than 6 or 7 on a side, so that a great deal of time is spent runing after the ball, Neither do they throw so fair ball, They are affraid the fellow in the middle will hit it with his bat-stick."[44] Oliver Wendell Holmes, Sr. played at Harvard in 1829.[45]

Older scholars may have had some interest in the game as well. Connecticut lexicographer and writer Noah Webster may have been referring to a baseball-type game when wrote his journal entry for March 24–25, 1788: "Take a long walk. Play at Nines at Mr. Brandons. Very much indisposed."[46]

Indeed, the sabbath restrictions were breaking down. In 1836, a Georgetown University student wrote to a friend, "...the Catholics think it no harm to play Ball, Draughts or play the Fiddle and dance of a Sunday...."[47]

Such was the case apparently even in Rhode Island, according to James B. Angell: "[Sunday] was the day for visiting relatives and friends and largely for fishing and hunting and ball-playing.[48] At least one minister played the game. In his diary, Rev. Thomas Robbins detailed his ball play and that of local boys, while a divinity student at Williams College and during his teaching days. "I exercise considerable, playing ball," he wrote on April 22, 1796. In February and March, 1797, he noted that the Sheffield, Connecticut, boys were playing ball, apparently "smartly" on one occasion. The April 24th entry recorded: "Play ball some. The spring as yet rather backward." Three years later, at Danbury, Connecticut, on an unseasonably warm January day, Robbins remarked, "My boys play ball freely." And right around Christmas that same year, in another warm spell, the boys were at it again. For December 27th, Robbins wrote: "Boys play at ball till night without the least inconvenience."[49]

There was some dissent. On August 19, 1785, Thomas Jefferson urged his nephew Peter Carr to avoid ball games and take up hunting as recreation. "Games played with the ball and others of that nature, are too violent for the body and stamp no character on the mind," the future president counseled.[50]

Despite Jefferson's opinion, however, children's books continued to recommend or at least document baseball-type games for youths. Edgar and Jane, the protagonists of a British children's book, published in Baltimore in 1806, *The Children in the Wood*, wandered into a British town where some children "were playing at trap and ball."[51] In an 1806 book of poems for children, Ann Gilbert described some sort of ball play as common on the village commons:

The Village Green

Then ascends the worsted ball;
High it rises in the air;
Or against the cottage wall,
Up and down it bounces there.[52]

In a sequel volume published the next year, Gilbert included a poem warning boys about breaking windows during ball play:

Ball

MY good little fellow, don't throw your ball there,
You'll break neighbour's windows I know;
On the end of the house there is room and to spare;
Go round, you can have a delightful game there,
Without fearing for where you may throw.

Harry thought he might safely continue his play,
With a little more care than before;

So, forgetful of all that his father could say,
As soon as he saw he was out of the way,
He resolved to have fifty throws more.

Already as far as to forty he rose,
And no mischief happen'd at all;
One more, and one more, he successfully throws,
But when, as he thought, just arriv'd at the close,
In popp'd his unfortunate ball.

Poor Harry stood frighten'd, and turning about,
Was gazing at what he had done;
As the ball had popp'd in, so neighbour popp'd out,
And with a good horsewhip he beat him about,
Till Harry repented his fun.

When little folks think they know better than great,
And what is forbidden them do;
We must always expect to see, sooner or late,

That such wise little fools have a similar fate,
And that one of the fifty goes through.[53]

In an 1807 edition of *The Prize for Youthful Obedience,* a hermit who had been watching some children playing ball games approved of their play and promised "to provide 'bats, balls, &c.' at his next visit."[54] An 1802 volume, *Youthful Sports* actually touted cricket as a sport superior to what it called "bat and ball":

Cricket.

THIS play requires more strength than some boys possess, to manage the ball in a proper manner; it must therefore be left to the more robust lads, who are fitter for such athletic exercises. It must be allowed to be good diversion, and is of such note, that even men very frequently divert themselves with it. Bat and ball is an inferior kind of cricket, and more suitable for little children, who may safely play at it, if they will be careful not to break windows."[55]

Two succeeding children's recreation manuals in 1810 painted a rosier picture of trap ball. *Youthful Amusements* recommended it highly:

Trap Ball.

Without any exception, this is one of the most pleasing sports that youth can exercise themselves in. It strengthens the arms, exercises the legs, and adds pleasure to the mind.

If every time the ball be bowled to the trap, the striker be permitted to guess the number of bat's lengths from the trap, it greatly contributes to teach lads the rule of addition. And should he be so covetous as to overguess the distance, he will, as he deserves to do, forfeit his right to the bat, and give it to another playmate.[56]

Youthful Recreations went even further, offering that it should be the right of every child to have an hour of recreation each day with sports, among bat and ball-type games: "To play with *battledore* and *shuttlecock* or with a *trap* and *ball,* is good exercise; and if we had it in our power to grant, not only to the children of the affluent, but even such of the poor as are impelled by necessity to pick cotton, card wool, to sit and spin or reel all day, should have at least one hour, morning and evening, for some youthful recreation; and if they could obtain neither battledore nor shuttlecock, trap, bat, nor ball, they should at least play at *Hop-Scotch*."[57] The next year, *The Book of Games,* a look at sports at a British academy, gave a ringing endorsement to trap ball and supplied the most detailed description of it in the period.[58] *Remarks on Children's Play*, in 1819, repeated the same comments in the 1810 *Youthful Amusements* book.[59]

At the turn of the century, baseball-type games continued to provoke clashes in cities, towns, and villages. Some of their governments responded with prohibitions on such games, much as did the province of New Hampshire for Christmas Day in 1771. At its town meeting in March, 1795, Portsmouth, New Hampshire attempted to abolish cricket and any games played with a ball. The ordinance read as follows:

"VOTED III,

> That if any person or persons shall after the thirty-first day of May next, within the compact part of the town of Portsmouth,...play at cricket or any game wherein a ball is used,... he, she, or they, so offending, on conviction thereof shall forfeit and pay to the overseers of the porr of said town for the time being, for each and every offence, a sum not exceeding three dollars and thirty cents, nor less than fifty cents, and costs of prosecution,....[60]

Down the coast Newburyport, Massachusetts, passed a similar restriction two years later, adding soccer to its list of offending games:

> 12th. Voted and ordered, that if any person shall play at foot-ball, cricket or any other play or game with a ball or balls in any of the streets, lanes, or, alleys of this town, such person shall forfeit and pay a sum not exceeding one dollar nor less than twenty-five cents.[61]

In 1805 the town of Portland, Maine, promulgated a more detailed prohibition entitled "A By Law to check the practice of playing at Bat and Ball in the Streets":

> ...[N]o person shall play at the game of bat and ball, or shall strike any ball with a bat or other machine in the streets, lanes, or squares of the town, on penalty of *Fifty Cents* for each offense.[62]

A decade later and fifty miles inland, Worcester, Massachusetts considered outlawing playing ball because of numerous complaints:

> At a legal meeting May 6, 1816

> To see if the said Inhabitants will adopt any mode, or make such regulations as will in future prevent the playing Ball and Hoops in the public Streets in said Town, a practice so frequent and dangerous, that has occasioned many great and repeated complaints.[63]

Note that the town council characterized ball playing as *frequent*. The crowning irony to all of this came a month later in, of all places, Cooperstown, when that village promulgated an ordinance forbidding the playing of ball in the center of town fully twenty-three years before Abner

Doubleday supposedly drew up his diamond and rules! The June, 1816 ordinance read as follows:

> *Be it ordained,* That no person shall play at Ball in Second or West street, in this village, under a penalty of one dollar, for each and every offence.[64]

Tom Heitz has suggested that the one dollar fine was equivalent to the cost of replacing a window in those days, so perhaps the law was setting up an insurance program of sorts to cover breakage and had little hope of completely discouraging players from playing.[65]

Still boys and men continued to play ball. Keene, New Hampshire, farmer Abner Sanger noted in his journal entry for April 27, 1782: "Caleb Washburn, young Benjamin Hall, Tom Wells, the younger and El play ball before my barn."[66]

At the turn of the century at Exeter Academy ball-playing was commonplace, according to a historian of that school: "The only games seem to have been old-fashioned 'bat and ball,' which, in the spring, was played on the grounds around the Academy building, and football. The former differed widely from the moden game of base ball, which was introduced later. The old game had fewer rules, and was played with a soft leather ball." Note, however, the author's characterization of the game as old-fashioned, implying a longevity of familiarity.[67] In 1836 Albert Ware Paine recalled playing in Bangor, Maine, in the 1810s and 1820s: "But a day seems to have elapsed since meeting with our neighboring boys, we took delight in flying our kite and prancing our horses on the green or engaged ourselves in the more active sports of 'playing ball' or goal.'"[68] New York City octogenarian Charles Haswell reminisced that if "a base-ball was required, the boy of 1816 founded it with a bit of cork, or, if he were singularly fortunate, with some shreds of india-rubber; then it was wound with yarn from a ravelled stocking, and some feminine member of his family covered it with patches from a soiled glove."[69] Sometimes memoirists mentioned baseball only to say that they avoided the game or regretted what they considered a waste of time and industry. Thus Wilmington, Delaware ship captain John Hamilton wrote about his boyhood in the 1790s that reading about foreign countries "took precedence [over] Kites, Marbles, Balls, Shinny Sticks, and all other Boyish Sports."[70] Similarly, Cannon's Ferry, Delaware, doctor William Morgan remarked about his adolescence in the 1790s, "My sixteenth, seventeenth and eighteenth yeares were spent in youthfull folley. Fidling, frolicking, ball playing and hunting as far as I could be spared by my father from his employ. These are called inocent amusements and ware not caried very far by me."[71] Sometimes, however, ball games led to further adventures. Jonathan

Mason, Jr., a Boston merchant, remembered a special game of ball on the Boston Commons in the 1790s or early 1800s:

> Another early remembrance of the common besets me. One morning, the day after what was called the Negro election, Benj Green, Martin Brimmer, George E Head, Franklin Dexter and myself were playing ball on the common before breakfast: and the ball fell into a hole where one oif the booth's stakes had been driven the day before, which was filled up with paper, rubbage etc. putting the hand down something jingled and we found several dollars in silver which had probably been put there for safety and the owner becoming intoxicated late in the day had gone off and forgotten them. I can't recollect that we advertised them. We were small boys then all of us, and I was the youngest.[72]

And even though he claimed he had never heard the word "baseball" in the 1820s, Middletown, Connecticut, resident John Howard Redfield remembered that baseball-type games were pervasive:

> The remainder of Election week was given more or less to relaxation and amusement. This period usually coincided with the vacation, or gap bewteen the winter and summer terms of school. Ball was the chief amusement, and if weather permitted (and my impression is that it generally *did* permit) the open green about the meeting-house and the school-house was constantly occupied by the players, little boys, big boys, and even *men* (for such we considered the biggest boys who condescended to join the game).... These grown-up players usually devoted themselves to a game called "wicket," in which the ball was impelled along the ground by a wide, peculiarly-shaped bat, over, under, or through a wicket, made by a slender stick resting on two supports. I never heard of baseball in those days.[73]

Clearly, as these prohibitions, depictions in children's books, and remembrances indicate, baseball and its predecessors were entrenched in the young republic's athletic repertoire by 1820.

Other evidence hints that the games had spread to the South and to Canada. John Drayton, a South Carolina politician and historian, referred to ball playing in his state about 1802: "[A]musements are few; consisting of dancing, horse racing, ball playing, and rifle shooting."[74] Another South Carolinian, Charles Fraser, recalled in 1854, how vibrant were the sports of his childhood in Charleston in the early art of the century: "The manly sports of ball, shinee, jumping, running, wrestling, and swimming, are now laid aside as unworthy of modern refinement. But they were as common among the elder boys of my time, as marbles, tops and kites were among the little ones."[75] Ely Playter, a York, Ontario, tavernkeeper, may have meant baseball or a baseball-type game when he wrote in his diary for April 13, 1803: "I went to Town ... walk'd out and joined a number of men jumping & playing Ball, perceived a Mr. Joseph Randall to be the most active...."[76] Incipient commercialism may also have been invading the games. The New York *Evening Post* for September 20, 1811, contained an advertisement for "Trap Ball, Quoits, Cricket, &c." at Dyde's Military Ground.[77]

The most bizarre bit of evidence of baseball's spread may have occurred in conjunction with a tragic incident just after the close of the War of 1812. The British were still housing numerous American prisoners at Dartmoor Prison in England, awaiting repatriation arrangements. Needless to say, tempers ran high and the British officers occasionally tormented the Americans.

As had other prisoners-of-war before them, some of the Americans whiled away their incarceration by playing baseball. For example, American prisoners-of-war back in North America at Cornwall, Ontario, mixed ball with their boxing. Wrote one prisoner, "The men remained in the gaol yard and fought several times and in fact played [ball — the editor mistakenly translated the word as "hell"] all day."[78] Similarly one prisoner, Benjamin Waterhouse, recalled the Americans at Dartmoor were in "high spirits and good humour" about going home and reflected it in their play: "I distinctly remember that the prisoners appeared to enjoy their amusements, such as playing ball and the like, beyond what I had before observed."[79] On April 6th, such was the case. As inmate Nathaniel Pierce recalled, "...first part of this day the Prisoners divirting themselves Gambling playing Ball &c."[80] During the afternoon, however, things went awry. A batter hit the ball over one of the interior walls and the British sentries would not allow the players to retrieve it. As prisoner Charles Andrews later wrote, "...some boys who were playing ball in No. 7 yard, knocked their ball over into the barrack-yard, and on the sentry in that yard refusing to throw it back to them, they picked a hole in the wall to get in after it."[81] Another inmate, Joseph Valpey, Jr., described the scenario in more detail:

> On the 6th day of April 1815 as a small party of prisoners were amusing themselves at a game at ball, some of the number striking it with too much violence it went over the wall fronting the prison the Centinals on the opposite side of the same were requested to heave the ball back, but refused, on which the party threataned to brake through and regain the ball and immediately put their threats in execution, a hole was made in the wall sufficently large enough for a man to pass through....[82]

The British officers misconstrued this breach of the interior wall as some sort of riot and ordered troops to fire at the ball players. By the end of the melee there were seven dead and thirty-one wounded prisoners.

By the 1820s, the games were taking on the more organized form of clubs. In his autobiography, New York politician Thurlow Weed claimed to have been a member of a town ball club in Rochester in 1825:

> Though an industrious and busy place, its citizens found leisure for rational and healthy recreation. A base-ball club, numbering nearly fifty members, met every afternoon during the ball-playing season. Though the members of the club embraced persons between eighteen and forty, it attracted the young and the old. The ball-ground, containing some eight or ten acres, known as Mumford's meadow, by the side of the river above the falls, is now a compact part of the city.

Weed went on to list ten of the better players on that club and point out that a couple of them rose to prominence as lawyers in New York City.[83] Although some historians think that the mounting popularity of baseball in the intervening decades may have colored Weed's memoir, Samuel Hopkins Adams, in the story, "Baseball in Mumford's Pasture Lot," in his book, *Grandfather Stories*, corroborated Weed with a scene in which Grandpa Adams informed his grandson and friends that he had played baseball back in Rochester in 1827. "When I first came here, the Rochester Baseball Club met four afternoons a week. We had fifty members. That was in 1827," the old man recounted. The club played in "Mumford's pasture lot, off Lake Avenue." Furthermore, he told them, "The cream of Rochester's Third Ward ruffleshirts participated in the pastime," which was clearly baseball, not town ball, as the old man described the positioning of the fielders and mentioned that it took three outs to retire the batting side.[84]

Yet it would be a mistake to see baseball and baseball-type games as very modern by the 1820s, at least not in the sense that sport historians such as Allen Guttmann have stipulated. Presumably there was an equity in the rules, that each player played under the same conditions, but there may have been exceptions to that. There was certainly no bureaucratization overseeing baseball-type games. There may or may not have been specialization; players most likely played nonspecific positions on the playing field and probably the pitcher, or "feeder" was not a very important position yet. How much players were experimenting to perfect the rules or methods of playing the game is also unclear.

Quantification, at least in the form of statistics that carried over time, were nonexistent, and if there were any "records," they didn't make it into any "recordbook."[85] Local players may have kept up an oral memory of great players and great plays, but it is just as likely that the emphasis was on play, spontaneity, and communal recreation. Baseball and similar games were still folk games, with all their rubbery aspects and irregular patterns. That does not mean, however, that they were any less important to the populace than are modern sports today. Baseball and baseball-type games existed with some degree of frequency, because they filled a cultural hunger for physical play and communal recreation, a yearning of time immemorial. The above sources, and probably others still undiscovered in the record, attest to the American phase of this long process.

Henry Dearborn and his fellow soldiers deserve thanks not only for helping to convince the British to lose the war, but for marching four miles that day in April, 1779, "to find a place leavel enough to play ball," and all the ball-playing students, such as Longfellow, merit our remembrances as well.

Finally though, the origins of the game may have to remain shrouded in mystery. Perhaps, as Harold Seymour wrote, "To ascertain who invented baseball would be equivalent to trying to locate the discoverer of fire."[86] Perhaps it was an entirely "natural" occurrence. As James D'Wolf Lovett stated, "It seems to be the natural instinct of a boy as soon as he finds the use of his arms, to want to 'bat' something."[87] Possibly the instinct is quite deep-seated and the Freudians and other psychoanalysts can weigh in with theories such as Adrian Stokes' provocative interpretation that cricket developed as a form of sexual sublimation.[88] Or maybe Kenneth Patchen's explanation in his poem, "The Origin of Baseball," comes as close as any:

> Someone had been walking in and out
> Of the world without coming
> To much decision about anything.
> The sun seemed too hot most of the time.
> There weren't enough birds around
> And the hills had a silly look
> When he got on top of one.
> The girls in heaven, however, thought
> Nothing of asking to see his watch
> Like you would want someone to tell
> A joke — 'Time,' they'd say, 'what's
> That mean — time?', laughing with the edges
> Of their white mouths, like a flutter of paper
> In a madhouse. And he'd stumble over
> General Sherman or Elizabeth B.
> Browning, muttering, 'Can't you keep
> You big wings out of the aisle?' But down

Again, there'd be millions of people without
Enough to eat and men with guns just
Standing there shooting each other.

So he wanted to throw something
And he picked up a baseball."[89]

Notes

1. Henry Wadsworth Longfellow to Stephen Longfellow, April 11, 1824, in Samuel Longfellow, ed., *Life of Henry Wadsworth Longfellow with Extracts from His Journals and Correspondence*, 2 vols. (Boston: Ticknor and Company, 1886), v. 1, 51.

2. Robert W. Henderson, *Ball, Bat, and Bishop* (New York: Rockport Press, 1947).

3. Goodstein, who is not particularly a baseball historian, has uncovered evidence of Graves' involvement in financial misdealings and shooting a spouse, as well as committals for mental illness, in years prior to his testimony for the Mills Commission. The Mills Commission also ignored testimony that baseball existed before 1839, especially a letter from a man who had played the game in Portsmouth, New Hampshire as a school child in 1830. See also "Origins of Baseball" in Jonathan Fraser Light, ed., *The Cultural Encyclopedia of Baseball* (Jefferson, North Carolina: McFarland and Company, 1997), 530; Harold Seymour, "How Baseball Began," *New York Historical Society Quarterly*, v. 40, n. 1 (October 1956), 369–385; and Uriel Simri's little-known dissertation, "The Religious and Magical Function of Ball Games in Various Cultures," West Virginia University, 1966.

4. Erwin Mehl, "Baseball in the Stone Age," *Western Folklore*, v. 7, n. 2 (April 1948), 145–161 (quotation is from page 161), and Mehl, "Notes on 'Baseball in the Stone Age'," *Western Folklore*, v. 8, n. 2 (April 1949), 152–156.

5. Robert Crowley, "The Scholars Lesson," in J. M. Cowper, ed., *The Select Works of Robert Crowley* (London: N. Trubner and Company, 1872), 73.

6. Robert Moynihan, "Shakespeare at Bat, Euclid on the Field," in Alvin L. Hall, ed., *Cooperstown Symposium on Baseball and the American Culture (1989)* (Westport, Connecticut: Meckler Publishing Company, 1991), 319–323.

7. See Mark Alvarez, *The Old Ball Game* (Alexandria, Virginia: Redefiniton, 1992), 10–12. See also "Origins of Baseball," in Light, ed., *The Cultural Encyclopedia of Baseball*, 528–531.

8. O. Paul Monckton, *Pastimes in Times Past* (Philadelphia: J.B. Lippincott Company, 1913), 52.

9. Thomas L. Altherr, ed., *Sports in North America: A Documentary History, Volume I, Parts I and II, Early American Sports to 1820* (Gulf Breeze, Florida: Academic International Press, 1997).

10. Ron MCulloch, *How Baseball Began* (Los Angeles: Warwick Publishing Company, 1995), 4 and 6; and Per Maigaard, "Battingball Games," *Genus*, v. 5, n 1–2 (December 1941), 67. An 1866 book on outdoor games also refers to a game called "ball-stock," which is German and origin and resembles town ball. There is no way of ascertaining, however, from the book, if the game existed before 1839. *The Play Ground; or, Out-Door Games for Boys* (New York: Dick and Fitzgerald, Publishers, 1866), 112–113.

11. McCulloch, *How Baseball Began*, 3. Ann McGovern, in a book targeted for adolescents, *If You Lived in Colonial Times* (New York: Scholastic Incorporated, 1992 [1964]), stated on page 52, without documentation, "Most of all, boys liked to play ball. They played with a leather ball filled with feathers."

12. Mehl, "Baseball in the Stone Age," 147.

13. For an excellent discussion of the place and role of folk games and sports in pre-colonial and colonial English culture, see Nancy Struna, *People of Prowess: Sport, Leisure, and Labor in Early Anglo-America* (Urbana, Illinois: University of Illinois Press, 1996), *passim*, but especially chapter 1.

14. William Bradford, *Of Plymouth Plantation*, Harvey Wish, ed. (New York: Capricorn Books, 1962), 82–83.

15. Esther Singleton, *Dutch New York* (New York: Dodd, Mead and Company, 1909), 290.

16. M. Halsey Thomas, ed., *The Diary of Samuel Sewall 1674–1729, Volume II: 1709–1729* (New York: Farrar, Straus and Giroux, 1973), 718.

17. Harold B. Hancock, ed., "'Fare Weather and Good Helth': The Journal of Caesar Rodeney, 1727–1729," *Delaware History*, v. 10. n. 1 (April 1962), 64.

18. John Brickell, *The Natural History of North-Carolina* (Dublin: James Carson, 1737), 336.

19. Bruce C. Daniels, *Puritans at Play: Leisure and Recreation in Colonial New England* (New York: St. Martin's Press, 1995), 174.

20. Benjamin Rush to Benjamin Rush Floyd, April 21, 1812, in Lyman H. Butterfield, ed., "Further Letters of Benjamin Rush," *Pennsylvania Magazine of History and Biography*, v. 78, n. 1 (January 1954), 43.

21. *A Little Pretty Pocket-Book, Intended for the Amusement and Instruction of Little Master Tommy and Pretty Miss Polly* (London: J. Newbery, 1767), 88, 90, and 91.

22. "An Act to prevent and punish Disorders usually committed on the twenty-fifth Day of December,....," 23 December 1771, *New Hampshire (Colony) Temporary Laws, 1773* (Portsmouth, New Hampshire, [1773–1774]), 53.

23. Lloyd A. Brown and Howard H. Peckham, eds., *Revolutionary War Journals of Henry Dearborn 1775–1783*, (Freeport, New York: Books for Libraries Press, 1969 [1939]), 149–150.

24. Tom Heitz, conversations with the author, June and August, 1996.

25. [Simeon Lyman], "Journal of Simeon Lyman of Sharon Aug. 10 to Dec. 28, 1775," in "Orderly Book and Journals Kept by Connecticut Men While Taking Part in the American Revolution 1775–1778," *Collections of the Connecticut Historical Society*, v. 7 (Hartford: Connecticut Historical Society, 1899), 117.

26. [Joseph Joslin, Jr.], "Journal of Joseph Joslin Jr. of South Killingly A Teamster in the Continental Service March 1777–August 1778," in "Orderly Book and Journals Kept by Connecticut Men While Taking part in the American Revolution 1775–1778," *Collections of the Connecticut Historical Society*, v. 7 (Hartford: Connecticut Historical Society, 1899), 353–354.

27. [Samuel Shute], "Journal of Lt. Samuel Shute," in Frederick Cook, ed., *Journals of the Military Expedition of Major General John Sullivan against the Six Nations of Indians in 1779* (Freeport, NY: Books for Libraries Press, reprint of 1885 ed.), 268.

28. [Ebenezer Elmer], "Journal of Lieutenant Ebenezer Elmer, of the Third Regiment of New Jersey Troops in the Continental Service," *Proceedings of the New Jersey Historical Society*, v. 1, n. 1 (1848), 26, 27, 30 and 31, and v. 3, n. 2 (1848), 98.

29. Rebecca D. Symmes, ed., *A Citizen-Soldier in the American Revolution: The Diary of Benjamin Gilbert in Massachusetts and New York*, (Cooperstown, New York: New York State Historical Association, 1980), 30 and 49; and "Benjamin Gilbert Diaries 1782–1786," G372, New York State Historical Association Library, Cooperstown, New York.

30. [George Ewing], *The Military Journal of George Ewing (1754–1824) a Soldier of Valley Forge* (Yonkers, New York: Thomas Ewing, 1928), 35.

31. Eugene Parker Chase, ed., *Our Revolutionary Forefathers: The Letters of François, Marquis de Barbé-Marbois during His Residence in the United States as Secretary of the French Legation 1779–1785* (New York: Duffield and Company, 1929), 114.

32. Charles Knowlton Bolton, ed., "A Fragment of the Diary of Lieutenant Enos Stevens, Tory, 1777–1778, *New England Quarterly*, v. 11, n. 2 (June 1938), 384–385, but the original, more accurate journal, from which the above notations come, is at the Vermont Historical Society, Montpelier, Vermont.

33. William H. W. Sabine, ed., *The New-York Diary of Lieutenant Jabez Fitch of the 17th (Connecticut) Regiment from August 22, 1776 to December 15, 1777* (New York: pvt. ptg., 1954), 126, 127, and 162.

34. [Charles Herbert], *A Relic of the Revolution, Containing a Full and Particular Account of the Sufferings and Privations of All the American Prisoners Captured on the High Seas, and Carried into Plymouth, England, During the Revolution of 1776* (Boston: Charles H. Peirce, 1847), 109.

35. Marion S. Coan, ed., "A Revolutionary Prison Diary[:] The Journal of Dr. Jonathan Haskins," *New England Quarterly*, v. 17, n. 2 (June 1944), 308.

36. John Smith Hanna, ed., *A History of the Life and Services of Captain Samuel Dewees, A Native of Pennsylvania, and Soldier of the Revolutionary and Last Wars*, (Baltimore: Robert Neilson, 1844), 265 and 266.

37. John A. Spear, ed., "Joel Shepard Goes to the War," *New England Quarterly*, v. 1, n. 3 (July 1928), 344.

38. *Collegii Yalensis, Quod est Novo-Portus Connecticutensium, Statuta, a Præside et Sociis Sancita* (New Haven, Connecticut: Benjamin Mecom, 1764), 9; and *The Laws of Yale-College, in New-Haven, in Connecticut, Enacted by the President and Fellows* (New Haven, Connecticut: Thomas and Samuel Green, 1774), 11.

39. *Dartmouth College Laws and Regulations*, 1780, Dartmouth College Library, Special Collections MS 782415.

40. *RULES for the Good Government and Discipline of the SCHOOL in the UNIVERSITY of PENNSYLVANIA* (Philadelphia: Francis Bailey, 1784).

41. *The Laws of Williams College* (Stockbridge, Massachusetts: H. Willard, 1805), 40.

42. John Rhea Smith, 22 March 1786, in "Journal at Nassau Hall," Princeton Library MSS, AM 10841, quoted in Varnum Lansing Collins, *Princeton* (New York: Oxford University Press, 1914), 207.

43. Daniel Webster, *Private Correspondence*, Fletcher Webster, ed., 2 vols. (Boston: Little Brown and Company, 1857), v. 1, 66. See also Vernon Bartlett, *The Past of Pastimes* (London: Chatto and Windus, 1969), 45.

44. Williams Latham, "The Diary of Williams Latham, 1823–1827" (unpublished), quoted in Walter C. Bronson, *The History of Brown University, 1764–1914* (Providence: Brown University, 1914), 245. James D'Wolf Lovett remembered that Boston boys in that era didn't find the shortage of players so problematic. If his crowd couldn't summon up enough players for town ball or baseball, the boys reverted to playing the simpler games of one old cat, two old cat, three old cat, or whatever configuration fit. Lovett, *Old Boston Boys* (Boston: Riverside Press, 1906) 127–128.

45. John A. Krout, *Annals of American Sport* (New Haven, Connecticut: Yale University Press, 1929), 115.

46. [Noah Webster] "Diary," reprinted in Emily Ellsworth Fowler Ford, ed., *Notes on the Life of Noah Webster*, 2 vols. (New York: pvt. ptg., 1912), v. 1, 227.

47. Georgetown student letter, August 27, 1836, Georgetown University Library, quoted in Betty Spears and Richard Swanson, *History of Sport and Physical Activity in the United States*, 2d Ed. (Dubuque, Iowa: William C. Brown Company, 1983), 85.

48. James B. Angell, *The Reminiscences of James Burrill Angell* (London: Longmans, Green, and Company, 1912), 14.

49. Increase N. Tarbox, ed., *Diary of Thomas Robbins, D.D. 1796–1854*, 2 vols. (Boston: Beacon Press, 1886, v. 1, 8, 29, 32, 106, and 128.

50. Thomas Jefferson to Peter Carr, August 19, 1785, in Julian P. Boyd, ed., *The Papers of Thomas Jefferson*, 23 vols. (Princeton, New Jersey: Princeton University Press, 1953–), v. 8, 407.

51. Clara English, *The Children in the Wood, An Instructive Tale* (Baltimore: Warner and Hanna, 1806), 29.

52. [Ann Gilbert] *Original Poems, for Infant Minds*, 2 vols. (Philadelphia: Kimber, Conrad, and Company, 1806), v. 2, 120. Gilbert's verse re-appeared in an 1840 pamphlet, *The Village Green, or Sports of Youth* (New Haven: S. Babcock), 5, with the word "worsted" changed to "favorite" and with an accompanyiing woodcut showing four boys playing baseball.

53. [Gilbert], *Original Poems, for Infant Minds*, 2 vols. (Philadelphia: Kimber, Conrad, and Company, 1807), vol, 1, 88–89.

54. *The Prize for Youthful Obedience* (Philadelphia: Jacob Johnson, 1807), Part II [16].

55. *Youthful Sports*, (Philadelphia: Jacob Johnson, 1802), 47–48.

56. *Youthful Amusements* (Philadelphia: Johnson and Warner, 1810), 37 and 40.

57. *Youthful Recreations* (Philadelphia: Jacob Johnson, 1810), no pagination.

58. *The Book of Games; or, a History of the Juvenile Sports Practised at Kingston Academy* (Philadelphia: Johnson and Warner, 1811), 15–20.

59. *Remarks on Children's Play* (New York: Samuel Wood and Sons, 1819), 32.

60. *By-Laws of the Town of Portsmouth, Passed at their Annual Meeting Held March 25, 1795* (Portsmouth, New Hampshire: John Melcher, 1795), 5–6.

61. *Bye-Laws of Newburyport; Passed by the Town at Regular Meetings, and Approved by the Court of General Justice of the Peace for the County of Essex, Agreeably to a Law of This Commonwealth* (Newburyport, Massachusetts, 1797), 1.

62. *The By Laws of the Town of Portland, in the County of Cumberland, Second Ed.* (Portland, Maine: John McKown, 1805), 15. Italics in the original source.

63. Worcester, Massachusetts Town Records, 6 May 1816, reprinted in Franklin P. Rice, ed., *Worcester Town Records, 1801–1816, Vol. X* (Worcester, Massachusetts: The Worcester Society of Antiquity, 1891), 337.

64. Cooperstown, New York village ordinance, 13 June 1816, reprinted in the Cooperstown, New York *Otsego Herald*, n. 1107, 13 June 1816, 3.

65. Tom Heitz, conversations with the author, June and August, 1996.

66. Lois K. Stabler, ed., *Very Poor and of a Lo Make: the Journal of Abner Sanger* (Portsmouth, New Hampshire: Peter E. Randall, 1986), 416.

67. Frank H. Cunningham, *Familiar Sketches of the Phillips Exeter Academy and Surroundings* (Boston: James R. Osgood and Company, 1883).

68. Albert Ware Paine, "Auto-Biography," reprinted in Lydia Augusta Paine Carter, *The Discovery of a Grandmother* (Newtonville, Massachusetts: Henry H. Carter, 1920), 240.

69. Charles Haswell, *Reminiscences of an Octogenarian 1816 to 1860* (New York: Harper and Brothers, 1896), 77.

70. John Hamilton, "Some Reminiscences of Wilm't'n and My Youthful Days — &c., &c." *Delaware History*, v. 1, n. 2 (July 1946), 91.

71. Harold B. Hancock, ed., "William Morgan's Autobiography and Diary [:] Life in Sussex County, 1780–1857," *Delaware History*, v. 19, n. 1 (Spring–Summer 1980), 43–44.

72. Jonathan Mason, Jr., "Recollections of a Septuagenarian," 3 vols., Downs Special Collections, Winterthur Library, Document 30, v. 1, 20–21.

73. Edmund Delaney, ed., *Life in the Connecticut River Valley 1800–1840 from the Recollections of John Howard Redfield* (Essex, Connecticut: Connecticut River Museum, 1988), 35. Italics in the original source.

74. John Drayton, *A View of South-Carolina, As Respects Her Natural and Civil Concerns* (Charleston, South Carolina: W. P. Young, 1802), 225.

75. Charles Fraser, *Reminiscences of Charleston, Lately Published in the Charleston Courier, and Now Revised and Enlarged by the Author* (Charleston, South Carolina: John Russell, 1854), 88.

76. [Ely Playter] "Extracts from Ely Playter's Diary," April 13, 1803, reprinted in Edith G. Firth, ed., *The Town of York 1793–1815: A Collection of Documents of Early Toronto* (Toronto: The Champlain Society, 1962), 248.

77. *New York Evening Post*, n. 2867, September 20, 1811, 2.

78. G.M. Fairchild, Jr., ed., *Journal of an American Prisoner at Fort Malden and Quebec in the War of 1812* (Quebec: pvt. ptg., 1090), no pagination.

79. [Benjamin Waterhouse] *A Journal of a Young Man of Massachusetts, Late a Surgeon on Board an American Privateer, Who Was Captured at Sea by the British, in May, Eighteen Hundred and Thirteen, and Was Confined First, at Melville Island, Halifax, then at Chatham, in England, and Last, at Dartmoor Prison* (Boston: Rowe and Hooper, 1816), 186.

80. "Journal of Nathaniel Pierce of Newburyport, Kept at Dartmoor Prison, 1814–1815," *Historical Collections of Essex Institute*, v. 73, n. 1 (January 1937), 40.

81. [Charles Andrews] *The Prisoners' Memoirs, or Dartmoor Prison* (New York: pvt. ptg., 1852), 110. In another memoir, prisoner Josiah Cobb referred to the ball being thrown over the wall by accident, something that happened somewhat frequently. [Cobb] *A Green Hand's First Cruise, Roughed Out from the Log-Book of Memory, of Twenty-Five Years Standing: Together with a Residence of Five Months in Dartmoor*, 2 vols. (Boston: Otis, Broaders, and Company, 1841), v. 2, 213–214. For the testimony of other prisoners, see I.H. Waddell, *Dartmoor Massacre* (Pittsfield, Massachusetts: Phinehas Allen, 1815), 6–21.

82. [Joseph Valpey, Jr.] *Journal of Joseph Valpey, Jr. of Salem, November, 1813–April, 1815* (Detroit: Michigan Society of Colonial Wars, 1922), 60.

83. Harriet A. Weed, ed., *Life of Thurlow Weed*, 2 vols. (Boston: Houghton Mifflin, 1883), v. 1, 203.

84. Samuel Hopkins Adams, *Grandfather Stories* (New York: Random House, 1955 [1947]), 146–149.

85. Allen Guttmann, *From Ritual to Record: The Nature of Modern Sports* (New York: Columbia University Press, 1978), chapter 2, and Guttmann, *A Whole New Ball Game: An Interpretation of American Sports* (Chapel Hill, North Carolina: University of North Carolina Press, 1988), 6.

86. Seymour, "How Baseball Began," 376.

87. Lovett, *Old Boston Boys*, 125.

88. Adrian Stokes, "Psycho-analytic Reflections on the Development of Ball Games, Particularly Cricket," *The International Journal of Psycho-analysis*, v. 37 (1956), 185–192.

89. Kenneth Patchen, "The Origin of Baseball," in Patchen, *Selected Poems* (New York: New Directions, 1957), 15–16.

Baseball as a Symbiosis of Interests: A Survey of Men and Women at Minor League Games in the Midwest

Dave Ogden

Introduction

John Hocking has described two components of a baseball game: the field event (the activities between the chalk lines) and the stadium event (activities in the stands).[1] Brad Shore is more vivid in his description. Baseball, he says, is "a kind of oscillating engagement, an alternation between attention to the public spectacle at hand and the withdrawing of attention into more private or domestic pursuits, such as small talk or buying a hot dog...."[2]

This study focused on whether men and women perceived their involvement in this "engagement" differently and whether such differences reflect traditional gender-based learning theories and the sports sociology literature. Are men and women interested in attending baseball games for different reasons? Are men more inclined than women to follow the field action and discuss the game? Are women more inclined to attend to significant others and to view the occasion as a group or family outing?

Literature Review

Society has traditionally associated males with aggressiveness and competition and females with nurturance and passivity. The family unit and the school greatly influence the formation of the perceived "balance of power" among the sexes in social situations and relationships.[3] Mass media is another agent in reinforcing traditional gender roles. Such exposure has a significant impact in the formation of perceptions of the self and of what society expects in interest, attitude and behavior.[4]

Women are taught to think of themselves as caregivers and nurturers, while men learn that their success and social fit "hinge on accomplishments in a competitive world."[5] For males, "the need for self-esteem is clearly regarded as higher and more valuable than the need for affiliation," and the need for self-actualization is even greater. Females, on the other hand, "place greater emphasis than men do on communion, that is, on the experience of living within a community of others."[6]

Playing sports is one way in which youngsters are prepared for a competitive world and learn how to build self-esteem. Sports is also another way in which gender ideals are enforced, since boys more so than girls are encouraged by their fathers to participate, and more is expected of boys.[7] In a study of youth soccer, coaches paid more attention and devoted specific instruction to boys and provided "female athletes with less specific and technically oriented instructional feedback, feedback which is so necessary to develop into a more skilled and competitive athlete."[8] Youth baseball is no different. One study found that coaches gave female tee-ball players little encouragement, compared with the encouragement given to the male players.[9]

At home females' interest in sports may be further constrained. Evidence of that can be seen in the television viewing patterns of parents with their children. Fathers are more likely to watch sports with their young sons, rather than with their daughters, and older girls are "the least likely to watch sports programs."[10]

Females may find that as they grow older their opportunities to express their opinions and thoughts on sports remains limited. Women generally are not considered members of the "inner fan circle" and seldom engage in "sports talk."[11] Other research that shows that females have more trouble than males "asserting their authority or considering themselves as authorities" and "in expressing themselves in public so that others will listen."[12] Women's talk is "typically devalued by men and women alike" and their interest or pursuit of knowledge in certain intellectual and cultural areas is often considered "incompatible with female capabilities."[13]

In addition, women, especially those whose learning styles depend on a feeling of connectedness with others, may refrain from discourse that appears argumentative. Women tend to take such discussions "personally" and "continue to fear that someone may get hurt."[14] Could that be the case when sports is the topic of discussion? Sports talk for men often turns into a competition via display of one's sports knowledge.[15] Women whose learning styles reflect a maturity and balance of perspectives "resent the implicit pressure in male dominated circles to toughen up and fight to get their ideas across." These women, who enjoy sharing information for the construction of knowledge, prefer "real talk," in which "domination is absent, reciprocity and cooperation are prominent."[16]

Are such differences in learning styles reflected in the behavior of men and women at ball games? Do men and women perceive their experiences and roles as baseball spectators differently? This study provides answers to those questions.

Methods

Self-completion surveys were distributed during the 1998 season to more than 1,100 spectators at 40 games of the Omaha Royals (Triple-A affiliate of the Kansas City Royals) and the Sioux City Explorers (of the independent Northern League). In all, surveys were used from 1,074 respondents (648 men and 426 women). Respondents had to be at least 21 years of age to participate. Mean age of male respondents was 42 years and the mean age of female respondents was 42.2 years.

The 37-item survey instrument was based on issues raised in the sports sociology and learning theory literature and borrowed from instruments previously used in spectator research at ballparks.[17] Early versions of the instrument were refined and restructured and items were refined and rewritten after pilot studies with the instrument at several 1998 Major League Baseball spring training games in Florida and at several Omaha Royals games early in the season. Chi square, independent samples t-test, and multiple regression were the primary statistical techniques used to analyze the data.

The ballpark survey was supplemented with a follow-up phone interview of 30 respondents who indicated on the survey their willingness to participate in this second stage of data collection. The phone interview provided more indepth information on the respondent's history of exposure to baseball, perspectives on the role of baseball in family relationships, and perception of recent issues in Major League Baseball and the state of the professional game.

Results

As baseball spectators men and women differed little, if at all, in some respects. Men and women attended the same number of games in 1997 and

1998 (about eight each year). Men and women agree that baseball games serve as opportunities to be with friends and family, according to items on a five-point Likert scale (see Table 1). Their actual attendance reflected their perspective. One gender was as likely as the other to report attending with family and friends.

Men and women also agree (as indicated by a Likert item on the ballpark survey) that the pace of most baseball games is not too slow. Most female respondents interviewed by phone (and some male respondents) expressed strong feelings. Patrick, a serviceman in the Navy, was one of those, who said that the absence of time impositions "makes baseball unique" and "separates it from football and basketball." Joni, a self-described "fanatic," called it "the beauty of baseball.... It takes what it takes to play a game, no longer and no shorter."

TABLE 1
INDEPENDENT SAMPLES T-TEST FOR LIKERT-SCALE ITEMS

	Men		Women	
	M	SD	M	SD
1. Enjoy game to be with friends	4.14	.752	4.16	.831
2. Like to discuss plays	3.75****	.927	3.48	1.00
3. Enjoy crowd activities	3.17	1.13	3.62****	1.11
4. Like PA to provide stats	4.00**	.876	3.86	.875
5. Enjoy game to be with family	4.26	.905	4.36	.856
6. Enjoy argument or confrontation	2.69	1.24	2.59	1.30
7. Enjoy watching team mascot	3.68	.993	3.96****	.888
8. Enjoy talk shows/Web/chat groups	3.33****	1.09	2.90	1.07
9. Visit about family/work	2.62	1.15	2.89****	1.20
10. Enjoy keeping score/stats	2.58****	1.11	2.35	1.04
11. Support team when losing	4.30	.717	4.26	.712
12. Pace of games too slow	2.69	1.12	2.63	1.14

Note. Judgments were made on five-point scales.
(1 = strongly disagree, 5 =strongly agree)
**$p < .01$
****$p < .001$

Sylvia, a 79-year-old retiree, said:

> The game must be played as it is, or it no longer is baseball. Things take time to happen and it takes time to set up situations. You can't mess with the mechanics of that. If it takes time to throw a strike or to strike a batter out, then it takes time. That's baseball.

Both genders also disliked violence and angry outbursts by players (see Table 1). Men and women interviewed via phone cited Albert Belle, Roberto Alomar and Felix Martinez as players who discredit the game because of their involvement in brawls and confrontations.

In many respects, however, men and women differ as spectators. One of those is in how family and friends influence decisions to attend games. One third of the women said they came to a game because their significant other wanted them to come or they wanted to be with that person or the family. Slightly less than 25 percent of men reported those reasons for their decisions. Almost 53 percent of the men said their attendance at the game was their "personal choice," compared with 43 percent of women who stated that. $\chi2$ (5, N = 1070) = 20.45, p = .001 (see Table 2).

TABLE 2
FACTOR ON WHICH RESPONDENT
BASES DECISION TO ATTEND GAME

	Men	*Women*
Personal choice	342 (52.8%)	185 (43.7%)
Spouse/other wanted me to come	22 (3.4%)	38 (8.9%)
To be with family/significant other	139 (21.5%)	102 (24.1%)
Friend/associate wanted me to come	32 (4.9%)	24 (5.6%)
To be with friend	26 (4%)	13 (3.1%)
Other reason	86 (13.2%)	61 (14.4%)

Note. Percentages in each column do not add up to 100% because of rounding.
df = 5, $\chi2$ = 20.45, p = .001

These findings are bolstered by a chi-square analysis showing a significant difference between the number of women who reported coming to the game with "spouse or significant other" and the number of men who did so. $\chi2$(1, N = 1073) = 9.787, p = .001. Almost 55% of the women respondents reported coming to the game with their spouses or significant others, compared to 45% of the men (see Table 3).

TABLE 3
WHO ACCOMPANIED RESPONDENTS TO THE GAME

	Men	*Women*
Friend(s)	195 (30%)	136 (30%)
Family other Than spouse	302 (46.7%)	194 (45.7%)
Spouse	292 (45%)	233 (54.8%)
Came Alone	44 (6.7%)****	7 (1.6%)

Note. Results are from chi-square on individual items in multiple
  response question. For men N = 648, and for women N = 425.
**$\chi2$ (1, N = 1073) = 9.78, p < .01.
****c2 (1, N = 1073) = 14.99, p < .001.

Women were also more apt than men to pay attention to those who accompanied them. A chi-square analysis on a series of dyads in the ballpark survey showed that women were significantly more likely than men to prefer "talking with family or friends" than to "second guessing the manager's call" to $\chi 2$ (1, $N = 1035$) = 25.21, $p < .001$.

Slightly more than 77% of women chose the former over the latter, while 62% of men made that choice. Women were also more likely to get caught up in the crowd, and what Hocking (1982) calls "the stadium event." A chi-square analysis of another dyad showed a significant difference between the percentage of men (52%), who preferred "talking with others about game strategy" more than participating in crowd activities, and the percentage of women (27%) who did so, $\chi 2$ (1, $N = 1039$) = 60.36, $p < .001$. (see Table 4, p. 13).

These findings were magnified by the responses of those interviewed by phone. Paul, a 68-year-old insurance salesman, and Larry, a 60-year-old feed truck driver, typified the male responses when they said they don't like to talk about anything other than what's happening on the field. "Some people come to games to socialize," said Larry. "Mostly, I just like to watch the game."

Laura, a 43-year-old accountant and a self-described "ho-hum" fan, reflected the feelings of other women who were interviewed by phone.

> I talk about the concessions, or if we see somebody we know, or if they're doing things like "the wave." I think they do those things ... because it gets boring and fans don't get as involved unless there's something happening. But he [her husband] doesn't get distracted from the game like I do.

TABLE 4
PREFERENCES FOR PAIRED ITEMS
DESCRIBING BALLPARK EXPERIENCE

	Men	Women
Pair A		
Watching plays	511 (80.4%)	255 (62.9%)
Special events	125 (19.6%)	151 (37.1%)
Pair B		
Second-guessing manager	242 (38%)	92 (23%)
Talking with family/friends	394 (62%)	307 (77%)
Pair C		
Talking strategy	326 (51.8%)	112 (27.4%)
Clapping/cheering	304 (48.2%)	297 (72.6%)

	Men		Women	
Pair D				
Watching a play	520	(82.4%)	287	(71.9%)
Gift giveaways	112	(17.6%)	113	(28.1%)

Note.
Pair A: df = 1, χ2 = 39.14, p < .001.
Pair B: df = 1, χ2= 25.21, p < .001.
Pair C: df = 1, χ2= 60.36, p < .001.
Pair D: df = 1, χ2= 18.13, p < .001.

Men more so than women use media to follow baseball (see Table 5). Men watched an average of almost six hours of baseball each week on TV, compared with about four hours of baseball viewing each week for women. Men reported that they listened to baseball three-and-a-half hours each week on the radio. Women listened one-and-a half hours weekly. Men read about baseball in the newspaper almost five times each week, with women reading about half as many times.

TABLE 5
INDEPENDENT SAMPLES T-TEST ON
NUMBER OF HOURS SPENT WEEKLY
FOLLOWING BASEBALL VIA MASS MEDIA

	Men		Women	
	M	SD	M	SD
Newspaper	4.75****	3.07	2.41	2.79
Radio	3.56****	9.47	1.51	3.62
TV	5.63****	9.34	3.69	6.24
Web	.79**	3.04	.34	1.86

Note. Newspaper is measured in number of times read each week.
**p < .01
****p < .001

It's not surprising then that men interviewed by phone were more self-assured and confident in their knowledge of the game. Women deferred to others for such knowledge. When asked from whom they sought information when they didn't understand a play, women said they depended on their husbands, mass media, or the person next to them for their information, or they stayed uninformed. But for most men, such sources were a last resort. The majority said that their expertise was enough to carry them through most situations. Scott said it's "very rare" for him not to understand a play or an umpire's call, and Tom stated that "there's very seldom a call I don't understand." Bryan, 30 and a marketing manager, described his level of knowledge in stronger terms.

I've been around this game a lot, and I've seen and played a lot. I wouldn't think at this point in my life that there would possibly be a play that I wouldn't understand. I suppose there could be something happen on the field, like some arcane rule that I wouldn't know about. But I doubt that will happen.

The feelings men and women have toward the game, however, are not as divergent as their self-perceived knowledge. Both feel the game is a relaxing way to spend time with family and friends, and both are optimistic about baseball's future. Many phone respondents felt the McGwire-Sosa home run chase in 1998 re-established interest in the game. These respondents also feel the sting from the 1995 Major League Baseball players' strike and think that baseball's burgeoning economic structure could alienate increasing numbers of spectators. Said one of the phone respondents: "A family with lots of kids can find it pretty expensive. They [professional baseball organizations] need to get their prices down.... Baseball doesn't listen to its fans."

Discussion and Conclusions

Both men and women consider an outing to the ballpark as a good way to spend time with family and friends, but men and women diverge in their particular interests in the event itself. Results indicate that women are more likely to serve a support role, in coming with family and spouse, and emulating behavior consistent with interests of their group. Men, on the other hand, also use the game as a family outing, but their interests, more so than women's, lie in the action on the field and communication with other "fans."

Male significant others or husbands took the lead in choosing to see the game, with women significantly more often reporting that they came to the game at the request of or to be with their spouse or significant other. These results support research that shows women watched sports "because it gave them something to do with their friends or family."[18] The results also lend credence to other findings that women's enjoyment of baseball "may stem from joint participation with their male partners, rather than from the characteristics of the sport themselves."[19]

The way women in the study approached an outing to the ballpark clearly reflects learning styles and ways of knowing attributed to females by the literature.[20] Their main interest was that of the group or person with whom they attended, and they sought affiliation with the larger group of spectators through stadium activities.

Participation in these activities, like cheering and clapping with the crowd, creates connections between individual spectators.[21] Reaping whatever an experience has to offer by establishing or re-establishing connections with others is one of the hallmarks of feminist learning. For women, attachment to the community enriches life and intimacy with the community comes before identity with the community.[22] Being connected with others drives the learning process for women, and women more so than men are displaying that style through their spectatorship.

In doing so women sustain the social order that frames the baseball spectating experience. They are not passive members of the crowd. They help to create the milieu from which springs activities and events outside the field action. Their support role does not mean sacrifice. Unlike some of the literature on women's learning, women do not necessarily subjugate their interests to that of their family's, significant other's or spouses in attending games.[23] Women were as focused on activities of the crowd and group immediately surrounding them as men were on the game itself. Women weren't simply idling away time as their husbands or significant others attended to the game. They didn't mind the slow pace of the game and used that time attending to family and/or friends or to the larger stadium community in which they were enveloped. Not only their attention, but their conversation was also directed toward family and friends.

Men interacted, as well, and a majority of them also came to the game to enrich their relationships with family and friends. But they sought connection to enrich their vicarious involvement with the game. Men talked about baseball with others during games and, compared with women, felt as if they had a larger community with whom to engage in everyday discussions about baseball. As concluded by other authors, baseball talk is still a "man's world."[24]

Men are also the greatest media consumers of baseball. This study confirms that, with men spending more than five hours a week watching baseball on TV, Major League Baseball's emphasis on regional coverage and its multiple network packages are solid strategies for marketing to male audiences. Local broadcasters and regional cable networks are gambling $380 million in rights fees that those strategies work.[25] This study should give sportscasters confidence that carrying the games of their area's Major League Baseball teams is a good investment for reaching male audiences.

On the other hand, the Major Leagues have good reasons for targeting women as consumers at the ballpark. According to this study, women attend as many games as men. Indeed, women more so than men seem to enjoy what has been called "intra-audience effects," in which "the mass of spectators watching a sport show create conditions in which perception is influenced by interaction between spectators. Imitation as a way of establishing contact appears here in the most striking form...."[26] As discussed earlier, Hocking bisects the game into two events: the field event and the stadium event, with intra-audience effects a part of the latter.[27] By providing evidence of women's interest in the stadium event and men's interest in the field event, this study explains how spectators view the relationship between the two events. The ballpark experience creates a symbiosis between those events and the interests upon which they are focused, with the action on the field being punctuated by the response of and activity in the crowd. Many spectators in this study want that action to remain unpressured and unfettered by time. The responses of men and women in this study is that tinkering with the game's pace should be limited. Many women recognize what Brad Shore calls the "oscillating engagement," in which lulls in the field action accommodate events or activities in the stands.[28]

Gender differences in interest in the field and stadium events may serve as a sociological explanation for this "oscillating engagement." Although baseball reflects a divergence of interests, it creates a convergence of those interests to give depth and richness to the overall experience for the fans. Becoming a baseball "fan" often begins through relationships already forged via earlier experiences with family and friends. At the same time, the interchanges and relationship-building that is integral to a cohesive social group can take place within the relaxed cadence of the baseball game.

It must be remembered that interest in the field event versus the stadium event does not strictly follow the gender line. After all, a majority of men and women named favorite baseball teams, and the majority of men said they preferred talking with family or friends rather than "second-guessing the manager" (although the percentage of women who also cited that preference was significantly higher).

The extent to which each gender actually engages in stadium event activities needs further research. Such research would require actual observation of crowd activities to determine, among other things, who initiates or participates in crowd activities, such as clapping, cheering, and the "wave," or who is wearing baseball-related apparel.

How much a person's interest has to do with childhood exposure to baseball is another area worthy of exploration. Are there differences in length and intensity of childhood exposure between gender? If there are differences, is there any relationship between them and differences in the amount of baseball spectatorship and media use for baseball? The answers to these questions could have profound implications for professional baseball's future and for its long-term marketing strategies.

Notes

1. John E. Hocking, "Sports and Spectators: Intra-audience Effects," *Journal of Communication*, Winter 1982, pp. 100–108.

2. Brad Shore, *Culture in Mind: Cognition, Culture and the Problem of Meaning* (New York: Oxford University Press, 1996), p. 78.

3. Jack Mezirow, *Transformative Dimensions of Adult Learning*, (San Francisco: Jossey-Bass Publishers, 1991).

4. C.A. Tuggle, "Sportscenter Tonight," *Journal of Broadcasting & Electronic Media*, Winter 1997, pp. 14–24.

5. M.B. Nelson, *The Stronger Women Get, the More Men Love Football*, (New York: Harcourt Brace & Company, 1994), p. 97.

6 Danielle D. Flannery, "Changing Dominant Understandings of Adults as Learners," in *Confronting Racism and Sexism*, eds. Elisabeth Hayes and Scipio A.J. Colin (San Francisco: Jossey-Bass, 1994), p. 21.

7. D. Stanley Eitzen and George H. Sage, *Sociology of American Sport,* (Dubuque, Ia.: Wm. C. Brown Company Publishers, 1982).

8. P. Dubois, "Gender Differences in Value Orientation Toward Sports: A Longitudinal Analysis," *Journal of Sport Behavior*, vol. 13 no. 1, 1990, p. ____.

9. M. A. Landers and G. A. Fine, "Learning Life's Lessons in Tee Ball: The Reinforcement of Gender and Status in Kindergarten Sport," *Sociology of Sport Journal*, No. 13, 1996, pp. 87–93.

10. M. St. Peters, M. Fitch, A. C. Hurston, J. C. Wright, and D. J. Eakins, "Television and Families: What Do Young Children Watch with Their Parents?" *Child Development*, no. 62, 1991, p. 1414.

11. Gregory Stone, "Some Meanings of American Sport: An Extended View. In Gerald Kenyon (ed.) *Proceedings of C.I.C. Symposium on the Sociology of Sport* (Chicago: The Athletic Institute, 1969), pp. 5–19.

12. M. F. Belenky, B. M. Clinchy, N. R. Goldberger, and J. M. Tarule, *Women's Ways of Knowing: The Development of Self, Voice, and Mind*, (New York: Basic Books, Inc., 1986), pp. 4–5.

13. *Ibid.* p. 17

14. *Ibid.* p. 105.

15. Nelson, pp. 108–109.

16. Belenky, Clinchy, Goldberger and Tarule, p. 146.

17. Barrett A. Lee and Carol A. Zeiss, "Behavioral Commitment to the Role of Sport Consumer: An Exploratory Analysis," *Sociology and Social Research*, no. 64, 1980, pp. 405–419.

18. Walter Gantz and Lawrence A. Wenner, "Men, Women and Sports: Audience Experiences and Effects," *Journal of Broadcasting and Electronic Media*, no. 35, 1991, p. 238.

19. M. E. Roloff and D. H. Solomon, "Sex Typing, Sports Interests, and Relational Harmony," in *Media, Sports, & Society*, ed. Lawrence A. Wenner (Newbury Park: Sage Publications, 1989), p. 307.

20. Flannery, pp. 17–26.

21. Hocking, pp. 100–108

22. Carol Gilligan, *In a Different Voice: Psychological Theory and Women's Development*, (Cambridge: Harvard University Press, 1982).

23. E. J. Tisdell, "Feminism and Adult Learning: Power, Pedagogy, and Praxis," in *An Update on Adult Learning Theory*, ed. Sharan B. Merriam, (San Francisco: Jossey-Bass Publishers, 1993), pp. 91–103.

24. D. Anderson and G. P. Stone, "Responses of Male and Female Metropolitans to the Commercialization of Professional Sport 1960 to 1975," *International Review of Sport Sociology*, vol. 16 no. 3, pp. 5–21. Collins, P.H. (1990). *Black Feminist Thought*. London: Harper Collins Academic.

25. K. McAvoy, "Show Me the Money," *Broadcasting & Cable*, 29 March 1999, pp. 24–30.

26. Hocking, pp. 100–108.

27. *Ibid.*

Joe DiMaggio and the Ideal of American Masculinity

William Simons

For many, the mere mention of Joe DiMaggio's name conjures up a series of indelible tableaux. His place in American culture far transcends baseball. DiMaggio personifies the ideal of American masculinity. Joseph Durso noted in *The New York Times*, "In a country that has idolized and even immortalized its twentieth century heroes, from Charles A. Lindbergh to Elvis Presley, no one more embodied the American dream of fame and fortune or created a more enduring legend than Joe DiMaggio. He became a figure of unequaled romance and integrity in the national mind...."[1] From the intense realism of Ernest Hemingway's *The Old Man and the Sea* to the whimsical satire of *Doonesbury*, DiMaggio is the standard by which others measure their masculinity.

Joe DiMaggio is a hero, an exemplar of American masculinity. More than any other player in baseball history, he symbolizes the masculine ideal. Honus Wagner, Christy Mathewson, Lou Gehrig, Bob Feller, Stan Musial, and Mark McGwire have been role models, but their place in the popular culture has neither been as prominent nor enduring as that of DiMaggio. Caveats emerge when other baseball superstars are evaluated as male role models. Driven by inner demons, Ty Cobb, a racist and sociopath, trampled upon basic decencies. Joe Jackson and Pete Rose are forever linked to gambling scandals. Despite baseball and military heroics, Ted Williams too often lost control of his tempestuous emotions. And the eponymic sluggers who preceded and followed DiMaggio in the Yankee outfield, Babe Ruth and Mickey Mantle, were, according to *USA Today* reporter Erik Brady, "overgrown adolescents."[2] DiMaggio was an adult. If Ruth represented disreputable masculinity, DiMaggio epitomized masculine respectability.

And our racial protocols have impeded the emergence of a black DiMaggio in the American culture. Paternalism pervaded depictions of Joe Louis and Jesse Owens even as they were hailed as symbols of American democracy. Jack Johnson and Muhammad Ali polarized contemporaries. And Michael Jordan's prominence has yet to survive decades of retirement. Segregation deprived players in the Negro Leagues of the recognition they merited. Before his premature death, Josh Gibson, arguably the greatest power hitter of all-time, suffered from the recurrent delusion that Joe DiMaggio would not shake his hand. Circumstances rendered the courageous Jackie Robinson, who transformed baseball and America, a figure of controversy. Public perceptions of Willie Mays, perhaps even a better all-around player than DiMaggio, emphasized enthusiastic ebullience rather than heroic gravity. Milwaukee, distant from the nation's media centers, contributed to Hank Aaron's comparative obscurity during much of his career, and racism limited contemporary appreciation for the records set in his final seasons. Barry Bonds and Ken Griffey, Jr., excel in a game no longer the undisputed national pastime.

Indeed, the fact that DiMaggio was baseball's best player when it was the undisputed national pastime elevated his place in the national culture. So too did his good fortune in playing for sports' most storied franchise during its most successful era in the city that then dominated the nation's media. The fabled romance with Marilyn Monroe, appreciative prose by Ernest Hemingway and Paul Simon, official anointment as baseball's "greatest living ballplayer," and a dignified presence in highly visible Bowery Savings Bank and Mr. Coffee commercials kept the DiMaggio flame burning brightly throughout the years. Nearly a half-century after he played his last major league game, DiMaggio's illness and death received the attention that the demise of a former president might receive. A *Newsweek* cover story, special thirty plus page wraparound tributes in both New York's *Daily News* and *Post,* the lead front page story in nearly every other newspaper in the nation (including the *Wall Street Journal*), editorial tribute, commentary from intellectual and cultural authorities, television specials, many flags at half-staff, and the renaming of the West Side Highway marked DiMaggio's death.

In life DiMaggio perhaps endured longer than any other figure as a heroic symbol in the national consciousness. He even outlasted Jimmy Stewart. From his brilliant 1936 rookie season until his death over 62 years later in 1999, Joe DiMaggio was a living hero. Davy Crockett, Abraham

Lincoln, Teddy Roosevelt, James Dean, Babe Ruth, Clark Gable, John Kennedy, Bobby Kennedy, Martin Luther King, Jr., and Elvis Presley, for example, did not even live 62 years. For Thomas Jefferson, Andrew Jackson, Robert E. Lee, Andrew Carnagie, Thomas Edison, Charles Lindbergh, Franklin Roosevelt, Dwight Eisenhower, John Wayne, Mickey Mantle, and Jonas Salk, the interval between apotheosis and death was far less than for DiMaggio. And so many tragic Audie Murphys and Jim Thorpes outlived their honor. But neither time nor physical decline diminished DiMaggio's appeal. In DiMaggio's final years, Americans still felt a chill as the last introduction at Old-Timers' games gave us one more glimpse of "the greatest living ballplayer."

In the final inning of his long life, DiMaggio retained his heroic aura. Had illness and death not intervened he would have thrown out the first ball at both the 1998 World Series and the 1999 Yankee home opener. As baby boomers entered middle age, they developed belated appreciation for the accomplishments of their parents, the generation that endured the Great Depression and defeated Hitler. And DiMaggio was one of the last remaining icons of that era. Director Steven Spielburg termed his popular 1998 film "Saving Private Ryan" a tribute to his father's generation. And Tom Brokaw's 1998 book *The Greatest Generation* rose to the top of the best sellers list extolling the virtues of the men and women who came of age during the Great Depression and World War II. As one of the last surviving icons of that era, DiMaggio benefitted from the renewed respect granted his generation. The Associated Press termed "Current Yankees Awestruck by Joltin' Joe." So powerful a hold did DiMaggio have on the American mind that a respondent to a survey taken by *The Daily Star* of Oneonta, New York, a week after the Yankee Clipper's death answered "Joe DiMaggio" to the query "Who do you think will be the most influential sports figure in 1999?"[3]

It was not merely sports that DiMaggio influenced. He provided an ideal for respectable masculinity. In *Manhood in America: A Cultural History* (1996), sociologist Michael Kimmel argues "that the quest for manhood — the effort to achieve, to demonstrate, to prove our masculinity, has been one of the formative and persistent experiences in men's lives." Although a "multiplicity of masculinities... collectively define men's actual experiences," an idealized normative standard exists in the American consciousness. Although Kimmel is critical of the ideal, believing that devotion to it has rendered its adherents emotionally inarticulate, he emphasizes its prominence in American culture. Kimmel asserts that the dominant masculine ideal possesses the following attributes: not allowing domination by others, control over oneself, emotional autonomy, exemption from home and family, self improvement and economic success, honor and morality, rendering the world safe for women and children, stoic confrontation of pain and hardship, recognition by others of one's achievements, protection of reputation and serving as role model for others in an all-male domain.[4] Classic American heroes — James Fenimore Cooper's frontiersman, John Wayne's cowboy, and Humphrey Bogart's urban detective possess these attributes. But none more so than Joe DiMaggio's baseball player.

DiMaggio possessed many admirable qualities, but his limitations received abbreviated attention. Introverted and insecure, DiMaggio, for example, suffered from ulcers and insomnia. And, according to various Monroe biographers, including Robert Slatzer, DiMaggio was so obsessed with Marilyn that he stalked his former wife for a time.[5] Moreover, his inability to sustain relations led to estrangement from his only child. This is not to suggest that DiMaggio was a fraud, but our focus is the icon of popular culture, not that most private of men. A small coterie of revisionists and iconoclasts raised caveats. When DiMaggio held out for more money in the spring of 1938, it was one of the few times he was widely resented. But redemption came quickly. Yet a 1966 *Esquire* article by Gay Talese portrayed an aging DiMaggio as bored, lonely, and discontented.[6] Furthermore, a *Newsday* article, following DiMaggio's death, bore the title "Joe Was a Hero to Many, but Not All."[7] Likewise, Ottaway News Service columnist Ken Lovett wrote on March 20, 1999, "DiMaggio ... certainly should not be held up as a role model."[8] Moreover, a *New York Daily News* article by Bill Madden and Luke Cyphers claimed that in his final years DiMaggio could not protect himself from the exploitative machinations of his business manager.[9] And *New York Times* pundit Robert Lipsyte gave this posthumous assessment of DiMaggio—"Private to the point of paranoia."[10] Nonetheless, in the main currents of the American mind, DiMaggio is a peerless hero. The DiMaggio of popular culture meets Kimmel's eleven criteria of the masculine ideal.

Not Allowing Domination by Others

The ultimate test of an individual's capacity to avoid domination by others is to leave this life on one's own terms. In life Joe DiMaggio valued privacy, dignity, courage, and grace. He departed this world with his cherished virtues intact. During his 99-day hospitalization, he fought gallantly against pneumonia, cancer, and media intrusion. DiMaggio mounted several remarkable comebacks. The Yankee Clipper survived the last rites of the Catholic Church and a premature announcement of his death by NBC. Emerging from a coma, he issued directives. DiMaggio's resilience amazed the doctors. At his insistence, the public was misled about the severity of his illness. And DiMaggio made the decision that he would die at his Hollywood, Florida, home. On March 8, 1999, Joseph Paul DiMaggio died, as he lived, gracefully. With three family members, two friends, and hospice attendant Javier Ribe present, DiMaggio, radiant of face and lucid of mind, spoke his final words: "I love all of you." It was, recalled Ribe, "one of the most beautiful and peaceful deaths that I have ever seen."[11]

DiMaggio had planned his funeral with meticulous detail, even to where to get the cold cuts following the service. Attendance at the funeral was by invitation only. About 80 people, primarily family and friends, entered the vast cathedral. No celebrities.

Commissioner Bud Selig and American League President Gene Budig were the only baseball representatives admitted. George Steinbrenner and Reggie Jackson were excluded. Police kept throngs of reporters and onlookers across the street. No baseball mementoes adorned SS Peter and Paul Roman Catholic Church. His brother Dominic, the last survivor amongst Joe's eight siblings and formerly the Red Sox center fielder, gave a simple yet moving eulogy. As the *New York Daily News* observed, "With a dignity that echoed his years as a Yankee superstar and American icon, Joseph DiMaggio was laid to rest...."[12]

Control over Oneself

DiMaggio's manner of death reflected the demeanor of his life. His self-control was nearly absolute. Ty Cobb, Leo Durocher, Ted Williams, and Albert Belle are amongst the many as noted for their emotional outbursts as for their baseball talents. It is impossible to imagine DiMaggio taunting opponents, kicking an umpire in the shins, spitting at fans, or trying to run over children. As to why he did not engage in dramatic displays of emotion, Deadpan Joe explained, "I can't. It wouldn't look right."[13] As a baseball player, DiMaggio almost never lost control over himself. The most atypical incident involved kicking the dirt around second base when Brooklyn outfielder Al Gionfriddo's spectacular catch deprived him of a home run during the 1947 World Series.

Thomas Jefferson envisioned God as the Supreme Architect. In fashioning a perfect creation, Jefferson's God exhibited an "economy of nature," wasting no energy and engaging in no superfluous activity. It was, believed Jefferson, the task of humanity to emulate the Creator. That is how

DiMaggio played baseball, wasting no energy and engaging in no superfluous activity. Creating the illusion of slow motion through his balletic grace, DiMaggio made the difficult look easy. A *New York Times* editorial asserted, "The combination of proficiency and exquisite grace which Joe DiMaggio brought to the art of playing center field was something no baseball average can measure and that must be seen to be believed."[14] Honus Wagner's awkward mastery, Mickey Mantle's powerful but undisciplined swing, and Willie Mays' dramatic catches with hat askew were all foreign to DiMaggio's economy of energy. It was said that DiMaggio made few theatrical plays in the field; his mastery and self-control were such that he had no need for dramatics. DiMaggio "was the perfect Hemingway hero", observed David Halberstam. He exhibited stoic "grace under pressure."[15] DiMaggio's self-control was so finely honed that he even conveyed quiet dignity endorsing Mr. Coffee.

Emotional Autonomy

Mr. Coffee was an appropriate endorsement for DiMaggio. He drank a good deal of coffee. He was also a moody, irritable, silent, chain-smoking loner. Like the frontiersman, cowboy, and urban detective, Joe DiMaggio was emotionally autonomous. He led the league in room service. "The essential American soul," wrote D.H. Lawrence, "is hard, isolate, stoic."[16] That was DiMaggio's character. He was not a chatty middle infielder. DiMaggio's domain was the vast and remote frontier of Yankee Stadium's center field. As George F. Will observed, DiMaggio, like Charles Lindbergh, "wore an aura of remoteness."[17] Inner directed, DiMaggio was not defined by others. When his wife Marilyn Monroe, fresh from entertaining troops in Korea, giddily announced, "Joe, you never heard such cheering!" DiMaggio quietly responded, "Yes, I have."[18] Dave Anderson of the *New York Times* recognized that the Yankee Clipper maintained privacy "even better than he played."[19] Sportswriter Jimmy Cannon knew that DiMaggio was both central to and apart from his Yankee teammates: "There were guys who played with him for years and considered him a stranger, but on the field he was the closest anyone ever came to them. His greatness was part of the whole of the team and the loneliness was defeated because this is where he belonged...."[20]

Exemption from Home and Family

Emotionally autonomous frontiersmen, cowboys, and urban detectives were exempt from ties to home and family. So too was Joe DiMaggio.

In his eulogy, brother Dom noted that Joe never found a lifetime partner. His two marriages were of brief duration. DiMaggio's discreet liaisons with anonymous showgirls created no ties that bind. He never truly inhabited the San Francisco house that his widowed sister Marie kept for him. A peripatetic bachelor by inclination, DiMaggio lived out of trains, airplanes, and hotel rooms.

Even from his few friends and relatives, including brother Dom, Joe went through periods of estrangement. Thus it is not surprising that DiMaggio did not form lasting connections to home and family. The most tragic estrangement was with his son Joe, Jr., who in middle age, despite an Ivy League education, lived in a trailer park and worked in a junkyard. In 1946 Joe and Joe, Jr., then a child, posed together on the cover of *Sport*. Again, in 1961 when Joe, Jr., was a young man, they shared a *Sport* cover. Father and son wore Yankee uniforms in the *Sport* photographs. Baseball was not a sufficient bond, however. Feeling the burden of his name, Joe, Jr., a good player, quit baseball in adolescence. Baseball was the essence of the father. And an emotionally inarticulate father playing catch with his son finds generational communication tenuous when the father's legacy burdens the son. At the end of the movie *Shane*, a boy cries for the cowboy to return, but the man knows it is his destiny to live apart from home and family. Joe DiMaggio also knew.

Self-Improvement and Economic Success

Self-improvement and economic success are both quintessential American goals. Benjamin Franklin's *The Autobiography of Benjamin Franklin* pays homage to those virtues as do subsequent generations of motivational literature. Joe DiMaggio was a self-made man. As a baseball player, DiMaggio drove himself relentlessly. A meritocracy, sport produces an elite of talent. Remarkable ability and maximum effort brought DiMaggio to the top of his profession. He became, in David Halberstam's apt phrase, "the preeminent *athlete*" of his generation.[21] DiMaggio's pursuit of self-improvement extended beyond his baseball craft.

DiMaggio reinvented himself. He learned to dress well, making Taub's list of ten best-dressed men in 1939. Through extensive dental work, DiMaggio further enhanced his appearance. He confronted his shyness and insecurities by attending the Dale Carnegie Institute. As host of a television baseball show in the early 1950s, he was awkward and wooden. By the 1970s, DiMaggio had transformed himself into a poised and polished commercial spokesman for Mr. Coffee and The Bowery Savings Bank.

DiMaggio, the son of an Italian immigrant fisherman, was a classic Horatio Alger hero. He rose from humble obscurity to fame and riches. Spectacular baseball success and tough contract negotiating made him the game's highest paid player. Baseball folklore is replete with tales of former stars like Grover Cleveland Alexander who squandered their money and died in poverty. In contrast, DiMaggio augmented his largess after retiring as a player. He invested his money wisely. DiMaggio was a well-paid commercial spokesman. And during his last years, DiMaggio earned millions of dollars in the sports memorabilia industry. His autograph commanded a higher price than that of any other living American.

Honor and Morality

DiMaggio pursued the American dream of economic success, but his honor was not for sale. In 1951 injuries and age diminished DiMaggio's baseball performance. Nonetheless, DiMaggio's stature in the game was such that Yankee owners Don Topping and Del Webb offered him the same $100,000 contract he had received in 1951 to return for another season even if he chose to play only home games or limit his role to pinch hitting. The Yankee owners told DiMaggio he would remain the game's highest paid player in the 1952 campaign. Topping confessed, "We tried everything we possibly could to get him to stay. But we couldn't convince him. I don't know why he had to quit. Sick as he was last season he did better than most of the players hanging around."[22]

But "hanging around" would have violated DiMaggio's moral code. At the December 11, 1951, press conference announcing his retirement, DiMaggio spoke of honor: "I once made a solemn promise to myself that I wouldn't try to hang on once the end was in sight. I've seen too many beat-up players struggle to stay up there, and it's always a sad spectacle."[23] An honorable man lives by a moral code. No matter how high the compensation or reduced the obligations, DiMaggio would not sacrifice his honor. DiMaggio's words made clear that he would retire on his own terms: "I feel that I reached the stage where I can no longer produce for my ball club, my manager, my teammates, and my fans."[24]

DiMaggio's professional honor was not for sale, nor was his personal honor. Joe DiMaggio was a man of integrity. His life was not for sale. When DiMaggio died, Monica Lewinsky was on the cover of *Time* magazine. Promoting her book, Lewinsky gave explicit details about tawdry sexual encounters with President Bill Clinton. And Clinton himself, publicly engaging in strategic concessions and unpersuasive denials, embodies the sexual antithesis of DiMaggio.

As for DiMaggio, he dated a number of showgirls. He married Dorothy Arnold, an actress, and Marilyn Monroe, the woman every man desired. Comparing Frank Sinatra unfavorably to DiMaggio, Monroe revealed to a confidant Joe's great sexual prowess. But DiMaggio never spoke to a third party about private moments with Marilyn Monroe, Dorothy Arnold, or any other woman. An honorable man does not make public his romantic and physical intimacies. And Joe DiMaggio never violated his moral code.

DiMaggio was outraged by the scene in "The Seven Year Itch" where the gust from a subway grate revealed more of his wife Monroe than he was willing to share with the public. A romantic hero, DiMaggio loved Monroe with a powerful emotional intensity. Through the years, he received several offers, worth millions of dollars, to write a book about his relationship with Monroe. DiMaggio always refused. A gentleman is discreet; he does not kiss and tell. It is immoral. Joe DiMaggio's integrity and memories were not for sale. Not at any price.

Rendering the World Safe for Women and Children

Joe DiMaggio helped render the world safe for women and children. His chivalry toward Marilyn Monroe was not confined to keeping her confidences inviolate. In the years after their divorce, Marilyn, vulnerable and unstable, would repeatedly turn to DiMaggio's strength when overwhelmed by her emotions. Although tormented by her promiscuity, DiMaggio never refused Marilyn's desperate pleas for help. Joe was always there in her times of crisis. When a psychiatric hospital refused to discharge Monroe, DiMaggio won her release with the warning, from a man who did not make idle threats, that "if you don't give her to me, I will take this place apart, piece of wood by piece of wood."[25] Then, DiMaggio, his playing career a decade in the past, took Marilyn to the safety of the Yankee spring training camp. Long divorced, Joe gallantly secured a separate hotel room for Marilyn. Buoyed by Joe's strength, Marilyn felt better. For a time.

In the end, even DiMaggio could not save her. Stalked by her neuroses and celebrity, Marilyn took her own life in August 1962. If DiMaggio could not protect Marilyn in life, he would shield her in death. Barring celebrities and the media, DiMaggio took control of her funeral. When DiMaggio was warned that important people expected to attend Monroe's funeral, he turned them away with a fierce retort: "Tell them if it wasn't for them, she'd still be here."[26] In death DiMaggio gave Marilyn a poignant dignity that eluded her in life. For DiMaggio, the gallant romantic, even death did not end the tragic relationship with his beloved Marilyn. DiMaggio sent roses three times a week to Marilyn's crypt.

Joe and Joe Jr. never established a strong father-son relationship. The man and the boy both loved Marilyn, and their best times together were with her. And Marilyn's death briefly brought father and son together again. At the time of DiMaggio's own death, he had not seen Joe, Jr., for years. In death, however, DiMaggio finally bridged the gap. Joe, Jr., served as pallbearer for his father. And DiMaggio's will established a trust fund that would grant his son $20,000 a year, a judicious sum to grant a man with a checkered occupational history. To have a comfortable life, Joe, Jr., would need to work to supplement the stipend. But $20,000 a year would provide a safety net.

DiMaggio, in death, through his will, made his only child's life more comfortable. In life, Joe DiMaggio rendered the world safer for many children. His brother Dom's eulogy said, nothing gave Joe more pleasure than establishing the Joe DiMaggio Children's Hospital at Memorial Regional Hospital in Hollywood, Florida. About a week after the Yankee Clipper's death, a beautiful half-page photograph of Joe DiMaggio appeared in the *New York Times*. It was taken near the end of his life. In the photograph, DiMaggio tenderly holds a sick infant. Love radiates from DiMaggio's face. Beneath the photograph were the words, "Most Americans know Joe DiMaggio as the Yankee Clipper, the legend in baseball, the American Dream. For the kids at the Joe DiMaggio Children's Hospital he is all that and more.... Joe DiMaggio was always an inspiring visitor and a loving namesake to this non-profit children's hospital. His support and commitment have helped to give many children that extra encouragement needed to promote healing and restore hope."[27]

Stoic Confrontation of Pain and Hardship

Joe DiMaggio felt the pain of children, but he stoically confronted his own pain and hardship. DiMaggio suffered numerous injuries during his career. But he mounted many remarkable comebacks, frequently playing while experiencing intense pain. Playing hard, DiMaggio repeatedly punished his body. Few other big men have ever slid into bases with such force. X-rays revealed the toll DiMaggio's style of play inflicted on his back. And painful bone spurs, requiring multiple surgeries, made even walking excruciating. DiMaggio epitomized Hemingway's definition of courage as grace under pressure. After injury and surgery forced the aging DiMaggio to miss the first 65 games of the 1949 season, he waged one of the most exceptional personal comebacks in sport history. In his first three games after returning to active play, DiMaggio hit four home runs, knocked in nine runs, and made 13 catches in the outfield. Then late in the 1949 campaign, DiMaggio contracted a virulent case of viral pneumonia. Weakened and suffering from nausea, he lost 18 pounds. But a drawn, emaciated DiMaggio demanded that manager Casey Stengel play him in two crucial, late September games against the Boston Red Sox. The measure of a man is what he does with what he has left. By that standard, DiMaggio was not simply a great athlete; he was a great man. Ashen, gaunt, and limping, a very ill DiMaggio singled and doubled, pacing the Yankees to victory over the Red Sox. And then in the final contest of the season, DiMaggio played eight innings before physical collapse on the field forced his exit. DiMaggio's courageous example and brilliant play ensured another Yankee pennant. Throughout his baseball career, DiMaggio never complained about the frequent illnesses and painful injuries he endured.

Nor did DiMaggio engage in self-pity away from the diamond. He did not bemoan hardship or pain. Even after the tragic loss of Marilyn, the public saw only his stoic class. And when finally confronted by age and mortal illness, DiMaggio died with courage. Morris Engelberg, friend and attorney, witnessed the Yankee Clipper's demise: "DiMaggio fought his illness as hard as he played the game of baseball and with the same dignity, style, and grace with which he lived his life."[28]

Recognition by Others of One's Achievements

Jimmy struts into the bar with a dog. He claims the dog can talk. Buster bets $50 that Jimmy is a liar. Jimmy asks the dog how sandpaper feels. The dog answers, "Rrrough!" Buster laughs derisively. Jimmy immediately asks the dog what is on top of a house. The dog responds, "Rrroof!" Buster gestures contemptuously. Then Jimmy quickly asks the dog who was the greatest baseball player of all time. The dog growls, "Rrruth!" Buster snatches the money and tosses Jimmy and the dog out of the bar. The dog turns to Jimmy and says, "I should have said DiMaggio."

There are endless variations on the above story. Clearly, however, the punch line draws a laugh because many people believe that, despite the relative brevity of his career, Joe DiMaggio was baseball's preeminent player.

DiMaggio did not labor in obscurity. A plethora of articles and books attest to the appreciative recognition by others of his achievements.

"There were more powerful hitters, flashier fielders and speedier runners, but nobody combined these skills as efficiently, elegantly and effortlessly as the Yankee Clipper," asserted baseball historian Robert W. Creamer.[29] Casey Stengel termed DiMaggio "the greatest player I ever managed."[30] Ted Williams contended, "I've never seen anyone who played the game with more perfection. He was the best player I ever saw."[31] "He was," editorialized *The Daily Gazette* of Schenectady, New York, "a hero to children and adults for the way he played the game — with consummate skill, but also with grace and dignity."[32] "Other players ... racked up better numbers. But no player," argued writer Glen Stout, "ever, not even Ruth, played better when playing well meant the difference between his team winning and his team losing."[33] "If you said to God, 'Create someone who was what a baseball player should be,' God would have created Joe DiMaggio," mused ex–Dodger manager Tommy Lasorda.[34] When DiMaggio died, the *Los Angeles Times* noted, "Many still consider him the best all-around player in baseball history."[35]

DiMaggio's play in the field was peerless. His glove and arm were legendary. The art of base stealing languished in DiMaggio's generation, but he was the best base runner of his era. And no one who ever saw it ever forgot DiMaggio's classic swing. He had a career batting average of .325, hitting .381 in 1939. In only 1,736 games, DiMaggio batted in 1,537 runs. Only five sluggers — Babe Ruth, Ted Williams, Lou Gehrig, Jimmy Foxx, and Hank Greenberg — retired with higher lifetime slugging percentages than DiMaggio, and none of them possessed DiMaggio's glove, arm, or base-running skills. Taking into account three prime seasons lost to World War II military service, numerous injuries, and that in DiMaggio's era the distance from home plate to the wall in his left-center field power alley at Yankee Stadium was 457 feet, his 361 home runs are impressive. Home run hitters typically strike out frequently. DiMaggio however, struck out only eight more times than he hit home runs. By contrast, Mickey Mantle hit 536 home runs but registered 1,710 strikeouts. A number of great players, including Ted Williams, Carl Yastrzemski, and Ernie Banks, never played on a team that won the World Series. As the heart of the Yankees, DiMaggio led New York to ten pennants and nine world championships during his 13 year career. DiMaggio's remarkable achievements earned him baseball's highest honors. Thrice he was named the American League's Most Valuable Player. The Baseball Hall of Fame, the game's equivalent of Mount Olympus, proudly displays DiMaggio's plaque. And in 1969, sportswriters formally voted DiMaggio baseball's "greatest living ballplayer."

Moreover, many pundits regard DiMaggio's 1941 record 56 consecutive game hitting streak as sport's most remarkable record. Commentators often simply refer to it as *The Streak*. Harvard paleontologist, man of letters, and cultural guru Stephen Jay Gould asserts, "DiMaggio's streak is the most extraordinary thing that ever happened in American sports."[36] According to Gould, DiMaggio's hitting streak is the only sports record that transcends the protocols of statistical probability. Sportswriter Bill Madden labels the streak the "Feat to Top 'Em All."[37] It inspired the Les Brown band to record the 1941 song, "Joltin' Joe DiMaggio," with the refrain, "Our kids will tell their kids his name, 'Joltin' Joe DiMaggio."[38] *Time* called the streak "a feat of consistency no other player has come close to matching."[39] In a book, *Streak*, devoted to the feat, Michael Seidel wrote, "Amid the turmoil of world war and the preparation for our undetermined role in its conduct, the attention paid to DiMaggio's streak ... provided a heroic, factual focus for a land whose imagination seemed primed for increments of power."[40]

Tributes to DiMaggio extend beyond his baseball triumphs. He was honored for his character. In 1977 the Yankee Clipper received America's highest civilian award, the Medal of Freedom. Former President Ronald Reagan called DiMaggio "a symbol of all that is good and decent."[41] When former Secretary of State Henry Kissinger sat beside DiMaggio at the 1996 World Series, Kissinger said that the honor was his. Even the satiric *Doonesbury* identified DiMaggio as America's "moral authority."[42] At DiMaggio's April 23, 1999, memorial service at St. Patrick's Cathedral, dignitaries from sport, entertainment, business, and government came to pay homage. And on Sunday April 25, 1999, a granite and bronze tribute to DiMaggio was dedicated in Monument Park at Yankee Stadium.

The encomiums that followed DiMaggio's death celebrated the man more than the athlete. Bill Clinton observed, "When future generations look back at the 20th century, they will think of the Yankee Clipper."[43] *Time* columnist Roger Rosenblatt wrote, "DiMaggio's persona was wholly the product of abstracts: pride, fidelity, natural aristocracy and, above all, ability."[44] Sportswriter David Kindred recognized DiMaggio's "majestic presence."[45] Columnist George F. Will wrote that DiMaggio "proved that a healthy democracy knows and honors nobility when it sees it."[46] Steve Campbell, Albany *Times Union* sportswriter, referred to DiMaggio as "regal."[47] Writing for the *Wall Street Journal*, Michael McCarthy claimed DiMaggio represented "a bedrock American ideal: that prosperity awaits he who will earnestly shoulder a day's work."[48] In the *New York Times*, Bob Hebert pontificated that DiMaggio "became the designated hero of the colossus, the pre-eminent god of this secular creation myth."[49] The Rev.

Armand Oliveri asserted, "Joe had achieved greatness, but that his real greatness was the way he carried himself."[50]

Paul Simon wrote that DiMaggio was "as proud and masculine as a battleship." The lyrics to his song "Mrs. Robinson," explained Simon, acknowledge DiMaggio as a hero. And a hero, Simon ruminated, allows us to "read with a new clarity our moral compass."[51] In the age of Clinton and Lewinsky, the lyrics of "Mrs. Robinson" possess even more poignant meaning than when they were composed 30 years ago.

Protection of Reputation

Heroes protect their reputations. Natty Bumppo, Wyatt Earp, and Sam Spade did. So did Joe DiMaggio. In *Othello*, Shakespeare called reputation "the immortal part of myself" and wrote:

> Who steals my purse steals trash; 'tis something, nothing;
> Twas mine, 'tis his, and has been slave to thousands;
> But he that filches from me my good name
> Robs me of that which not enriches him,
> And makes me poor indeed.[52]

Andrew Jackson's mother exhorted him to bypass legalisms in the case of slander and to settle the matter himself. Although we no longer fight formal duels, DiMaggio would have agreed with Shakespeare and Mrs. Jackson. As David Halberstam observed, Joe DiMaggio was the "keeper of his own flame." DiMaggio, wrote Halberstam, "guards his special status carefully, wary of doing anything that might tarnish his special reputation. He tends to avoid all those who might define him in some way other than the way he defined his self on the field."[53]

The faux intimacy of television leaves no mystery. Taking place prior to the ubiquity of television, the prime of Joe DiMaggio lent itself to story telling and epic legend. Staten Island *Advance* sportswriter Jerry Izenberg recognized that radio helped nurture the DiMaggio legend: "Then conjure up DiMaggio— as they did at their radios. Project — as they did — through the imagination that only radio could generate, the grace, the style, the magnificent tableau of DiMaggio's perfect timing."[54] And DiMaggio was determined to give those who actually saw him play indelible memories. Asked why he always drove himself so hard, DiMaggio responded, "Because there might be somebody out there who's never seen me play before."[55] DiMaggio retired from active play "because I don't want them [the fans] to remember me struggling."[56] Sportswriter Marty Appell wrote,

"He also knew when it was time to quit playing, and later, he knew when it was time to stop playing in Old Timers Games, and even when to stop wearing a uniform."[57] Proud and remote, DiMaggio protected his public image. DiMaggio, noted *New York Times* sportswriter George Vecsey, "set the conditions for his appearances on Old-Timers' Day. He was always described as the 'greatest living ballplayer' ... "[58] DiMaggio, observed Paul Simon, "understood the power of silence."[59] The Yankee Clipper, wrote Simon, "never in word or deed befouls his legend and greatness.... In these days of presidential transgressions and apologies and prime-time interviews, we grieve for Joe DiMaggio and mourn the loss of his grace and dignity."[60]

Serving as a Role Model for Others

Serving as a role model for others is Michael Kimmel's final attribute of the ideal of American masculinity. And DiMaggio's fulfillment of all of Kimmel's other attributes rendered him a role model. Reacting to DiMaggio's death, New York Governor George Pataki said: "He was every American boy's hero, including mine."[61] Wellington Mara, owner of the NFL's New York Giants, commented on DiMaggio: "I always felt that he was a model of professionalism that any athlete in any sport would do well to attempt to emulate."[62] And countless American males have wished that they could play baseball, woo a beautiful woman, and display class like Joe DiMaggio. Even the film *Grease* cited DiMaggio as a role model.[63]

Ernest Hemingway's novella *The Old Man and the Sea* provides the most memorable depiction of DiMaggio as a role model. Santiago, an old Cuban fisherman who does epic battle with a great fish, repeatedly evokes DiMaggio as the measure of a man. In talking to his young friend Manolin, Santiago implicity evokes baseball as a metaphor for life. The boy Manolin loyally considers Santiago the best of fishermen, and Santiago knows "the great DiMaggio" is the greatest baseball player. Santiago strives to emulate the masculine ideal DiMaggio represents. As he girds for heroic struggle, Santiago resolves, "I must be worthy of the great DiMaggio." Evoking DiMaggio as a masculine mantra, Santiago counsels Manolin to "Think of the great DiMaggio." As a bond between himself and the great Yankee, Santiago notes that DiMaggio's "father was a fisherman." The old man dreams of taking "the great DiMaggio fishing." Since DiMaggio knew poverty in his youth, Santiago believes that the Yankee "would understand" his struggles. When the great fish nearly exhausts his endurance, Santiago reminds himself "of the great DiMaggio who does all things perfectly even with the pain of the bone spur in the heel." Santiago steels himself by asking, "Do you believe the great DiMaggio would stay with a fish as long as I will stay with this one?" Santiago is "sure" that DiMaggio would. And when Santiago finds dignity in his valiant struggle, he says, "I think the great DiMaggio would be proud of me today."[64]

Joe DiMaggio's renown has met the test of time, and death will not erode his place in American culture. DiMaggio represents the ideal of American masculinity. He will remain the standard by which men measure themselves. Should anyone ever do the impossible and exceed DiMaggio's mark of hitting in 56 consecutive games, protection of his reputation will require no asterisk. For the qualities that made DiMaggio great are not quantifiable. Courage. Dignity. Grace.

Notes

An earlier version of this paper appeared as "Joe DiMaggio and the Ideal," in Richard Gilliam, ed., *Joltin Joe: The Best of Joe DiMaggio* (New York: Carroll & Graf, 1999).

1. Joseph Durso, "Joe DiMaggio, Yankee Clipper, Dies at 84," *The New York Times*, March 9, 1999, A1.

2. Erik Brady, "Ultimate Celebrity Had Air of Mystery," *USA Today*, March 9, 1999, 1A.

3. "Who Do You Think Will Be the Most Influential Sports Figure in 1999?" Oneonta *The Daily Star*, 3.

4. Michael Kimmel, *Manhood in America: A Cultural History* (New York: The Free Press, 1996), passim.

5. Robert F. Slatzer, *The Life and Curious Death of Marilyn Monroe* (Los Angeles: Pinnacle Books, 1974), 246.

6. Cited in Jack B. Moore, *Joe DiMaggio: A Bio-Bibliography* (New York: Greenwood Press, 1986), 197.

7. "Joe D Was a Hero to Many, But Not All," *Newsday* (Queens Edition), March 14, 1999, B6.

8. Kenneth Lovett, "Lawmakers Use DiMaggio to Play Politics," Oneonta *The Daily Star*, March 29, 1999, 5.

9. Bill Madden and Luke Cyphers, "Joe D & Morris: The Final Days," *New York Daily News*, April 25, 1999, 6.

10. Robert Lipsyte, "A National Turns Its Eyes to Center Field, One More Time," *The New York Times*, April 25, 1999, SP1.

11. "DiMaggio Uttered, 'I Love All of You' Then Slipped Peacefully Away," *New York Post*, March 12, 1999, 2.

12. Michelle Caruso and Owen Mortiz, "DiMaggio Laid to Rest, *New York Daily News*, March 12, 1999, 3.

13. Quoted in Durso, "Joe DiMaggio," D4.

14. Quoted in Durso, "Joe Dimaggio," D4.

15. David Halberstam, *Summer of '49* (New York: William Morrow and Company, 1989), 48.

16. "Yankee Great Is Dead at 84," *The Boston Globe*, March 9, 1999, D8.

17. Clipping, Joe DiMaggio File, National Baseball Hall of Fame.

18. David Kindred, "Joe DiMaggio," *The Sporting News*, March 22, 1999, 27.

19. Dave Anderson, "60 Years in Public Eye: His Privacy, Pride, Ego and Dignity," *The New York Times*, March 9, 1999, D5.

20. Reprinted in Jimmy Cannon, "Greatness and Grace," *New York Post*, March 9, 1999, 103.

21. Halberstam, 260.

22. Gene Schoor, *Joe DiMaggio: A Biography* (Garden City: Doubleday & Company, 1980), 189.

23. William Sanford and Carl Green, *Joe DiMaggio* (New York: Crestwood House, 1993), 29.

24. Joseph Durso, *DiMaggio: The Last American Knight* (Boston: Little, Brown Company, 1995), 203.

25. Richard Ben Cramer, "The DiMaggio Nobody Knew," *Newsweek*, March 22, 1999, 58.

26. Cramer, 58.

27. "The Legend Lives On" *The New York Times*, March 14, 1999, 31.

28. Bill Bell, Dave Goldiner, and Gene Mustain, "Yankee Clipper Joe DiMaggio Dies at 84," *New York Daily News*, March 9, 1999, wrap 2.

29. Robert W. Creamer, "All the Tools," *Sports Illustrated*, March 15, 1999, 52.

30. Clipping Joe DiMaggio File, National Baseball Hall of Fame.

31. Reprinted in Peter Gammons, "He Was All By Himself," *The Boston Globe*, March 9, 1999.

32. "A Classic American Hero," *The Schenectady Daily Gazette*, March 19, 1999, B6.

33. Glenn Stout, *DiMaggio: An Illustrated Life*, edited by Dick Johnson (New York: Walker and Company, 1995), 227.

34. "DiMaggio Dies at Home at 84," Binghamton *Press and Sun Bulletin*, March 9, 1999, 7D.

35. The Lost Angeles Times Syndication "Baseball Loses One of Its Best," *Albany Times Union*, March 9, 1999, A4.

36. Quoted in Paul Gray, "Left and Gone Away," *Time*, March 22, 1999, 92.

37. Bill Madden, "Feat to Top, End All," *New York Daily News*, March 9, 1999, wrap 12-13.

38. Mark McGuire, "Hall Visitors Mourn Legend," *Albany Times Union*, March 9, 1999, A4.

39. Gray, 92.

40. Michael Seidel, *Streak: Joe DiMaggio and the Summer of '41* (New York: McGraw Hill, 1988), 3.

41. "We Love You, We'll Miss You," *New York Daily News*, March 9, 1999, wrap 4.

42. G.B. Trudeau, *Doonesbury*, Universal Press Syndicate, 1998.

43. "We Love You, We'll Miss You," wrap 4.

44. Roger Rossenblatt, "A Hero in Deep Center," *Zone*, March 22, 1998, 122.

45. Dave Kindred, "Joe DiMaggio," *The Sporting News*, March 22, 1998, 25.

46. George Will, "DiMaggio Proves Democracy," Oneonta *The Daily Star*, March 4, 1999, 4.

47. Steve Campbell, "No. 5 Was Always No. 1," *Albany Times Union*, March 9, 1999, C1.

48. Michael McCarthy, "Ordinary Joe: America Saw Itself in DiMaggio and It Liked What It Saw," *The Wall Street Journal*, March 9, 1999, A1.

49. Bob Herbert, "A Designated Hero," *The New York Times*, March 10, 1999, A19.

50. Associated Press, "A Dignified Funeral for Joe D." Oneonta *The Daily Star*, March 12, 1999, 15.

51. Paul Simon, "The Silent Superstar," *The New York Times*, March 9, 1999, A23.

52. "Othello," *The Complete Works of Shakespeare* (Roslyn, New York: Walter J. Black, 1937), 1189.

53. Quoted in Durso, "Joe DiMaggio," D4.

54. Jerry Izenberg, "A Monument for a New York Icon," *Staten Island Advance*, C3.

55. Halberstam, 48.

56. Halberstam, 272.

57. Marty Appel, "Life After Baseball," *Yankee Magazine*, April 1999, 51.

58. George Vecsey, "DiMaggio Left a Mark in the Sands," *The New York Times*, March 9, 1999, D1.

59. Simon, A23.

60. *Ibid.*

61. "We Love You, We'll Miss You," wrap 4.

62. "Yanks Mourn the Legend," *Daily News*, March 9, 1999, wrap 6.

63. "Grease," Paramont, 1978.

64. Ernest Hemingway, *The Old Man and the Sea* (New York: Charles Scribner's Sons, 1952), passim.

From Bloomer Girls' Baseball to Women's Softball: A Cultural Journey Resulting in Women's Exclusion from Baseball

Gai Ingham Berlage

Women and girls were actively involved in amateur, semi-professional and professional baseball from 1866 to 1935. On playgrounds, in high schools, in colleges, on industrial teams, on professional barnstorming teams, women and girls played baseball and excelled. Based on women's early involvement in baseball, it would have seemed only natural that women would continue to be a part of baseball history and that baseball would be considered a co-ed sport today. But, shortly after 1933 softball had almost completely replaced baseball as a sport for women. The change from baseball to softball occurred at all levels. Companies that had sponsored women's baseball teams now sponsored women's softball. Public and private schools that had previously ordered baseball equipment for girls now ordered softball equipment. How was it possible that the transition from baseball to softball would become so complete that the history of women's baseball would be forgotten and not rediscovered until the 1990s?

Cultural definitions of femininity not only limited women's opportunities to play baseball, but also determined the type of game they could play. If baseball was to be a male domain, women could not be envisioned as playing the same game. Women might play modified games, but the "real" game was for men only. From the mid–1800s to the mid–1930s, there existed a constant cultural tension between society's definition of femininity and its definition of sport as a male domain. The development of softball in the 1930s provided an escape valve. With a little imagination and the help of cultural conditioning, all those modified games of baseball that women had been playing could now culturally be redefined as the precursors of softball or simply as early women's versions of softball.

In the early years, the 1860s through much of the 1930s, women and girls played baseball in school and in the community with some degree of social acceptance. Today there is little or no encouragement for girls to play baseball. It is expected that girls will play softball. Because of the movie *A League of Their Own*, many young girls are aware that women played baseball during World War II. Most girls, however, are unaware that women were playing much earlier. The public assumption is that with the exception of World War II, women always played softball. The irony is that more girls and women played baseball prior to 1940, than do today.

Until the late 1930s there were girls who played baseball on the sandlot, on the playground and in some colleges. Although softball was invented in 1887, it didn't become popular until the 1930s. In 1933 the Amateur Softball Association made the term softball official and this term was substituted for the modified baseball games girls had been playing. In 1939 Little League baseball was started as a program for boys only. There was no protest. It was accepted that baseball was a boys' sport. From 1939 through 1973 girls were banned from playing Little League baseball.

Prior to the 1930s, it was acceptable for women to play baseball as long as they played what were considered feminine versions of the men's game or appeared feminine in appearance while playing the men's game. Their opportunities to play were, however, circumscribed by traditional definitions of femininity and by their social class. Women who didn't conform to cultural definitions of femininity or who appeared unattractive ran the risk of being labeled masculine, a freak or a homosexual. The public was also suspicious of the motivation of some of the early male promoters of professional women's baseball. These male promoters were accused of being more interested in promoting prostitution than baseball. However, the majority of women who played on women's or men's professional teams suffered little or no stigma.

Today because of Title IX and other equal rights legislation, girls have the legal right to play baseball and yet, proportionately fewer girls play today than did in the early 1900s. The reason is softball. It has evolved as the culturally accepted sport for females. Girls and women can play softball at the high school, college, Olympic, and professional level. Softball has become the opportunity structure for girls; consequently girls opt to play softball rather than baseball.

Although distinctions between male and female roles were probably greatest during the Victorian Era, 1876–1900, this was the period when women got their chance to play baseball. The Victorian Era was an amazing period in American history. American society was in the midst of rapid social and economic change as the result of industrialization, massive immigration, and the depression of 1873. During this period women's lives changed dramatically. Medical attitudes about health, exercise and women's fashion, especially, corsets changed. The invention of the safety bicycle gave women new freedom of movement and encouraged them to wear bloomers, which made exercise more practical. With the establishment of women's colleges and the beginning of the women's suffrage movement, questions were raised about the equality of men and women. The image of the "new" woman, who was independent, educated, and athletic replaced the Victorian image of the "true" woman who was weak, frail and dependent.

By the late 1800s baseball had come to typify all that was good about America. It had captured the spirit of the nation and was the national sport. It was thought to be the great assimilator of the masses. The expectation, however, was that men played baseball and women cheered them on.

The second half of the 1880s set the stage for an unlikely convergence. A small group of Victorian ladies left their parlor couches, their smelling salts, and their feminine frailty behind to participate in the new national pastime, baseball. They defied cultural definitions of femininity that decreed that women were by nature frail, in need of protection, and with limited energy. By playing baseball, they challenged the medical opinion that if women participated in strenuous exercise they would jeopardize their ability to have children. By playing baseball, they also challenged the notion that sports were solely a male domain. Interestingly enough, it was upper and working-class women rather than middle-class women who had the greatest opportunities to play. Upper-class women had the freedom to experiment with playing baseball in private settings such as their homes, exclusive clubs, and private schools. Mostly out of view of the general public, their playing was largely ignored. Even if it came to public attention, the games were seen as "ladylike" amusement for the idle rich. Baseball games played by refined upper-class ladies in long dresses were defined more as social than sporting events. Consequently, when these society women played genteel "social games of baseball," they were not seen as unfeminine. They were participating in feminine versions of the men's game of baseball.

Working-class women also had more freedom to play baseball than middle-class women did. Having already breached Victorian notions of femininity by working outside of the home, they had little to lose by playing baseball. Working on the farm or in the factory required strength and endurance, appearing frail was not a characteristic that working-class women could emulate. Strength rather than frailty was a desirable attribute. Consequently, when promoters formed women's barnstorming teams as novelty entertainment, they were able to recruit working-class women. To be paid to play and to have an opportunity to travel was very appealing to working class women.

Baseball had begun as a genteel game played by private men's clubs. After the Civil War the game spread to the masses and the emphasis switched from genteel sportsmanship to winning at any cost. The proletariat game became identified with ruffians. So there were now two very different images of the game.

Upper-class games were more social events than sporting events. The Knickerbockers, an upper-class gentleman's club, was the first club to invite their wives, daughters and girlfriends to see them play. In 1867, they designated the last Thursday of the month, as Ladies' Day.[1] On these occasions, tea was served and gentlemanly conduct on the part of the contestants was expected.[2]

Eventually some upper-class women decided they would rather play than watch. They formed their own private baseball clubs. In keeping with proper upper-class deportment, appropriate dress and conduct during games became very important. A baseball club in Pensacola, Florida, in 1867, had a rule that if a player got entangled in her hoop skirt and fell; she was immediately expelled from the club.[3]

Some society women also played baseball on their private estates. An article in *Baseball Magazine* 1908 noted that shipping magnate, Clement A. Griscom had a baseball diamond at his summer home so that the daughters of his friends could play. According to the author, the baseball parties organized by Grisom's wife had become quite the rage.[4]

A 1911 Collier's magazine article was devoted to the newly formed women's "social baseball club" at the exclusive Society Country Club at Belfield, the wealthy German section of Philadelphia. Apparently it was acceptable for women to play "social" baseball as distinguished from competitive baseball which was manlier. Their uniforms left no doubt in people's minds that this was a feminine version. Rather than wearing regulation men's baseball uniforms, the women in keeping with their feminine role wore long skirts and blouses with a B emblazoned. The long skirts also restricted their movement and made for a slower paced game.[5] These women of leisure and of privilege had the freedom to amuse themselves playing baseball without any fear of public sanction.

Upper-class girls were also able to play baseball at some of the first women's colleges. These northeastern colleges sometimes referred to as the "seven sisters" were Mount Holyoke, Vassar, Smith, Wellesley, Bryn Mawr, Radcliffe and Barnard. The earliest of these women's colleges, Mount Holyoke was formed as a seminary in 1837 and became a four-year college in 1861. Vassar was formed in 1865, Smith and Wellesley in 1875, Bryn Mawr in 1885, Radcliffe 1878 and Barnard 1889. These women's colleges were developed to give women an education equal to that of men, but in separate institutions. In this way, it was hoped that women's special needs could be met and their femininity preserved. Educators at these schools were progressive in that they believed a healthy mind required a healthy body. Physical exercise became an important part of the college curriculum. Educating women and requiring them to do physical exercise were radical ideas. Many doctors believed that women physiologically could not withstand the rigors of a college education and that exercise could lead to permanent ill-health and the inability to have children.[6]

A *New York Times* editorial titled "College Sport and Motherhood" warned girls and their parents of the danger of sports for girls. It said, "Every girl, it seems, has a large store of vital and nervous energy upon which to draw in the great crisis of motherhood. If the foolish virgin uses up this deposit in daily expenditures on the hockey or tennis court, then she is left bankrupt in her great crisis and her children have to pay the bill."[7] Others in the society thought that a college education would make women unfeminine and therefore, unmarriageable.

Some doctors were beginning to question this view of women's health especially since so many immigrant women appeared robust even though they worked long hours doing physically demanding chores. These doctors believed that the ill-health and fainting spells that upper-class women experienced might be due to a lack of physical exercise and to tight corsets.

Progressive women physicians and physical educators at these women's colleges believed that calisthenics and other types of gymnastics exercise were essential for the girls' health. But these physical educators had a problem; most of the girls didn't like doing calisthenics and didn't want to do them. Many of the girls were enthralled with baseball and asked if they couldn't play baseball like their brothers. The educators were delighted that the girls were showing an interest in some type of exercise and encouraged them to play baseball. Vassar had the earliest baseball teams with teams of eight players in 1866 and then nine players in 1876. Smith had teams in 1879, Mount Holyoke in 1891, Wellesley in 1897, Barnard in 1910, Radcliffe in 1915 and Bryn Mawr in 1925.[8]

Playing baseball at these women's colleges was very different from that at men's colleges. Feminine decorum meant that women in the early years had to play baseball in long sleeved dresses with full skirts that reached to the floor. Their baseball caps were the only part of their uniforms that were similar to men's. In later years long skirts would be replaced by the greater freedom of bloomers. Needless to say, the voluminous long full skirts affected play. At Smith College, a student, Gertrude May Cooper, created a booklet with drawings showing the proper way to catch and retrieve a ball in a long skirt. There was the special skirt catch which was illustrated by showing a girl with her feet set apart and the ball being caught in the skirt material. And of course, there was always the problem of how to retrieve the ball if it accidentally landed under the skirt. Although the rules and the baseball equipment were the same, the feminine uniforms and the manner of play established that this was a feminine version of the male game.

Private girls' schools such as Miss Porter's in Farmington, Connecticut, and Miss Hall's in Pittsfield, Massachusetts, also allowed girls to play baseball. When the girls approached Miss Porter, the headmistress of Miss Porter's school, in 1867 she gave the girls permission to play baseball as long as they selected a field that was approached by going through other fields where there would be no passersby. Miss Porter worried about public reaction to their playing and her fears were well founded. Later that spring, Trinity College, a men's school in nearby Hartford, challenged the girls to a game. Everything was fine until some of the girls' parents heard about it. The parents quickly put a stop to the game.[9]

By the early 1900s girls in public schools also had the opportunity to play some form of baseball. For example, in 1919 baseball was an organized activity in New York's Public School Athletic League. A 1920 survey of Cleveland schools indicted that 91 percent of high school girls played baseball.[10] In rural areas little girls often grew up playing baseball along side their brothers and no one thought much about it.

But not all baseball games were of the upper-class variety. By the late 1870s professional baseball was becoming popular and there were at least five salaried teams. In 1871, the National Association of Professional Base Ball Players became the first professional league.[11] Professional baseball changed baseball's upper-class image. Winning now became more important than sportsmanship and the public image of ballplayers became that of ruffians rather than that of genteel upper-class men. Husbands were reluctant to bring their wives to games because of the rowdy behavior of fans. Proper women didn't attend games.

In order to change professional baseball's image, a few baseball owners came up with the idea of having "ladies days." By inviting women to come out to the ballpark, owners hoped to inhibit men's unruly behavior, to create the image of baseball as family entertainment, and to increase attendance. In 1883 the Athletics and the Orioles became the first professional teams to designate Thursday as Ladies' Day. Other teams immediately followed.[12] Being a female fan became quite acceptable, because it fit nicely into role female role expectations. Here were women in a supportive role, cheering on the men. Their presence was also thought to provide a good moral atmosphere to restrain men's more base instincts. Proper gentleman would not offend a lady by using uncouth language.

Being a female fan was very different from being a player. Playing baseball was a male activity. Women might dabble in feminine sports such as riding, tennis or golf, but "real sports" such as baseball or football were the domain of men.

Taking advantage of the double-sex standard, male promoters in the 1860s organized professional women's teams as novelty entertainment. The draw was the sensationalism of seeing the weaker sex play the masculine game of baseball. At first women's teams played against other women's teams. In 1867 an all black women's team, the Dolly Vardens was formed in Philadelphia. Not much is known about team except that their uniforms were red calico dresses and the ball was made of yarn. They definitely were theatrical entertainment.[13] The first of the white women's professional teams to gain widespread publicity were the Blondes and Brunettes in 1875. The teams as their names suggest were composed of nine blonde players and nine brunettes. The teams were the creation of Frank Myers, S.B. Brock, and Thomas Halligan. An article in the *New York Clipper*, September 18, 1975, stated, "[The owners] under the impression that there is money in it, propose to give exhibitions in the principal cities."[14]

There were other women's teams throughout the 1870s and '80s. The 1890s, however, heralded a new age in women's baseball. Just having women players was not enough; the public now wanted to see women with serious baseball skills. Women's barnstorming teams that played against men's sprung up across the country. The new novelty was the "battle of the sexes." One of the early successful teams was Franklin's young Ladies Baseball Club Number 1 of 1890-1891. The players wore striped dresses belted at the waist, polka dot scarves, dark stockings, ankle high schools and baseball caps. They were so successful that they annihilated many of the men's teams that played them. However, the promoter, W. S. Franklin may not have been particularly forthright in declaring that the team was composed totally of females. There may have been a few male ringers on the team dressed as women.[15]

At about the same time a number of teams calling themselves Bloomer Girls appeared across the country. There were the Boston Bloomer Girls', the Texas Bloomer Girls', the Chicago Bloomer Girls' and various other Bloomer Girls teams from other parts of country. The women now played in bloomers rather than long dresses. In later years, women on these teams played in regulation looking men's uniforms.

Bloomer Girls' teams rarely played against other women's teams, but instead played against men's teams. These women were known for playing serious baseball. However, many a team had one or two male ringers on the team, usually playing the position of catcher, pitcher or shortstop. Apparently financial incentives were great enough that these teams had little trouble recruiting a few males even if they had to wear dresses.

By the end of the 1920s most of the women's teams had disappeared and the number of amateur and semi-professional men's teams had declined. The country had changed. There were now many forms of competing entertainment. Radio broadcasts of professional baseball games also drew fans away from their local teams. A few highly competitive Bloomer Girls' teams managed to survive into the 1920s and 1930s. These teams had highly skilled players who competed successfully against men's amateur and semi-pro teams. Their games were given serious coverage by the press as can be seen from an article that appeared in the *Literary Digest*, July 28, 1923. The writer stated that the Kansas City Bloomer Girls' had defeated one of the best men's semi-pro teams in New Jersey.[16] The New York Bloomer Girls' were probably the last of the Bloomer Girls' teams. Their last season was 1935.

Starting in 1898 there were also a few women who had the skills to play on men's teams. Although these women were exceptional baseball players, they were recruited primarily for their novelty drawing power. Most were from working-class backgrounds. The first of the phenoms was Lizzie Stride or Stroud whose professional baseball name was Lizzie Arlington. She came from a coal-mining town and had grown up playing baseball. Captain William J. Connor, owner of the Philadelphia Reserves, hired Arlington in 1898 as a gimmick to increase gate receipts. When the crowds failed to materialize Connor lost interest in his new star. Then Ed Barrow, President of the Atlantic League hired her to pitch in some minor league exhibition games. She played her first regulation minor league game on July 5, 1898. Again she failed to attract the anticipated crowds and she disappeared from the line up.[17]

Lizzie Murphy, like Arlington, was from a working-class background. She made a career out of playing semi-professional baseball from 1918 to 1935. Her career began when she was eighteen and started playing for a Warren, Rhode Island, amateur men's team. Soon she was playing for Eddie McGinley's Providence Independents, a semi-pro team that barnstormed throughout New England. Then she was discovered by Eddie Carr. From that point on she played for Carr's All Stars and traveled throughout New England and Canada. She played first base and was advertised as the "the queen of baseball" and as "Spike" Murphy, the best woman ballplayer in the country. Eddie Carr was so proud of his find that he had a picture of her on his letterhead.[18]

Lizzie Murphy was also thrilled to be playing for Carr's All Stars since the team had some ex-major leaguers on the roster. In later years she recalled that she had played with Mack Hollis, a former Rochester player and Artie Grace, who had played for the Boston Red Sox. The team also played against well-known teams such as the Cleveland Colored Giants and the Boston Braves of the National League.[19]

Murphy's greatest thrill came when she played against the Boston Red Sox on August 14, 1922. She played first base for the American All Stars against the Red Sox in a benefit game at Fenway Park. Murphy played two innings and her team won 3–2.[20] Murphy goes down in history as the first woman to have played against a major league team.

In an odd twist a fate, vaudeville would provide the opportunity for another woman, Mabel Schloen, to play against a major league team, the Cincinnati Reds. Schloen's baseball career began in 1922 when she was invited to play with the East Rutherford Cubs, a semi-professional baseball team in New Jersey. Her real ambition, however, was not to be a ballplayer but to be an actress. Her beauty plus her baseball skills became the launching pin for her vaudeville career. In 1924, she entered the *New York Daily Mirror* beauty contest and became a finalist. Harry Linton, a "Follies" producer, signed her to do baseball skits for his shows. She continued to play baseball during the summer months with East Rutherford. As a publicity gimmick, Linton arranged for her to play in exhibition games with the local men's baseball teams in the towns the Follies toured. In 1924, she played three innings in Fenway Park in Boston catching for future Hall of Famer Walter Johnson, the Washington Senator pitcher. She also played for the Providence Grays, a team managed by Rube Marquard, another Hall of Famer. And in 1926 she played in an exhibition against the Cincinnati Reds. Newspaper articles proclaimed her a serious ballplayer even though she was an entertainer. In the late 1920s, Schloen quit baseball and moved to Hollywood to pursue her acting career fulltime.[21]

Josephine Parodi whose professional baseball name was Josie Caruso is another woman who was hired to play semi-professional ball for purely financial reasons. In 1929 Dick Jess, a promoter, contacted a New York newspaper and stated that he was scouting Upper Manhattan and the Bronx for a good girl baseball player whom he could turn into a diamond star. He was sure there was a female Babe Ruth waiting to be discovered. He selected eighteen year old Josephine Parodi to be his star. He had her play under the name Josie Caruso, perhaps trying to draw on the fame of the very popular opera star of the time, Enrico Caruso. The team was billed as "Josie Caruso and Her Eight Men." The team played semi-professional and amateur teams throughout the East and drew large crowds. Josie became a national celebrity after she appeared in movie newsreels across the country. In 1931, she married and stopped playing.[22]

Financial concerns also launched the baseball careers of three other women who played during the 1930s depression years. As the result of the Great Depression baseball attendance suffered and owners of teams searched for ways to increase attendance. Promoters hit on the idea of having a woman ballplayer play against Major Leaguers. In 1931 seventeen year old Virne Beatrice "Jackie" Mitchell was signed by Joe Engel, owner, promoter and president of the Chattanooga Lookouts, a Class Double-A minor league team. As a publicity stunt he had her pitch in an exhibition game against the New York Yankees. With much fan fare on April 2, 1931, she struck out Yankee sluggers Babe Ruth and Lou Gehrig.[23] The debate continues today as to whether or not she legitimately struck them out. Mitchell to her dying day believed that she surprised them with her sinker pitch.

After the Yankee exhibition game, Mitchell was scheduled to other games for the Lookouts. Her baseball career, however, came to an abrupt end. Baseball Commissioner Kenesaw Mountain Landis ruled that women were banned from playing Major or Minor League baseball and her contract was null and void.[24]

In 1934 Babe Didrikson, famous for having won two Gold and one Silver Medal in the 1932 Olympics, was hired as a promotional gimmick to pitch in some major league exhibition games. She pitched for the Philadelphia Athletics against the Brooklyn Dodgers and the St. Louis Cardinals against the Boston Red Sox as well as other teams.[25] The House of David, a men's semi-professional barnstorming team, also hired her for about $1,000 a month. She played approximately 200 games from early spring to late fall.[26] She was exploited for her celebrity status.

In 1936, Frances "Sonny" Dunlop played for the Fayetteville Bears against the Cassville Blues in a Class D minor league game in the Arkansas-Missouri League. Since there was no advance publicity, baseball officials failed to stop her play. A *Fayettesville Daily Democrat* journalist wrote, "As far as it is known here, Miss Dunlop probably is the first girl in history to play an entire game of organized baseball."[27]

Dunlop was the last woman to play minor league baseball. In 1952 when Eleanor Engle, as a publicity stunt by the Harrisburg, Pennsylvania Senators, a Class B minor league team, the reaction from Major League baseball was swift and vitriolic. George Trautman, minor league president, declared her contract null and void and called the signing a travesty. He warned that severe penalties would be levied against any club that signed or attempted to sign a woman. Baseball commissioner Ford Frick agreed with him. An official ruling on June 21, 1952, banned women from playing either major or minor league baseball.[28]

Although most of the women who played on men's teams were from working class backgrounds and were hired by professional promoters for publicity purposes, one woman player is an exception to that rule. Alta Weiss came from an upper-middle class family and her promoter was her proud father. Dr. Weiss had three daughters and no sons. When his daughter, Alta, showed an interest in baseball, he was thrilled. He had a gymnasium built onto his barn so that Alta could practice her pitching skills during the winter months. He even had John Berger, an employee of his, practice with her all winter. He was determined to make her into a star. At the same time, he expected her to do well in school and to follow in his footsteps as a doctor. At seventeen she became the star pitcher for the Vermilion Independents, a men's semi-pro team in Ohio. She proved such a big draw that that special trains had to be run from Cleveland and surrounding towns to accommodate the more than 13,000 fans who came to see her play in the final seven games of the 1907 season.[29]

At the end of the season her father realized his daughter's economic potential and bought half interest in the team and changed the name to Weiss All-Stars. The press loved her and made her into a celebrity. In 1922 her last year of play, *The Cleveland Press* taunted its American League club with an eight-column banner line, "If the Nap Pitchers Can't Win Regularly, Why Not Sign Alta Weiss to Help?"[30]

Alta was a pioneer not only on the ball field but also in medicine. She was the only female in the Class of 1914 at the medical school at Columbus, Ohio. She continued to play baseball until 1922 while maintaining her medical practice.[31]

There may be other women who played ball during the 1920s and '30s or earlier whose histories are yet to be discovered. But by the late 1930s, the novelty of having a woman player was no longer seen as a financial advantage. Softball was firmly defined as the sport for women, and hardball for men. Cultural conditioning meant that women accepted baseball as an exclusively male endeavor. Young women now aspired to be softball players. The women ballplayers of the 1920s, '30s and earlier were quickly forgotten. So much so that when Philip K. Wrigley established the All American Girls' Baseball League in 1943, it was considered an unprecedented idea. The earlier history of women's baseball was no longer public knowledge.

Softball as a girls' sport had gotten its foothold in 1926 when Gladys Palmer published a modified set of rules for girls' baseball. Palmer believed that baseball as played by men was unsuitable for girls. However, she thought that a modified girls' version had educational merit.[32]

In April 1927 the Sub-Committee on Baseball of the National Committee on Women's Athletics of the American Physical Education Association met for the first time. These physical educators were adamant that women's sports should be less strenuous than men's should. At this meeting Palmer's 1926 rules were slightly modified. This version of baseball with smaller base paths helped pave the way for softball to be accepted as alternative form of baseball for women.[33]

In 1933 the Amateur Softball Association made the term *softball* official, and this name was substituted for the modified baseball games that girls had been playing.[34] Softball was now seen as distinct sport from hardball. Even though both men and women played softball, it came to be accepted as the female equivalent of hardball. The image of softball nicely coincided with the image of women as the weaker sex. Here was a game similar to baseball, but one that was less strenuous and less dangerous. The game because of its smaller diamond and softer ball seemed to be ideally suited for women.

In 1933 with the introduction of the first national men's and women's softball tournament at the Chicago World's Fair, softball gained national recognition. The tournament received excellent coverage because the financial backing came from the Chicago *American*, a Hearst newspaper. Fifteen teams competed in the women's division. The *American* reported that 70,000 attended the championships.[35]

During the 1930s softball flourished. It was an ideal sport for the depression years. It was inexpensive sport that a lot of people without much previous experience could participate in at the same time. The game also required less space than baseball. Between 1935 and 1940, under Franklin D. Roosevelt's New Deal, the Works Progress Administration (W. P. A.) built 3,026 athletic fields. Most had softball diamonds.[36] Y's, churches, playground organizations, and schools all began to sponsor softball teams. During the '30s and '40s businesses and factories also organized softball teams and industrial leagues for their employees. According to the ASA by 1936 there were 92,545 softball teams in the United States. [37]

In 1939 it was estimated that 60 million people watched softball games. That was about ten million more than watched baseball. And interestingly, more people attended women's games than men's.[38]

In 1942 the newly formed International Girls' Major League made up of thirty-two of the stronger women's softball teams in the country was featured in *The Saturday Evening Post*. The writer stressed the masculine characteristics of the players and especially of the Savona sisters when he wrote, "The frailest creature on the diamond is frequently the male umpire ... Miss Olympia, although built like a football halfback, looks frail compare to Miss Freda ... Olympia runs the bases, slides like a man and catches like a man. If she could spit, she could go with Brooklyn."[39]

Women's softball had an image problem. Players were often pictured as being masculine, physical freaks or lesbians. Some teams had burlesque-type names such as Slapsie Maxies's Curvaceous Cuties, Barney Ross's Adorables, and the Dr. Pepper Girls of Miami Beach.[40]

The Amateur Softball Association (ASA), the major governing body of softball, became concerned with the media image of women softball players as unfeminine. To try to counteract that stereotype, in 1942 the ASA sponsored its first beauty contest in conjunction with the ASA world championships. The winner became Miss Softball of America.[41] This accommodation also helped to create the image of softball as a female sport.

In 1943 the All-American Girls' Softball League (AAGSBL) was formed. The League started with four teams that played a 108-game schedule. All the teams were located in mid-sized war production cities within 100 miles of Chicago. In each locale, softball had been popular since the 1930s.[42] The league began by playing with a 12-inch ball that was the same size as regulation softball, but harder. The distance between bases was 65 feet rather than 90 in baseball. The pitching mound distance was 40 feet from plate to mound, slightly shorter than regulation softball and considerable shorter than baseball. The pitcher used a windmill underarm motion rather than overhand. Leading off the base, stealing bases and sliding were all permitted as in baseball. These were forbidden in softball.[43]

Midway through the 1943 season as a media ploy Wrigley asked the press to refer to the game as "Girls Baseball" rather than softball. It wasn't until 1945 that the league officially changed its name to the All-American Girls' Baseball League (AAGBL).[44]

When Wrigley formed the AAGSBL in 1943, he antagonized many of the owners of other women's softball teams in the Chicago area by recruiting their top players. Some of these owners sought legal help. Told that since the women were amateurs Wrigley could legally recruit them, they formed their own league. The National Girls Baseball League (NGBL) was formed in 1944 with four semi-pro softball teams from the Chicago area. The NGBL name was designed to challenge the unique baseball status of the AAGBL and to give the AAGBL direct competition. The NGBL was actually a softball league and its only relation to baseball was its name. Competition between the two leagues for players and publicity was constant. This eventually led to raids on players and salary wars. Although the NGBL never received the financial backing or the publicity of Wrigley's league, it operated successfully until the 1950s.[45]

The NGBL served as an ongoing catalyst for the AAGBL to strive to remain unique. This competition served to continually make AAGBL rules more like major league baseball's, so that by the last season of play in 1954, AAGBL teams were playing by official baseball rules. Because of this, the AAGBL became the only women's league ever to have professional baseball status. Throughout its existence the NGBL continued to use underhand pitching and an official-sized softball.

Promotion for women's softball in the 1950s emphasized players' beauty and sensuality. Feminine ballplayers in bathing suits were used to advertise the Women's World Softball Tournament in the late 1950s.[46] Feminine ballplayers fit in nicely with cultural and advertising norms of women as sex objects.

Ironically, it was the establishment of softball in the 1930s that virtually ended girls' chances to participate in baseball. Culturally softball became identified as the female equivalent of men's baseball. That cultural distinction remains today. Little League and Major League baseball no longer have to bar women from playing to keep them out of the game. Little girls are culturally conditioned to want to play softball instead.

On the 100th anniversary of baseball in 1987, Darlene Mehrer, a Chicago woman baseball enthusiast, wrote an article expressing her dismay that softball was ever invented. She said, "How, in one short century, has the ersatz sport (softball) so strangled the consciousness of the country in the grip of its flabby tentacles that the mention of women's *baseball* gets no reaction other than blank amazement?" In disgust she said, "Happy Birthday, Softball, Wish You'd Never Been Born." She equated the origin of softball in Chicago with other great Chicago tragedies. "Lots of things started in Chicago—the Chicago Fire, the St Valentine's Day massacre, the Black Sox Scandal. Softball fits right in."[47]

Notes

1. Harold Seymour, *Baseball: The Early Years* (New York: Oxford University Press, 1960), 328.
2. Tristram Coffin, *The Old Ball Game: Baseball in Folklore and Fiction* (New York: Seaview Books, 1981), 87.
3. Ted Vincent, *Mudville's Revenge: The Rise and Fall of American Sport* (New York: Seaview Books, 1981), 95.
4. Roy Somerville, "Feminine Baseball De Luxe," *Baseball Magazine*, May 1908, 19.
5. Seymour, 487–488.
6. Gai Ingham Berlage, *Women in Baseball: The Forgotten History* (Westport, CT: Praeger, 1994), 10.
7. Cited Robert Lipsyte and Peter Levine, *Idols of the Game: A Sporting History of the American Century*, (Atlanta: Turner Publishing, 1995), 124.
8. Berlage, 12.
9. *Alumnae Bulletin Miss Porter's School*, 1938; *When I Was at Farmington* (book of former students memories published in 1938), 119; letter to author from Madge Buerger, Executive Secretary Alumnae Association, Miss Hall's School, 14 November 1989.
10. Merrie Fidler, "The Establishment of Softball as a Sport for American Women, 1900–1940," in *Her Story in Sport: A Historical Anthology of Women in Sports*, ed. Reet Howell (West Point, NY: Leisure Press, 1982), 530.
11. Jack Selzer, *Baseball in the Nineteenth Century: An Overview* (Cooperstown, New York: Society for American Baseball Research, 1986), 7.
12. Seymour, 329.
13. Court Michelson, *Michelson's Book of World Baseball Records* (Chicago: Adams Press, 1985), 84.
14. "The Female Baseball Club," *New York Clipper*, 18 September 1875.
15. Bob McCoy, "Keeping Score," *Sporting News*, 5 July 1982; Debra Shattuck, "Playing a Man's Game: Women in Baseball in the United States, 1866–1954" (M.A. thesis: Brown University, 1988), 42.
16. Cited in Larry Keith, "Not Every Bloomer Held a Girl," *Sports Illustrated*, 4 January 1971, E3.
17. "Women Players in Organized Baseball," *SABR Baseball Research Journal*, 1983, 160.
18. Elizabeth Williams, "Warren Woman Recalls Life as Baseball Star," Providence *Evening Bulletin*, 2 Feb. 1938.
19. *Ibid.*
20. Dick Reynolds, untitled paper on Lizzie Murphy, 4–5, NBHFL.
21. Jill Agostino, "Star Quality: Schloen Was a Hit on the Diamond and in Vaudeville," *New York Newsday*, 29 September, 1994.
22. Douglas Noble, M.D., Paramus, N.J., letter to author, 17 June 1992; articles from Josephine Parodi scrapbook.
23. "When Baseball's First Feminine Pitcher Struck Out 'Mighty' Babe," *Chattanooga News*, 32 April 1931.
24. Bob McCoy, "Keeping Score: A Crafty Softpaw," 5 July 1982, newspaper clipping, NBHFL.
25. Babe Didrikson Zaharias as told to Harry Paxton, *This Life I've Led* (New York: A.S. Barnes & Co., 1955), 183; William Johnson and Nancy Williamson, *"Whatta-Gal": The Didrikson Story* (Boston: Little, Brown, 1977), 128.

26. Johnson and Williamson, 128–129.
27. Quoted in "Women Players in Organized Baseball," *SABR Baseball Research Journal*, 1983, 161.
28. "Baseball Rules Out Chattanooga Girl," 23 June 1952, newspaper clipping, NBHFL.
29. Debra Shattuck, "80 Years Ago in Vermilion: A 'Skirt' on the Mound Stuns Baseball Fans," *Vermilion Photojournal*, 31 August 1987, sec.C.
30. Sesquicentennial Historical Committee, *Ragersville, Auburn Township, Ohio, 1830–1980: The Sesquicentennial Story of a Community* (Berlin, Ohio: Berlin Printing, 1980), 197.
31. Sesquicentennial Historical Committee.
32. Morris Bealle, *The Softball Story* (Washington, D.C.: Columbia Pub. Co., 1957), 165.
33. *Ibid.*
34. *Ibid.*, 29.
35. Felicia Halpert, "How the Game Was Invented," *Women's Sports and Fitness*, vol. 9 no.7, July 1987, 50.
36. Littlewood, 14.
37. Littlewood, 14.
38. Leo Fischer, "Softball Steps Up," *Reader's Digest*, June 1939, 135.
39. Robert Yoder, "Miss Casey at the Bat," *Saturday Evening Post*, 22 August 1942, 16, 48.
40. "Ladies of Little Diamond," *Time*, 14 July 1943, 74.
41. Littlewood, 29.
42. Merrie Fidler, "The Development and the Decline of the All-American Girls Baseball League, 1943–1954," (M.S. thesis: University of Massachusetts, Amherst, 1976), 54.
43. Data compiled by National Baseball Hall of Fame.
44. Sharon Roepke, Diamond Gals: The Story of the All American Girls Professional Baseball League, 2d ed. (Flint, Mich.: AAGBL Cards, 1988), 6; Merrie Fidler, "The All-American Girls Baseball League, 1943-1954," in *Her Story in Sport: A Historical Anthology of Women in Sports*, ed. Reet Howell (West Point, NY: Leisure Press, 1982), 591.
45. Susan Cahn, "No Freaks, No Amazons, No Boyish Babes," *Chicago History Magazine*, Spring 1989, 33.
46. Paul Dickson, *The Worth Book of Softball: A Celebration of America's True National Pastime* (New York: Facts on File, Inc., 1994), 197.
47. Darlene Mehrer, "Happy Birthday Softball, Wish You'd Never Been Born," *Base Woman*, July 1987, 3.

Mixed Signals: The Story of Effa Manley and the Negro Leagues (A Play)

Julianna Skluzacek

The time is 1989 — the place is the basement of a Newark home in which Effa and Abe Manley lived during their ownership of the Eagles, 71 Crawford Street. Left there are old file cabinets and piled up cardboard boxes and a single chair.

Also on the stage to the right is a set of bleachers. Three murals depict pictures of Effa and scenes from old Eagles' photos. Center there is an old, yet elegant chair with a small table. In all conversations the actor playing Effa plays both parts. As the lights come up we see a young, nicely dressed woman of the 1940's period as she steps for the shadows behind the boxes. She speaks to a young man who has come to move the files out. He has begun to eat his lunch when she appears. You do not see the man.

Effa speaks:

So, you finally found all of this. I'd forgotten where I put it until Abe reminded me the other day. (Pause) How did I get in here? I know the way. (Pause) You came with the truck to pick these things up? Don't let me keep you from eating your lunch. Ah, Tastee Cakes — my, my food, I do miss that — among other things. (Pause)

Why, I'm Effa Manley. You know, "the" Effa Manley, owner of the Newark Eagles, or what is it one writer called me — the "Queen of the Negro Leagues?" (She laughs.) Well, I never felt or lived like royalty but I did love baseball. (Pause) Goodness, son, I'm not still alive! Hey, hey, hey.

Come on back here. I'm harmless — at least now I'm harmless. Not too many people who thought that when I was alive as I raised more than an eyebrow in my time. (Walks about the boxes and crosses over to chair to sit.) It feels strange being back in this old house that Abe and I shared for so many years. Let me explain it to you.

They say that sometimes when a spirit feels someone or something reaching for it, you can — ah well, I don't know — rematerialize and be seen by those living on this earthly plane. (This amuses her) Might have been the discovery of these files — boxes containing thousands of pieces of paper that chronicle the twelve most important years of my life. I put this stuff down in the basement after Abe died. Forgot it was here. I sold the house, moved to California — but not to forget. I always want to remember and now I want you to remember too.

And possibly, I just yearned to come back one more time and have the last say about the Negro Baseball Leagues and how I feel about what has happened — and what still needs to happen. I know — you just came to pick this stuff up and you weren't expecting to run into some smart-talking lady with an attitude. But I have a story that needs to be told. And what Effa wants ... You see, time is the culprit. So many of us have gone and those who are left won't be around long to ask. So, I'm going to tell you about myself and those boys of mine who made me so proud to be a part of that world and those years. Sit yourself right back down there. (Pause) Why you? Because I don't know how long I'll be here and no matter how thin the pancake, there are always two sides to it. We didn't get to write the history books and there is more to black baseball's story than Branch Rickey's heroic experiment. Branch Rickey? He was the owner of the Brooklyn Dodgers — the man who brought Jackie Robinson up to be the first black player in the majors. Don't you know anything? Never mind him for now I'm getting ahead of myself. I'll get to Mr. Rickey in due time.

I think you should know something about me first. After all, I am one of the most important characters in this story. (Pause) Yes, really. Do you know any other woman before or since who co-owned and ran a major league baseball team, who fought for black rights and was a woman in times when most of your grandmothers were still trying to get out of the kitchen? And, (She sits and slowly crosses her legs) what other woman's legs could stop a runner in his tracks on the way to a stand-up triple faster than a hungry dog gobbling up dinner scrapes. (She laughs deeply.)

Here are the basic facts. My mother was Bertha Ford Brooks and she was a seamstress and she was white, in case you were wondering — everyone else did. I was born March 27, 1900. Now, I know you're thinking — she doesn't look 99 to me. Well, you didn't think I'd come back at the age

I was when I passed over? Effa always liked looking good and some things never change. What was I saying? Oh yes, about my birth. My birth certificate lists my mother's husband, Benjamin Brooks, as my father. He was a black man. I had 6 brothers and sisters but it never occurred to me to ask why I was this little blonde haired, light-skinned child. I just played with all the other kids on my block with no question. What I learned later from my mother was a surprise but strangely enough, it didn't significantly alter my life. I knew the world in which I wanted to journey.

When I was a teenager, oh I must have been 15 or 16. There was a white boy at school who had the worst crush on me. He'd follow me around and stammer hell occasionally. I thought he was quite cute but something kept holding him back from asking me out. Finally, one day I whirled around on him, "Why do you just keep fawning over me like some sick dog. Just ask me out." "My mother would kill me if I went out with some colored girl — even a light skinned, pretty one like you." I was mad when I came through the door of our apartment. I was screaming and carrying on when my mother looked at me so serious, "You have just a much right as any girl to go out with that boy." (Slowly Effa crosses and is drawn back into another time. In the following scene she does both hers and the voice of her mother.)

EFFA: Ma, you said that once before when I was little and that teacher wondered why I played with the black kids at school. Come on, Ma. I'm old enough to notice the way some people whisper when I walk into the store or pass by on the street.

MOTHER: Effa, when I was young and still married to Benjamin, I worked for a very rich white man, John Bishop. I'm not making excuses, child. I'll just simply tell you that I became pregnant by him. I knew the moment they laid you in my arms that there was no part of Benjamin Brooks in you.

EFFA: But Brooks is on my birth certificate. I've seen it. It's my name.

MOTHER: That is true. It was easier that way for all of us.

EFFA: So that's why he left. Because of me?

MOTHER: No, it was not that simple. Benjamin sued Bishop for alienation of affection and got $10,000 from him. I could never get over him taking that money. It seemed like a payment for you — my Effa. Girl, do you understand what this means? You can live or eat or work anywhere you want.

EFFA: But, Mama, this is where I want to be. I love my family and — these people. But do these people want me? I hate being different.

MOTHER: Effa, there is nothing wrong with being different. Every day I walk down the street and see people with the same looking faces. But you — there is no one like you. With your eyes and a way of walking into a room that makes everyone catch their breath. I suspect your life is going to be extraordinary. And only you can make that life.

To the audience: My mother was very wise. She then held me and told me I belonged where I felt loved. That is how I came to make my choice to live in the black world and I have never been sorry about that. My decision to live in the world of my childhood was not always easy and I know I even gave myself mixed signals about what I wanted. I decided to keep the story of my birth a secret. Let people wonder — and my, did they ever wonder. I was my own woman with dreams that did not include following the rules. My mother taught me I could do anything a man could and I was out to show the world just that. But always in the back of my mind was that it cost a white man $10,000 to keep me a secret.

I graduated Philadelphia's William Penn High School in 1916 and I did not look back. There was a brief marriage to a man who I met on the Atlantic City Boardwalk. I'm telling you that man wanted me to stay home and cook dinner every night and hand over my paycheck for him to spend. Well, out he went. I got my own apartment in Harlem and supported myself as a hatmaker.

When I started living on my own, I was lucky enough to share the same apartment building with Hall of Fame Negro League pitcher Smokey Joe Williams. He was retired and working as a bartender. His stories about playing for New York's Lincoln Giants, barnstorming his way across America mesmerized us. How much do you know about what we called the Negro Leagues? Do you know the names of any black ball players besides Sammy Sousa? Hey, put that box down. You're going nowhere because this is the part that I was getting to and this is the part you need to hear. (she waits for him to sit). I've got 60 minutes to tell you because you're on your lunch hour? All right, I better get talking.

Now, New York summer nights could be unbearably hot. Soon, the entire building would be catching a breeze on the front stoop. It didn't take much persuading to get Smokey Joe to talk for hours about his years playing in the Negro Leagues during the '20s. (Effa uses Smokey Joe's voice)

Do you know who Moses Fleetwood Walker is? Let me tell you. In 1884 he signed with an all white Toledo team. It was just one step down from the majors and all of black baseball buzzed with the news. However, it only took one year for racism from the other players to force him off the team. Men refused to play the Toledo team if Fleetwood took the field. He received death threats and there was no powerful commissioner at that time to put a stop to the outrageous behavior. The summer of 1887 things heated up when white players refused to even appear in pictures with their black teammates. That winter none of the black players in the top five minor leagues had their contracts renewed. The curtain was drawn not to open again for fifty years.

Even though a war was fought because of it, America was not able to merge black and white into a single nation. Major league baseball symbolized this deep divide. Oh sure, Smokey Joe said there were still some all black teams hanging on playing in the predominately white minor leagues. The Cuban Giants was an outstanding team that played in the Middle States League. But in 1890 they made the fatal error of winning the league title. Soon after the Eastern League banned all black teams as well. So what happened to all these great ball players who had no teams? Well, a vacuum by its very nature draws matter into it. With no venue to participate in a game they loved, black players formed their own leagues. And where else but in that vibrant but highly segregated town of Chicago would the Negro Leagues have their birth with the Chicago League? Every historical movement demands a person of vision to help energize folks and make ideas become reality. Rube Foster was that man. The year was 1920 when Rube helped to found the Negro National League which included the Atlantic City Bacharachs one of the finest teams to play in the Eastern Colored League. At the mention of the Bacharachs, a young voice chirps, "Tell us about Pop, Smokey." (As Smokey) "John Henry "Pop" Lloyd? My he was something to watch. Couldn't be beat as a third baseman ... and hitter? My, my! I remember once a St. Louis sportswriter was asked to name the best player in baseball history. He responded, 'If you mean in organized baseball my answer would be Babe Ruth, but if you mean in all of baseball, the answer would have to be an Atlantic city colored man named John "Henry" Pop Lloyd.'" (Effa becomes herself again.) Pop, like many other Negro leaguers, went on to contribute so much to his community.

Black baseball continued to boom, but the problems that killed it in the '40s also almost destroyed it when the depression came. The black leagues were run by chaos. The teams did not own their own stadiums; they had no office or business staff. The Brooklyn Royal Giants ran itself from a restaurant — outrageous. Some teams played 60 games, some 25.

Then tragedy struck when the powerful Rube Foster became ill and then died a few years later. With no cash reserves, the Depression and declining crowds hit the Eastern Colored League and it collapsed. Players were forced to go on the road barnstorming to feed their families. Why is it that tough economic times always hit blacks the worst?

These men traveled from town to town sometimes riding the rails. Often they would get to a place to play ball only to not make enough money to get home. Hotels wouldn't let them sleep in their beds so the men carried their belongings along with their baseball gloves in bedrolls. Players could go days without eating if they didn't have any money to buy food. And even when they did have the money they couldn't always get served. Chet Brewer, who played for the Union Giants traveled with his team on an old bus with long benches on each side of it. They'd sleep in the bus, wash and hang their underwear out the windows to dry and try to find places that would serve them. Ole Jim Crow was alive and active. In Elkhart, Indiana, they ordered 36 hamburgers from a small cafe. While they were cooking, one of the fellows says, "I'll just have a piece a pie while I'm waiting." To which the waitress replied, "I'm sorry, we don't serve you like this." So, they just stood up and said, "Fine since we can't eat here, you people have a good time eating all of those hamburgers." And we walked out. Smokey Joe told us how players even slept in the local black funeral home while barnstorming — sometimes on cots and sometimes in the coffins themselves.

The depression continued to take its toll on this nation — both black and white. But black baseball was never truly dead. We just went someplace where the sun was still shining — Cuba, Mexico and South America. Teams still hung together playing the game they loved wherever they could find an opponent and a ballpark. The 1930s brought a whole new golden age for the Negro Leagues. And it was at this time that my story with black baseball and my life with Abe Manley began.

It was at the 1932 World Series in Yankee Stadium that I met Abe Manley. I don't remember now who introduced us but Abe cut an imposing figure. (Effa relives this) Effa: It's very nice to meet you as well, Mr. Manley. You appear to be an avid baseball fan. Babe Ruth? Well, yes he is quite an impressive hitter and I've always been a fan of his. (Pause) Of course, I know that Josh Gibson from the Pittsburgh Crawfords is every bit as good — got the same big ego, too. (pause) You are surprised that I know who he is. Well, Mr. Manley, what is it you would like to know about baseball? Yes, I have seen the Hilldale team play in Philadelphia but I've never seen you there. Yes, you may, indeed, have my telephone number.

And so began our courtship. There were many reasons why I shouldn't have married Abe Manley. He made his fortune in the numbers but got out of the business when the white mobsters moved in. They actually blew up the front of his club, the Rest-A-While, in Camden because he refused to pay them protection money. Abe was smart and he sensed the wind changing with the local police who had tolerated the numbers business for years. So he left it and moved to Harlem where I met him. Abe was also about 15 years older than I was. I thought that was romantic although it had its drawbacks later on. He offered security and a glamorous life. As a light skinned woman — Abe did not know I was white when he met me — I was Abe's ticket into high black society — or what they called upper shadie — a place where he was not welcome as a numbers owner. Abe

Manley was also a gentle human being. A quality not easy to find in some of the younger but rougher men I had known.

Abe asked me to marry him and off we went to Tiffany's to purchase a 5-carat diamond ring. We shocked all the sales girls. Word spread through the store that an old Negro man had bought a 5-carat ring for a young white girl. We were married on June 15, 1933. It was the second marriage for us both. I was 33 years old and my life was just beginning. (Jazz music begins to play.)

I loved life in Harlem. Unlike other large American cities where blacks lived on the fringes of town, Harlem was located in the heart of Manhattan. There was great music at the clubs, always a party or gathering to attend. At the same time, blacks were beginning to crusade for the equal rights they had been promised after the Civil War. As I chose to not tell anyone about my racial background, they just all assumed that with my olive skin I was partially black.

At that time, the department store L. M. Blumstein had five stores located in Harlem. The Citizens League for Fair Play organized a protest because the store would not hire blacks for any other job other than janitorial or elevator operator. Heck, there were men with college degrees running the elevators. Unacceptable! I joined the league as secretary — where I first learned I had a good head for numbers and organization. The Reverend John Johnson had all 1,000 members of his congregation save their receipts from Blumsteins. An appointment was made to see the management. They politely listened to the committee — acknowledged that 75 percent of their business came from blacks and then turned them away. Our next step was an all out boycott against buying at Blumsteins. The first day of the picketing one of the volunteers failed to show up so down I went to the store and picked up my sign that said "DON'T BUY WHERE YOU CAN'T WORK." By July 3, they called another meeting. This time I made sure I went along. I sat there while all these men argued back and forth. Lots of talking but no action. Just like in the Negro Leagues later on. Well, I couldn't take it any more.

"You know, Mr. Blumstein, we think as much of our young colored girls as you do your white girls, but there's no work for them except to work as someone's maid, or become prostitutes." When I said that, Blumstein's lawyer almost went through the roof, "Oh, Mrs. Manley, don't say such a thing." "I am only telling you the truth." Blumsteins could not hide from the truth, not in that office or on the street outside. They capitulated. So we targeted other businesses and one-year later, 150 blacks had been hired in clerical jobs on 125th Street.

While all of this was going on, we were looking for a new business. We found a perfect fit for a Babe Ruth fan and Hilldale team fanatic. As I said, Abe had gotten out of the numbers' business after they bombed his club. He was looking for another business when the Brooklyn Eagles Negro League ball team came up for sale in 1935.

The Eagles' first year was a hard one. We got clobbered our first game by the Homestead Grays. We lost a lot of money that season as it was still the Depression and you could not make ends meet while paying so much stadium rent and sharing the gate receipts with booking agents. In addition, there were so many black teams in the New York area, we were slicing up the market into too small of pieces. Abe and I decided to move the Eagles. We bought the Newark Dodgers who played at Ruppert Stadium in Newark, merging the two teams together and that's how the Newark Eagles were launched.

For the first two years, Abe wouldn't let me have a word to say. Then it got to be a place where he would let me make a suggestion or offer a criticism, and finally, right out of a clear sky one day, he said, "Honey, I think I'll let you take over now." It thrilled me, but I wasn't sure of myself. I was scared I'd do something wrong, but he soon got rid of that fear for me. Whenever I showed signs of hesitating about making a move, Abe put on his hat and coat, went out and got into the car and drove off. It made me mad at first but it taught me not to be afraid to make a hard decision. It really was for the best and Abe must have known that. Abe Manley might have been a numbers man but he was lousy at bookkeeping. So I handled the business end of the Eagles. Abe was elected to vice-president of the league the second year and then served as secretary. He got the title and I did all the work. It got so I attended league meetings to represent the Eagles.

What Abe was good at was finding the best baseball talent that was out there. He could look at a wet behind the ears, young player and see that he would be great someday. It was a real skill — one that would put us on top of the world one day. So while Abe was out scouting, I negotiated the contracts each year with the players, handled the schedule and travel arrangements and made the equipment purchases. Some people did not understand why I insisted on my players looking as good as possible. I did not want any shabby uniforms or worn out equipment on the Eagles' field. Maybe we couldn't belong to the white majors even though we played like we did, but I sure wanted us to look like we belonged there. It was a matter of pride. Our bus, though not new, was clean and polished at all times.

I thought I might miss New York and the vibrant life of Harlem but Newark was a great city back then. Newark black society would socialize at the Grand Hotel. I became secretary for the local NAACP, fundraising for them along with the Urban League and the Boy's Club. Abe didn't care much for socializing but I loved the parties that featured famous men like the jazz pianist Eubie Blake and Joe Louis, the fighting champ who became a good friend of mine even after I moved to California. But I was always going to be that woman who owned the ball club. (She goes to greet some-one who snubs her.)

I didn't care. I had my team and my boys. It wasn't easy being a woman in a world so dominated by men. That hasn't changed much, has it, sir? At first the men deeply resented my presence. Cramped their style, they said, and I had little tolerance for the over inflated egos of some of the owners, especially Gus Greenlee. I would not stand for any funny busi-ness when it came to money or fair play and, I think they were intimidated by how smart I was. Sometimes I had to use all of my weapons, whether it was the distraction of a well-shaped leg or a timely tear. Eventually I earned their trust and they sent me to the East-West Game in Chicago to make sure the money was divided up equally and that people weren't cheated.

The quality of Negro League baseball was shown off best by the play-ing of the All Star East-West Game. It became the highlight of the season. Fifty-thousand people, black and white would gather at Comiskey Park. You did not go to the ballpark dressed like today. Everyone had on his or her Sunday best. Dressed to the nines, we were. It was the place to see and be seen. (Music of the era begins to play as Effa walks over to one of the boxes and takes out a hat and gloves which she puts on.) Black entertain-ers came in from all over the country. Billie Holliday, Lena Horne, Louis Armstrong, Joe Louis. There were also plenty of white politicians because they knew they needed the black vote.

Every year the fans, both black and white, flocked to the East-West Game in Chicago. There were no color lines when it came to enjoying great baseball. There they were, sitting side by side, buying food, standing in line for drinks and even sharing the same bathrooms. In 17 years there was never a racial incident — there in Chicago, one of the most racist towns in the country. Why we could not all play and live together like that all year was a mystery to me. The color lines of America dissolved for a few hours each year in a ballpark.

Abe and I understood what black baseball meant to the people. It gave us heroes at a time when there were few black ones around. The white press? It never covered black baseball. It was up to black sportswriters to tell our stories. One of the issues they were always harping on was the dis-organization of the team owners. We too felt there was too much barn-storming going on. In fact, teams often did not even stick to the league schedule. Owners would take their teams where they could get the best crowds and make the most money. There was so much talent on the teams but it was being wasted. The power struggles between the Crawfords' Greenlee and the Greys' Posey were of epic proportions; like medieval lords ruling over their kingdoms each fighting the other for more power and land. Just another justification the white owners cited for keeping the black teams out of the major leagues. The biggest lie? That we could not play as well as them. Well, let me tell you we not only played as well — we played better.

Black baseball was a different game — fast, daring and fans loved it. There were no coaches or one correct way of doing things. Everyone had his own style. It was a hitter's game with many more bunts, hit-and-run plays, and stretched out singles. Heck, Cool Papa Bell of the Crawfords stretched out singles to triples on a regular basis. He was so fast that he could turn out the light and jump in bed before it got dark. There were no illegal pitches. You could get anything from a spitball to shine balls, emery balls, and darkened "dirt" balls. All it took was a little nick in a ball or some spit on it to make it jump all over the place. Pitchers loved to throw straight at your head. Max Manning called them chin dusters. After sending a batter flying out of the box, Max would laugh and holler, "Hey, don't take it personally. I'm just trying to make a living." Another Eagle, Leon Day joked, "You've heard of tight pitches called chin music? Well, I gave them a whole symphony." Sometimes players sharpened up their spikes on their shoes and they'd come flying in with the spikes high looking to draw blood. It was black baseball that introduced shin guards for catchers. They needed them.

Through the years, Negro League teams competed against white major leaguers such as the Babe Ruth or Dizzy Dean All-Stars. We beat them so consistently, the commissioner forbade them to play us. Our superior playing was an embarrassment to them. We knew we were good enough, but they were not going to admit it.

Unfortunately, the constant in fighting kept the Negro Leagues in chaos and helped eventually to lead to our demise. We really needed a commissioner with no ties to any of the teams. There were none forthcoming.

The Eagles too had their share of problems with trying to enforce signed player contracts. Leroy Satchel Paige is probably the most well known Negro Leaguer. Eagle Lennie Pearson reluctantly faced him when Paige pitched for the Crawfords. After taking three consecutive strikes, he walked back to the dugout where Monte Irvin asks, "How did he look?" "I don't know, I haven't seen the ball." Did you know Paige was suppose to be a Newark Eagle? Mr. Paige may have been a living legend but he did not know the meaning of the word contract. The summer of 1938 Paige jumped from the Crawfords midseason to go play for more money in the Dominican Republic. He returned to the states later that year but he had never signed his '38 contract with the Crawfords. Owner Greenlee was fed up and sold Paige's contract to the Eagles for $5,000, a lot of money back then. We may have thought we had Paige but Satchel never thought twice about taking off again and jumping contract when he once again decided to take a big money offer from the South American leagues. The spring of 1939, despite our contract, he signed with the Kansas City Monarchs, which he had no right to do. The next winter he went back to Puerto Rico to play and wrote me an ambiguous letter. He subtly suggested that if I were to agree to be his "girl" he would come and play for the Eagles. That infuriated me. No man was purchasing my silence again. I let him know that was not going to happen. I went after the league presidents Martin and Wilson. (She moves back in time again to the scene.)

"Do not sit there and pretend to tell me that you didn't know that I have a contract from the Crawfords and a receipt for $5,000 that tells me Mr. Paige is an Eagle. (Pause) What do I expect you to do? My dear gentlemen, we expect you to order Wilkinson to send Paige to Newark NOW. If organized baseball is not strong enough to do this, it is not strong enough to call itself organized. And if you choose not to do this Abe and I will take the Eagles out of the league."

The result? Well, we didn't get Satchel but we did get two other players for him of no real talent. But in a sense we had won because it was the first time that a claim for a jumping player had ever been reconciled. Abe and I fought these battle because we had a vision of what the Negro Leagues could be.

Are you still with me? (Pause) Good. Oh dear, I need to hurry along. Your lunch hour is half over and I'm beginning to feel somewhat vapory.

Remember when I mentioned that Paige went to play in South America? Let's talk a little about the players who traveled in the winter and even the summer to play in the South American leagues: Mexico, Cuba, Puerto Rico and the Dominican Republic. (Latin music begins.) Why did they do this? Well, the political dictators like Trujillo in the Dominican Republic had plenty of money to spend on their ball teams and their players. A man could make enough money to take care of his family for the year in just a couple of months. The money was so good even white ballplayers went south to play in the cold months. And there, in those warm climates filled with light and sun, black and white played on the same teams; shared the same locker room facilities and dined and slept in the same hotels. That's one of the best reasons I could see for playing down there. These proud, gifted athletes could walk down the street arm and arm with their wives, feeling safe, and able to live truly like free men. There were no special color sections or signs on the water fountains. That was an appeal that we could never have conquered. Eagles' pitcher Max Manning spent four winters in Cuba playing. He said it had to be better than playing in the majors. Eagle's third baseman Ray Dandridge echoed the feelings of the players, "In Mexico, a good player was a good player." White and black players learned they could count on each other. They even shook hands after the games. But this is a story that the white press ignored. They did not even acknowledge the existence of Martin Dihigo from Havana who was a national hero in the Mexican leagues.

The 40's brought the Golden Era of the Negro Leagues. (music begins to play from WWII) It was World War II that put black baseball on the map. At first, blacks were denied the boom that the country was experiencing because of the build-up of defense industries. Then President Roosevelt passed the Fair Employment Practices Committee. Newark became a boomtown. There were new industries everywhere and blacks were bringing home decent paychecks. The black population grew and they loved coming to ballgames. The war also brought travel restrictions — it was hard to get a train ticket — and gas rationing was strictly enforced. People had to stay close to home to find entertainment.

Finally, in 1943 we finished a season in the black after years of taking money from our personal income to support the team. A Sunday afternoon in Newark included church, an Eagles game and dinner with friends or out on the town. It was the place to be. And we supported the war effort with war bond rallies at the stadium. Abe and I always believed we had a responsibility to be a positive part of the community and we expected that from our players as well. Throughout the years, the Eagles raised money for causes like the NAACP and the anti-lynching campaign.

As the war ran on, more of our young players entered the service. But when it ended, our players came back and Abe went to work building us the great team that set us up for the 1946 season. The end of World War Two found the Negro Leagues at the height of their success.

Our hopes were high with the return of Max Manning, Day, Doby, Ruffin, Irwin, Parks, Israel and Biz Mackey as manager. The black sportswriters picked the Eagles as the pennant favorites. The 1946 season started out with a no hitter pitched by Leon Day against the Philadelphia Stars. Watching Leon pitch was like hearing Ella ease out the notes of a Gershwin tune — graceful, fluid. Unfortunately we went into a terrible slump after a winning opener.

> EFFA: Abe, we have got to do something quick or this pennant race is going to be over before it begins.

ABE: I've been thinking about it. Biz and I think we should trade Murray Watkins to Philadelphia for third baseman Patterson and then ...

EFFA: The fans are going to scream, Abe. They voted Murray most popular player last year — remember?

ABE: Effa, don't even speak about Watkins and Patterson in the same breath. The only reason I can get him is because he's not getting along with the manager. Besides, putting together the team has always been my job and things are not going to change now. It's your.... (job)

EFFA: This is just like when you traded away McDuffie. You were so unreasonable and ...

ABE: Effa, that was an entirely different set of circumstances and you know it.

EFFA: Yes, but to tell everyone you traded him for two broken bats and a jockstrap.

ABE: Effa — Effa, come back here. Don't you walk of the room when I'm still talking.

EFFA: Abe was a quiet and accepting husband but I really pushed him during my relationship with Terrie McDuffie. (She is uncomfortable as she begins.)

You see, Abe had started having some health problems and he spent a lot of time playing cards with his buddies late into the night. I grew tired of attending parties by myself. The good times and laughter grown hollow. Women? Not comfortable in my presence as I had little interest in conversations about home and children. Men? They found me alluring. Lovers, yes. Friends, no. This man's world was solitary at times. And Abe? I loved Abe but our age difference was causing certain problems in areas of the marriage. A girl can't do books all the time. (To the boy) You got me talking about myself. You quiet guys are tricky that way. Back to a safer topic — the '46 season.

Besides trading Watkins, Biz and Abe put Ruffin in as starting catcher and moved Monte Irvin in from the outfield to shortstop a position where we had trouble. That meant Harvey was playing regular in the outfield. We took off like a rocket. The sweetest series of the summer was beating our perennial nemesis — the Homestead Grays in 3 out of 4 games. The Grays' team included three future Hall of Famers — Josh Gibson, Buck Leonard and Cool Papa Bell. The first half of the race ended with the Eagles 25 and 9 but it was still a long road to Labor Day. One day after a home game one of the fans hollered at me, "Girl, good trade!" "Stop your smiling, Abe."

We finished the second half 22 and 7. The city was on fire with the Eagles. We drew 120,292 people to the games. It was our best season ever netting us $25,000. (She opens a file and takes out a paper and reads from it) No one could beat a lineup that featured Monte Irvin batting at .394, Larry Doby at .342, Johnny Davis at .338, Pat Patterson at .337; Len

Pearson at .322. And when Day pitched that meant adding a .431 hitter to the powerful brew. And our pitching? We did not need Satchel. As we were about to prove with Max Manning, Leon Day, and Rufus Lewis. This was the lineup as we moved into the '46 World.

Writers called it the last of the great ones. Things were changing. It was the first year of integration into the white majors. Jackie Robinson had been drafted by Branch Rickey to play for the Brooklyn Dodgers. Integration hadn't yet drained us of our talent as only five black players had been signed to play in the white majors. Our opponents? The Kansas City Monarchs, a team that included four men who would play in the integrated leagues: Willard Brown, Frank Thompson, Connie Johnson and Satchel Paige. We beat the Monarchs earlier that year in a barnstorming game, 7 to 4 at Ruppert Stadium. The victory tasted especially fine as Satchel pitched. We were ready for them and they wanted to beat us just as much as we wanted to beat them.

The Negro League World Series was not just played at the teams' home ballparks but all over the country. (Effa again is back in another time.) The series begins on September 17 at the Polo Grounds in New York City. There are over 19,000 fans present. Kansas City wins two to one.

But the second game is at our home field, Ruppert Stadium. It's a glorious day. I bought the boys brand new white home uniforms. My, they look fine when they hit the field for warm-ups. Eagles seven to four.

September 23 — the third game is a long bus ride to Kansas City. We take a licking losing fifteen to five. I try giving hitting instructions from our box but ever since the time I crossed my legs to give my bunt signal (She slyly crosses her legs.) distracting a batter so much he got knocked out cold, Biz told the boys to ignore me.

The fourth game is played at Kansas as well. Eagles' victory; eight to one. The series is tied 2–2. Game five packs Chicago's Comiskey Park. It's Kansas City — five to one. No one is happy when we return to Ruppert in a position that demands we win the next two games on Friday, September 27 and Sunday, September 29.

The sixth game is a scoring feast — a nine to seven win. That Sunday morning, Abe and I barely talk to each other we are so nervous. Everything we have worked for over the years is here hanging in the balance — on one ball game on one day in the autumn of 1946.

We arrive at the park — every nerve fiber alive and dancing. We are able to move out early by scoring in the first when Patterson, safe on an error, is moved along by Doby drawing a walk. Then Monte singles him home. My, that boy can play. The crowd's spirits sink in the top of the sixth when Monarch first baseman John "Buck" O'Neil slugs a homer. But our boys have a glint of hard-edged determination in their eyes that has been sensed by the pitcher. He walks both Doby and Irvin. Next up — Johnny Davis. Come on, Johnny, don't leave them stranded out there. Bring 'em round. Suddenly — he smacks a hard line drive scoring them both. (She cheers.) We are up three to one. We are all on our feet. I hardly have any voice left. The Monarchs have a little steel left in them as well. They bunch up three hits at the top of the seventh and score a run. Eagles ahead — just 3 to 2. The fans are whisper quiet at the top of the ninth. I'm torn between a feeling of wanting to leave and not being able to move. Like the champions they are, the Monarchs try one more time to clinch the game. One out — Mickey Taborn, catcher, singles, but our man, Wilkes, throws him out at second when the fool tries to stretch it to a double. That man should know better with our infield. "And don't you try that again, sir!" TWO OUTS! Just one more. A roar swells within the stands and then, silence once again. The streets of Newark are deserted. Everyone is either at the game or has their ears pasted up next to a radio. Ford Smith singles and Chico Renfroe draws a walk. Two potential runs on base. I know we have an opportunity to come back in the bottom of the ninth but not one Eagle wants the pressure of that situation. Souell steps into the batter's box.

Eagles' pitcher Rufus Lewis sizes him up. My eyes are riveted to the playing field. Souell fouls off a pitch as the crowd groans. The tension is suffocating. Next, a ball. The count is 1 and 1. My nervous system can take no more. (She lowers her head.) Then, as if from another world, I hear the sickening sound of bat striking ball — crack! I'm almost afraid to look up. Has Souell homered? Just as I raise my eyes I see our first sacker, Lenny Pearson, fondly squeezing that little old round white ball ... Souell popped up! The place erupts into pandemonium. I barely remember the next minutes. I was drained of all energy, but Abe is on the field crying and hugging everyone. Next, that picture — like a still photograph captured by my mind's eye for all time — our boys — those fine men of unparalleled skill celebrating joyously on the field. I breathe in that moment. But for now we are all off to the Grand Hotel to relive the stories of glory that would be my late night companions in later years. (She takes off her hat and crosses back to the chair, sitting quietly.)

(To the young man) I know — we both need to go. That's all right because what happened over the next two years I am hardly able to talk about still. Jackie Robinson was a crack in the dam that grew from a trickle to a raging rapid. I could not face it at the time but the Negro Leagues' days were fading quickly. You see, I remember who played in that last World Series but I also recall who did not. Jackie was absent from the Negro League rosters as well as former Eagle Don Newcombe. Also gone that year to the white minors was catcher Roy Campanella. There was a painful part about that great '46 season. Even though it had been one of the most exciting Black World Series of all time, the sportswriters had their eyes on these history making players who braved the early days of integration. For awhile Robinson and the Negro Leaguers commanded the same space in the black dailies but the equal treatment ebbed away as the season wore on. As Robinson and the others proved they could keep up with their white teammates, they got even more coverage. I couldn't blame the papers. These men were every black person's heroes.

Abe and I truly thought there was a place for the Negro Leagues in major-league baseball. But that would only happen if the white owners of the majors desired a lasting liaison. And they did not. They wanted our fans and the money they spent but not us. We were doomed and we knew it when Branch Rickey and the other owners showed up to rape our ball teams. Yes, I say rape because that is what happened. All over black baseball, white teams were picking up black players and not compensating their teams one cent. We all spent years and considerable dollars developing these great players. Integration was a bittersweet celebration for us.

When Rickey signed Jackie Robinson to play in the Brooklyn Dodgers minor league team in '45, he treated him like a free agent, as if he did not have an existing contractual agreement with any team. The Monarchs simply lost him. But who could complain? It would look as if we were against integration. When he signed our Newcombe, I had to gag myself to keep from going after Rickey in the press. But in private I was so angry.

Rickey managed to out maneuver us completely. Rickey told the press that the Negro Leagues were so badly organized that we were the poorest excuse for a league. He said we were run by gangsters and he accused us of not having signed contracts with our players. Now, if you go through all these boxes you will discover that we always got a signed contract every spring with all of our players. That's the way Abe and I did business. I took our fight to the papers but it was not enough. We begged the black fans to come to the rescue of Negro League baseball. We were looking at 400 young men and their families being dumped into the unemployed as well as the people who worked in our offices and at the stadiums. However, it was too thrilling to see black players on the previously forbidden white fields. Time has shown me that we shouldn't have blamed the fans. Our attendance fell by more than 50 percent in 1947. To save money with salaries, we reluctantly sold pitcher Larry Doby to the previously all white team, the Cleveland Indians. Bill Veeck, who had been trying to integrate the American League, came to Abe and offered $10,000 for his contract. The price was far too low, but we admired Larry and didn't want him or the press to think we were denying him such an important opportunity.

I still wasn't going to let Veeck get away with stealing such a fine ball player.

"Mr. Veeck, you know if Larry Doby were white and a free agent, you'd give him $100,000 to sign with you merely as a bonus. If you feel you're being fair...." The result? We got $5,000 more for Doby. After we lost Doby, the Eagles began to lose ground. The sale of Doby also created a morale problem on the team. No one begrudged Larry his success but they must have wondered why they weren't chosen. All of the Eagles were worthy to play in the white majors. We lost the pennant in '47 and finished third in '48. Only 35,000 fans turned out for the entire season.

> EFFA: Abe, I have gone over the books and over them. We can not sustain these losses another season. We'll have nothing left.
> ABE: I know, Effa. You decide. I can't.
> EFFA: It's time to admit history has passed the Negro Leagues by.
> ABE: I'll take a swing down to the colleges, maybe Cuba, look for some new talent.
> EFFA: Abe, stop. We have to sell the team. I hate the thought as much as you do. This has been my home — these people my life. Baseball doesn't want us anymore. And you're not well enough to keep fighting this battle.

We announced we were disbanding and selling the team to a Memphis dentist. One of our remaining most valuable players and assets was Monte Irvin. The white majors were very interested. I was not about to take another loss on a player so I hired a good lawyer. We struck a deal with the New York Giants for $5,000, though, Monte was clearly worth more. The $5,000 we split with the lawyer, and then split the remaining $2,500 with Young, the buyer of the team. I convinced Abe that if I was leaving baseball I was going out well dressed — I bought a magnificent mink stole with the money.

Sadly, there were many fine players who never got called. I know Max Manning told a Giant's agent, who called, to deal with us if they wanted him. We asked a fair price for Max. He was never contacted again. I regret that now. While Max and I seldom agreed on anything, he was as fine a pitcher as any the Eagles had. Neither Max nor most of the players were bitter about it. They handled it with more grace than I. The Eagles' Bob Harvey said it best, "I wanted to play baseball and I did. I wanted to play with the best and against the best and I did. Miss the major leagues? I never did."

Our lives were fairly quiet after we left baseball. Soon Abe's health deteriorated. I think his heart was broken. That man loved baseball like no other owner has since. When he died it was the end of an era. Monte and Larry were the lead pallbearers. I'll remember Abe's tales of traveling with the boys on the bus, laughing, relishing their songs and companionship. I envied him that experience. It was the one element of baseball into which, I, as a woman, could not force my way.

The leagues stumbled through the 50s and slowly faded away. I moved out to California but never completely out of baseball. When they established a special committee to admit Negro League players into the Hall of Fame, I contributed to the campaign by writing letters to the decision-makers. But there are still many black players who deserve to be in the Hall of Fame. Now young man, (looks at audience) and all of you, remember these stories I have told you and tell them well and often. See it. A brilliant emerald field baptized in sunlight — those beautiful young men — black diamonds afire with a joyous passion for this game, baseball. There's Monte, Larry, Max, Ray Dandridge, Josh Gibson, Cannonball Dick Redding, Willie Wells, Buck Leonard, Lennie Pearson, Leon Day, Smokey Joe and thousands more. They play neither for money nor fame but for — love and because it was our national pastime too.

(There is the sound of a truck arriving.) I see it's been an hour and I hear that your truck has arrived. Thank you, for listening. You have a girlfriend? Ah well, never mind there are some things a spirit can't do anymore. Don't forget my boys, you hear, and take good care of my things. (Effa straightens her stockings then reaches into one of the boxes to take out her mink stole. She approaches an audience member [preferably a man] to hold it for her and she wraps it around herself and walks slowly off the stage. The lights linger for a moment on the panels as the music rises.)

Part 4

BASEBALL AND
AMERICAN BUSINESS

Baseball Is Polluted: The Modern Way to Spell BASEBALL — $Business, $People, $Collecting, the $Sport and $More

Ronald P. Anjard

You've heard the old saying ... "it's American as baseball and apple pie."

As I look back, probably as you also look back, what we remember about baseball are sounds ... the crack of the bat, the umpire crying out "Play Ball," the sound of a ball snapping into a glove, the cheers of the fans, vendors yelling out "popcorn, cracker jacks," the seventh inning stretch tune — "take me out to the ball game" ... I also remember great teams such as the Yankees, the Dodgers, the Indians, the Braves ... and on ... and I even remember the old stadiums ... Yankee Stadium, Fenway Park, Tiger Stadium, Ebbets Field and on ... We remember the thrill of watching Mickey Mantle "knock it out of the park," and Bob Feller's terrific fastball, ... and we even remember special records such as Ted Williams' .400, Tony Gwynn's seven silver bats, Don Larsen's perfect game, Joe DiMaggio's hits in the most consecutive games... Cal Ripken's most consecutive games played and 1998's Sosa and McGwire's home run record derby ... and on. There's also spring training which lets fans get close and meet the players. Many of us played ball in our youth. I also think about baseball cards, autographed cards and balls and bats and stuff ... actually meeting and talking to the players. There's all sorts of memorabilia! Baseball has been on the cutting edge of social change ... Before *Brown v. the Board of Education*, before the Montgomery bus boycott, before Martin Luther King, Jr., there was Jackie Robinson who broke the color barrier of baseball and inevitably, changed American life. Baseball, true, is a game. But it is far more. Baseball defines, in other ways what no other game does, who and what we are as a people. Baseball has been one of the great leveling forces of our democracy. When I think about all these aspects, it seems obvious why baseball became our nation's sport.

Today, unfortunately, baseball faces a potential Armageddon because of records ... another type of record ... MONEY RECORDS — these are "the fortunes" — the monies now paid to ballplayers and club owners; these are the price to attend a game, especially with your family. "Take me out to the ball game" has now a whole new image ... we now go out and see the millionaires!! ... How many of us, you and me, earn in a lifetime what a high percentage of today's players earn in just one year? Will you or I earn $10+ million in our lifetime as Kevin Brown does now for the Dodgers in this season? I checked and great Dodgers such as Pee Wee Reese, Duke Snider, Gil Hodges, Don Newcombe, Jackie Robinson — all made $18,000. I shouldn't ask how many of you will ever earn in your lifetime the $105 million that Kevin Brown will receive just for his present contract for just a few years. Once players and teams had an allegiance: Just look at the old baseball cards to see how many years — often an entire lifetime — a player played for just one team. Today's baseball cards almost tell it all: Players may be with a club 1–2–3 seasons ... sometimes they play for three teams in the same season. Loyalty, team spirit ... what spirit?

How can you build team spirit when so many players are traded or lost each year, and how must the lower-paid players feel when they work with a new team member earning $5–$9 million per year. Curious. In his book, *You're Missing a Great Game*, former St. Louis manager Whitey Herzog explains why he doesn't like what he is seeing. "One of the problems with baseball today is that the players haven't learned the game right and have no interest in learning it." Herzog blames their big contracts and agents who negotiate on their behalf. "Players know the score.... They know what they're getting paid for and it ain't fundamentals." Today's spirit is primarily for the money! Players are kept or traded, often based on their negotiated salary's impact on the team's overall budget ... rather than their current baseball skill and team spirit. Newspapers list the team members who earn at least $1 million per year. Last year, the Yankees did not have the most millionaires; two teams, one being Baltimore, had more. Even the "poor" Padres pay every regular fielder — infielder and outfielder — at least $1 million. Montreal had just one $1 million player —

Rondell White. The Expos had only a $8,317,00 payroll. From the data, you can predict their league finish. So, how many baseball millionaires were there? In 1998, there were 326 millionaires, and the average salary for all players in the majors on opening day in 1998 was $1,341,406; the average salary rocketed 19.3 percent to $ 1,720,050 for opening day, 1999. In 1999 the Padre payroll was in excess of $48 million; they ranked 15th of the 30 teams in 1999. In contrast the NY Yankee payroll was #1 at $85 million, the Dodgers at $79+ million, and Baltimore at $78+ million. In contrast the Kansas City (#25) payroll was $23.7 million and #30, Montreal was at $17.3 million. The Yankee average is $3.04 million per player in contrast to the Padres at $1.7+ million, KC at $880,000 and finally the Expos at $619,304 per player. One last statistic: For St. Louis, Mark McGwire represents 19 percent of their total payroll and Sammy Sosa represents 15 percent of Cubs' total budget.

Baseball stadiums are now being replaced with new, expensive stadiums in which the owners personally make millions. The President of the San Diego Padres, who earlier designed and built Camden Yards, is now in the process of building a new Padre "Yard." The fans don't gain, the players don't gain — primarily the owners gain money. In fact, the fans actually lose — typically the price of seats has literally exploded, often. The comparable price of seats — based on season ticket prices — for the Yankees is about $50 per game ($4,050 per season per person — adult or child — for the 81 games), while the Padres' ticket is $22 for the best seat.

Unfortunately what has developed in baseball is the development of the have and have-not teams: the clubs which can spend major dollars for players salaries and those which simply can't. There are six haves and the rest are have-nots! Recently an editorial in the San Diego *Union Tribune,* titled "Baseball Dilemma: How Can Small Market Teams Survive?" said that baseball's future hinges on the survival of small-market teams. Ticket prices and ticket sales could not keep up with the Padres' escalating payroll — "the price required to field a winning team" — even though the Padres drew record crowds. The editorial goes on to say, "baseball is on an economic collision course. Skyrocketing player salaries, combined with the ever-widening competitive imbalance that exists between the rich teams and the poor teams, are fast approaching critical mass." You can literally plot the average salary of teams against the percentage of games won, and have a direct, linear, fantastically statistical correlation. This therefore directly relates to winning the pennant and winning the Series. In past years, it has been primarily the major money teams which have won the Pennants and the Series ... the Padres in 1998 were a major exception. Of related interest is Burt Solomon's book, *"Where They Ain't,"* which deals with the origin of the baseball owner's monopoly on franchise rights. It describes how, at the turn of the century, "the owners of the National League clubs colluded with club owners in competitive leagues to fashion the monopoly that continues to benefit them." In the late 1940s the monopolistic power was broadsided by the players, but the owners fought back. In *Hard Ball* James Quirk and Rodney Fort explain how cities and fans suffer at the hands of monopolistic owners.

A few further and important comments about owners and their economics. Data from *Forbes Magazine*, December 14, 1999, clearly indicates that owners use very selective accounting. In all professional sports, including baseball, 113 professional teams surveyed by *Forbes* generated $479 million in operating income (earnings before interest, taxes and depreciation). This is based on revenues of $7.9 billion. This "a shade over 6 percent of revenues." In 1997, 12 of 28 baseball teams reported losses as high as $20+ million; two reported marginal profits (less than $1 million). While owners reported losses, *Forbes* analyses indicated that about 50 percent of these actually lost money. "It all comes down to how one defines revenues. Owners typically exclude most of the revenues from stadium naming rights and advertising, luxury suites, club seats, concessions and parking, and team merchandise stores." Add back these revenues and the profits and suddenly many losing clubs emerge from red ink to black. "Although not as big a piece of the revenue pie as television fees and tickets, these ancillary revenues are highly profitable — and growing fast." What is more, the team owners have saddled taxpayers with much of the capital costs for new stadiums, such as in San Diego, "making ancillary revenue even more profitable." According to Andrew Zimbalist, who teaches sports economics at Smith College: "One of the major motivations ... for going into new stadiums is because most of the revenue sources are not shared with players." "Corporate sponsorship is another rapidly growing revenue source for owners." Other teams, seeking to emulate Baltimore and Texas, have literally bet their futures on new ballparks — Seattle, Detroit, Houston, Milwaukee and San Francisco all move into new stadiums in 2000 and the Padres are right behind them. Cincinnati and Pittsburgh are making progress toward new stadiums also.

Over one-third of the teams *Forbes* analyzed now carry a corporate logo. The Yankees' $53-million-a-year-cable deal could "allow them to sign the best ballplayers money can buy." The "most valuable" baseball teams in 1997 were: the NY Yankees, Baltimore Orioles and the Cleveland Indians; the most profitable were: the Rockies, Yankees, Orioles, Braves and Indians. In February, March and April, I wrote the key management of the Yankees in which I complained that they did not support fans in many ways and at the conclusion of which I said: "I was once proud to be a Yankee fan ... But I am 'totally' unproud of any association with a management who so flagrantly shows its fans that you don't care and obviously indicate 'don't bother us' ... I deeply resent your 'no consideration' treatment." Their vice president's inappropriate response finally was that "any continued attempts at harassing Yankee's employees will be addressed accordingly."

A 1998 newspaper article was titled "Costs are driving baseball to a lockout." The article said that if nothing changes over the next three years, that baseball will be shut down by a spring training lockout in February 2002. Low revenue clubs are shrieking and high revenue teams say they're playing by the rules. Former Oakland GM Sandy Alderson, one of the new executive vice-presidents in the baseball commissioner's office, said that "15–18 teams have been eliminated from contention next season because they can't afford to compete." The line of demarcation last year was $48 million. Of the 12 teams with payrolls above that figure, eight went to the playoffs and all but one had winning records. The exception was the Baltimore Orioles (79–83) which actually spent a major-league-high $74.2 million. Further, of the 18 teams below $48 million, only 3 (17 percent) had winning records: San Francisco (89–74), St. Louis (83–79) and Toronto (88–74). Understand that the Giants and Cardinals were just below (0.1–0.4 million or less than 0.1 percent) this magical $48 million limit. Thus in reality, only one team, Toronto, with a winning record, was under this $48 million "boundary." It already appears that unless a club is willing to spend at least $50 million in the 1999 season, it has little chance of having a winning season. In December 1998, the Baltimore payroll was already $75+ million, the Dodgers at $72 million, Atlanta at $ 70+, and the Yankees at $68+ million. "The gap's going to get larger and larger and larger," according to Padres GM Kevin Towers. I was in Kansas City when the Royals fans protested. As part of a "Share the Wealth" demonstration against payroll disparities between small-market teams like the Royals and big-market teams like the Yankees, 3,500 paid fans walked out row-by-row in the inning of a Royals-Yankees game. During the game, protesting fans turned their backs on the Yankee batters and cheered whenever the Royals were at the plate. This might prove to be the just the tip of the iceberg.

A closer look at free-agent spending shows that eight teams have dominated the market. Of $900+ million given to 75 free agents (in late December 1998) 78 percent of this was spent by just eight teams: LA, Baltimore, Arizona, Yankees, Angels, Texas, Atlanta, and the Mets. This does not count $123 million given to Piazza and Leiter before they could become free agents. Most teams now say when they look at top names, "too rich for us."

Some sports enthusiasts ask, "What process has fattened the players' wallets?" Arbitration keeps the salary escalator going up. The advent of salary arbitration in 1974 actually started baseball's revolution. Players with at least three years of major league service but fewer than six can argue their case before an independent arbitrator. In 406 cases decided, just five players have had their pay cut. To one baseball owner, the arbitration system is ludicrous. Arbitration was actually put in place to protect players who fall short of the six years service required to become a free agent. It eliminates the possibility of a team clamping on a young player's earnings.

In the 1998 season, revenues ranged from $170 million (believed to be the NY Yankees) to a low of $35 million (NY Mets). Revenue sharing in 1998 was 80 percent and increased to 85 percent in 1999 and to 100 percent in 2000; but some teams are not convinced this will be enough. As a result, some low-revenue owners have talked about having a "work stoppage" as a means to extract more revenues from the large market teams. Baseball "leaders" fear that if NBA owners gain concessions from their players, it may encourage baseball's hawkish faction to again seek a salary cap. The Diamondbacks' owner, Colangelo, said that "without some kind of lid on the top and also some profit sharing, some revenue sharing, you can't solve the problems in every one of the cities." Commissioner Bud Selig expects the top six teams will transfer $140 million to the bottom six teams this season. But the problem with revenue sharing has been the way the funds are actually used; seeing no point in boosting payroll that can't grow big enough to produce a winner, some teams use the money to make profit. Mariners chairman John Ellis, a member of Baseball's Executive Council, wants large-revenue teams to share proportionately with teams in the middle (where Seattle resides). "Ultimately, we need to create a partnership with players where we say, okay, guys, we divide up our revenues with you, all revenues from baseball. You take X percent and we'll take Y percent and now you can figure out how you want to divide it up," Ellis said. "What we do in baseball in the next four or five years will ensure baseball's great popularity the first 20–30–40 years of the 21st century."

There are many other aspects to baseball ... one is collecting a wide variety of memorabilia. This is now big business — a Babe Ruth signed baseball sells from $1,500 to $3,000. A McGwire signed bat sells for $150–$200. Recently a bat signed by baseball greats Joe DiMaggio and Mickey Mantle was being sold for $5,900; a bat just signed by Joe D. was offered at $7,800. Amazing. For the days the players were paid so much less, such as the $18,000 mentioned earlier for the Dodger greats, Joe DiMaggio, before he died wouldn't sign anything for less than $150; this seemed

OK to most of us as he really only made money on his autographs. Today, fans still go out to the stadiums — regular season, spring training, pre-season games for autographs — for themselves, for their kids, and sometimes for resale. Fans meet the players, share with the players, get autographs. My daughter Michele takes great photos of players and gives them a copy. More than one professional has said to other players that she was their number one fan. Yet, with all the millions of dollars the players individually earn, often they don't want to be bothered by fans asking for autographs. Ex-Yankee and Seattle Mariner manager Lou Pinella as well as ex–Padre manager, now Cubs Manager Riggleman, and others, have explicitly told their players not to sign anything for fans at games, and they "hear" about it from their manager if they do. I have personally written and complained and readvised these managers that the players and their own salaries were being paid by us, the fans ... and without us, they wouldn't be millionaires. None of these managers ever had the "chutzpah" to respond. In addition to baseball cars, baseball balls, caps, photos, bats, mini-helmets, batting helmets, jerseys, gloves, pennants, magazine covers, and even toys such as bobbin' heads, are all not part of the collectible scene. There are many special events in which players are invited to come and autograph for the fans — sometimes the price is a number of baseball card packages, sometimes it's $5–$10, and in some cases it is expensive, and in some cases such as Joe DiMaggio, worth it, yet in other cases, it isn't! So baseball collectibles have grown from the bubble gum and card packs of old to a wide variety of big business. Some people and even players cheat. Some autographs are not authentic. I personally returned some items sold as Mark McGwire's autographs (ball, bat, photo) which did not compare with known personalized signed autographs, and which were returned for credit. One very major player's wife actually sold a variety of items which we knew he never signed or would not sell away. So money has become a bigger part of baseball memorabilia, sometimes big-money and in some cases just cheaters. Even the focus in memorabilia unfortunately has also turned to money.

To me and others, the icing on the baseball money mania is "sponsorship." Soon our players can start looking like *Nascar* autos. The cartoon by San Diegan great S. Kelly says it all — "say it ain't so."

Baseball is now facing a major armageddon, because the major focus has turned to money and no longer on the sport. Soon, only the well-financed fans will be able to take their families to games ... Soon, something effective must be done for the Haves and the Have-Nots to co-exist and all have a chance at winning baseball golden-rings, the Pennants and World Series. Do fans really need a lockout or a players' strike? The sound of the ball "smackin' the leather glove" is being replaced, unfortunately, by the smack of the leather wallet. Now, we have a major variation of "it's American as baseball and apple pie," but now baseball is written with huge dollar signs. Baseball — the nation's sport — is now becoming just another big business.

Stamp Out Smokeless Tobacco and Snuff in Baseball

Daniel Green

Although smokeless tobacco and snuff are banned in all the minor leagues of professional baseball and by the National Collegiate Athletic Association, the use in the major leagues continues unabated.[1]

The contract signed by owners and players in the fall of 1996 included only an educational program on the effects of smokeless tobacco and snuff, according to Richard Weiss of the Major League Players' Association (personal communication, February 1997). Historically, the Players' Association has objected to contract clauses that address behavior motivation. "The acceptance of a drug program in the major leagues is considered a significant breakthrough," stated Jimmie Lee Soloman, Director of Minor League Operations (personal communication, February 1997). However, major league players are stubborn when it comes to change, even when confronted with documented facts about the dangers of smokeless tobacco and snuff. At this writing, all thirty player representatives favor the ban but it will be very interesting to see if they vote in that manner when the contract is up for final discussion and approval before the 2001 deadline.

History

Tobacco and baseball seem intertwined. Chewing tobacco was popular 150 years ago when professional baseball started. Players used tobacco juice to combat dust, to soften their gloves, or to make spitballs. The bullpen was named after an advertisement for Bull Durham cigarettes; the first baseball card was an advertisement for Piedmont Cigarettes. Most baseball stars used tobacco products. Babe Ruth, who died of throat cancer at age 53, chewed tobacco, dipped snuff, and smoked many cigars. On the other hand, Honus Wagner detested smoking. The famous shortstop did not want his reputation used to encourage bad habits among adolescents. He had his baseball card destroyed before it hit the stands (although six survived and hold the highest value of any baseball card in existence).[2]

In the 1950s, each New York club promoted its own brand of cigarette; Chesterfield for the Giants, Lucky Strike for the Dodgers, and Camels for the Yankees. When Nolan Ryan first played for the Mets in the late 1960s, about a third of the teams smoked and a handful chewed.[3] At the time, dip was unheard of. However, free samples began to appear in the clubhouses in the 1970s and eventually dipping became popular.[2] Although a federal law banned television advertising of smokeless tobacco in 1986, players continue using it, undeterred by the death of Curt Flood at age 57 of oral/throat cancer, or Brett Butler's surgery and rehabilitation from throat cancer. Although athletes, such as baseball's Ryne Sandberg, football's Franco Harris, and Olympic Gold Medalist wrestler Bruce Baumgartner, have spoken out against the use of smokeless tobacco, Major League players continue to use the products.[3, 4]

If players will not listen to reasoned arguments about tobacco's dangers, there is nothing left but to seek to ban these products — if for no other reason than to curb the rapid increase in the number of young people who use smokeless tobacco products.[2] Consider these statistics:

- *The number of males, age 18 and older, who use snuff doubled in the twenty years from 1970 to 1990;*
- *Tobacco use rose an alarming ninefold, from 0.7 percent to 6.2 percent, among men aged 18 to 24;*[5, 6]
- *In 1990, twenty percent of white male high school seniors reported they used smokeless tobacco.*[7] *A 1990 survey conducted in Dane County, Wisconsin (Madison area), found that 22 percent of twelfth grade male students regularly use smokeless tobacco. More young man in Dane County now use smokeless tobacco than smoke cigarettes. Evidence also exists that young women are experimenting with these products.*
- *In addition, a Minnesota-Wisconsin youth tobacco survey showed that 10 percent of male high school freshmen use smokeless tobacco products weekly.*

There is no doubt that there exists a correlation between advertising and tobacco use. In the first four years that Camel cigarettes advertisement featured Joe Camel, the number of smokers younger than age 18, who preferred Camel, rose from one percent to 30 percent of the market. Furthermore, Joe Camel is as familiar to six-year-old children as Mickey Mouse.[8, 9]

Since advertising promotes awareness and use of tobacco, a Wisconsin Research Laboratory and Department of Public Instruction conducted a Youth Risk Behavior Survey (YRBS) in 1990. These results revealed that 52 percent of high school males and 19 percent of the females had tried ST or Snuff.[10] We may need possible legislation to keep advertisements like the two page advertisement for SKOAL that appeared in late 1996 in *Sports Illustrated*. When I protested to *SI*, they stated, "The median age of the SI subscribers is 36.8 years and the percentage of subscribers under the age of 18 is small."[11] Are there young people under the age of 18 reading Mom and Dad's copy of *SI*? According to Dr. Tom Green, "In *Sports Illustrated*, 33 percent of whose readers are males under 18 years, cigarette advertising expenditures were $29.9 million in 1985."[12, 13]

Sports figures, such as Walt Garrison of the Dallas Cowboys and Carlton Fisk who played for the Chicago White Sox and Boston Red Sox, have lent their names to advertising in which smokeless products are misrepresented as a safe alternative to smoking. Moreover, tobacco products are insidiously advertised on athletes' clothing and on race cars.[1, 8] Sales of smokeless products have increased 200 percent in a ten year period while cigarette smoking has declined in some age groups.[14, 15]

Performance and Health

Contrary to the myth, smokeless tobacco has a deleterious effect on performance, slowing reaction, movement and response times. Smokeless products are as addicting as any other tobacco product.[4] Experts note that the concentration of nicotine in a can of snuff is generally significantly higher than that found in a package of cigarettes.[4] Snuff labeled as "low nicotine" may have a high alkaline content which dramatically increases the body's absorption of nicotine, thus canceling out any good effect of a low nicotine product.[4]

"A can of snuff a day is equivalent to the amount of nicotine from three to four packs of cigarettes," according to a *New England Journal of Medicine* article.[16] In addition, consumers are usually unaware of the 2,500 different chemical compounds that have been found in smokeless tobacco and snuff. The most common compounds include sand, grit, sugar, sodium, tobacco, nicotine and carcinogens, such as metallic compounds (i.e., arsenic, cadmium and nickel), radioactive compounds, such as lead and polonium, polynuclear hydrocarbons (chemicals found in tars), and nitrosamines.[17, 18] All of these compounds can be deadly, however nitrosamines are the most dangerous and potent.

Nitrosamines are from preservatives found in nitrites and nitrates. The US Food and Drug Administration limits the amount of nitrosamines in food to no more than 60 parts per billion. The amount of nitrosamines in smokeless tobacco products can be 1,000 times higher than that found in foods and 2,000 to 80,000 parts per billion is found in snuff.

Tobacco use has been linked to increased blood pressure, stroke, oral cancer, heart attacks, and also cancer of the pharynx.[19, 20] Clearly something must be done to eradicate this scourge from our society.

Educating the Public

An assertive and aggressive educational program is needed if we are to eliminate the use of tobacco products in major league baseball, and, by extension, from the youth of our country.

Jones[21] observed 23 minutes in the fifth game of the 1986 World Series. The value of free advertising in those 23 minutes was estimated to be $36 million, the salaries of some of our major league teams. According to a 1993 calculation by the Nielsen Ratings Service, three million adolescents watched a typical World Series game.

To begin with, all major league teams should regularly receive the latest information about the dangers of smokeless tobacco and snuff. These materials have been sent by me to the President and CEO, who will vote on the next major league contract; the field manager, who is with the team on a daily basis from spring training until the end of the season; and the player representative from each team who will also vote on the next contract. These individuals should be made aware of the current statistics on oral and pharyngeal cancer, they should also have information about how to assist players in quitting their use of the tobacco products before spring training starts. This information has been sent yearly and will be sent until contract negotiations are completed.

I recommend intervention at spring training sites by dental professionals armed with literature promoting cessation of smokeless tobacco and snuff use.[22] Joe Garagiola and the late Bill Tuttle have done an outstanding service in this regard, as has Dr. John C. Greene and staff, Dean of University of California, San Francisco Dental School. They, and others, have provided oral examinations, in addition to printed materials.

Nicotine in snuff is not all absorbed, but a single can of moist snuff contains 300 mg of nicotine, which is five times the adult lethal dose. Nicotine immediately affects the nervous system as a stimulant, then causes depression and wears off. This up and down sensation causes addiction. A person with an addiction needs nicotine every 20–30 minutes while they are awake to maintain a sense of feeling "good."

Nicotine also affects the heart and circulatory system. When nicotine enters the bloodstream it causes the arteries to tighten and become smaller. This means that the heart has to pump faster and harder to push blood through the arteries, causing an increase in blood pressure.[23]

When comparing blood pressure levels between ST users and smokers, there is a definite increase in blood pressure for those who used ST.[23, 24]

Snuff has sodium, as do certain foods, but the amount differs. Bacon has 1.09 percent and dill pickles have 1.43 percent sodium. However, snuff has three times the sodium that is in these two foods. Nicotine and sodium together increase blood pressure, causing stress on the heart. Constant stress can lead to heart disease, stroke, and possible heart attack.[23, 24]

As a healthcare professional, I insist that the US Federal Trade Commission mandate that all ingredients and side effects be listed on the packaging of smokeless tobacco and snuff.[25]

We must also improve our methods of communicating with young people about these dangers of smokeless tobacco and snuff.

In the past year, federal and state legislators have shown their willingness to use the law and the courts to make tobacco companies financially accountable for the public's use of their products. States have increased taxes on tobacco products and show no signs that these increased will be discontinued. One can only hope that these financial sanctions will cripple the large tobacco companies and reduce the consumption by the public.

Tobacco kills more Americans than AIDs, alcohol, car accidents, fires, illegal drugs, murders and/or suicides combined.

The next Major League Baseball Contract is up for consideration in 2001. This gives ample time to demand the removal of smokeless tobacco products from the clubhouses of our national sport.

Respectfully Submitted,
H. Daniel Green, D.D.S.

Where to Write:
Major League Baseball Players Association
12 East 49th Street
New York City, NY 10017
Fax: (212) 752-3649

Chicago Cubs
1060 West Addison
Chicago, IL 60613

Chicago White Sox
333 West 35th Street
Chicago, IL 60616

Milwaukee Brewers
County Stadium
Milwaukee, WI 53214

How to Hit a Home Run:
Use your letterhead, so that the organization will immediately identify you as a professional.
Organize your thoughts so they fit on one page. Present a cogent explanation of the dangers of smokeless tobacco.
Be positive and offer constructive criticism; don't threaten!

Notes

1. Palmer, C. "NCAA Forbids Tobacco Usage." ADA News 25 (4), 21 Feb 1994.

2. Major League Players Association Office, 12 E. 49th Street, New York, NY 10017. Richard Weiss' staff, 7 Feb 1977. Oral communication.

3. Office of the Commissioner, Major League Baseball, 350 Park Avenue, New York, NY 10022. William Murray's staff, 4 Feb. 1977. Oral communication.

4. Stavisky, Eli. "Smokeless Tobacco: One Strike Could Mean Out," Pennsylvania D.J., Jan–Feb 1991, 18–19.

5. Dental Health Adviser, Smokeless Tobacco. A Strike Against You. (Knoxville, TN: Whittle Communications, 1988).

6. "Quitting Spitting, More Than Enough Reasons to Stop Using Spit Tobacco Now!" American Cancer Society, 1996, ACS Pub. #96-250M, #2090-TOB.

7. Chew or Snuff Is Real Bad Stuff. Bad Breath. Mouth Sores. Cancer. Some of the Things the Ads Don't Tell You About Chew and Snuff. National Cancer Institute, 1993. U.S. Department of Health and Human Services, National Institutes of Health, pub. #93-2976.

8. Greene, J.C., Walsh, M.M., Masouredis, C., Report of a Pilot Study. *A Program to Help Major League Baseball Players Quit Using Spit Tobacco.* JADA, Vol. 125, May 1994, 559–567.

9. Tilashalski, K., Rodu, B., Mayfield, C., *Assessing the Nicotine Content of Smokeless Tobacco Products.* JADA, Vol. 125, May 1994, 590–594.

10. Smokeless Tobacco Fact Sheet. American Cancer Society. Wisconsin Division, Inc., May 1993, WD-247.

11. *Sports Illustrated*, Time and Life Building, Rockfeller Center, New York, NY 10020. Written communication, Nov. 1996.

12. Green, T. Pennsylvania D.J., Vol. 62, #2, 13–19.

13. "Health Consequences of Smoking: Report of the Surgeon General," 1982.

14. National Institute on Drug Abuse. *National survey results on drug use from monitoring the future survey,* Vol. 2, 1975-1992. U.S. Department of Health and Human Services, Public Health Service (Bethesda, MD: National Institutes of Health), 1994. NIH publication 93-3598.

15. Allen, K.P. and others. *Teenage Tobacco Use: Data Estimates from Teenage Attitudes and Practices Survey*, United States, 1989. (Hyatteville, MN: U.S. Department of Health and Human Services, National Center for Health Statistics, 1993) (advance data from Vital and Health Statistics, No. 224).

16. Schroeder, C. "Smokeless Tobacco and Blood Pressure." *New England Journal of Medicine*, 1985, 312: 919.

17. Tobacco Education Program, slide lecture series. American Cancer Society, Pennsylvania Division, March 1989.

18. Hampson, S. "Sodium Content of Smokeless Tobacco." *New England Journal of Medicine*, 1985, 313:919.

19. Connolly, G.N., Orleans, C.T., Kogan, M. "Use of Smokeless Tobacco in Major League Baseball," *New England Journal of Medicine*, 1988, 313: 1281–1285.

20. Robertson. P.B., Derouen, T.A., Ernster, V. et al. "Smokeless Tobacco Use: How it Affects the Performance of Major League Baseball Players," *JADA*, vol. 126, Aug. 1995, 1115–1124.

21. Jones, R.B. "Use of Smokeless Tobacco in the 1986 World Series," *New England Journal of Medicine*, 1987, 316: 952.

22. Greene, J.C., Walsh, M.M., Masouredis, C. "Report of a Pilot Study: A Program to Help Major League Baseball Players Quit Using Spit Tobacco, *JADA*, 1994, 125: 558–567

23. Schroeder, Chen. "Smokeless Tobacco and Blood Pressure." *New England Journal of Medicine*, 1985, 312: 919.

24. Hampson, 313: 919.

25. Tilashalski, K, Rodu, B. Mayfiels, C. "Assessing the Nicotine Content of Smokeless Tobacco Products," *JADA* 1994, 125: 590–594.

Baseball, Culture, Criminal Justice, and the Academy

Robert P. Engvall

Introduction and Purpose Statement

A myriad of cultural "observers" in numerous disciplines have long considered baseball's impact upon the American way of life. The discipline in which I spend the majority of my academic life, criminal justice, has seldom been a discipline in which baseball's cultural impact has been assessed or even considered. Perhaps this is so because as a criminal justice professor, it might, seemingly at least, be more difficult to determine the cultural connections between baseball and crime than might be made the more obvious connections between baseball and the social aspects of human nature that a sociologist might make. The connections may also be less obvious than those between baseball and "romance" that an English professor might discover, or even between baseball and our mindset, as a psychologist might assess. Still, though perhaps more tenuous, the parallels between our great American pastime and another great American pastime, crime, can be quite readily made.

When I began work on this paper, my goal, in keeping with the contradictions present within society and within baseball, was as grand as it was actually quite simple: I wanted to show how baseball has impacted our criminal justice system. As I have read more and studied more about the history of this game (and perhaps most importantly, as I have had the chance to speak with and listen to Eliot Asinof at this very conference), I have come to the conclusion that baseball has had less effect upon our cultural social systems such as the criminal justice system, than these systems have had upon baseball. That is not to say that baseball has had no impact, but like the chicken and the egg, the debate over which came first is largely misplaced. The impact of each might be assessed, but which has the greater impact is not entirely worthy of our time. I think, in fact, that Voigt (1976) was correct when he wrote: "sports seldom shape cultural change, but usually lag behind by reflecting the prevailing customs and values of an era" (p. 109). Our criminal justice system, as are all of our social systems, is the product of persons who themselves are the products of their social environments. The prevailing values and customs of each era have shaped the sports of that era. Since baseball has the longest and most storied history of the American sports, it is baseball that perhaps deserves the most attention when considering the connections between our social system of criminal justice and the social pastime of organized professional baseball.

Baseball and Criminal Justice

A focus upon the antecedents of baseball and the early history of baseball as our national pastime has paralleled the cyclical nature of history. One hundred years ago, in 1899, baseball was already embedded within American culture. The impact that this game has had upon the American way of life and as a consequence, the impact baseball has had upon numerous "disciplines" within the academy, while seldom fully contemplated, is easily identifiable. Studying a society by how that society spends its leisure time, and what focus a society places upon leisure time activities is not a particularly novel concept. Still, it remains an effective measure of the people that comprise a society of individuals. My work here, at this conference, has been to attempt to measure the impact of baseball upon our criminal justice system, and perhaps more practically, to identify connections between baseball and the social system that is our criminal justice system. By doing so, and in combination with the various other presentations made at this symposium, we might better be enabled to understand both the richness of the game that we all love and talk about, and our society which has allowed that game such an important place. Even more importantly, however, we might be able to use baseball as a medium to help us better understand each other across disciplines. Pizzi (1999) identified sports as a medium through which we might study our culture and be enabled to better assess our social systems. This symposium has allowed baseball to be that medium, this presentation and this paper, I hope, has allowed for the use of baseball as a medium through which all of us might consider our criminal justice system.

The early history of baseball reflected the fact that baseball was only following, rather than paving, new paths. Baseball paralleled American society in the 19th century. A society deeply divided by race in the 1800s has given way to a society, while still divided by race, is even more deeply divided by income levels. Still, baseball was played by civil war soldiers, black and white, sharing a common love for the game, and a common desire to escape their temporal realities. Today, baseball is still played by children of all backgrounds and from all income levels, albeit on diamonds that differ in their quality. While race remains divisive in America, baseball led the way in integration (at least among the professional sports) in the face of loud and hostile criticism. Baseball led the way in free agency, now a staple of big time sports in America. As baseball by and large followed the paths set by American society, it also set itself apart from society by forging new paths. Baseball as a game of contradictions, like life also a mass of contradictions, are both reflected in our criminal justice system; yet another social system featuring a tangled web of contradictions.

Jacques Barzun wrote, in a statement often quoted, as it was in the introduction by Stephen Gould to Asinof's (1963) *Eight Men Out*, "whoever wants to know the heart and mind of America had better learn baseball." Having never been to the Hall of Fame prior to this symposium, I was struck by the fact that these same words graced the entrance. Much has been made lately of the heart and mind of America, a country where our young people have taken to killing their peers in high school cafeterias, and our elected leaders, of both parties, seem less bent on goodwill and statesmanship, than on self-aggrandizement and one upsmanship. Perhaps baseball remains as a way in which we might discover the heart and mind of America.

Asinof commented upon the games complexities fraught with so many variables that "fixing" the outcome was problematic. Life, too, is complicated, and those variables that have recently been assessed with regard to the Littleton, Colorado, high school shooting (and the spate of recent schoolground shootings throughout the United States) have been found to have been too complex to allow any one factor to receive more than only a share of the blame. Crime is a complex subject. It isn't all about poverty ... after all most poor people aren't criminals. It can't be all about troubled childhoods, as most of those having had difficult childhoods aren't criminals either. It is indeed quite complicated, and any assessment of the "reasons" behind crime are generally tenuous and open to quite able arguments refuting them, or at least refuting them to a certain degree.

Baseball, economics, labor, and crime were all connected during baseball's first strike in 1912. Zimbalist (1992) reports that on May 16, 1912, members of the Detroit Tigers struck over the suspension of their teammate, Ty Cobb, for fighting with a fan who had taunted him from the stands. If we are to think that 1999 is the first time we've collectively felt the world was going to hell in a handbasket, we might summon the words of a *New York Times* editorialist who wrote on May 17, 1912, of the strike's underlying cause: "the growing resentment of all authority and discipline throughout the world" (Zimbalist, 1992, p. 8). Perhaps again, however, we've made too much of a simply explained event ... after all, Ty Cobb has seldom been described as a paragon of virtue. He has been personally assailed even in the "feel good" movie *Field of Dreams*, in which his contemporary, the character of Shoeless Joe Jackson, describes him in extremely unflattering terms. Calhoun (1987) goes one further in describing Cobb as having an "almost psychopathically vicious disposition" (p. 229). Lest we think Calhoun might have overstated the case, Al Stump, who ghostwrote Cobb's autobiography described Cobb as "the most violent, successful, thoroughly maladjusted personality ever to pass across American sports" (Scheinin, 1994, p. 308). However, offensive we might find Cobb's conduct in attacking a fan ... our feelings only become worse once we uncover the facts of the incident. It seems that the reason Cobb went into the stands to attack the fan, actually a fan with a disability no less, was because the fan derided Cobb by using a racial epithet usually reserved for African-Americans. The fact that Cobb's teammates supported Cobb, may speak less for team unity than it does for a deep and abiding racism prevailing at the time that made it societally understandable to attack a person who had hurled such an insult (Shropshire, 1996, p. 35).

Whatever the personality of Cobb, and however loathsome he may have been, the bar has now been lowered to curb level when we think of the advent of perhaps the most notorious athlete, and the one with the most notorious ties to the American system of criminal justice, one O. J. Simpson. Simpson has emerged perhaps not only as a symbol of potential greatness gone very awry but his case symbolized the deep racial divisions that permeate this country despite advances that sports generally, and baseball in particular, may have contributed. Certainly Branch Rickey's decision to sign Jackie Robinson gave baseball a place in history that has quite appropriately been on the forefront of improving racial divides. Still, the racism that is present in society has not gone away, however much baseball can do to improve race relations. Shropshire (1996) refers to racism in society and in sports as simply a "historical reality" (p. 9). Even with the good that baseball has done toward improving race relations, and the signing of

Jackie Robinson surely takes its place at the forefront of improving race relations in this country, there remains so much that can be done. The 1995 World Series between the Atlanta Braves and Cleveland Indians, two franchises with long histories (granted much of the Braves' history belongs to the cities of Boston and Milwaukee) brought "racial unconsciousness" to the forefront with Braves' fans "tomahawk chop" leading the way toward racial insensitivity. Lest we think that we cannot do more, societally, and in our sports culture, the tomahawk chop was not only not condemned by the baseball establishment, but its use in Atlanta was condoned by management, stadium personnel, and most true fans who would never consider themselves racist in any manner. In their defense, and in our own, perhaps they were and are less racist, than they were and are, merely incredibly insensitive.

The early history of major league baseball reflected the unfolding ethical dilemma present in the United States. How to deal with racial issues in a nation which freed its slaves, but could not bring itself to grant equality to the freedmen. Segregation was occurring throughout society, and so too was baseball a segregationist reflection of the dubious racial decisions that allowed African-Americans to be free, but not to be allowed the opportunities that white persons had. Separate facilities for swimming, and even for drinking water, spoke volumes about a society that was far from ready to embrace positive interaction between and among different races. Baseball, in this context, wasn't more racist, it was merely racist in a manner consistent with surrounding society.

In the early 1990s, David Justice, then of the Braves, now ironically a member of the Indians, was quoted by *Sports Illustrated* on the subject of race relations.

> There are a lot of good guys on this team, but there are a few who I know use the "N" word when I'm not around ... how many white players do you see get abused in the paper? We see it happen all the time with black players. No matter what you do, you're still a nigger. Baseball is just an extension of life [Shropshire, 1996, p. 149].

Indeed, baseball is just an extension of life. As such, baseball is filled with characters who collectively possess every character trait that participants in all other "pastimes" also share. While Cobb may have been the most celebrated "thug" of his day, there are those today with whom we generally don't want our children to emulate, not all of whom, or perhaps even most of whom, are professional athletes. Other athletes have also emerged upon the scene that make all of us question their fitness, not only for membership among our elite groups of professional athletes, but perhaps even

for membership among all of us within society. Dennis Rodman in basketball, and perhaps even, Pete Rose and Albert Belle in baseball come to
mind. It is, perhaps, incredible irony, that the man who broke Ty Cobb's
hit record, Pete Rose, has a character that has allowed himself to be as
openly and properly criticized as was the character of Cobb. Stories of
Rose's behavior from such sources as George Will and numerous others,
should cause none of us to shed a tear over his exclusion from the Hall of
Fame. Perhaps, as Leo Durocher so noted, and as parlayed into millions
by American businessmen such as Donald Trump, Bill Gates, and Michael
Eisner, finishing first doesn't necessarily always correlate with being a nice
guy. Perhaps as well, we, (and most directly I as of this moment) should
guard against the tendency to overstate either the nastiness or the charm
present among major league ballplayers. For every Albert Belle, Pete Rose,
and Ty Cobb, there is a Tony Gwynn, Cal Ripken, Jr., and Kirby Puckett,
three ambassadors of the modern game with whom any parent would feel
comfortable knowing their children were emulating.

The Black Sox Scandal of 1919, as quite ably studied by Asinof, is
without a doubt the best known instance in which the connection between
crime and baseball became more than fodder for social scientists' academic discussions. The eight White Sox players banned for life for their roles,
real and perceived, in dumping the 1919 World Series comprise the heart
of the scandal that most intimately connected baseball with crime. Unfortunately, that scandal, like scandals in other segments of our society, was
not the last scandal, but merely perhaps the end of a more innocent era in
which we believed baseball was apart from the nastiness present in much
of life. Baseball in the early twentieth century was tarnished by this scandal, but it was a scandal that foreshadowed what was about to happen in
America during the Roaring Twenties. Asinof (1963) wrote of the "residue
of fear," a fear borne of an awareness, on the part of baseball players, of
the "1920s gambling-gangster world with which they had all come in contact" (p. xiii). The importance of gambling in American culture and of the
risk versus reward structure of capitalism itself can easily be seen without
a trip to Las Vegas or Atlantic City. Gambling, coming in such diverse
forms as casinos run by native Americans on reservation lands, to riverboat casinos, and state lotteries as easily accessible as the local convenience
store, have made for an environment as we near the year 2000 in which it
is difficult to consider sports without gambling. We now might even wonder why a player drops a routine flyball, or why a hitter misses a sign;
could it be more than a simple error? Might there be a reason, financial or
otherwise, that a player might fail to make a seemingly routine play? Prior
to the Black Sox scandal, the impact of gambling on the game was much

less subtle. There are accounts of players actually being tackled by gamblers in order to prevent a catch from being made, or even the "violent" and seemingly unthinkable "stonings" that could occur when a fan pelted a player about to make a catch (Asinof, 1987, p. 11).

Several historians, including Riess (1980) and Boyer (1995) have concluded that baseball during that era had become emblematic of America's social structure. "Its teamwork showed democracy in action; its fans were found among all classes of society; it taught America's traditional values to successive waves of immigrants; and it served as an annual ritual which united cities behind their teams" (Boyer, 1995, p. 332). The importance placed upon professional baseball and the reverence with which it was held in society might help explain that despite the fact that all eight players implicated in the black sox scandal were ultimately acquitted of the charges against them, Commissioner Landis banned all eight from ever playing professional baseball again. Tampering with the fans emotions it seemed was enough; breaking the law, at least the technical law, was not necessary. In some sense then, baseball was above the law, an institution holding a far more revered place in our culture than even the constitution and the rule of law. What judges might say was heard, but when the commissioner spoke, people listened.

Scandal during the rise of professional baseball was not limited to players. In 1882, Umpire Richard Higham was banned from baseball for letting professional gamblers in on how he was going to call games (O'Brien, 1998). After the formation of the national league in 1876, which replaced a league begun in 1871 organized by the players, owners exerted their control and "banned" gambling. The "ban" was somewhat transparent, however, as even the owners allowed some gambling by the players as it was seen as way in which the players could make a little money on the side, thereby allowing the owners to keep salaries low. Prior to the Black Sox scandal, there were attempts made to fix the World Series in 1903 and 1905, and in 1912, the losing manager, Connie Mack, openly speculated that his players had colluded with gamblers to throw the series.

Indeed, baseball's early years were ugly. Resembling the American frontier to the west, baseball was big, raucous, and very violent, with incidents of violence both on and off the field. Drinking, gambling, and corruption were every bit as present in baseball parks, as it was in the saloon we've seen popularized by American television westerns. In a famous incident occurring in 1873, Bob Ferguson, a third baseman for the Brooklyn Atlantics was umpiring a game between Baltimore and New York, when New York's catcher, Nat Hicks, mouthed off to the ump. The umpire, Ferguson, didn't let the comment go by, he instead picked up a bat and pounded Hicks, breaking the catcher's arm. But, reminiscent of gang members today, when the police attempted to arrest Ferguson, Hicks' minimized his injuries ... essentially refusing to "snitch" on a fellow player (Scheinin, 1994). Mark Twain referred to baseball in this era as "the very symbol, the outward and visible expression of the drive and push and rush and struggle of the raging, tearing, booming nineteenth century." Gambling stories centering upon baseball, some of which were fact and others fiction, began to have a serious impact on the game.

As organized baseball matured, like the American frontier, it became more respectable, and the roughhouse mentality faded away. But a change from "blue collar" status toward "white collar" status doesn't necessarily mean a drop in crime, just as it doesn't seem to in society. The nature of the crime changes and the dress of the participants gets better, but crime doesn't wither away. Baseball perhaps reflects better than most other social institutions, that poverty does not, in itself, cause crime. Just as wealth does not, in itself, preclude one from becoming a criminal (despite the evidence that leads us to believe the wealthy will be less likely prosecuted, and less likely punished severely if prosecuted). Still, the effects of poverty, at least relative poverty certainly played a role in the Black Sox scandal, a scandal at least partly borne out of the miserly ways of Charles Comiskey, whose players made literally one-half of what their opponents, the Cincinnati Reds were making during the 1919 pennant year. Just as poverty does not nor did not excuse those who perpetrate a crime, so too can we not dismiss it as a reason for a mindset that allows criminal intent to enter and take root.

As the times changed, and gambling became not only less frowned upon, but actually encouraged by most states, baseball's engagement with our criminal justice system changed course. Like larger society, baseball's "trouble-makers" were still addicts, but rather than gambling addicts, they were now drug addicts. In October of 1983, three members of the Kansas City Royals, Willie Wilson, Jerry Martin, and Willie Aikens, were serving time in a federal penitentiary on drug charges (Sands & Gammons, 1993). Steve Howe became the first player in major league history to be banished from the sport for a drug violation. Howe had had his chances, with his ultimate penalty coming only after seven previous drug-related suspensions (Sands & Gammons, 1993). Recent months have seen recurrent drug related instances of questionable conduct engaged in by Daryl Strawberry, further evidence that, as it is in larger society, illegal drug use in baseball remains a problem.

Whether Pete Rose should ever be admitted to the Hall of Fame, and whether Marge Schott should be admitted to her own team's facilities are questions that transcend the sport of baseball and are questions that concern our society's ability to consistently and coherently address such social issues as gambling and racism. As we reflect upon the founding of the Hall of Fame 60 years ago, a time in which the country was suffering through a protracted economic depression and the uncertainty of Germany's military buildup and expansion in Europe, celebrating a "game" may have seemed both periphery to "real life," and vitally necessary to renewal of the human spirit. As we consider the "grandeur" of the $105 million contract recently given to Kevin Brown by the LA Dodgers, we still live in a land in which poverty afflicts children, and healthcare remains inaccessible to all. Contradictions between the money we spend upon entertainment and the money we fail to spend on "reality" still abounds and criticism of sport generally and baseball in particular is fodder for editorialists from far and wide.

As I contemplate our criminal justice system and our increased emphasis upon "getting tough on crime," and the subsequent public policy decisions to build more and more prison cells and punish more and more of our citizens, I wonder aloud if there can be connections between our American nature that thrives on competition and lauds our sporting heroes and our nature that seeks to increase our collective ability to punish citizens who fall out of line. Baseball, like life, is made most fascinating by both its inherent contradictions and its consistency.

Just as gambling went from something evil, that could only be engaged in in back rooms and with "shady" characters to state sanctioned lotteries, and riverboat casinos sponsored by heros of the past and present, so too did baseball's gambling, which never could really stop, go from fixing games to mere betting on one's own team. The gambling woes of Pete Rose, well chronicled elsewhere, which resulted in his ban from baseball in 1989, at least bore no evidence that he ever attempted to throw or "have thrown" a game (although, it must be admitted that betting greater amounts when as manager he was starting a "better" pitcher, than when he was starting someone lesser, cannot be said to be in the best interests of the game).

The Mirror May Actually Have Two Faces?

Whether the issue is crime itself, or issues that tend to contribute to crime, such as poverty, racism, even gambling and drug abuse, the contradictions present in baseball are those that exist in our lives. The contradictions between the "haves" and the "have-nots," between those with the most talent, and those with lesser talents, and those with the money and those with lesser money. The contradictions between a marketplace that "rewards" entertainers and "punishes" schoolteachers. The contradictions present in a society that laments "welfare" for the poor, as it simultaneously finances stadiums with massive amounts of public money in which millionaire players perform for billionaire owners in luxury suites.

As divisions in society grow, so too do divisions within baseball. As loyalty from employee to employer and from employer to employee dissipates in our larger society, so too does free agency capture the essence of a "gentlemen's sport" that has become perhaps as mercenary as the rest of the marketplace. According to Hall (1997), only 15 players remained with their teams during the ten year period of 1987 to 1997. Fifteen out of 700.

What is good about baseball is good about America, and what is bad about baseball tends to mirror that which is bad about America. It is truly America's pastime, and a study of its history provides an excellent window into what Americans value. Through that window we can see a society that values "getting tough on crime," while it simultaneously, if to a lesser extent, laments the "unfairness" that we all know permeates our criminal justice system.

Major League Losers, by Mark Rosentraub, chronicles many of the major "moves" made by cities in building stadia for their teams, and in the threats made by team owners if these demands weren't met. "Welfare" for millionaire owners is how Rosentraub describes it. Our emotional attachment to teams causes us, as taxpayers and citizens, to make economic judgments that we otherwise would not consider. Would we spend millions on welfare for the poor, if we know that a few would profit greatly, and most would see no impact? Of course not, but we would, it seems, spend millions on welfare for the rich, even though we know the direct beneficiaries of the subsidies will be those who need it the least.

As luxury boxes become a central and "necessary" feature of new ballparks, the divide in our society between those who have the most and those who have the least, is again ably reflected by baseball. As anyone who has been to the new Comiskey Park can verify, the addition of several levels of luxury boxes for those who have, did not improve the viewing in the upper decks for those who don't have. Higher ticket prices reflect the higher altitude of seats, and perhaps the escalating salaries and rewards for both owners and players reflect a further separation between the fans and the participants. More accessibility to more games via cable TV, again reflects a society in which those who can afford access, get all the baseball they want, and those who cannot afford cable TV get even less access than they have been afforded previously. At the risk of falling into a socialist dialogue, this is not to deny the presence of capitalism as a force throughout American history. Those with the most resources have always had the best seats, just as they've driven the nicest cars, and worn the nicest clothes. The difference, baseball wise, is that now those with the most resources aren't really even in the same stadium. They sit in climate controlled luxury at appropriate levels, out of touch with those surrounding them ... by choice. In contrast, those struggling to make one or two games a year, have no real choice, and must sit farther away and remain largely "out of touch" with the field and the players. Baseball's coming of age in America along with the growth of cities, allowed for civic pride to be built upon one's team. Rich and poor alike could share in the joys and sorrows of what was essentially a "blue collar" sport accessible to all. As America has yuppified, so too, sadly, has baseball. Can we blame the sport ... probably not. It is probably an inevitable outgrowth of the times, and baseball as a reflection of society, not a dictator of societal values and virtues, must follow, rather than lead. If we cannot blame poverty, entirely at least, for crime, than we probably should not blame economic largesse for the changes in baseball. These sociological institutions, crime and baseball, are effected by far more than that. They are a part of our national character and our character is reflected in the way in which we react to each of them.

Kids want to be like Mike, men want to be like Mike, and women want to be with Mike ... perhaps that explains why those with the means often take great pains to be near these modern day heroes. Mike Lupica's recent work *Mad As Hell: How Sports Got Away from the Fans and How We Get it Back*, describes the reluctance of owners to sell their teams, even when they whine about the millions they lose, as a function and/or a symptom of their need to be "somebody." Without the attention that goes with owning a "major league" sports franchise, many of these owners would simply be old, rich, white guys, whose names would not be known outside their immediate families. By owning a franchise, these people are able to associate with the type of "celebrities" and attain the type of "celebrity" that bankers, lawyers, and CEOs seldom attain on their own.

Is it coincidence, that with the rise of new "corporate" ownership, has come a new "corporate" mentality that parallels the corporate mentality pervasive in society? Since 1970, each time a baseball labor contract has expired there has been a work stoppage. This despite the average salary increase of over 20 percent annually between 1975 and 1990 (Zimbalist, 1992, p. xv). Baseball's inability to work out labor disputes more positively, again merely reflects the tenor of a society which has seen wholesale firings of air traffic controllers who had gone on strike, and a myriad of downsizings and outsourcings that have left unions embittered, embattled, and usually with a dwindling powerbase. Whether baseball is ahead of or behind the curve in labor relations depends, I suppose, upon which side of the fence one resides. The fact that players have stood together in the face of "union-busting" techniques, collusion, and public relations fiascos … speaks well of union strength, particularly in a time of decreasing union strength in most other sectors of private industry in this country.

Collective action for the betterment of society in the face of an individualistic society and a capitalist economic system that lauds individual achievement over group welfare, is yet another societal contradiction with which baseball labor agreements, like most labor agreements, must contend. John Updike spoke of baseball's individualism in his description of Ted Williams' final game at Fenway Park: "of all team sports, baseball, with its graceful intermittencies of action, its immense and tranquil field sparsely settled with poised men in white, seems to me best suited to accommodate, and be ornamented by, a loner. It is essentially a lonely game" (Updike, 1960, p. 112). Calhoun (1987) addressed what he viewed as the "individualism" inherent in the game of baseball. "While each individual stands alone, each is also individually accountable" (p. 229). As in life, sometimes it is the mistakes that are remembered the most, and the mistakes that leave a legacy that sometimes outweighs the rest … i.e. Bill Buckner's failure to field a ground ball in the 1986 World Series against the Mets. That ball has been auctioned for tens of thousands of dollars … worth far more, apparently, than any of Mr. Buckner's home run balls, or game winning RBI balls. The importance of the individual has been echoed by Voigt (1967) who has described baseball as a game of inner-directed 19th century values, oriented to individual achievement and personal responsibility. He has viewed the hundred or so years of the reserve clause era as conceptually in line with American values in which business owners have been free to run their businesses as they see fit.

Seymour (1990) wrote of the growing impact of baseball at the turn of the century: "Baseball was seen to be taking priority over other aspects of life. Crime fell off during one Giant-Yankee World Series. In 1908 citizens reportedly showed more interest in which clubs would be taking part in the World Series than in the outcome of the election" (p. 4). In 1999, our citizenry quite clearly shows ever less interest in elections, while our passion for sports tolerates work stoppages, lock-outs, unimaginable contract demands, and unparalleled marketing tie-ins. Those who aren't interested in the games themselves are being attracted to stadiums by what the noted sociologist Christopher Lasch referred to as "irrelevancies." Exploding scoreboards and now swimming pools beyond the centerfield fence have little to do with the game on the field. Luxury skyboxes have televisions that aren't even always tuned to the game being played below. Whether the fact that people are in the stadium but don't care about the game, is progress or not, is I surmise, a matter of opinion. That these people may "need" to be seen at a baseball game, perhaps speaks to the impact of the game on our society; that they don't care about the game, speaks as loudly, however, to the lack of impact the game has upon our real lives.

Sports becomes corrupted, according to Christopher Lasch when the unpredictability of the outcome is lost. When the White Sox "threw" the World Series, the game is corrupted. When boxing and/or wrestling promoters "fix" the outcomes, the matches are corrupted. Many commentators are now proclaiming that without revenue sharing and/or other programs that might lessen the gap between the rich franchises and the poor franchises, the game itself will be corrupted. Fans will not flock to see teams in small market cities lose again and again, and even, ultimately, fans will avoid Yankee stadium when teams like my beloved Twins come in, since the outcome of the games is so seldom in doubt. Whether this will come to pass, at this point, remains largely speculative.

Conclusion

As the lines between entertainment and reality are continually blurred, we see such phenomena as "Court TV" which allows live broadcasts of real trials to be beamed into our living rooms. The trials that make TV are those that have entertainment appeal, and like the Simpson trial, they are trials in which the verdict, one way or the other, is not a certainty. If baseball players are not larger than life, if they are "merely" entertainers, no different from musicians, comedians, actors, and more and more lawyers and judges, then perhaps the "myths" that surround baseball will diminish. Perhaps conferences like this will lose their appeal, and English professors will cease writing about the romanticism of baseball. Perhaps we should all inject a dose of reality into our veins and gain a better understanding of the place of "entertainment" within our society. That place is surely profound, and the need for "diversion" from all of our daily routines cannot be diminished. Still, the importance of baseball is surely less than the importance of our criminal justice system. The impact of one upon society is surely greater than is the impact of the other.

It seems that it is true that "if we build it they will come." It is true whether the "it" is a ballpark or a prison. It is my hope that we will, societally, recognize the importance of building more ballparks, so that more will come to participate and to be entertained, so that perhaps fewer will need to be imprisoned. Is it a leap of faith to believe that more youth baseball programs and more and greater connections between professional baseball and youth programs will lead to less crime and less need for prisons? Yes, indeed it is. A leap of faith not unlike my "need" every spring to follow the Twins in their quest for the pennant ... whether that following is based on any shred of reality or not.

I watch the games, I read the boxscores, and pay close attention to the standings, not just of "my" team, but of all the teams. While I may be merely vicariously living out my baseball youth, along with millions of other overgrown "kids" I am also living my life concentrating on those things that are important to me, and baseball, while just a game, is part of that life. Concentrating on those things that are important, like family, friends, work, and play contribute to the social life of all of us, and ultimately, contribute to a lessening of the burden on already overburdened social systems, such as the criminal justice system.

If indeed baseball reflects the surrounding social systems, then the reflection cast back from the criminal justice system is not altogether positive. It is a system that many perceive to be racist, unfair, far too dependent upon money, and often downright corrupt. If baseball reflects some of this racism, unfairness, dependence upon greed and corruption, it is not baseball that should bear the brunt of the criticism. It is we who, as we criticize, must bear the brunt of that criticism. We have created this "monster," and now we should perhaps tame it. The question for us, as we ponder the "place" of baseball in society, is what "monster" should be tamed? Which social system is the most monstrous? Do we need educational reform, healthcare reform, welfare reform, criminal justice reform? Any directions that baseball has taken have come with us at the wheel. We should not be surprised that our driving has not been altogether perfect. All we need to do is look critically at any of our social systems and we might find vast room for improvement. Baseball remains a true reflection of the larger society that surrounds it; perhaps we should all take a better look into our own personal mirrors and assess the reflection that is cast back upon us, not with the goal of berating or breaking the mirror, but of better addressing the reflections that the mirror sends back. Whatever is wrong with professional baseball, and however its ills might be cured, blaming baseball without assessing the larger culture, is akin to blaming the mirror we all look into each morning for our increasing wrinkles and decreasing hairlines. Expecting the mirror to change, without changing the source of the reflection is, quite obviously, rather misguided.

Rosentraub (1997) perhaps put it best:

> Sports are important, but ... the professional sports wizards cannot give us anything that we do not already possess. Sports can teach valuable lessons, but so can any number of other institutions. Sports can provide entertainment, but so do movies, concerts, nature trails, bicycle paths, and countless other activities. Sports can bring people to downtown areas, but so can other civic events. Sports are a helpful and beneficial diversion, but they do not have the power and abilities ascribed to them by believers in the Wizard [p. 73].

Of course we know that Rosentraub is largely correct. Still, even among professors who should perhaps "know better" and who perhaps should be spending our evenings exercising on bicycle paths instead of relaxing at ballparks, we cannot escape the lure of baseball. It is a lure that I can hand down to my sons, and one that they might remember far more than the other "benefits" I will bequeath to them. It lures us because it is us, and it is what holds us together as a people far more than most other social activities might ever hope to accomplish. As a professor, I've attended other conferences, including several with my family. This is the one my sons will remember. Perhaps that is the point of all of it.

References

Asinof, E. *Eight Men Out*. New York: Holt, Rinehart, & Winston (1963).

Boyer, A. "The Great Gatsby, The Black Sox, High Finance, and American Law." In S.W. Waller, N.B. Cohen, and P. Finkelman (Eds.). *Baseball and the American Legal Mind* (pp. 436–450). New York: Garland Publishing, Inc. (1995).

Calhoun, D.W. *Sport, Culture, and Personality*. Champaign, IL: Human Kinetics Publishers, Inc. (1987).

Hall, S.S. "The Loyalist." *The New York Times Magazine*. p. 66 (1997, October 5).

Lupica, M. *Mad as Hell: How Sports Got Away from the Fans and How We Get It Back*. New York: G.P. Putnam's Sons (1996).

O'Brien, T.L. *Bad Bet: The Inside Story of the Glamour, Glitz, and Danger of America's Gambling Industry*. New York: Times Books (1998).

Pizzi, W.T. *Trials Without Truth: Why Our System of Criminal Trials Has Become an Expensive Failure and What We Need to Do to Rebuild It*. New York: New York University Press (1999).

Rosentraub, M. *Major League Losers: The Real Cost of Sports and Who's Paying for It*. New York: BasicBooks (1997).

Sands, J. & Gammons, P. *Coming Apart at the Seams: How Baseball Owners, Players & Television Executives Have Led Our National Pastime to the Brink of Disaster*. New York: MacMillan Publishing Company (1993).

Scheinin, R. *Field of Screams: The Dark Underside of America's National Pastime*. New York: W.W. Norton and Co. (1994).

Seymour, H. "Baseball: Badge of Americanism." In A. L. Hall (Ed.), *Cooperstown: Symposium on Baseball and American Culture* (pp. 1-22). Oneonta, NY: State University of New York College at Oneonta (1990).

Shropshire, K.L. *In Black and White: Race and Sports in America.* New York: New York University Press (1996).

Vlasich, J.A. *A Legend for the Legendary.* Bowling Green, OH: Bowling Green State University Press (1990).

Voigt, D.Q. *America Through Baseball.* Chicago: Nelson-Hall Publishers (1976).

Zimbalist, A.. *Baseball and Billions: A Probing Look Inside the Big Business of Our National Pastime.* New York: Basic Books (1992).

The Curt Flood Act: Legislative History and Labor Relations Implications

Karen Shallcross Koziara

Background

Major league baseball has both rich traditions and an ever appealing newness. Each spring is full of promise and every season some dreams become reality. However, baseball is also a complicated business. One of baseball's historical realities is that economic forces long have affected relationships between players and owners. In turn, these relationships have had an impact on the game itself. For example, the reserve system, which tied players to one team and prevented them from selling their services to the highest bidder, first became an issue in the 1880s. This practice endured because it was legally protected by baseball's exemption from the Sherman Antitrust Act of 1890. In one form or another, the extent to which clubs "own" players has been a contentious employment issue for most of the 20th century.

There were several efforts to organize major league ball players into a union prior to the 1950's. These attempts were vigorously opposed by the owners, and did not have lasting success. In the 1950s the current union, the Major League Baseball Players Association (MLBPA) began representing major league players. With the leadership of Marvin Miller and the protections provided by the National Labor Relations Act (NLRA), in 1968 MLBPA began formal collective bargaining for the first time in major league baseball. (Miller 1991). Historically relationships between the owners (The American League of professional Baseball Clubs and The National League of Professional Baseball Clubs) and MLBPA were adversarial, and often turbulent. The first of eight work stoppages occurred in 1972. All of these stoppages tried the patience and understanding of baseball fans, but none more so than the 1994-95 strike which lasted 232 days and resulted in cancellation of the 1994 World Series.

The public reaction to the state of baseball's labor relations was not lost on MLBPA and the major league owners. The current agreement contains several provisions designed to increase cooperation between the parties. In one of these provisions MLBPA and the owners agreed to jointly request and cooperate in lobbying Congress to remove baseball's antitrust exemption with respect to collective bargaining. That contract provision resulted in the Curt Flood Act of 1998.

Objectives

This paper focuses on the background, content, and implications of the Curt Flood Act of 1998. One objective is to provide a brief historic context for the Curt Flood Act. The Sherman Act's impact on collective bargaining generally, and multiemployer bargaining in particular, as well as baseball's antitrust exemption, are reviewed. The recent legislative history leading to enactment of the Curt Flood Act, including the positions of the owners, the union, and other interested observers is discussed.

A second objective is to analyze the likely impact of the Curt Flood Act on baseball labor relations. This is a particularly important objective because supporters of the bill touted it as the cure to fix what ails baseball labor relations. For example, Senator Orrin Hatch said in hearings on the bill, "Clarifying that anti-trust laws apply to major league baseball is something that will benefit sports fans across the country, young and old, rich and poor, Democrat and Republican...." (U.S. Senate Committee on the Judiciary 1997, 1). He explained, "While there are different factors contributing to baseball's recently tumultuous labor relations, there's one root cause about which we in Congress can do something. With their current anti-trust status, major-league baseball owners can ... conspire and collude, without restraint — the precise practices the anti-trust laws were designed to prohibit" (*Ibid.*).

Will this law indeed "level the playing field" and lead the way to a new, less tumultuous and more peaceful era in baseball labor relations? This is a complicated question to answer because it involves the interface of antitrust legislation and the National Labor Relations Act (NLRA). Bargaining in baseball, as in other professional sports and many non-sports industries, is conducted on a multiemployer basis. Multiemployer bargaining occurs when individual employers agree to act in concert when negotiating with the union which represents their employees. Multiemployer bargaining appears to violate the Sherman Antitrust Law because it involves concerted actions by employers. However, the courts have found that multiemployer bargaining is protected by the NLRA if its objective is not to restrain trade.

This paper analyzes labor relations in other industries to predict the impact of the Curt Flood Act on baseball. In other words, to what extent will baseball's labor relations tactics and climate be affected by antitrust coverage? Is this the time for baseball fans to ready themselves for a strike and lockout free future?

The Sherman Antitrust Act and Labor Relations

The 1890 Sherman Antitrust Act was designed to control monopolies and other business practices which restrained trade. Section 1 of the Act provides a broad definition of what practices are illegal. "Every contract, combination in the form of a trust or otherwise, or conspiracy, in restraint of trade among the several states ... is hereby declared to be illegal." Section 7 continues, "Any person who shall be injured in his business or property by any other person or corporation by reason of anything forbidden or declared to be unlawful by this act, may sue therefor in any circuit court of the United States." The law also empowers the courts to issue injunctions and other criminal penalties, including triple damages against violators.

This language is broad and sweeping, and it led to questions of whether or not union activities such as strikes and boycotts were illegal restraints of trade. In general the courts found that primary strikes, or those aimed at only the employer directly involved in the dispute, were lawful. Secondary boycotts and picketing, or those aimed at otherwise uninvolved businesses, were usually, but not always, illegal. (See, for example, *Loewe v. Lawlor* 1908), *Gompers v. Bucks Stove and Range Company* 1911). Some courts, however, found primary boycotts, and even primary picketing, illegal (*Truax v. Corrigan* 1921).

During the early 1900s organized labor made a number of attempts to get a legislative exemption to the Sherman Act. Theoretically, Sections 6 and 20 of the 1914 Clayton Act exempted labor unions from the Sherman Act, However, it was not until passage of the 1932 Norris-LaGuardia Anti-Injunction Act that the labor exemption was operationalized. This law limited the Sherman Act's application to labor unions by restricting the use of injunctions in labor disputes. Together the Sherman Act and the Norris-LaGuardia Act provide that labor unions are not illegal combinations or conspiracies in restraint of trade. Currently, for a union to be found in violation of the Sherman Act requires a showing that it (1) conspired with a nonlabor group, and (2) created an unreasonable restraint of interstate commerce.

However, these laws do not exempt certain agreements and activities between unions and employers from the Sherman Act. The case law outlining which of these activities is lawful is called the nonstatutory exemption to the Sherman Act.

THE NONSTATUTORY EXEMPTION

The National Labor Relations Act is the major legislation regulating private sector labor relations in the United States. It protects the rights of employees to join unions, and to negotiate with employers and enter into contracts over the terms and conditions of employment. Given the broad language of the Sherman Act, some contracts between unions and employers raised questions of illegal restraints of trade. In deciding these cases, the courts usually have found agreements between unions and employers do not violate the Sherman Act as long as the union is acting in its own self interest and unilaterally. Contracts in which the employer and union agree to harm other employers are not exempt from the Sherman Act. In general, the Supreme Court has given the NLRA priority, and accommodated the Sherman Act to the NLRA. This reflects the recognition that the NLRA was enacted specifically to regulate collective bargaining.

MULTIEMPLOYER BARGAINING

Multiemployer bargaining involves a number of employers in one industry bargaining jointly with the union that represents their workers. This type of bargaining relationship is most common when employers compete directly with each other in a local product market. Multiemployer bargaining is particularly common in construction, but it occurs in a number of other industries including transportation, retail trade, manufacturing and health care.

Multiemployer bargaining is a consensual relationship, meaning that both the union and all the involved employers must agree to bargain on this basis. The fact that the union and the employers all agreed to this arrangement means that they all see it as to their advantage. For employers, common wage rates and working conditions prevent employment conditions from being used as a basis of competition among them. This is also advantageous for the union. For employers a united front also prevents the union from "whipsawing", or playing one employer off against the another. Employers also gain by pooling their resources to reduce the individual expense of negotiating contracts. Other benefits for the union include having only one set of negotiations instead of many, as well as one uniform contract to oversee.

The NLRA does not explicitly address multiemployer bargaining. However, the National Labor Relations Board (NLRB) accepts this bargaining structure as legitimate, but does not require it. Individual employers and the union may decide prior to negotiations whether or not to take part in multiemployer negotiations. Once negotiations begin, however, they are required to continue to bargain on a multiemployer basis unless this approach is abandoned by mutual agreement, or in unusual circumstances.

When deciding cases involving questions about whether multiemployer bargaining resulted in antitrust violations, the Supreme Court has used the nonstatutory exemptions principles discussed previously. The Sherman Act must be accommodated to the provisions of the NLRA because Congress enacted the NLRA to regulate the collective bargaining process. As the Court explained in one precedent setting case in coal mining (*United Mine Workers of America v. James A. Pennington* 1965), "A union may make wage agreements with a multiemployer bargaining unit and may in ... its own union interests seek to obtain the same terms from other employers. No case under the antitrust law could be made out on evidence limited to such union behavior." It went on to explain that a union forfeits its antitrust exemption when, "It has agreed with one set of employers to impose a certain wage scale on other bargaining units. One group of employers may not conspire to eliminate competitors from the industry and the union is liable with the employers if it becomes a party to the conspiracy." In the Pennington case the court found that the union did conspire with employers to eliminate industry competitors and thus lost its antitrust immunity.

In the Bonanno Linen (1982) case the Supreme Court further developed the nonstatutory exemption in the linen supply industry. In this case the Court considered a situation in which an employer had withdrawn from a multiemployer unit without the union's consent after a bargaining impasse had been reached. After the impasse began, the union instituted a strike against the employer, Bonanno, and the other employers locked out their employees to defend the multemployer unit from whipsaw strikes. Bonanno then withdrew from the multemployer unit, and hired permanent striker replacements in order to continue operations. The remaining employers and the union eventually negotiated a new agreement. After the settlement, the union charged that Bonanno had refused to bargain in good faith when it withdrew from the multiemployer unit. It requested that the terms of the new contract agreed to by the other employers be extended to Bonanno. The court decided that the bargaining impasse was not an "unusual circumstance" and thus its existence did not justify the employer's unilateral withdrawal from the multiemployer unit. Pointing out that permitting withdrawal after impasse would undermine the usefulness of multiemployer bargaining, the court stated, "As a recurring feature in the bargaining process, impasse is only a temporary deadlock or hiatus in negotiations" (*Ibid.* 408). In other words, the court determined that the multiemployer unit did not end with a bargaining impasse. Given that most impasses are temporary, employers have an obligation to remain in the unit unless unusual circumstances, such as an employer facing extreme financial pressures or the unit becoming substantially fragmented, occur.

BROWN V. PRO FOOTBALL, INC.

The Supreme Court's decision in *Brown v. Pro Football, Inc.* (1996) illustrates the current status of the nonstatutory exemption in a setting very similar to major league baseball. The contract between the National Football League (NFL) and the football players' union expired in 1987. In 1989, while negotiating for a new contract, the NFL developed a plan to allow each football club to have a "development squad" of up to six players. These players would play in practice scrimmages and sometimes substitute for injured players in league games. The NFL owners proposed that these players receive $1000 per week. The union countered with an offer that squad players get the same benefits and protections as regular players. When negotiations on this issue reached an impasse, the NFL unilaterally implemented its proposal by providing each club with a uniform players' contract which included the $1000 per week salary for development squad players. In 1990, 235 development squad players sued the NFL and its member clubs claiming that the clubs' concerted imposition of the $1000 week salary violated the Sherman Act.

The Court ruled that the NFL's unilateral implementation of the developmental squad salary system after bargaining to impasse did not violate the Sherman Act. It reasoned that the nonstatutory exemption allows employers in a multiemployer unit, once an impasse is reached, to implement their last good faith offer. The Court explained that multiemployer bargaining was a well established and common bargaining method with benefits to both labor and management. To subject this practice to question under antitrust law would result in antitrust courts questioning the wages, hours and other substantive bargaining issues, "the very result the implicit labor exemption seeks to avoid ... and ... place in jeopardy some of the potentially beneficial ... effects that multemployer bargaining can achieve." It further reasoned that the employers' actions were directly related to the bargaining process, and the NLRB, not antitrust courts, had primary responsibility for policing the collective bargaining process. It concluded that the NFL's action were protected by the nonstatutory exemption from the Sherman Act for as long as the football players chose to have a union represent them. If the players decertified the union, the bargaining relationship would end and the nonstatutory exemption would no longer apply. Under these circumstances the players could bring suit under the Sherman Act.

Major League Baseball's Antitrust Exemption

Major league baseball's exemption from the Sherman Act resulted from the Supreme Court's 1922 decision in the Federal Baseball case. The case resulted from the newly developed Federal League challenging the National and American Leagues for players and major league status. The American and National Leagues responded to the threat posed by the Federal League with suits filed against players who left the established leagues to play for Federal League teams. The Federal League responded with a suit against the National and American leagues for violations of the Sherman Act. This litigation faced many delays, at least some of which were caused by Judge Kenesaw Mountain Landis, who was the presiding judge of the court in which the suit was filed. Shortly thereafter Landis was chosen by the owners to be baseball's commissioner. During these litigation delays, the rival owners met and agreed to merge their interests. Most Federal League owners were either bought out or offered ownership in existing major league teams. However, the owner of the Federal Baseball Club of Baltimore was offered a minimal settlement and responded with an antitrust suit aimed at major league baseball for damages to his business (Abrams 1998, 55–56).

In deciding Federal Baseball, the Supreme Court found that the Sherman Act did not apply because baseball games were neither trade nor commerce, but "purely state affairs" (*Federal Baseball Club, Inc. v. National*

League of Professional Clubs 1922). Although Justice Holmes, who wrote the opinion, acknowledged that the baseball clubs played against each other for money, and crossed state lines to do so, they were not involved in interstate commerce as envisioned by the antitrust laws. The fact that the clubs and the players moved across state lines in the course of their competition was merely incidental, "not the essential thing."

A number of years later cases in the other major professional major league sports came to the courts. These courts acknowledged the outdated, if not erroneous, decision in Federal Baseball. However, they neither extended the precedent to other major sports, nor altered it with respect to baseball.

The Supreme Court had another opportunity to review the baseball exemption from the Sherman Act created by Federal Baseball when St. Louis Cardinal outfielder Curt Flood challenged being traded to the Philadelphia Phillies in 1969. At that time baseball's reserve system allowed each club to "reserve" for itself the services of the players it signed to contracts. The reserve system meant that players were owned by the club unless traded to another club or released. Obviously this system sharply limited the individual choices players could make about their professional lives. Even more important, it reduced the ability of players to use market forces to enhance their bargaining power with respect to salaries.

In deciding that the reserve clause did not violate antitrust law, the Supreme Court stated that baseball was a business engaged in interstate commerce. However, it chose not to overturn the Federal Baseball precedent. It acknowledged the possibility that its decision involved "inconsistency or illogic," but due to baseball's historic exemption, illogic or inconsistencies should be settled in Congress rather than by the Court (*Flood v. Kuhn* 1972).

The Curt Flood Act: Recent Legislative History

THE MAJOR LEAGUE BASEBALL REFORM ACT OF 1995

Subsequent to the Flood decision, Congress considered a number of bills that would have ended baseball's exemption from the Sherman Act. This attention heightened during the 1994-95 work stoppage. In 1994 a bill which would have eliminated the exemption for baseball for purposes of collective bargaining narrowly failed to be reported out of the Senate Judiciary Committee. When the 1994 strike curtailed the World Series and with no apparent resolution to the dispute in sight, similar bills were introduced into the House and Senate in early 1995.

The Senate Judiciary Committee's report on S. 627, the Major League Baseball Reform Act of 1995 explained in detail why Congress was interested in addressing baseball's antitrust exemption. It began with the premise that free markets, protected by antitrust laws, are the basis for our economic system. Further, although the Supreme Court had sheltered major league baseball, Congress had never declared that baseball would be the only industry exempt from antitrust regulation. The Committee stated that the 1994-95 strike reemphasized the need for Congress to insure major league baseball followed the rules required of all other unregulated businesses. The Committee explained, "The strike ... was not prompted by the players' demand for more money, but by their lack of any alternative when faced with the owners' threats to impose unilaterally terms and conditions of employment that could violate the antirust laws" (Senate Committee on the Judiciary 1996, 2–3).

The report further pointed out that between 1972 and 1994 baseball experienced eight work stoppages, more in number than in professional hockey, football and basketball combined. For the senators supporting this legislation, the 1994-95 strike was motivation to modify baseball's "anomalous" antitrust exemption. The exemption was given as a reason for the frequency of baseball strikes. The difference between baseball and other sports is that if an impasse occurs and the owners implement new terms of employment, other athletes may challenge this concerted action by owners under antitrust law. The fact that baseball owners can not be so challenged makes them more willing to bargain to impasse and create a work stoppage than other owners. Baseball players, not having the antitrust option available, are "forced to either accept the new conditions or strike" (Senate Committee on the Judiciary Report 1996, 10-11).

POSITION OF THE MAJOR LEAGUE
BASEBALL PLAYERS ASSOCIATION

The Judiciary Committee's report contains reasoning very similar to that provided by the representatives of the Major League Baseball Players Association (MLBPA). The MLBPA focused on the effect of the antitrust exemption on labor negotiations. When Donald M. Fehr, the MLBPA's executive director, appeared before the committee he explained, "When bargaining breaks down, other athletes can still make the choice between labor laws and the antitrust law.... But as far as the baseball owners are concerned, when negotiations break down, baseball players can choose between the labor laws and the labor laws. How can they (the owners) argue that has no effect on negotiations?" He also pointed out that in basketball ever since the mid–1970s every collective bargaining agreement had been "wrapped up in a consent decree arising out of an antitrust case" (Senate Committee on the Judiciary 1995, 3).

Fehr also made the point that baseball should be subject to the same law that regulated other sports and industries in interstate commerce. He did not think that the fact that baseball had not in the past been subject to antitrust regulation was a meaningful argument for continuing the status quo.

POSITION OF THE OWNERS

The baseball owners argued that baseball is not a business, or at least not a business like other businesses. Their representatives made the case that the industry is notable for its lack of profitability. Prior to the 1994 strike, owners predicted industry-wide losses of about $100 million dollars. The Judiciary Committee report pointed out the impossibility of verifying that information due to the complexity of baseball financing. It also explained, "Profitability is not a factor in determining whether a particular enterprise is engaged in interstate commerce or should be subject to the antitrust laws" (Senate Committee on the Judiciary 1996, 12).

Other owner concerns included the possible impact of removing the exemption on relationships with the minor leagues. Most minor league teams have business relationships with major league clubs. This relationship is formalized in the Professional Baseball Agreement, which stipulates that major league clubs contribute financially to minor league player costs. Both the major and minor league owners feared that applying antitrust laws to baseball would jeopardize this relationship. James F. Rill, appearing for the owners, explained these concerns. Because nearly all minor league teams rely on the major leagues for essential financial support, removal of that support could sharply reduce the number of minor league teams. There would also be less money available for player development, and these costs would shift to minor league clubs, colleges, and the athletes themselves. Rill explained, "Given the risk of treble damages liability, there certainly would be a strong incentive on the owners' part to play it safe and abandon the existing system" (Federal News Service 1995, 2).

Franchise relocations and broadcast relationships were other issues of importance to the owners. Rill explained that baseball had not experienced the "traumatic relocations" of other professional sports because the baseball owners could "collectively agree" on whether teams could relocate.

Loss of the antitrust exemption could result in more franchise movement, including possible movement from small markets to larger markets with existing clubs, but capable of supporting additional teams (*Ibid.*). Both S. 627 and the Curt Flood Act of 1998 explicitly stated that they did not apply to baseball's minor leagues, franchise relocations, or broadcast relationships (*Ibid.*, 15).

The 1994–95 Strike

The 1994–1995 negotiations began after the expiration of the existing contract on December 31, 1993. The 1994 partial season was played under the terms of the expired contract. The strike of 1994–95 began August 12, 1994, over salary caps and revenue sharing, two issues important to the owners. Both were seen as important to protecting the economic viability of "small market" teams.

Many people, including players, thought the strike would be relatively brief, and that the owners would give into MLBPA as in the past. However, one knowledgeable observer credited Acting Commissioner Bud Selig as the person who managed to keep the owners united, even in the face of cancellation of the 1994 World Series (Holtzman 1998, 276).

The strike had great costs for all involved. The final 52 days of the 1994 season and the World Series were canceled. Owners' losses totaled about $376 million, and players lost about $350 million in salaries (*Ibid.*). As noted earlier, the public relations losses were huge. Although overall attendance was higher in 1998 than in 1997, it is still not at pre-strike levels.

All in all, the strike was a public relations nightmare. One indicator of the impact of the strike on the public's perception of baseball was the fact that three Hall of Fame inductees felt compelled to address the situation in the 1995 and 1996 induction ceremonies. In 1995 Richie Ashburn suggested that it was time to get "this mess straightened out." He put the onus to do so on all involved with a quote from Casey Stengel after a triple play ended the 1962 Mets' 120 loss season. "Fellers, he (Stengel) says, "I don't want anybody to feel bad about this ... this has been a real team effort. No one or two people could have done all of this" (Ashburn 1995, 11). In 1996 Jim Bunning provided the owners with a clear admonition, "Get your house in order. Figure out how you want to share your revenues without going to the players and asking them to foot the bill. Get an agreement ... a long term agreement, a minimum of ten years" (Bunning 1996, 16). However, Mike Schmidt's comments were particularly poignant:

Our game has reached a crossroads. (pause) I don't believe it can survive unless the team owners and players become one. Take a look at
the empty seats at every game or drive by an empty playground where
kids used to be playing ball. (pause) That concerns me, and baseball
it should scare you! Just a new basic agreement will not bring the fans
back, even great baseball won't ensure their return, there must be a new
level — a higher level of cooperation and understanding. We need to
recapture and re-energize the spirit of baseball fans. If we make the
fans number one they will come! [Schmidt 1995, 14]

S. 53: The Curt Flood Bill

In December 1996 the owners and MLBPA signed a memorandum of
understanding which included a section in which they agreed to work
together for legislation providing players with the same antitrust protections as members in other sports. This agreement was subsequently incorporated into the collective bargaining agreement negotiated by MLBPA and
the baseball owners effective January 1, 1997 (Basic Agreement 1997, 107).

In January 1997, on the first day of Congress, S. 53, the Curt Flood Act
of 1997 was introduced. S. 53 was essentially the same as S. 627. It stated
that the antitrust laws would apply to the business of baseball with the
exception of matters involving the minor leagues, franchise relocations,
and broadcasting (U.S. Senate Committee on the Judiciary 1997, 5). However, two major events occurred between the Senate hearings on S. 627 in
1995 and the hearing on S. 53 in 1997. First, the full impact of the 1994-95
strike had become apparent to both players and owners. Second, the
Supreme Court's decision in *Brown v. Professional Football, Inc.* made it
clear that the nonstatutory exemption did not allow players to bring
antitrust suits against concerted actions by employers even after a bargaining impasse as long as a bargaining relationship existed.

During the hearings on the Curt Flood Act, Donald Fehr reiterated
the positions he took on S.627. He pointed out that the failure of antitrust
law to cover baseball provided baseball players with fewer options than
players in other sports once an impasse is reached. He again explained that
"In 1994 the players effectively had only one choice: accept the owners unilaterally imposed terms and conditions of employment or strike" (U.S.
Senate Committee on the Judiciary 1977, 10). He also stated that the current situation gave the owners an incentive to try to break the union
because, "Then they could set the terms and conditions free of any restraint
that would otherwise be imposed by the antitrust laws. That is not the case
... in the other professional team sports" (*Ibid.*, 8). In other words, if the

owners in other sports managed to break the unions representing their players, the nonstatutory exemption accorded the owners as members of a multiemployer unit would be lost. Thus, any concerted actions they took with respect to wages and other working conditions would be vulnerable to antitrust suits. The same would not apply to baseball owners as long as baseball's antitrust exemption existed.

Given the decision in the Brown case that players represented by a union can not raise antitrust objections to owners' concerted activities even after a bargaining impasse, treatment on a par with other professional team sports did not appear desirable from a union perspective. Either the players would have to decertify the union, or the union would find itself unable to represent the players, for antitrust litigation to occur. However, Marianne McGettigan, who led the congressional lobbying effort for MLBPA, provided an explanation of the continued importance of the Curt Flood Act to the union even in the face of the Brown decision. Her focus was on the importance of free agency to the players.

Free agency as provided for in the 1997–2000 (2001) agreement allows a player who has completed six or more years of major league service to elect to become a free agent and sell his services on the open market. Free agency substantially increases players' individual bargaining power and prevents clubs from controlling their professional lives as was possible under the reserve clause. Because free agency is part of the collective agreement, if a bargaining impasse occurs it is one of the provisions the owners could change or do away with unilaterally (McGettigan 1999). Given that the reserve clause and free agency have been central issues separating clubs and players since the 1880s, the loss of free agency would dramatically erode the gains players have made in this area. Under these circumstances, decertifying the union and using antitrust litigation might make practical sense. This is particularly relevant given that litigants can sue for triple damages under the Sherman Act.

Interestingly, Fehr focused much less on the negative effect of the antitrust exemption on baseball negotiations then he had in previous hearings. In contrast, he explained that the 1997 agreement had built into it a number of provisions with the objective of getting "The players and owners to work together on a day-by-day basis to operate the game, to rebuild the game, to reach out to fans" (U.S. Senate Committee on the Judiciary 1997, 8). The hope was that one result "Will be that the next time we negotiate, the relationship will be fundamentally different than it has been at anytime in the past." He acknowledged that this would be a large task given baseball's bargaining history, but said, "Our task for the next go-around is to make sure that that record is broken, and broken with as loud a thump as we can manage" (*Ibid.*).

He also explained the circumstances that led the owners to agree to jointly lobby Congress for a law removing baseball's antitrust exemption for purposes of collective bargaining. In the other major professional sports the collective bargaining contract expires at the end of month in which the championship games take place. In baseball the collective agreements had expired on December 31. This created a situation in which clubs would be negotiating contracts with individual players under the terms of the expiring contract rather than a newly negotiated contract. The owners wanted to change the expiration date of the contract to October 31. Fehr said that the owners believed this change would enhance their bargaining position because it would provide time to start negotiations and, "If necessary, declare an impasse and impose new terms and conditions of employment for new individual contracts for the following season"(*Ibid.*, 11). The union was willing to trade this issue for the owners' agreement to work together on the antitrust issue.

Given this agreement, it is not surprising that the owners did not appear to give reasons as to why S. 53 should not become law. Further, after the Curt Flood Act was reported out of the Senate Committee on the Judiciary, Donald Fehr and Commissioner Allan (Bud) Selig jointly sent Congress letters requesting amendments to the proposed legislation (Congressional Record 1998, S9497).

Further, in July, 1998, on the day after he was elected Commissioner, Selig made the following remarks about the future of baseball labor relations:

> I don't believe it is possible for either side to think about a work stoppage in the next generation. We have to find smarter better ways to solve our problems. I'm so convinced of that, and I told the clubs the same thing yesterday in a very emotional speech when I was alone with them.... If anybody thinks, though old fashioned methods are going to work, they're wrong. I don't know how much more blunt I can be than that [Knisley 1998].

The comments of both Fehr and Selig's suggest that lessons were learned from the 1994-95 strike. In this vein, even the simple act of jointly sending a letter to Congress may be a sign of progress. given the relationship between Fehr and Selig during the strike. Former U.S. Secretary of Labor Robert Reich provides an example of that relationship from a meeting with them to help mediate the dispute shortly after the strike began in 1994. Reich described both Fehr and Selig as "stubborn, pugnacious, distrustful." About the meeting, he said, "Both men talk endlessly in monologues that never quite respond to questions asked or comments given. Each is convinced that the other is out to screw him. Neither will budge. If there is a hell, it is a small room in which one is trapped for eternity with both of these men" (Reich 1997, 190).

The Curt Flood Act: Major Provisions

The Curt Flood Act, an amendment to the Clayton Act, was signed by President Clinton in October of 1998. The Flood Act is designed to ensure that baseball players have the same rights under antitrust law as that enjoyed by other professional athletes. Specifically Section 27a provides, "The conduct, acts, practices, or agreements ... in the business of organized professional major league baseball relating to or affecting employment ... are subject to the antitrust laws to the same extent (as) ... if engaged in by persons in any other professional sports business affecting interstate commerce." This section ends with the proviso that, "Nothing in this subsection shall be construed as providing the basis for any negative inference regarding the caselaw concerning the applicability of the antitrust law to the minor league baseball."

The above provision was reinforced by language added by amendments that permit only major league players or former major league players to bring suit under the law. Another amendment specifies that the law will not affect the application to baseball of the nonstatutory labor exemption from the antitrust laws (P.L. 105-297, Section 27).

Implications

Congressional action on baseball's historic exemption from antitrust law was a long time coming. In many ways, the Curt Flood Act reinforces significant parts of that exemption. The law specifically removes the minor leagues, franchise relocations and broadcasting from its reach. In any future antitrust litigation involving baseball, the courts will note that Congress took action, but specifically excluded these issues, thus leaving most of the antitrust exemption intact.

Given the Supreme Court's decision in *Brown v. Professional Football, Inc.* the Curt Flood Act is unlikely to have much impact on labor relations in baseball. The decision makes it very clear that as long as a bargaining relationship exists, major leagues owners have the right as members of a multemployer unit to meet, discuss, and act in concert with each other even after a bargaining impasse occurs. Players can only sue owners for antitrust violations if no bargaining relationship exists. In theory the players could decertify the union in order to sue the owners. However, such litigation would be expensive, protracted, and a generally ineffective alternative to collective bargaining. It is unlikely that the players would adopt this strategy except as a last resort.

It is, however, a strategy that the players might use if the owners pursued a position to impasse and then implemented unilateral terms and conditions of employment. This would particularly be the case if the owners implemented salary caps, as they did in 1995, or did away with free agency. Such a decertification strategy could result in chaos with a variety of unpredictable litigation and individual bargaining outcomes. The dire consequences of this action, including the unpredictability of costs, particularly in the face of potential treble damages, could prevent the owners from pursuing this course. If the law discourages this conduct, it would provide a fitting legacy to Curt Flood.

By itself the Curt Flood Act probably will do little to change baseball labor relations. The economic realities faced by the owners create the potential for a continuation of a difficult and conflict ridden relationship. Although the 1997 contract provides for revenue sharing, it did not resolve the financial differences between the affluent and non-affluent clubs, and salaries continue to escalate.

Commissioner Selig believes more revenue sharing between the revenue-rich teams and the less affluent clubs is important for competitive balance in major league baseball. Currently the clubs share national broadcast and licensing revenues equally, which in 1998 meant $16.5 million for each club. As a result of the revenue sharing provisions in the current agreement, after the 1998 season, the 13 clubs with the highest revenue providing $100 million to the 13 clubs with the lowest revenue (Badenhausen, Sicheri, and Pinto 1999, 122). Believing that this amount is not sufficient, in 1999 Selig appointed a four person committee including former Federal Reserve Chairman Paul Volker to plan for increased revenue sharing.

However, revenue sharing is a divisive issue. The above referenced *Forbes* article reported that several clubs, including the Montreal Expos, Cincinnati Reds and Oakland A's, actually lowered payrolls after benefiting from revenue sharing. At the same time the New York Mets, Los Angeles Dodgers and Boston Red Sox, all big contributors to revenue sharing, lost more than $5 million each. The article concluded that in theory revenue sharing would allow poorer teams to compete on the market for players. However, in practice revenue sharing rewards "cheapskate" owners and punishes teams spending money to get players who deliver a higher quality product. One sports valuation expert was quoted as saying, "Increasing revenue sharing significantly would put a serious drag on player salaries because there would be little incentive for owners to put the best product on the field."

Nonetheless, economic realities remain a problem for poorer clubs. For example, early in 1999, Minnesota Twins owner Carl Pohlad acknowledged his club had no chance to be competitive because, "I'd say, in order to compete, you have to have a minimum of a $50 million payroll." The Twins cut the 1999 payroll to somewhere between $10 and $15 million, down from $27 million at the beginning of the 1998 season. In contrast the 1999 Yankees had a projected payroll of $80 million. The Twins hoped for increased revenue sharing, as well as a new stadium (Schmuck 1999). Richer clubs, such as the Yankees, have little reason to embrace additional revenue sharing.

These economic realities have the potential to make future negotiations very difficult. Some owners want additional revenue sharing, others do not. Several baseball owners have indicated that they would seek major changes in the existing contract when it expires. Some baseball owners prefer salary caps or maximums to increases in shared revenues. From the owners' perspective, the role that Selig chooses to play will be very important. He is credited with having a "consensus" style, but he will face a real challenge in getting agreement among the owners. He is seen as being one of the "great phone guys" who regularly talks to and understands the positions of the various owners, but also as someone who will "not make a move" without the support of the owners (Knisley 1998). An important challenge Selig will face is getting a workable consensus among the owners, rather than having the owners again look to the union to solve the industry's economic problems.

Donald Fehr's earlier quoted comments indicate that he hopes for a more cooperative and peaceful bargaining relationship with the owners. However, he also has made it very clear that the players would vigorously resist changes in the free agency and salary arbitration provisions in the contract. Interestingly, he tempered these remarks by saying, "The memories of what we went through four years ago remain reasonably vivid. If that remains when we get to bargaining, that should have a beneficial effect" (Blum 1999).

Perhaps the most positive aspect of the Curt Flood Act with respect to baseball labor relations is the fact that the owners and the union did cooperate over its passage. It appears that both Selig and Fehr, and hopefully, other officials, realize the destructive impact of the 1994-95 strike. Of course, after other work stoppages fans thought that the parties would have learned how costly their actions were, and worked to avoid future Phyrric victories. This time, however, the conscious choice of the parties to work together over the antitrust issue shows an understanding of the need to build trust and cooperation both for the good of the business of baseball and the game of baseball.

References

Abrams, Roger I. *Legal Bases: Baseball and the Law.* Philadelphia: Temple University Press (1998).

Ashburn, Richie. Induction Ceremonies. National Baseball Hall of Fame and Museum, Inc. 30 July: 11 (1995).

Badenhausen, Kurt, Willliam Sicheri, and Richard Pinto. "Baseball Games." *Forbes* 163 (May 31): 112–15 (1999).

Blum, Ronald. "Men Without Caps." *Sporting News.*1 February (1999).

Bonanno Linen Service v. NLRB, 454 U.S. 404 (1982).

Brown v. Pro Football, Inc., 518 U.S. 231 (1996).

Bunning, Jim. Induction Ceremonies. National Baseball Hall of Fame and Museum, Inc. 4 August: 16 (1996).

Curt Flood Act. 1998. P.L. 105–297, Section 27.

Federal Baseball Club, Inc. v National League of Professional Baseball Clubs, 259 U.S. 200 (1922).

Federal News Service. Prepared statement of James F. Rill before the U.S. Senate Judiciary Committee, Subcommittee on Antitrust, Business Rights and Competition (1995).

Flood v. Kuhn, 407 U.S. 258 (1972).

Gompers v. Buck Stove and Range Company, 221 U.S. 418 (1911).

Holtzman, Jerome. *The Commissioners: Baseball's Midlife Crisis.* New York: Total Sports, (1998).

Knisley, Michael. "Wedded Bliss — For Now." *The Sporting News.* 20 July: 16 (1995).

Loewe v. Lawler, 208 U.S. 274 (1908).

McGettigan, Marianne. "The Curt Flood Act of 1998 The Players' Perspective." *Marquette Sports Law Journal* 9: 375–88 (1999).

Miller, Marvin. *A Whole Different Ball Game.* New York: Birch Lane Press (1991).

Reich, Robert B. *Locked in the* Cabinet. New York: Knopf (1997).

Schmidt, Michael J. Induction Ceremonies. National Baseball Hall of Fame and Museum, Inc. 30 July: 14 (1995).

Schumck, Peter. "Cutting Back in Minnesota." *Sporting News.* 4 January: 53 (1999).

The American League of Professional Baseball Clubs and The National League of Professional Baseball Clubs and Major League Baseball Players Association (1997). *Basic Agreement.*

Truax v. Corrigan, 257 U.S. 312 (1912).

United Mine Workers of America v. James A. Pennington, 381 U.S. 657 (1965).

U. S. Congress. Senate. Committee on the Judiciary. 1995. *Hearings on the Major League Baseball Reform Act of 1995.* Washington D.C.: GPO.

U.S. Congress. Senate. Committee on the Judiciary. 1996. *Report on the Major League Baseball Reform Act of 1995.* Washington D.C.: GPO.

U.S. Congress. Senate. Committee on the Judiciary. 1997. *Hearings on S. 53.* Washington D.C.: GPO.

Part 5

BASEBALL AND THE FAN

The Fans' Role in Shaping Baseball: A Voice Too Long Silent?

J. David Pincus, Stephen C. Wood and Fritz Cropp[1]

1. Introduction: A Changing Game?

Major League Baseball has never been better — and worse — off than it is today.

The same can be said of baseball fans, whose love of the game seems to transcend whatever worsening business and structural problems confront America's beleaguered but still popular national pastime. The exciting, precedent-setting 1998 season witnessed the historic home run record-shattering race between Mark McGwire and Sammy Sosa, the gloriously balanced Yankees that won 120 games and the World Series, and the quiet conclusion of iron man Cal Ripken's remarkable consecutive games streak. With such a year, baseball appears to be undergoing a revival as it fights its way back from the depths of the strike-plagued season of 1995. As a business, baseball's powers-that-be have recognized the players and umpires union, but fans have never had a formal voice in the shaping of Major League Baseball.

Baseball's truest and most enduring appeal lies not so much in its playing as in its window to American history and cultural mores. Social historian Jacques Barzun's famous observation drives this point home: "Whoever wants to know the heart and mind of America had better learn baseball."[2] Thirty-four years later, journalist Neal Gabler echoed Barzun's sentiments that baseball's essential meaning runs far deeper than its "excitement quotient" as a stage show, springing from its reflective ability to help us see ourselves, warts and all, while nudging us to change before the times pass us by: "... it was always the game with the longest bloodlines, the one by which an individual could measure his life just as the country could measure its life: by teams and dynasties and legendary plays."[3]

Differences Abound

Baseball today isn't the same game, or business, it was just a generation or two ago when Barzun offered his insight on the nature of baseball. Major League Baseball (MLB) has changed in significant ways, some intended and visible, others inadvertent and subtle. Perhaps more than at any time in its long and colorful history, baseball's fundamentals, as a sport and commercial enterprise, are being questioned, redefined and gradually overhauled. Baseball continues to evolve from league realignment to interleague play, from expanded playoffs to expanding leagues, from skyrocketing player compensation packages to soaring TV, radio and merchandising agreements, from shifting franchises to stadium financing schemes to revenue sharing, and from player strikes and owner lockouts to free agency and salary arbitration.

More than anything, MLB has become a "big money" commercial venture more evocative of General Motors and IBM than the leisurely game once played for sheer enjoyment on Elysian fields. Team budgets are counted in hundreds of millions of dollars and player contracts are inundated with thick legalese rivaling the most complex corporate mergers. Taken together, the changes marking the evolving nature of baseball on and off the field have been dramatic and traumatic. For no stakeholder group is this more true than the fans. Fans who see baseball as "their" game, and its clubs as "their" teams. Fans who ultimately hold the game's fate in their hands, a power, history tells us, they have never fully realized nor effectively wielded.

Baseball fans are an idiosyncratic collection of individuals ranging from those for whom a baseball game is practically a religious experience to those for whom a baseball game is an occasional recreational option. But taken as a whole, "Fans are the only ones who truly care," writes New York *Daily News* columnist Dick Young. "There are no free-agent fans ... who say 'Get me out of here. I want to play for a winner.'"[4] Some fans of baseball are emotionally attached to their teams and players, and to the game itself. Former Dodgers Hall of Fame manager Tommy Lasorda commented during the 1981 players strike: "I know the fans will be back eventually. They can't get this kind of entertainment for the price anywhere."[5] In the bitter aftermath of the rancorous 1995 strike, 14 years after Lasorda's prediction, the fans' tolerance and loyalty was tested as never before.

THE QUESTION(S)

The central question that drives this analysis is: *To what extent are fans' preferences and ideas being considered by Major League Baseball and team officials in determining baseball's direction and "best interests?"* Specifically, do the fans play any such role? Have they ever? If so, has it made any difference? How do those responsible for the game's prosperity, popularity and integrity (club owners, players, managers and coaches, umpires, commissioner and other league executives) gauge the tenor of fans' sentiments? Do they care enough about what fans think or respond their collective voice?

The thesis of our argument is that, in the game and business of baseball, it is good business to treat fans as stakeholders, not just revenue streams.

We begin by reviewing the literature related to baseball fans' relationship with the game and teams. Next we analyze how the fans' role may have shifted and review prior and current efforts to organize fans' interests into a singular, credible voice. Included is an evaluation of all MLB teams' web sites, interviews with several MLB club executives, and an assessment of the various fans organizations including interviews with long-time consumer activist Ralph Nader and USFANS President Frank Stadilus. Finally, we offer an approach to establishing a credible fans voice in Major League Baseball.

2. Review of Literature: Slim Pickings, Few Discernible Patterns

The sports and social literature of the 20th century barely addresses the role of the baseball fan, or sports fans in general, in any meaningful way. Our exploration of the popular and academic literature, which spanned a number of allied disciplines, uncovered mostly anecdotal material. The bulk of our findings took the form of opinion and retrospective newspaper pieces written by irate sports writers and prominent individuals, usually during times of crisis (*e.g.,* strikes, lockouts, labor/broadcast negotiations). This fact alone seems to speak loudly to fans' largely silent, inert status within baseball's decision-making inner circle.

In baseball executives' minds, baseball fans seem to be an afterthought, powerless and voiceless — units of revenue generation. Owners know that fans must be kept happy enough to buy tickets, vast quantities of fatty, high cholesterol fast food, and all the rah-rah memorabilia they can carry home. But the literature reveals no tangible role for fans, advisory, decision-making or otherwise, in shaping how baseball is played on the field or managed in the boardroom. Whether this finding reflects fans' universal apathy toward operational/administrative issues or an inability or unwillingness to galvanize their voice, or owners' and league officials' belief that fans should be handled as obedient children who are "seen and not heard" or both, is a matter of speculation.

Fans seem to taken for granted by the game's financially sensitive top dogs. Also, fans have been ineffective at consolidating their potential influence into any sort of credible, organized force that the lords of baseball could neither ignore nor bamboozle.

PRECEDENT, ALBEIT LIMITED

For decades, some fans have tried to raise a collective voice. Evidence can be traced back to at least 1935, when Robert Palmer of Oakville, Connecticut, and others began an organization of pen pal fans through which "members will be able to swap views and otherwise become acquainted."[6] Five years later, many teams and popular players had sprouted fan clubs, from which its officers developed the American Association of Baseball Fan Clubs. Interestingly, 1940 also marked the first fans organization that did not revolve around a particular club or player. The Associated Fans of America was created for the purpose of providing a "common meeting for fans through correspondence, to disseminate baseball information and to uphold and further the cause of the games by presenting books and other literature to libraries, hospitals, such as veteran institutions, and other places."[7]

Yet, such efforts have been few and far between, and yielded relatively little evidence to suggest that fans' ideas, preferences and/or input have ever been solicited or taken seriously by baseball's decision-makers. In fact, the literature we examined reveals a persistent depiction of baseball-as-a-business and fans-as-revenue dichotmy. Such commercially framed characterizations reinforce Gutmann's (1988) claim that since the '50s, baseball has been steadily separating from its pastoral roots and moving beyond the Great American Pastime. In its own fumbling way, post–1950s baseball has been pushed to adapt to a fast-changing population and culture expecting more Hollywood "show and tell" and less pure sport.[8]

Since the end of World War II, baseball attendance has grown dramatically, paralleling the game's transformation from sport to sports entertainment. The distinction between "sport" and "sports entertainment" is an attempt to separate the playing or viewing of baseball for the love of the sport from viewing baseball as a multimedia event that generates revenue. Sport and sports entertainment must both incorporate sport and entertainment, but the primary emphasis is distinguishes one from the other. That gradual shifting in emphasis has spawned an increasingly diverse fan base substantially more receptive to promotion-minded assaults by bottom-line-hungry clubs.[9]

An Infusion of Marketing

How successful baseball has been at adapting to the culture surrounding it remains an unresolved issue. Considerable efforts have been made over the last 20 years to bolster the game's "entertainment" appeal. Major League Baseball is bigger, faster, louder. Standard practices such as oversized, cartoonish mascots, glitzy fireworks-spouting scoreboards and nightly corporate promotion giveaways of everything from decoder rings to Frisbees to bats are good examples of the shift from "sport" to "sports entertainment."

The march toward marketing baseball as a product with selling attributes much like soap or soap operas has been speeding up for some time, and continues unabated today. This observation was born out by our interviews with club and league executives. Fueled by the creative marketing wizardry of team owners like Bill Veeck and Charlie Finley, baseball has been attempting to become more "fan-friendly" as a competitive business strategy. Owners' desire to push in that direction reached new heights following the attendance-declining seasons after the '95 strike. "Clubs began promoting ... images of players signing autographs, kids running the bases and smiling faces all over the park ... teams geared their pitches to family-oriented fun, made to fit the family budget. It was designed to overcome the image of spoiled, unresponsive millionaires that turned off legions of fans during the strike."[10] Apparently, though, business "strategy" has not included much attempt to embrace fans as partners, as has often been the case with many American retailers.

Fans as Customers, Customers as Fans

Baseball's evolution has not only paralleled the struggles of our culture (*i.e.*, racism), but corporate America as well (*i.e.*, labor relations). We see this cultural and corporate reflection in the way baseball's growing corps of MBA-trained executives has increasingly relied on "customer-driven marketing strategies." Baseball executives cater to customers' dominant needs and desires, a strategy touted and increasingly deployed by competition-minded U.S. corporations since the 1970s. Some, like management consultants Adrian Slywotzky and David Morrison, have argued that baseball is jeopardizing its long-term profit potential by ignoring how the average fan views "value" while allowing the bulk of revenue streams to be siphoned into monster player deals. In a recent *Fortune* interview, the authors asked this fundamental question: "What is happening to the average consumer, the average fan? He or she is losing interest in the game. Baseball is not creating a better deal for the average customer, and that is why baseball is going to be in trouble — because the owners and players and the broadcasters are not asking, 'Who is the customer, and how can we keep giving him a better deal?'"[11] Perhaps, the next step should be to redefine, or at least clarify, the essence of a "better deal."

In 1998, Sandy Alderson, for 14 years the general manager of the Oakland Athletics, became Executive VP for Baseball Operations in the commissioner's office, equivalent to number three on baseball's management totem pole. When asked about his first priority, he didn't hesitate: "Give general managers and other operations people a voice in decision-making that takes place at the Office of the Commissioner...."[12] Any inclusion of a fans' role in shaping baseball was notably absent from his remarks. The notion that the current formal stakeholders of baseball should seriously cultivate and incorporate fans into the "corporate" decision chain appears to be alien to the business tenant of baseball. Corporate America seems to have awakened to the need for such inclusion, but Major League Baseball seems slow to open its collective eyes.

The fan-as-customer philosophy surfaced repeatedly in our literature analysis and interviews with club officials. The findings suggest what appears patently obvious to anyone who has followed the game in recent years. In the narrowly focused eyes of baseball owners/management, fans are perceived as "fan-nies" to fill seats in ballparks and luxury boxes, and, more and more, as ratings points to bolster Neilsen ratings. Consistent with that viewpoint, baseball's club owners and MLB management probably would argue that the fans possess no inherent right to have a say in the running of a sport/business to which they are merely consumers. After all, fans are occasional consumers with little more than a passing interest in how the game is actually operated as a business. For some fans, maybe most fans, that is probably true; for the diehard fan, nothing could be further from the truth.

Defining a Baseball "Fan"

Defining the essence of a baseball "fan," a concept open to differing interpretations, lies at the heart of any analysis of the fans' role in baseball decisions. Shaping any definition, more than any other factor, is one's perspective of a fan's basic "value" to a team or sport. By their very nature, driven by team rather than institutional loyalty, fans of baseball comprise a scattered, disparate group — not a single-minded mass — that appears to vary considerably along a host of demographic and geographic factors. For example, owners or executives tend to perceive fans in a purely economic context, as buyers of tickets, concession and merchandise, and as viewers/listeners comprising the broadcast audience, with whom they seek an exclusive commercial exchange. More precisely, owners and executives expect to develop marketing-driven relationships with fans/customers.

In contrast, fans should be viewed in terms that transcend the dollar sign. Fans should be viewed as "stakeholders" in the overall baseball venture who, as much as any party, hold the prospects of America's national pastime in their hands — even though they may not be aware of it. Yet, as our research indicated, fans have had virtually no meaningful voice affecting the character of "their" game, of America's game. Acknowledging baseball's long-standing tradition of decentralization – that is, teams operate independently, but within agreed upon central postulates governing the game — we argue that fan input/involvement (input at a minimum, involvement the goal) in umbrella issues/decisions affecting the ballpark experience and the game-as-a-whole is smart, forward-looking business. Examples of legitimate fan influence in shaping major league baseball could include selection of the commissioner, league realignment, free agency, club relocation policies, broadcast arrangements, revenue sharing criteria, and rule changes.

While team owners come and go, and while team owners own their teams in financial and legal terms, the fans, as long-term stakeholders and cultural or moral owners, warrant a voice in the shaping of baseball. Historically, such cultural or moral ownership has not been recognized by either owners or fans and, thus, fans have had no role in the decision-making process that governs baseball. Maybe the best illustration of this fact is the fans' total lack of standing or involvement in negotiations during the many strikes and lockouts that have plagued the game since the '70s. Rutgers Law School Dean and baseball salary arbitrator Roger Abrams (1998) speaks to this point in discussing the 1995 players strike:

> Again, as in prior work stoppages, the fans were left out of the equation. Although they pay the freight, either directly at the stadium

turnstiles or indirectly by patronizing baseball's commercial sponsors, fans do not have a seat at the bargaining table. National labor
policy is based on the premise that the adversarial relationship
between labor and management will produce agreements that serve
the public's interest by achieving labor peace. The assumption is that
if the products and services become too expensive as a result of a
costly agreement, the market response will inform management and
labor how to adjust their relationship in the future or lose their customers forever. This provided little solace to the fans....[13]

Though baseball fans lack organization, coordination, and voice, they
nevertheless yearn to be heard on issues that they believe hurt the game.
The latent, but inherent power of fans surfaced in late April 1999, when
more than 3,000 Kansas City Royals fans staged a walkout during a game
with the New York Yankees. The fans protested the widening economic disparity of player salaries that results in lessening competitiveness between
large- and small-market clubs.[14] Wearing t-shirts that read "$hare the
Wealth," KC fans in the left field bleachers stood, turned their backs on
the field of play during the Yankee half of the fourth inning and they lit-
tered the field with fake $100 bills as they departed the stadium. Fans'
largely unrealized influence also appeared during the 1998 All Star Game
when persistent fan outcries compelled Seattle Mariners star Ken Griffey,
Jr., to reverse his decision to forgo the popular home-run hitting contest.

Granted, the commercial dimension of baseball is critically important,
unavoidable and inherent to fans and clubs alike. Nevertheless, the relationship is more than one between buyer and seller. Based on our analysis, many fans see themselves as dispossessed, unappreciated and ignored.
In crafting and advancing the institution of baseball, adding fan representation to the mix of parties overseeing baseball's operation and reputation would, maintains sports journalist Mike Lupica, bring a sense of
balance to the competing, egotistical interests of the players union and
club owners.[15] This dynamic tension between viewpoints of fans as "fan-
nies" and fans as stakeholders is controversial, with no easy resolution. For
purposes of argument and to avoid unnecessary confusion, in this paper,
however, we have defined fans as stakeholders, or potential stakeholders —
much more than ticket-toting customers or balance sheet profit centers.

THE COMMISSIONER AS
FANS' VOICE: A HOLLOW RING

Baseball fans have never had a singular spokesperson or emissary or
organization to represent their collective interests and preferences. Some
critics and scholars have argued that, in theory, fans' interests have been

represented and protected by the commissioner, perceived by insiders and outsiders alike as baseball's CEO and guardian of "the best interests of the game." Indeed, most commissioners have at one time or another endorsed, and occasionally attempted to play, such a role on behalf of the fans (usually contrary to owners' wishes). Such upstart and naive efforts have been quickly thwarted by the team owners who have quickly reminded the commissioner of his own "best interests" and who pays his near-million dollar salary. More times than not, the result of such interventions have resulted in the muzzling of the commissioner, and a premature departure from office.

An illustration of this common pattern was offered by former Commissioner Peter Ueberroth: "My job," he said prior to his appointment, "would be to make the sport better, not only for the owners but for the players, managers, coaches, minor leaguers, and, most important, for the fans."[16] To an extent, he was true to his word when he played pivotal roles in helping settle umpires and players strikes; the latter in defiance of owners' clearly stated preferences. While fans and players liked his penchant for action and colorful rhetoric, Ueberroth soon lost the backing of owners, who seethed in silence at his cavalier defiance of them. They later resolved the issue by not renewing Ueberroth for a second term.

Similar words and actions dogged Commissioner Bowie Kuhn in the mid–1970s when he opened spring training camps in the face of an owners-initiated lockout of the players. "It is now vital," he said, "that spring training get underway without further delay. While nobody is more disappointed than I that we do not have solid progress to a final agreement, the fans are the most important people around and their interests now become paramount. Opening the camps and starting the season on time is what they want."[17] Kuhn's bold move in the name of the fans' best interests did little to endear him to his employers who openly resented his mistaken perception of the power. The relationship between the owners and Kuhn gradually waned and Kuhn, like other commissioners, was pushed out of office prematurely.

In a transparent move following Fay Vincent's forced resignation in 1992, owners appointed an interim commissioner: Bud Selig, then owner of the Milwaukee Brewers. Looking back, his selection as commissioner just before the start of the arduous labor negotiations seemed calculated to assure the owners a single-minded position. Appointing an owner as commissioner exacerbated the longest and most acrimonious strike in baseball history. Selig understood the owners' position and touted the party. The fact that he was recently made permanent commissioner over a number of prominent, credible outside candidates, including former

U.S. presidents and senators, may suggest that owners have, in effect, rewritten the commissioner's qualifications, job description and reporting protocol once and for all. Clearly, this action is a step away from involving fans as stakeholders, and closes the circle publicly and presumptuously around the owners.

Unfortunately for baseball fans, the bottom-line is that the commissioner of baseball, despite occasional honorable intentions and attempts to serve all of baseball's "best interests," is selected and paid by the owners, whose basic interests often clash with the fans'. Regrettably, the commissioner is not a source of fairness and equilibrium. The lack of independence to act as a neutral arbiter and governor of a sport/business sorely in need of transcendent leadership prevents the Commissioner from being an unbiased voice.

3. Original Research: Data Reinforce "Customer" Perspective

Since the review of literature revealed relatively little information concerning baseball fans generally and their role in baseball decision-making specifically, we examined present-day beliefs and practices toward fans. In order to gain a clearer sense of current baseball executives' attitudes and behaviors, we conducted a series of interviews to probe their current philosophy and thinking.[18] Further, we evaluated the teams' actual behavior with fans by using a systematic analysis of the fans' "orientation" in the web sites of Major League Baseball (see Appendix A).

The findings from the interviews and web site review buttressed the literature review that, for the most part, suggests baseball fans continue to be perceived by MLB management as "paying customers" first and foremost, not as stakeholders. In general, fans were viewed, discussed, and appear to be treated as the top target audience of teams' increasingly sophisticated marketing efforts to win their ongoing loyalty.

Web Site Analysis of MLB Clubs

The analysis of the electronic sites revealed that web sites are comprised mostly of information about tickets, seating at the ballpark, purchasing of team merchandise, interactive games, schedule and promotional dates, history/statistics concerning the team and its players. A conclusion that can be drawn from the web sites is that major league teams seem to be less-than-enthusiastic about contacting fans except on matters involving tickets and merchandise.

A small number of clubs carried on various forms of give-and-take with fans on issues, and also linked them to appropriate team executive personnel. The "Contact Us" (which includes e-mail links), "Chat," "Front Office," and "Frequently Asked Questions" categories represented MLB's attempt to offer fans an opportunity to interact on issues of substance. Granted, web sites are typically positioned as one-way information tools, yet as the medium's popularity and uses grow, sponsors are discovering their feedback and interactive value. Such discovery, however, often takes time, as well as trial and error, often requiring an organization to become comfortable with its web site on one level before it can move to the next. Interestingly, neither the Players Association's web site (the weakest of all by far), nor MLB's heavily visited web site, make much more than a token attempt to solicit or address fans' concerns.

INTERVIEWS WITH BASEBALL EXECUTIVES

Examining web sites provided us with a glimpse of how baseball clubs currently perceive and treat fans. Such data, while revealing and interesting, are necessarily limited in what they can tell us about club executives' deeper thinking and future plans concerning fans. Therefore, the web site evaluation was supplemented with "human" input directly from those at the top of the team hierarchies. Interviews were conducted with seven club marketing executives representing a mix of small- and big-market teams (see footnote 18).

Overall, executives spoke convincingly of their unflinching commitment to fans as *the* "most important" group and "lifeblood" of baseball. They seemed particularly sensitive to the fans' post-strike embitterment. Unquestionably, clubs have launched many programs for, and involving, fans designed to enhance the ballpark experience, and bolster community relations. The range of fan-focused efforts practiced by major league clubs runs the gamut from the traditional and superficial to the innovative and serious. We expected to find managements core perception of fans as purchasers of tickets and merchandise and followers via broadcast outlets – which we did. What did somewhat surprise us, however, was the depth and sophistication of some teams' attempts to understand their fans' ballpark preferences and subsequent attempts to accommodate the fans.

The Phillies, for example, are one of the more active and creative organizations we studied. Management reported conducting ongoing research on its current and former season ticket holders, as well as stadium vendors and employees, in an effort to improve the image of the ballpark in particular and the organization in general. Such data apparently played a pivotal role in management's decision to craft a stronger marketing emphasis on families and build in educational opportunities during games (*e.g.*, how to keep score, recognizing pitches). One practice unique to the Phillies is its annual requirement that every employee be a "fan for a day" (*e.g.*, park car in fans' lot, buy ticket, food and souvenirs from park vendors) and then complete a questionnaire about the experience.

Standing out among the teams' strategies to get close to their fans is an escalating emphasis on market/customer research aimed at uncovering insights into fans' thinking. Two teams, the Brewers and Indians, have hired outside research firms to conduct surveys and focus groups. Since 1996, Cleveland has used J.D. Powers & Associates, known for its consumer surveys for the auto industry, to talk with fans about how to make Jacobs Field more fan-friendly, in spite of the "Jake's" amazing consecutive sold out games streak, now approaching 400. Apparently, today's clubs sponsor research for its value in shaping their marketing vision, not for any "eyewash" or publicity value. The Twins' Director of Corporate Sales, for example, talks of "database mining" as easily as he does suicide bunts and double plays, claiming it to be a key to the organization's future direction, not just its sales strategy.

Community relations also seem to be high on clubs' priority list for connecting with fans and indirectly winning their "customer" loyalty. E-mail, web sites, focus groups, and annual reports drive these programs. Additionally, education programs that include scholarships, players' outreach and reading programs are increasingly common.

So, while some efforts are in place at the team level for fan involvement, at the national level fans remain clearly excluded. In January 1999, for example, Major League Baseball launched a Blue Ribbon Economic Task Force to "analyze all aspects of baseball's economic system and make recommendations and suggestions to the Commissioner...."[19] The line-up for the panel includes Senator George Mitchell, former Senate Majority Leader; Paul A. Vocker, former Chairman of the Board of the Federal Reserve System; Richard C. Levin, President of Yale University; and syndicated columnist George Will. How much of the distinguished panel's report will be made public or in any way help fans is still unknown, but the news release announcing the Blue Ribbon panel revealed MLB's intention of keeping the Players Association "fully apprised." By expanding the charge of the committee, MLB could have included the fans' perspective to help shape the issues in the negotiation mix, but chose not to.

PROMISING SIGNS

Taken collectively, the web site assessment and baseball management interviews reinforce the notion that MLB and its teams still hold the traditional view of fans as paying customers only, shunning the idea that as customers they can also be stakeholders or even potential advisors who possess value-added input. On one hand, such a conclusion is disappointing. On the other hand, cautious optimism is warranted as some clubs' good business sense has prompted them to learn more about what makes their fans/customers tick by listening to and studying them more closely. Through such research efforts, which hopefully are pushing open management's minds to the potential worth of fans' input, we see the basis for promise, a promise that MLB and club executives are gradually coming to see fans in a broader and more balanced light.

FANS' ORGANIZING EFFORTS

Over the years, a number of fans organizations have been conceived usually in response to a compelling issue or crisis. In the end, though, most have failed to sustain themselves, almost always falling short of meeting their lofty stated objectives. A couple have fared better than others, creating a bit of a stir or catching the attention of baseball denizens and the media, yet their impact on those who make the decisions shaping the game has been negligible, at best.

We examined the purposes, offerings and challenges facing fans' organizations. In two cases (FANS and USFANS), we spoke with the organizations' founders/operating heads to learn more about their ups and downs, top priority issues and plans to grow in size and influence.

NADER AND FANS

In 1977, famed consumer advocate Ralph Nader led a charge against "the rising crescendo of fraud and fast-buck artistry" in sports by establishing FANS (Fight to Advance the Nation's Sports). The organization grew to about 1,100 members, but did little except generate a cynical response from teams and sports writers. Shortly after FANS was launched, the *Washington Post* raised some serious issues in an editorial about its purpose and practices. First, regarding fan representation, how did Nader propose to represent competing fan interests?

> Take, for example ... the trade of Tom Seaver from the New York Mets to the Cincinnati Reds. Mets' fans, no doubt, thought it a

terrible trade that should never have been made. In contrast, Reds' fans thought it a marvelous coup. FANS, we suppose, would attempt to get around that problem by describing itself as representing the interests of the 'real' sports fans, as distinct from the parochial or fly-by-nighters.[20]

In that same editorial, the *Post* indicated that "A national convention of FANS would make the quadrennial political conventions look like tea parties."[21] Sports writer Dave Kindred, writing for the *Washington Post*, caustically noted that FANS "is good for lots of laughs." Noting Nader and Gruenstein's complaints about the rising price of hot dogs and beer, Kindred opined, "So right away you figure these guys don't have anything serious to gripe about.... Would FANS have us munch wheat germ at Fenway?"[22]

The Economist joined in the derision: As Nader appeared with a baseball cap on his head to announce the formation of FANS, it was "immediately greeted with hoots of derision and its acronym, FANS, was said to stand for 'Forget Anything Nader Says.'"[23] Clearly, FANS was not off to an auspicious start and lay fallow for 20 years.

Following the '95 lockout/strike, Nader discussed revitalizing a fans group. In a *USA Today* op-ed piece, Nader said, "We want to form a group of fans. We tried it 20 years ago but it ended because enough people didn't believe these dark days would ever come ... It's time we make the sports powers answer to those who make professional sports possible — the fans."[24] Jeffrey Flanagan of *The Kansas City Star* thought the timing good:

> We have the suspicion enough fans around the country are fed up with the fiscal hijacking going on by most owners to get new stadiums that FANS might be able to recruit more than 1,000 members this time. The degree of greed among owners, after all, has increased considerably since 1979. And less and less fans are willing to tolerate it.[25]

The issues had shifted to bigger stakes, and no longer was the talk about the price of hot dogs and tickets, but subsidized stadium scams — which somehow found Nader on the same side of an issue as the Heritage Foundation![26] Perhaps with a shift in issue orientation and more fans genuinely outraged, FANS would find new life. But, inexplicably, FANS-the-sequel suffered the same dismal fate as its predecessor.

In a telephone interview, Ralph Nader discussed some of the reasons he believes sports fans organizations fail. First, he warned against judging the concept of a fans organization a "failure" until a well-financed attempt had been made. He noted that FANS had about $10,000 in start-up funds and that today at least $200,000–$300,000 would be needed for a credible attempt. Second, he commented that given the nature of baseball fans they were "more likely to withdraw than charge forward. There is not a continuing priority in the game — they don't have a vested interest in the entire process."[27]

STADULIS AND USFANS

The year 1997 spawned a number of other fan-based organizations, among them United Sports Fans of America or USFANS, established by a group of Salt Lake City and Boca Raton businessmen. USFANS appears to be the most credible of the all the fans groups and one of the few still in operation.

The USFANS web site is clearly the most active of the fan-based Internet sites, widely promoting its advocacy efforts. Its stated purpose is to "make money for investors, provide discounts and benefits package to member fans, and serve as a powerful consumer advocacy organization on behalf of sports fans — giving them a strong voice on issues that affect them."[28] Frank Stadulis, a former IBM executive, is president of the organization, which currently boasts 12,500 members. He expects a significant influx of capital in the near future, already earmarked for efforts to expand the fan-member base. Annual membership dues is $19.95 ($9.95 for students); its organizational model includes an advisory board "comprised of renowned members from the sports world" (*e.g.,* baseball's Bill Giles and Gary Carter), and evolving franchising options (for about $10,000) reflecting Stadilus' position that sports like politics is a local phenomenon. A second USFANS office opened in Washington, D.C., in 1998 to influence pending legislation affecting the sports industry. The organization's web site includes an online survey, results of which are used to protest actions taken by teams or agents across all professional sports perceived by USFANS as detrimental to fans' interests.

During our interview, Frank Stadulis spoke at length about USFANS' purpose, structure and effectiveness to date. "It all boils down to money," he claimed, echoing Ralph Nader's plea not to condemn the idea of a fans group as unworkable until a solidly funded one came along. Stadulis believes that fans can "compete with very influential [owners] with a low level of investment." The power to influence major sports is real, he said, noting several recent examples. One came during the basketball lockout when Stadulis met with Brian McIntyre and Billy Hunter of the players union and asked that the lockout/strike "not be settled on the backs of the fans."[29] Throughout the negotiating process, USFANS conducted surveys of fans' perspectives, which were fed to the principal parties at the bargaining table. Stadulis maintains that things such as free fan autograph sessions happened as a direct result of his three or four meetings with owners and player representatives while the situation was unfolding.

Another tangible victory claimed by USFANS concerned the raising, and subsequent lowering, of post-season basketball ticket prices without notice from $25 to $47. Within 48 hours, in response to efforts by the USFANS to show club owners the error of their ways, fans were given a rebate.

When asked where baseball fits into the organization's multi-sport agenda, Stadulis indicated that at the present time baseball was USFANS' premier sport and would remain so. The organization's long-range plans call for selling stock in USFANS so that, in Stadulis' words, "the fans can own USFANS ... and proactively improve the nature of spectator sports."[30]

OTHER FANS ORGANIZATIONS

Over the past several years, the Internet has provided a ready outlet for frustrated fans to attempt to be heard.[31] FANS and USFANS have already been discussed. Sports Fans in Action, for example, reports 90,000 members over ten years, one need only visit the site to be counted as a member. And, since it does nothing to initiate correspondence or interaction, the claim that Sports Fans in Action influences decisions in major sports (*e.g.*, instant replays) appears to us to be inflated. In fact, such decisions may be made with fans in mind, but don't appear to be made as a result of any systematic consultation with fans. Sports Fans in Action's home page heralds its mission:

> ... to provide America's Sports Fan a COLLECTIVE VOICE relating to sports fan issues, sports products at discounted rates, and connectivity to the hottest sports-related Internet sites in the world. Our goal is to take a collective stand and improve the quality of sports fan issues through media presence, petitions and calls to appropriate parties as a large, organized body of Sports Fans that must be recognized at the bargaining table.[32]

In 1981, Ken Smith and Brian Thompson founded the National Fan Organization. One hundred thousand fans allegedly registered with the organization (no fees), but the paid membership hovered around 7,500 shortly after its inception. However, as of this writing, we have been unable to make contact with anyone from this organization — another fans group gone MIA.[33]

David Wasserman, a professor of molecular physiology and biophysics at Vanderbilt University and founder/president of Fans of the

National Pastime Advocacy Group (FNPAG), is probably a typical reflection of the state of these types of sites/organizations. A devout baseball fan, he believes fans deserve a voice, with the FNPAG web site evidence of his attempt to do something about it. While Wasserman prefers the term "participants" to "members," he admittedly has few. When we first contacted him through the web site in April 1999, only about 50 fans had visited the site in the five months it had been up. In June 1999, that due to lack of administrative help and time, Dr. Wasserman, in spite of his good intentions, had been forced to abandon the web site, with the future of the organization very much in doubt.[34]

The Seattle Fans Lobby's web site rhetoric is focused and fairly articulate: the lobby exists to "put an end to fan abuse. We are part of the problem. We fans aren't organized. We do not have a united voice to protest these abuses. To voice your opinions effectively: Be angry but well mannered. Snail mail still has the most impact. Faxes are your next best solution. E-mail tends to have the least impact."[35] The web site contains articles, surveys, and resource material (much of which wasn't available — often a sign of an ailing web site). Geared to issues of strong local interest to Seattle fans, the lobby seems, in many ways, the right idea for the right time. However, since it was posted in December 1996, the web site has recorded only 219 hits (although the counter may have been reset).[36]

CONCLUSIONS

For the most part, fans' organizations have been more hope and bluster than reality — far more successful as promising concepts than as working, ongoing entities. All but one (USFANS) has failed to attain any lasting viability, or impact on either the fans they sought to represent or the powers-that-be they sought to influence. The long-term effectiveness of USFANS is yet to be determined. Yet, fans' desire to have a voice in decisions that determine the nature of the sports, and teams, to which they give their loyalty may be as great as it's ever been. What appears to be missing from the assembled fan-driven web sites within baseball is any sense of unity, coordination or commonality — which may spotlight a large portion of the ineffectiveness that has characterized these types of organizations.

Given the inherent idiosyncratic nature of sports fans, particularly baseball fans, any single organization would be hard-pressed to represent fans of any one sport equitably, though some claim to do just that, while others limit their focus to a particular sport. Multi-sport representation, exemplified by USFANS, may be a strength or it may be a weakness. The composition of a board of directors for instance, would be affected, as would the issues tracked and lobbied, and the type and form of relationships established with key parties. USFans, for example, appears to address this latter concern by taking official advocacy stands only when opinions of those surveyed reach a 70 percent consensus on a given question or issue. Concerning board make-up, USFANS has constructed a diversified board with members hailing from several major sports.

Whether the three-year-old, all-sports organization can represent the varying needs and demands of multiple sports equally and effectively only time will tell. Certainly, USFANS is a step in the right direction and seems to give credence to consumer advocate Ralph Nader's claim that "the only way for fans to get back is through collective action."[37] At this point in its evolution, however, USFANS, still feeling its way and hampered by limited resources, can only react to "watershed national issues" as they arise across the spectrum of sports, according to its founder and president.[38] To bring baseball fans' needs and desires into the mainstream of the game's thinking and decision-making as soon as possible, an autonomous national baseball fans union/lobby should be established. The details of such an organization, its function, membership, leadership, public relations, structure and inherent difficulties, are detailed in an earlier version of this research presented at the Cooperstown Symposium on Baseball and American Culture.[39]

For baseball fans to gain a credible level of influence within baseball's inner circle, they must become full-time, vigilant players on a par with the other major players. The issues confronting baseball are too complex, and the relationships among the web of principals (i.e., owners, players, umpires, media, legislators, fans) governing the sport/business simply too intricate and dynamic to be left to any fans group whose full attention is not focused on baseball.

To have any realistic chance of gaining a secure foothold inside the decision-making circles of the game, fans must be organized, focused, credible and respected for their power to influence and tenacity to stay the course. Perhaps in time, if a baseball fans union can survive the difficult start-up period, it might be wise to seek affiliations with an umbrella group like USFANS as a means of enhancing the overall advocacy effort on behalf of fans of baseball.

The task of organizing the disparate and unorganized is tough enough under the best of circumstances, as history bluntly reminds us with examples such as the uphill climb of the players union. While there have been many attempts over the years to form a sports fans lobby or union, few, if any, have been able to deliver on their promise to long-frustrated baseball fans. The viability of USFANS, however, suggests that times are changing.

Summary: Baseball Fans Are Here to "Say"

Since the inception of Major League Baseball has operated as a closed system. For a long time, players had no say in their career. Frustrated by their exclusion, the players eventually formed a union, and in time gained the owners' attention and won their right to legally affect and help shape not only their destinies but that of the game of baseball. The umpires have followed a like course. By unionizing, both groups have boosted their stature and maximized their portion of the MLB pie and fortified their right to participate in discussions and decisions affecting the sport/industry responsible for their careers and livelihoods.

Baseball fans' should take their place around the conference table where its primary stakeholders shape baseball's kismet. Attaining their rightful place won't happen if they wait to be invited by those who aren't inclined to give up the control and rewards they've won through protracted negotiations. It is time, perhaps overtime, that fans step up to the plate and begin swinging the bat they've held idle in their hands for years.

We echo outspoken sports reporter Mike Lupica's cogent observation about the state of fandom today in his book *Mad As Hell*: "Fans still matter in sports. They're tired of being told they don't. It's time for them to do something about it, or forever hold their peace."[40]

Team	Website	Alumni	Ballpark	Box Scores/Stats	Chat	Children	Community	Contact Us	Fans	FAQ	Front Office	Game Day	History	Injury Report	Investor Relations
Anaheim Angels	angelsdugout.com			X						X					
Arizona Diamondbacks	azdiamondbacks.com		X				X	X	X			X	X		
Atlanta Braves	atlantabraves.com	X	X		X	X	X		X			X	X		
Baltimore Orioles	theorioles.com		X			X	X		X			X			
Boston Red Sox	redsox.com		X										X		
Chicago Cubs	cubs.com	X	X		X								X		
Chicago White Sox	chisox.com		X	X		X	X	X			X	X	X		
Cincinnati Reds	cincinnatireds.com	X		X		X		X				X	X	X	
Cleveland Indians	indians.com		X	X		X	X					X	X		X
Colorado Rockies	coloradorockies.com		X	X		X									
Detroit Tigers	detroittigers.com		X	X		X	X	X					X		
Florida Marlins	flamarlins.com		X	X		X	X						X		
Houston Astros	astros.com		X	X									X		
Kansas City Royals	kcroyals.com		X								X				
Los Angeles Dodgers	dodgers.com					X	X						X		
Milwaukee Brewers	milwaukeebrewers.com		X			X	X						X		
Minnesota Twins	wcco.com/sports/twins					X			X				X		
Montreal Expos	montrealexpos.com		X								X	X			
New York Mets	mets.com		X	X					X			X	X		
New York Yankees	yankees.com											X	X		
Oakland A's	oaklandathletics.com			X							X	X	X		
Philadelphia Phillies	phillies.com														
Pittsburgh Pirates	pirateball.com		X			X	X						X		
San Diego Padres	padres.com			X			X		X			X	X		
San Francisco Giants	sfgiants.com		X	X		X							X		
Seattle Mariners	mariners.org		X			X	X		X		X	X	X		
St. Louis Cardinals	stlcardinals.com	X	X	X		X		X				X			
Tampa Bay Devil Rays	devilray.com					X			X				X		
Texas Rangers	texasrangers.com		X					X				X	X		
Toronto Blue Jays	bluejays.ca			X					X				X		
Major League Baseball	majorleaguebaseball.com		X						X	X		X	X		
MLBPA	bigleaguers.com				X					X					

Team	Website	Links	Live Game Coverage	Magazine	Minor	Multimedia	News	Promotional Dates	Roster	Schedule	Shop	Tickets
Anaheim Angels	angelsdugout.com	X						X	X	X		X
Arizona Diamondbacks	azdiamondbacks.com			X			X				X	X
Atlanta Braves	atlantabraves.com				X	X	X		X	X	X	X
Baltimore Orioles	theorioles.com	X					X		X	X	X	X
Boston Red Sox	redsox.com		X		X	X	X		X	X	X	X
Chicago Cubs	cubs.com			X		X			X		X	X
Chicago White Sox	chisox.com				X	X	X		X	X	X	X
Cincinnati Reds	cincinnatireds.com				X	X	X		X	X		X
Cleveland Indians	indians.com					X	X	X	X		X	X
Colorado Rockies	coloradorockies.com					X						X
Detroit Tigers	detroittigers.com		X		X	X	X	X		X	X	X
Florida Marlins	flamarlins.com					X	X		X	X	X	X
Houston Astros	astros.com				X	X	X		X	X	X	X
Kansas City Royals	kcroyals.com			X			X		X	X	X	X
Los Angeles Dodgers	dodgers.com	X			X	X	X		X	X	X	X
Milwaukee Brewers	milwaukeebrewers.com						X					
Minnesota Twins	wcco.com/sports/twins			X	X			X	X	X	X	X
Montreal Expos	montrealexpos.com								X		X	X
New York Mets	mets.com					X		X		X	X	X	X
New York Yankees	yankees.com				X	X	X		X		X	X
Oakland A's	oaklandathletics.com										X	X
Philadelphia Phillies	phillies.com					X		X			X	X	X
Pittsburgh Pirates	pirateball.com	X	X			X		X	X	X	X	
San Diego Padres	padres.com						X		X		X	
San Francisco Giants	sfgiants.com					X	X		X	X	X	X
Seattle Mariners	mariners.org					X			X	X	X	
St. Louis Cardinals	stlcardinals.com			X	X	X	X	X	X	X	X	X
Tampa Bay Devil Rays	devilray.com					X	X		X	X	X	X
Texas Rangers	texasrangers.com					X	X		X	X	X	X
Toronto Blue Jays	bluejays.ca		X			X	X		X	X	X	X
Major League Baseball	majorleaguebaseball.com		X			X			X	X	X	
MLBPA	bigleaguers.com					X	X					

Notes

1. The authors wish to acknowledge and thank Jeffrey Pincus, Columbia, MD, and Michael Meliker, Bethesda, MD, for their important research contributions.
2. Guttman, Allen A. *Whole New Ballgame* (Chapel Hill, NC: University of North Carolina Press, 1988).
3. Gabler, Neal. "More Than a Game." *Los Angeles Times*, 13 September 1998.
4. Young, Dick. In, Paul Dickson (ed.) *Baseball's Greatest Quotations* (New York: Edward Burlingame Books, an imprint of HarperCollins Publishers, 1991: 486).
5. *Washington Star* July 31, 1981. In Paul Dickson (ed.) *Baseball's Greatest Quotations* (New York: Edward Burlingame Books, an imprint of HarperCollins Publishers, 1991: 240).
6. "The Fans' Corner." *Sporting News* 18 April 1935.
7. *Ibid.*, 14 March 1940.
8. Guttman, Allen. *A Whole New Ballgame.*
9. Voigt, David Quentin. *American Baseball: From Postwar Expansion to the Electronic Age, Volume III* (University Park, PA: The Pennsylvania State University Press, 1983: 283-290).
10. Lopresti, Mike. "Is Major League Baseball FAN-FRIENDLY?" *USA Today*, 15 July 1997: 1–2.
11. "Why Baseball Is in Trouble, How GE Makes Money, and Other Insights Into the True Origin of Corporate Profits." *Fortune*, 11 May 1998. An interview by *Fortune's* Anne Fisher with Mercer Management consultants Adrian J Slywotzky and David J. Morrison about their new book, *The Profit Zone: How Strategic Business Design Will Lead You to Tomorrow's Profits.* Reprinted in Marsh & McLennan Companies' "News Clips," Vol. XXV, No. 2, March/April, 1998.
12. "Alderson Promoting Baseball's Internal Change." *Arkansas Democrat-Gazette* 7 February 1999: 5C.
13. Abrams, Roger I. *Legal Bases: Baseball and the Law* (Philadelphia: Temple University Press, 1998: 186).
14. Horst, Craig. "Kansas City Fans Walkout in Protest of Salary Disparity in Baseball." *Northwest Arkansas Times*, 1 May 1999: B2.
15. Lupica,Mike. *Mad as Hell* (Chicago: Contemporary Books, 1996: 160–161).
16. Abrams,Roger I. *Legal Bases: Baseball and the Law.* Philadelphia.
17. *Ibid.*, 164.
18. Brazer, John, Director of Promotions, Philadelphia Phillies, April, 1999; Fred Claire, baseball consultant and former General Manager, Los Angeles Dodgers, May, 1999; Pat Courtney, public relations specialist and spokesperson, Major League Baseball, May, 1999; Bob Dibiasio, Vice President of Public Relations, Cleveland Indians, May, 1999; Jim Hawes, Corporate Marketing Manager, Baltimore Orioles, April, 1999; Rob Katz, Director of Promotions, Tampa Bay Devil Rays, May, 1999; Dean Rennicke, Director of Corporate Affairs, Milwaukee Brewers, May, 1999; Mike Roslansky, Director of Corporate Sales, Minnesota Twins, May, 1999; Rich Skirpan, Guest Services, Pittsburgh Pirates, April, 1999.
19. "Selig Names Blue-Ribbon Economic Task Force." *Major League Baseball,* news release, 13 January 1999.
20. "Fans." *Washington Post*, 29 September 1977: A14.
21. *Ibid.*
22. Kindred, Dave. "How Dare They? The Game Is Called Monopoly." *Washington Post*, 10 November 1977: G1.

23. "Ralph Nader, A Cause Too Far." *The Economist,* 24 December 1977: 30.

24. Nader, Ralph. "Baseball Really Better Without a Commissioner," *USA Today,* 16 June 1998: 13A.

25. Flanagan, Jeffrey. "Nader-Led FANS Has a Case Against Owners." *The Kansas City Star,* 19 February 1997: D2.

26. "Your Cash or Your Franchise." *The Kansas City Star,* 21 February 1997: B1.

27. Nader, Ralph. Telephone interview, 27 May 1999.

28. USFANS, www.usfans.com/usfans/public/release9.htm.

29. Stadulis, Frank. Telephone interview, 1 June 1999.

30. *Ibid.*

31. Our research uncovered several other internet sites aimed at capturing sports fans' interests, concerns, and needs for information and a soap box. There may be others, of course, but we're confident these ten cover the bulk of the waterfront: (1) USFANS (www.usfans.com) (2) Seattle Fans Lobby (www.txdirect.net/~soslobby/soshawks.html) (3) Sports Fans in Action (www.sportsfansofamerica.com) (4) All-sports (www.allsports.com) (4) National Fans Union (www.nfunion.com) (5) Sports Fans of America Association (6) Sports Network (7) National Association of Sports Fans (www.nasportsfans.com — listing denied) (8) The Angry Fan (no longer able to access) (9) Fans of the National Pastime Advocacy Group (no longer able to access), and (10) The National Fan Organization (unconfirmable status).

32. Sports Fans in Action, hompage, www.sportsfansofamerica.com.

33. "National Fan Organization." In *The Professional Mascot Handbook* by Karen Ahearn and Art Ballant (West Point: Leisure Press, 1982: 213–217).

34. Fans of the National Pastime Advocacy Group. Web site no longer available.

35. Seattle Fans Lobby, www.txdirect.net/~sosloby/soshawks.html.

36. *Ibid.*

37. Nader, Ralph. Telephone interview, 27 May 1999.

38. Stadulis, Frank. Telephone interview, 7 July 1999).

39. Details found in: Pincus, David., Stephen Wood, Fritz Cropp, Jeffrey Pincus, and Michael Meliker. "The Fans' Role in Shaping Baseball: A Voice Too Long Silent? The Case for a National Baseball Fans Union." The Baseball and American Culture Symposium, Cooperstown, NY, 1999.

40. Lupica, Mike. *Mad as Hell* (Chicago: Contemporary Books, 1996:15).

Baseball Fans and Cooperstown Symposium Participants

Michael V. Miranda

Baseball fans — who are we and why do we spend so much time on or with the game? Why can we answer the following questions, for example:

1) Hall of Famer Lou Brock was traded from the Chicago Cubs to the St. Louis Cardinals in 1964 for what pitcher?

2) Who is the only pitcher to hit two grand slams in the same game?

3) How many official at-bats did Eddie Gaedel have in his career?

4) How tall was Eddie?

5) Who was the car salesman who sold Joe Torre his first new automobile?

(The answers to these questions are provided just before the list of References Cited at the end of this paper.)

Why do we keep the answers to questions like these in our minds and readily available? It's because we are **FANS!**

My first Cooperstown Symposium was in 1997 when I was fortunate enough to have a paper I had written on Jackie Robinson accepted for presentation. While giving his welcome, symposium founder Al Hall made a comment about how comfortable baseball fans are at the symposium. By being given the opportunity to interact with others who are similar to themselves, sharing their deep emotional ties to and knowledge of the national pastime, Al stated that symposium participants feel more at home in Cooperstown at the symposium than they do almost anywhere else. This was especially true in academia, he said, when baseball-related research was usually not viewed with the same respect as research done on "scholarly" subjects (Hall, 1997).

I could not relate to the feeling that Al was speaking about at that time, but that is only because I had never before experienced a symposium. "I feel comfortable almost anywhere," I thought. But before the 1997 symposium, I was never among such a large group of baseball fans and scholars. I never before knew what it was like not to be one of the people in any setting to be the most knowledgeable about the game that my father taught me. But at that symposium, it was very different. At that symposium, everyone seemed to know much more than I did — and their enjoyment of the game was displayed proudly, without the fear that they might be judged to be frivolous or unconcerned about the real problems that intelligent adults fret about in the world. By the end of that first day, I knew and felt exactly what Al was talking about.

At my second symposium, in 1998, I found myself once again sitting in the Grandstand Theater at the National Baseball Hall of Fame and Museum awaiting Al Hall's opening comments with great anticipation. I started a conversation with a gentleman to my left who indicated to me with great pride that he was a Pittsburgh Pirates fan.

When I asked if he was from Pittsburgh, he said, "No ... California now. Originally from New York." "Then how did you become a Pirate fan?' I asked. It was then that he told me his story.

This fan had gone to his first sleep-away camp one summer when he was just eight years old. He cared and knew nothing about baseball and he was afraid at being away from home for the first time. On the first night of camp, his group's counselor thought that a good way to break the ice would be for the members of the group to indicate the name of their most favorite baseball team. The counselor answered this question first and said, "My team is the Pittsburgh Pirates." When it came to my new friend's turn, he thought that if the Pirates were good enough for the counselor, then they would be good enough for him. So, to fit in, to be accepted as "one of he boys," he said, "I like the Pirates, too!" And he has been a Pittsburgh rooter ever since.

These two events led me to the idea for this research.

In the fall of 1998, I mailed a questionnaire to all 652 people whose names were on the symposium mailing list as of July 1st, 1998. Every state except Alaska and Wyoming were represented as well as four foreign countries (Canada, England, Germany and Japan). The states with the highest number of individuals listed were New York (130), California (49), Pennsylvania (38) and Ohio (33). The states with the highest numbers of returned questionnaires were New York (44), California (20), Ohio (15) and Massachusetts, New Jersey and Pennsylvania (12 each). Table 1 in the Appendix provides the distribution of the 652 fans on the symposium mailing list and the 226 fans who responded to the questionnaire by state or country.

Eighty-six of the questionnaires were returned as undeliverable, leaving a total of 566 questionnaires which had apparently reached their addressees. The 226 responses represent a 40 percent return rate.

Of the 226 respondents, 115 had attended at least one symposium, with two having attended all ten symposia. Table 2 in the Appendix presents the number of symposia attended by each of the 226 questionnaire respondents.

According to the bibliography of symposium presentations compiled by Richard Gaughran (1997) and the program for the 1998 symposium, 227 papers were presented in the symposium's first ten years by 211 different people. Seventy-seven of these 211 presenters made their presentations as part of a group of two or more individuals while 134 presenters made their presentations as individuals. One hundred sixty-six of the 211 presenters were involved in just one presentation, while 45 have made multiple presentations. Table 3 in the Appendix shows the frequency distribution of presentations by each of the 211 presenters.

Our most prolific presenters have been Thomas Altherr with nine, and Gai Berlage, George Grella and Richard Gaughran with six each (Gaughran, 1997). (Tom, Gai and George are each on the program for the 1999 Symposium as well.) Fifty-nine of the 115 symposium attendees had not made a presentation at any symposium. Table 4 in the Appendix identifies the number of presentations made by the 56 questionnaire respondents who have given one or more presentations at the symposium.

The 115 questionnaire respondents who had attended at least one symposium attended an average of 2.2 symposia. The attendance of these 115 respondents each year is summarized in Table 5 in the Appendix.

Approximately 10 percent of these respondents have attended the symposium every year since they attended their first. The year of the first symposium attended for each of these 11 individuals is summarized in Table 6 in the Appendix.

Table 7 in the Appendix demonstrates that 50 of the symposium attendees who attended their first symposium from 1989 through 1997 have attended only one symposium.

The professions of the 115 questionnaire respondents who have attended at least one symposium are very significantly skewed toward education. Two-thirds of the 115 (67.8 percent) indicate that they are employed as a college professor or administrator (73) or as a high school teacher or administrator (5). Table 8 in the Appendix identifies the professions of all respondents who have been symposium attendees.

One hundred eleven fans who had never attended a symposium up to the time of this survey also responded to the questionnaire. No significant differences were found in the responses of these two groups to any of the key questionnaire items that have been analyzed for this paper, therefore the responses summarized for the remainder of this paper relate to all 226 questionnaire respondents as a whole.

Questionnaire respondents indicated that they "became a fan" from ages 2 through 29. Over 42 percent became fans at ages 7 (48) and 8 (48), while a total of 79.6 percent (155) became fans between the ages of 6 and 10. Table 9 in the Appendix presents the frequency distribution of this initiation into fandom.

The average age for becoming a fan was found to be 8.2 years, with the 208 male respondents averaging 8.1 years and the 18 female respondents averaging 9.2 years. For the group of 208 males, the median and modal age for becoming a fan were each 7.5 years and the range was from 2 to 29 years. For the group of 18 women, the range was from 3 to 29 years and the median and modal ages were each 8 years. A more detailed summary analyzed by current age appears in Table 10 in the Appendix.

These 226 fans gave a total of 311 reasons when asked the question "Why did you become a fan when you did?" Thirty-seven percent of the 311 answers related to the influence of another individual in the life of the budding fan, 30 percent related to the first experiences of either participating in or going to see a baseball game, 16 percent said that it was a specific team, player or game that led them toward becoming a serious fan, 13 percent credited some form of the media with getting them interested and 4 percent gave "other" reasons. A list indicating more specific information for all reasons given follows:

The influence of another person(s)—115 of the 311 responses (37%)

> Father—65 (57%)
> Mother—18 (16%)
> Other family member(s)—21 (18%)
> Friends—10 (9%)
> A player—1 (<1%)

First experience—93 (30%)
> Went to first professional game—52 (56%)
> Played Little League ball—24 (26%)
> Played ball with friends—17 (18%)

The media—42 (13%)
> Television—2 (<1%)
> Radio—19 (5%)
> Newspapers—8 (19%)
> Baseball cards—11 (26%)
> Movies—1 (<1%)

Specific teams, players or games — 49 (16%)
  Team — 29 (59%)
  Player — 10 (20%)
  Game — 10 (20%)

Other — 13 (4%)
  The "game" itself — 10 (77%)
  To become "Americanized" — 2 (15%)
  Moved to New York City — 1 (<1%)

Table 11 in the Appendix gives the percentages of the five broad categories indicated above broken down by age group. The only age group that did not list the influence of another person as the most common reason for becoming a fan was the 70 and over group. That group indicated that the experience of playing or attending their first games was the most common factor.

The players who were cited as the major reasons for the creation of a baseball fan are: Roberto Clemente, Joe DiMaggio, the double-play duo of Nellie Fox and Luis Aparicio, Mickey Mantle (2), Willie Mays (2), Stan Musial, Ted Williams (2), Carl Yastrzemski, the Baltimore Oriole pitchers of the mid–1960s and the Italian-American Yankees of the 1930s and 1940s.

The 1969 Mets were credited with making baseball fans of seven questionnaire respondents (perhaps due to the fact that so many questionnaire respondents were from the New York area), while two fans each identified the 1947 Dodgers, the 1956 Braves, the 1957 Braves and the creation of the Houston Colt .45s in 1962 as the reason for their interest in baseball. Each of the teams that received acknowledgement as being responsible for making fans of the questionnaire respondents are listed below:

> 1947 Dodgers (2), 1948 Indians; 1956 Braves (2); 1956 Dodgers; 1957 Braves (2); 1958 Braves; 1960 Pirates; 1960 Yankees; 1961 Yankees; 1962 Mets; 1967/68 Cardinals; 1967/68 Giants; 1968 Indians; 1968 Tigers; 1969 Mets (7); 1974 Dodgers; 1980 Royals; Colt .45s — when they were created in Houston (2); Braves — when they moved to Milwaukee; Dodgers — when they moved to Los Angeles; Orioles — when the St. Louis Browns moved to Baltimore; and the Yankee-Dodger rivalry.

Two fans identified the 1954 World Series as being responsible for starting their interest in baseball. Each of the specific series that were identified as being responsible for the creation of a fan are listed below:

> 1943 World Series; 1950 World Series; 1951 National League Playoffs; 1954 World Series (2); 1957 World Series; 1959 World Series; 1960 World Series; 1964 World Series; 1976 World Series; and 1977 World Series.

Several questionnaire respondents made very interesting comments about their becoming a fan. Some of these follow:

William Gordon, an attorney and instructor at Redlands Community College who now lives in Tulsa, Oklahoma, claims that he became a fan twice — at age ten and then again at age 35. He says, "My youngest son has been passionate about the game since about one-and-a-half years of age and I had to become a *real* fan to catch up."

Jeffrey Sammons of Bridgeton, New Jersey, a history professor at New York University, became a fan in 1957 "because of Hank Aaron, Warren Spahn, Lew Burdette and the Milwaukee Braves' defeat of the despised Yankees." Now, at age 49, Jeffrey is no longer a Braves fan because he "can't stand the Braves mascot, the tomahawk chop or that 'Indian' chant. Atlanta is not the same as Milwaukee was (and the Milwaukee team had great uniforms with the covered pockets)."

Jerry Desmond, the curator at the Chattanooga Regional History Museum grew up a Red Sox fan in Mapleton, Maine. He started out as a Red Sox fan, but his interest in baseball was born when he was riding in the back seat of a red convertible when he heard the Mazeroski home run that beat the Yankees in the 1960 World Series. Jerry proudly adds that he now has his own red convertible. He no longer is a Red Sox fan, however, "because Bucky (expletive deleted) Dent's home run in the '78 Playoffs turned (him) into an agnostic. If there is a God, he is unjust." Jerry is now a Cubs fan because, as he says, "There is no pressure." (One wonders if this is still the case since the Cubs' post-season appearance in 1998.)

Jack Charles, a retired high school English teacher who grew up in a small village in northeast New York, states that his dad started him off, "giving me and my brother a baseball on our birthdays each year, one apiece — a smart move, one I'm thankful for 'til this day."

Elinor Nauen lived in Minneapolis in 1960 and became a fan because "my parents were both immigrants and being a baseball fan was the most American thing I could find to latch on to." She was a Yankee fan in Minnesota because "they're the ones we heard about the most."

Brian Kantz, an editor in his 20s from Cleveland, says: "The real attachment for me, though, is the way it has brought my family together. I can't imagine a childhood that would be without me and my brothers playing catch or the family going down to Cleveland Stadium on a weekend afternoon to watch the Tribe. Baseball is about family and forming an attachment to your hometown team players ... My wife and I hope to share that kind of family love for the game once we have children of our own."

Jean Hastings Ardell of Corona del Mar, California, explains her attachment to the game by saying: "Baseball, as it is for many women, offered a convenient, non-threatening and congenial environment in which to connect with the male world (in my case, with my dad). Baseball connects me still to him though he's been gone for more than thirty years."

As Jean uses baseball to connect herself to her father, this is what John Vernon of Washington, D.C., has to say: "I feel that major league baseball does little to encourage the generations of young fans coming after us. However, I must say that my son, a slick-fielding infielder, shares my love for the game played right ... That we have this tie is important to me, especially since we have come to disagree, it seems, in all things beyond the sports realm. In this one sanctified area of human endeavor, we have the same appreciation of beauty and can talk about it excitedly. When that happens, I feel as if I were nine years old again and all things are possible. It's useful to lead from your heart every once in a while."

And an anonymous symposium participant in his 50s writes: "Yes, I am a fan. In 1964 I was discharged from the army at the Brooklyn Naval Yard after two-and-one-half years of missing baseball in Germany. I traveled across the river to Manhattan to have a reunion with my dad on Park Avenue. He asked me if I wanted to go out to dinner — my mother had passed away and it was just the two of us. I said, without hesitation, 'Are the Yankees in town?' We ended up along the first base rail where it juts out toward right field, duffel bag and all." He continues: "I had to go to a ball game before even going home — because somehow I couldn't really feel 'at home' without it. Such is baseball."

And R.G. (Hank) Utley of Concord, North Carolina, simply states "Baseball is good; Baseball is life; Therefore, life is good (especially at age 74)."

Hank also has a unique impression of the importance of baseball for a specific group of Americans: "I was a second lieutenant bombardier on a B-29 at Lincoln, Nebraska, Overseas Replacement Depot headed for the Pacific in October when we dropped the bomb. I did get to see the sixth game of the 1945 World Series in Chicago on the way home. Greenberg's bases loaded homerun on the last day of the season to win the pennant may not go down in history as one of the great home runs but it was the most *symbolic* of all time to thousands of G.I. fans. Hank went into the Army early (before the war) and he came back and through hard work picked up where he had left off. This was a message to all the G.I. baseball fans that we too could come back to a world that we left and start over again. That home run gave hope to millions. I know — I was there." And upon learning of this story, I don't think that we have to ask how R.G. got his nickname.

Another question on the questionnaire asked whether or not the respondents were fans of their hometown team and 82.3 percent stated that they were. This finding was quite stable across the sexes as 82.2 percent of all male fans responding and 83.3 percent of all women fans responding indicated loyalty to their hometown teams. Table 12 in the Appendix gives a more detailed breakdown.

The hometown teams that were rejected by the questionnaire respondents most often were he Yankees (8), the Cardinals (5) and the Dodgers and Phillies (4 each). The other rejected hometown teams were the: A's (3), Giants (2), Mets (2), Pirates (2), Red Sox (2), Braves, Cubs, Indians, Orioles, Reds, Tigers, Twins and White Sox.

When fans chose to root for teams other than the ones closest to their main place of residence, they chose to cheer most often for the Yankees (11), the Dodgers (7), the Braves (6) and the Giants (4). The other non-hometown teams selected as favorites were the: Red Sox (3), Mets (2), Orioles (2), A's, Cubs, Reds, Royals and Tigers.

Very often, non-hometown teams are chosen as the favorites due to a particular player or overall team success, but Paul Heising, a self-employed entertainment producer who grew up in New York City describes his choice in this way: "My father loved the New York Giants — so I loved the Brooklyn Dodgers."

Dave Mihaly, an architect from Port Richmond, California who grew up in Freehold, New Jersey explains his loyalty to the Baltimore Orioles as follows: "Everyone in my family was a Yankee fan. I wanted to be different, so I wrote a letter to Brooks Robinson asking for a picture. Not only did he send me an autographed color photo, he included 5' by 7" photo cards of every Oriole and two great posters of himself and Frank Robinson. The year was 1966. Maybe I made an impression on him. He certainly made a lasting one on me. I've been an Oriole fan ever since."

Sixty-seven percent of the fans who responded to the questionnaire, 152 out of the 226, said that there was a team or that there were teams that they hated. The most popular "teams to hate" were the Yankees (109), the Dodgers (18), the Giants (9) and the Cardinals (4). The other hated teams were the: Cubs (3), Phillies (3), Red Sox (3), Reds (3), Mets (2), Orioles (2), Tigers (2), White Sox (2), A's, Braves, Pirates, Senators and White Sox.

Here are comments made by some of the 109 Yankee-haters:

Brian Donoghue of Flushing, New York, an administrator for a mental health facility says: "In the mind of a child, it was a matter of good vs. evil (the Yankees, of course, being evil)."

Michael Bender, an insurance company project manager from North Babylon, New York says: "My Dad was a Red Sox fan and my grandfather was a longtime Dodger fan. I took my cue from them."

Brian Strum, an administrator from Brooklyn, hated the Yankees "because they were the rich man's team."

Another Brooklynite, Daniel Ross, now a publisher with the University of Nebraska Press, hated the Yankees because of "1941, 1947, 1949, 1952 and 1953."

Robert Gaunt, a retired United States Coast Guard officer from Grand Rapids, Michigan, hated the Yankees because "they continually fleeced talent from the Browns, Senators and others."

Thomas Altherr, a professor of history at Metropolitan State College of Denver, hated the Yankees "for all the right reasons: They were obnoxious and they won too often."

"Because my father said so" is the reason for hating the Yankees given by Scott Regan, a professor at Bowling Green State University who grew up in Albany, New York.

John Coski, a historian at the Museum of the Confederacy, answered my question with a question of his own: "Doesn't everyone who is not a Yankee fan hate the Yankees?"

But let's not neglect the reasons why some of the other teams were hated:

The Indians — "Because of their damn pitching" — Ross Lenhart, a businessman from Old Greenwich, Connecticut, who became a fan at age 14 in 1954;

The Red Sox — "Because of their treatment of Carlton Fisk." — Kevin Grzymala, a teacher from Buffalo, New York;

The Tigers and the White Sox — "I didn't care for the managers." — Ed Yoder, a professor at Penn State University who was raised in Millersburg, Ohio;

The A's — "Because, growing up in Philadelphia, you had to hate one of the teams." — Gary Gumpert, Professor Emeritus at Queens College in New York City;

And a Yankee fan who admitted to hating the Mets is Father Gabriel Costa, a professor of mathematics at Seton Hall University, who said he hates the Mets even though "I know, priests shouldn't hate."

I don't think that there is any baseball fan anywhere who doesn't remember going to his first major league game. The fans responding to my questionnaire were asked to identify the people with whom they attended their first games. Of the 198 fans who responded to this question, only 29 (14.6 percent) went to their first game with people other than members of their families.

That going to a ballgame is a family event is shown by the fact that over 55 percent of all respondents went to their first games with their father and/or their father and other members of their family and more than 13 percent went with their mothers and/or their mothers and other members of their families. An additional four percent of respondents went to their first games either with one or both grandparents or in family groups that included one or both grandparents. The full results appear in Table 13 in the Appendix.

Margaret Engel, a journalist from Chagrin Falls, Ohio, recalls: "*The Cleveland Press* gave students 32 pairs of baseball tickets if you got straight A's the last marking period. My twin sister and I would turn on the juice and get 64 pairs of tickets. Like thousands of other Cleveland kids, we took the Rapid Transit downtown and filled the bleachers in Municipal Stadium all summer."

Peter Williams, an English professor at County College of Morris, New Jersey remembers: "My first game was in the '47 Series [at age 10] for the Gionfriddo catch. I cheered. My father, who was a sports columnist and editor of the *New York World Telegram* and a friend of George Weiss, did not. He said DiMaggio was robbed. I pointed out that DiMag had himself robbed a number of hitters over the years, and the old man shut up."

The 226 fans who responded to the questionnaire go to approximately 1,739 major league and 843 minor league games each year. This averages out to 7.7 major league and 3.7 minor league games each. The age group of 40- to 49-year-olds goes to the most games with the 39 and under group following close behind. Table 14 in the Appendix presents the average number of games attended by age group.

One hundred sixty-six of the 208 male fans (79.8 percent) played organized baseball at some point in their lives while only one of the eighteen female fans (5.9 percent) did so. The group of males aged 39 and under was the group most likely to have had experience in organized baseball with the 50- to 59-year old group finishing second while the 40- to 49-year-old group was a very close third. Table 15 in the Appendix breaks down the respondents' participation on an organized team by age and sex.

The lone female who played organized baseball played on a men's town team. Fifty of the 166 male respondents who played organized baseball (30 percent) reached the high school level, sixteen (9.6 percent) played college ball and two played in the minor leagues. Three continue their playing careers in vintage base ball leagues. Table 16 in the Appendix indicates the levels at which the 166 male respondents who played organized baseball last played.

The experience of being part of an organized baseball team is one to be treasured. F. Travis Boley, the assistant curator at the Basketball Hall of

Fame, informs us that he "was a walk-on who sat on the bench at an NCAA Division II school. I played in *0* innings, but I *loved* being at the ballpark!"

One hundred fifteen of the 226 questionnaires were received from fans who had attended one or more of the Cooperstown Symposia. Attending the symposium is, of course, no easy task. One need only read the following paragraph in the letter that is sent out by Al Hall each year to realize this:

> Getting to Cooperstown is an adventure. The closest airports are Albany, Binghamton and Syracuse, each about one and a half hours away. Amtrak will get you as far as Utica, about fifty miles away. After you get on the ground, you will need to rent a car or arrange for limousine service [Hall, 1999].

When asked, the 115 symposium attendees gave 215 reasons for attending the symposium. Cooperstown itself was named as the reason for coming to the symposium over 30 percent of the time. Presenting a paper at the Symposium was given as a reason for attending 28 percent of the time. "The game of baseball" was listed over 17 percent of the time.

One unusual reason for attending the Symposium was "the Saranac Ale at the Tunnicliff Inn." That response was given by Peter Williams, a presenter at the first Cooperstown Symposium in 1989, the only symposium that he has managed to attend. Were it nor for the fact that I met Pete in 1997 when we each presented a paper at a conference in Brooklyn commemorating the 50th anniversary of Jackie Robinson's entry into the major leagues, I would be thinking about organizing a search party to see whether or not Pete has ever left the Inn. All of the reasons given for attending he symposium are summarized in Table 17 in the Appendix.

John Hammerlinck, a senior planner at the Minnesota Office of Technology and a resident of Bloomington, Minnesota, says that he attends the symposium because he "wanted to meet intellectuals who were not snobs."

Thomas Altherr, originally of Hamburg, New York, and now residing in Colorado, says: "For the first year, I thought it would be fun to be involved in the Fiftieth Anniversary of the Hall of Fame. In subsequent years, I went to meet old and make new friends, to keep aware of baseball scholarship, to get back to Cooperstown, to play Town Ball, etc."

Skip McAfee, a retired Executive Director of the American Society of Horticultural Science, presently of Columbia, Maryland, and a former resident of Dobbs Ferry, New York, explains his reasons for attending the Symposium as being the "subject matter, Town Ball, the venue (each year,

I go to the Otesaga Hotel, sit on a bench, look at Otsego Lake and reminisce about my childhood and baseball), Alvin Hall, and the camaraderie with attendees."

And Robert Norris, an environmental specialist who works for the State of Delaware states that he goes to the symposium "to join in fellowship with others that have a love for our great game. I have made friendships that will be life long."

Baseball journalist Red Smith has written:

> I had a bartender friend in Philadelphia years ago, a devoted baseball fan, who told me, and he said this with tears in his eyes, that the most beautiful thing in the world, more beautiful than any blonde, more beautiful than a mountain lake at sunset, was bases filled, two out, three and two on the batter, and everybody moving with the pitch [Novak, 1976].

And don't we know it!

Answers to questions at the opening of this paper:

1. Ernie Broglio (Samelson, 1996).
2. Tony Cloninger on July 3rd, 1966, for the Atlanta Braves against the San Francisco Giants (Davids, 1999).
3. None. He walked in his only plate appearance for the St. Louis Browns against the Detroit Tigers in 1951 (Samelson, 1996).
4. Three feet, seven inches (Samelson, 1996).
5. Bud Selig, who was the son of the owner of a large car dealership in Milwaukee when Joe first made the roster of the the the Milwaukee Braves. It was a 1960 Ford Thunderbird (Torre & Verducci, 1997).

References

Davids, Bob. "Baseball Briefs," *The SABR Bulletin*, Volume 29, Number 4, April 1999.

Gaughran, Richard. "The Cooperstown Symposium on Baseball and American Culture: A Bibliography." Compiled 1997. Hall, Alvin L. Letter to symposium participants, March 11, 1999.

Hall, Alvin L. Welcoming address at the Ninth Annual Cooperstown Symposium on Baseball and American Culture. Cooperstown, New York. June 11, 1997.

Novak, Michael. *The Joy of Sports* (New York: Basic Books, 1976).

Samelson, Ken et al. (Editor). *The Baseball Encyclopedia* (New York: Macmillan Books, 1996).

Torre, Joe & Tom Verducci. *Chasing the Dream: My Lifelong Journey to the World Series* (New York: Bantam Books, 1997).

APPENDIX

TABLE 1

Distribution of Fans on Symposium Mailing List as of 7/1/99 and Fans Who Returned Completed Questionnaires

	Rec'd.	Ret'd.		Rec'd.	Ret'd.		Rec'd.	Ret'd.
Alaska	0	0	Mass.	26	12	South Dakota	3	0
Alabama	3	1	Michigan	18	3	Tennessee	7	3
Arizona	4	1	Minnesota	5	4	Texas	11	5
Arkansas	4	4	Mississippi	3	0	Utah	4	3
California	49	20	Missouri	15	5	Vermont	5	0
Colorado	8	1	Montana	1	0	Virginia	22	4
Connecticut	14	4	Nebraska	7	3	Washington	7	2
Delaware	6	3	Nevada	2	0	West Virginia	1	1
Florida	24	4	N. Hampshire	2	2	Wisconsin	10	3
Georgia	11	5	New Jersey	28	12	Wyoming	0	0
Hawaii	1	0	New Mexico	2	0			
Idaho	5	2	New York	130	44	Wash., DC	9	3
Illinois	26	5	N. Carolina	9	5			
Indiana	15	3	North Dakota	4	3	Canada	16	1
Iowa	7	4	Ohio	33	15	England	1	0
Kansas	2	1	Oklahoma	1	1	Germany	1	0
Kentucky	4	3	Oregon	3	1	Japan	1	0
Louisiana	10	4	Pennsylvania	38	12			
Maine	6	3	Rhode Island	6	1			
Maryland	17	8	S. Carolina	5	2	TOTAL	652	226

TABLE 2

Number of Symposia Attended by Questionnaire Respondents

Symposia Attended	Number	Symposia Attended	Number
0	111	6	4
1	65	7	4
2	21	8	0
3	10	9	0
4	4	10	2
5	4		
		TOTAL	226

TABLE 3

Frequency Distribution of Presentations Made By Each Presenter

Number of Presentations Made	Number of Presenters
1	166
2	24
3	7
4	8

Number of Presentations Made	Number of Presenters
5	2
6	3
7	0
8	0
9	1
	TOTAL 211

TABLE 4

Number of Presentations Made by Questionnaire Respondents

Number of Presentations	Respondents
1	37
2	7
3	4
4	3
5	2
6	2
7	0
8	0
9	1
	TOTAL 56

TABLE 5

Symposium Attendance of Questionnaire Respondents

First Year	1989	1990	1991	1992	1993	1994	1995	1996	1997	1998
1989	16	4	5	3	4	7	6	4	3	3
1990		6	4	2	2	4	2	3	2	1
1991			12	5	5	3	4	3	4	2
1992				12	3	4	4	3	1	1
1993					9	3	3	3	4	1
1994						9	1	1	1	0
1995							13	5	3	2
1996								13	4	3
1997									11	3
1998										14
TOTALS	16	10	21	22	23	30	33	35	33	30

TABLE 6

Number of Respondents Who Have Attended Every Symposium Since Their First One

First Year Attended	'89	'90	'91	'92	'93	'94	'95	'96	'97
Number of Respondents	2	0	1	1	1	0	2	1	3

TOTAL 11

TABLE 7

Distribution of Respondents Who Have Attended Only One Symposium

Single Year Attended	'89	'90	'91	'92	'93	'94	'95	'96	'97	'98
Number of Respondents	7	1	3	6	3	7	8	7	8	x

TOTAL   50

TABLE 8

Professions of Questionnaire Respondents Who Have Attended the Cooperstown Symposium

Profession	Number	Profession	Number
College Professor/Administrator	73	Psychologist	3
		Accountant	2
Businessman/woman	9	Physician	2
Museum Administrator/Staff	8	Attorney	1
High School Teacher/ Administrator	5	Dentist	1
		Editor	1
Engineer	3	Pharmacist	1
Government Employee	3		
Mental Health Worker	3	TOTAL	115

TABLE 9

Age at Which Respondents Indicate That They Became Baseball Fans

Age Became Fan	Number	Age Became Fan	Number	Age Became Fan	Number
2	2	12	4	22	0
3	4	13	3	23	1
4	4	14	1	24	0
5	14	15	0	25	0
6	24	16	1	26	0
7	48	17	0	27	0
8	48	18	0	28	0
9	35	19	1	29	2
10	25	20	0		
11	9	21	0	TOTAL	226

TABLE 10

Summary of Data for "Age Became Fan" by Sex and Present Age

Current Age	Number	Mean	Median	Mode	Range
Males					
39 and under	33	7.85	8	8	2–22
40 to 49	57	7.39	7	7	2–13
50 to 59	78	8.47	8	7	3–29

Current Age	Number	Mean	Median	Mode	Range
60 to 69	34	8.68	8	8	5–16
70 and over	6	7.83	8.5	9	5–9
Total males	208	8.09	7.5	7.5	2–29
Females					
39 and under	5	10.60	7	7	7–29
40 to 49	6	8.83	7	5	5–19
50 to 59	6	8.67	8	8	3–18
60 to 69	1	8.00	8	8	8
Total females	18	9.22	8	8	3–29
TOTAL	226	8.18	8	8	2–29

TABLE 11

Reasons Given for Becoming a Fan by Age Group (percent)

Age	Individual(s)	Experience	Media	Specific Team, Player or Game,	Other
39 and under	41	26	9	24	0
40 to 49	31	30	14	17	8
50 to 59	38	31	15	15	2
60 to 69	44	32	15	7	2
70 and over	25	33	8	8	25
TOTALS	37	30	13	16	4

TABLE 12

Are Respondents Fans of Their Hometown Teams?

	Yes	No	Total
Males	171 (82.2%)	37 (17.8%)	208
Females	15 (83.3%)	3 (16.7%)	18
TOTAL	186 (82.3%)	40 (17.7%)	226

TABLE 13

People With Whom Respondents Attended First Baseball Game

First Game With:	Number	First Game With:	Number
Father	71	Parents and grandparents	2
Family	40	Brother(s)	1
Friends	29	Father and cousin	1
Parents	20	Father and grandfather	1
Father and brother(s)	16	Father and uncle	1
Uncle	5	Grandfather and brother(s)	1
Grandfather	4	Wife	1
Mother	3		
Mother and sister(s)	2	TOTAL	198

TABLE 14

Respondents' Average Annual Attendance at Baseball Games by Age Group

Age Group	Major League Games	Minor League Games	Total
39 and under	9.6	3.1	12.7
40 to 49	8.2	4.8	12.9
50 to 59	8.0	3.4	11.4
60 to 69	4.6	3.4	8.0
70 and over	5.0	2.8	7.8
TOTAL	7.7	3.7	11.4

TABLE 15

Respondents' Experience Playing Organized Baseball by Age and Sex

Sex	Age Group	Total Number	Number Who Played	Percent Who Played
Male	39 and under	33	27	81.8
Male	40 to 49	57	46	80.7
Male	50 to 59	78	63	80.8
Male	60 to 69	34	26	76.5
Male	70 and over	6	4	66.7
Total Males		208	166	79.8
Total Females		18	1	5.9

TABLE 16

Level at Which Male Respondents Last Played Organized Baseball

Level	Number	Level	Number
Little League	44	Senior League	13
Pony League	26	Minor League	2
High School	50	Vintage Base Ball	3
College	16		
Army	1	TOTAL	166

TABLE 17

Reasons Given by Symposium Attendees for Attending the Cooperstown Symposium

Reason Given	Number	Per Cent of Total Reasons Given
Cooperstown	65	30.2
To present a paper	61	28.4
The game of baseball	37	17.2
The friendship of attendees	21	9.8
To do research	19	8.8
To have fun	5	2.3
To play Town Ball	3	1.4
To hear a specific speaker	1	0.5
Lake Otsego	1	0.5
Al Hall	1	0.5
The Saranac Ale	1	0.5
TOTAL	215	100.1

Index